Electoral Politics in Zimbabwe, Vol II

Esther Mavengano · Sophia Chirongoma
Editors

Electoral Politics in Zimbabwe, Vol II

The 2023 Election and Beyond

Editors
Esther Mavengano ⓘ
English and Media Studies
Great Zimbabwe University
Masvingo, Zimbabwe

Sophia Chirongoma ⓘ
Midlands State University
Zvishavane, Zimbabwe

ISBN 978-3-031-33795-6   ISBN 978-3-031-33796-3 (eBook)
https://doi.org/10.1007/978-3-031-33796-3

© The Editor(s) (if applicable) and The Author(s), under exclusive licence to Springer Nature Switzerland AG 2023

This work is subject to copyright. All rights are solely and exclusively licensed by the Publisher, whether the whole or part of the material is concerned, specifically the rights of translation, reprinting, reuse of illustrations, recitation, broadcasting, reproduction on microfilms or in any other physical way, and transmission or information storage and retrieval, electronic adaptation, computer software, or by similar or dissimilar methodology now known or hereafter developed.
The use of general descriptive names, registered names, trademarks, service marks, etc. in this publication does not imply, even in the absence of a specific statement, that such names are exempt from the relevant protective laws and regulations and therefore free for general use.
The publisher, the authors, and the editors are safe to assume that the advice and information in this book are believed to be true and accurate at the date of publication. Neither the publisher nor the authors or the editors give a warranty, expressed or implied, with respect to the material contained herein or for any errors or omissions that may have been made. The publisher remains neutral with regard to jurisdictional claims in published maps and institutional affiliations.

Cover illustration: Marina Lohrbach_shutterstock.com

This Palgrave Macmillan imprint is published by the registered company Springer Nature Switzerland AG
The registered company address is: Gewerbestrasse 11, 6330 Cham, Switzerland

*To all lecturers who became the greatest of mentors and sources of inspiration.
Thank you, you will continue to change the world through your students*

Foreword

Capturing global imagination, Zimbabwe mounted a painful but significant armed struggle in the 1970s. This built on the earlier activism by trade unionists and nationalists. Central to these struggles were the themes of dignity and "one man (now, person) one vote." The disenfranchisement of black people on the basis of race outraged many and motivated the sons and daughters of the soil to take up arms to correct the injustice. Sadly, thousands paid the ultimate sacrifice. The right to vote, and for that vote to count, therefore, is integral to Zimbabwe's struggle for independence. Only revisionists and reductionists would seek to reduce the struggle to regaining the land or any other single issue.

Contributors to this volume explore multiple dimensions relating to elections in contemporary Zimbabwe. It is with regret that one must concede that instead of being a celebration of the sacrifices made by the daughters and sons of the soil, elections in Zimbabwe are often yet another occasion for the shedding of tears. It is a pattern that is replicated ad nauseum: every five years, Zimbabwe has sought to ensure that elections are held, and every five years, there is serious social dislocation. Instead of presenting a platform for the serious contestation of ideas for one of the continent's most educated citizenry, elections in Zimbabwe are consistently about name-calling, violence, intimidation, court cases and back to the campaign trail. However, to be fair, they have also been opportunities for innovation, colour, pomp and ceremony. It is only that these are always overshadowed by the negative dimensions generated by electoral politics.

This volume provides valuable insights into dimensions of Zimbabwean elections that have not benefited from concerted and consistent scholarly attention. These include issues relating to the exclusion of women (although some helpful literature has been produced), women with disability, the media and the role of traditional leaders. The latter dimension is particularly significant, as traditional leaders occupy a very strategic place in Zimbabwean society. Contributors to this volume have demonstrated appreciable levels of creativity, courage and conviction. They have overcome self-censorship and fear to offer helpful reflections on a key aspect of Zimbabwean life. I warmly commend this volume to scholars and students from diverse disciplines, as well as actors from civil society, the field of development, human rights and others.

Harare, Zimbabwe   Ezra Chitando

Ezra Chitando (Prof.) serves as Professor of Religious Studies at the University of Zimbabwe and Theology Consultant on HIV for the World Council of Churches. He is also Extraordinary Professor at the University of the Western Cape. https://orcid.org/0000-0003-2493-8151.

Acknowledgements

We would like to express our profound gratitude to all of those who supported us one way or another in the process of writing and publishing of this book. We would like to thank Prof. Ezra Chitando and Prof. Liberty Muchativugwa Hove for their input during the initial stages of developing the concept on Electoral Politics in Zimbabwe. We also received immense support during the production of this book from Ambra Finotello, Geetha Chockalingam, Ulrike Stricker-Komba and Shilpa Amarpuri, who are an amazing and excellent team at Palgrave Macmillan. We would not forget the significant role played by the reviewers of the chapters in this volume. You are greatly appreciated for you enormously contributed towards improving the ultimate quality of the chapters in this book.

Contents

1 Introduction: The Nexus Between Gender, Religion
  and the Media in Zimbabwean Electoral Politics 1
  Sophia Chirongoma and Esther Mavengano

Part I Gender and Electoral Politics in Zimbabwe

2 Electoral Participation as a Fundamental Right
  for Women with Disabilities in Zimbabwe 19
  Catherine Kudzai Bingisai

3 Unpacking the Issue of Gender and Electoral Violence
  in Christopher Mlalazi's *They Are Coming* 41
  Thamsanqa Moyo

4 Shona Women and Grassroots Politics in Zimbabwe:
  Prospects for the 2023 General Elections 55
  Maradze Viriri and Eunitah Viriri

5 Critical Thinking, Gender and Electoral Politics
  in Zimbabwe 73
  Ephraim Taurai Gwaravanda

6 Of Pains, Regrets and Suppressed Desires: Gendered
  Politics and Women Activism in Zimbabwean
  Electoral Politics 89
  Andrew Mutingwende

7	Rhetoric or Reality? Assessing the Efficacy of Policy and Legislative Interventions in Enhancing Women Political Participation in Zimbabwe Anesu Ingwani and Malvin Nyengeterai Kwaramba	107
8	Post-independence Election Violence: Re-thinking the Marginalisation of Women in Zimbabwean Politics Kudzai Biri	127
9	Voter Rights and Gender: An Analysis of the Importance of Voter Education in Zimbabwe Lillian Mhuru	143

Part II Media and Electoral Politics in Zimbabwe

10	Polytricking or Political Contestation? The Digital Space as Alternative Public Sphere in the Run up to the 2023 Public Elections in Zimbabwe Collen Sabao and Theophilus Tinashe Nenjerama	163
11	Music, Deceit, and Representation of Political Actors: Navigating the Connection of Chief Hwenje's Songs with Propaganda in Zimbabwe's Politicised Space Lazarus Sauti, Tendai Makaripe, and Wellington Gadzikwa	185
12	Melancholia and Polysemanticism in Winky D's Sonic Retentions: Subverting Expressive Barricades and Voicing the Electoral Process Through Performance Esther Mavengano	201
13	The Morbidity of Zimbabwe's Transformational Politics: Hope or Doom in the Post-coup Era? Gift Gwindingwe	227
14	The Rhetoric of Onoma: The Intersection of Memory and Power Dynamics in Naming and Name-Calling in Zimbabwe's Electoral Politics Esther Mavengano and Thamsanqa Moyo	247
15	The Effectiveness of Social Media in Mitigating Unfair Mainstream Media Electoral Coverage in Zimbabwe Lucia Chingwena and Isaac Mhute	263

Part III Traditional Leaders and Religious Discourses in Zimbabwe's Electoral Politics

16 Traditional Leaders as Vote Brokers and 'Kingmakers' in Zimbabwe's Elections   289
Gift Mwonzora

17 The Institution of Traditional Leadership and Partisan Politics in Zimbabwe   309
Jeffrey Kurebwa

18 The Role of Traditional Leaders and Culture in Zimbabwean Elections   331
Takavafira Masarira Zhou

19 A Critique of the Responsibility of Traditional Leaders in the Electoral Process: A Zimbabwean Experience   351
Sibiziwe Shumba

20 Abusing the Traditional Sceptre: Chiefs and Electoral Collusion in Zimbabwe   371
Edmore Dube

21 Traditional Leaders, Electoral Politics and Impregnability of the Rural Constituency in Zimbabwe   393
Pedzisai Ruhanya and Bekezela Gumbo

List of Appendixes   421

Index   431

Notes on Contributors

Catherine Kudzai Bingisai holds a Bachelor of Science Degree in Political Science and a Master of Science Degree in International Relations from the University of Zimbabwe. She is currently pursuing her doctoral studies in International Relations at Babeş-Bolyai University in Romania. Her research interests include but not limited to social linguistics, political economy, technology in elections, gender equality, food security and international organisations. She has attended several international conferences and workshops.

Kudzai Biri (Ph.D.) is an Associate Professor in the Department of Philosophy, Religion and Ethics of the University of Zimbabwe. Her area of specialization is Christianity and African Indigenous. She has published widely on religion and gender, religion and politics and religion and migration. Her recent book; *The Wounded Beast? The Bible, Tradition and Single Women* captures the resilience of African indigenous cultures that disempower and marginalise single women, in their diverse categories and challenges the Church to deploy inclusive sermons and challenge oppressive traditions.

Lucia Chingwena is a Sales and Marketing Specialist at For All Medical Aid Society. She holds a Master of Arts Degree in Strategic Communication from Midlands State University, Special Honors in Media and Communication Studies and B.A. in Media Studies from Zimbabwe Open University. She has strong interest in political communication research.

Sophia Chirongoma is a Senior Lecturer in the Religious Studies Department at Midlands State University, Zimbabwe. She is also an Academic Associate/Research Fellow at the Research Institute for Theology and Religion (RITR) in the College of Human Sciences, University of South Africa (UNISA). Her research interests and publications focus on the interface between culture, ecology, religion, health, politics and gender justice.

Edmore Dube (Ph.D. UZ) is a senior lecturer in the Department of Philosophy and Religious Studies, Great Zimbabwe University, Masvingo; with a huge interest in issues of justice and peace; critiquing *jambanja* (2018) and the 'armed state' (2019). He is a member of the African Consortium for Law and Religious Studies (ACLARS) and ATISCA. He has contributed to the ACLARS volumes on challenges besetting African heritage (2017) and impediments to human flourishing in Africa (2019), as well as the ATISCA discourse on religion and development (2019). He has co-edited a UNISA published volume on religious pluralism (2022).

Wellington Gadzikwa (Ph.D.) is a Senior Lecturer, Journalism and Media Studies at Africa University in Zimbabwe. He previously held the same position at the University of Zimbabwe. He is a published scholar with several chapters in books and peer reviewed journals. His research and publication interests are in journalism standards and practice, media framing, tabloids and tabloidisation. He also co-edited the book *Zimbabwe: The Mighty Fall of a Type of A Nation State* (2019) with Professor Maurice Taonezvi Vambe which presents a candid dissection of the post-Mugabe Zimbabwe.

Bekezela Gumbo is a Ph.D. student at the University of the Free State in South Africa. He also serves as the Principal Researcher at the Zimbabwe Democracy Institute in Harare, Zimbabwe. He also teaches comparative political development in Africa at Africa University. He has published widely on political transitions in Zimbabwe. His research interest is on the politics of transition and the quest for sustainable development in sub-Saharan Africa.

Ephraim Taurai Gwaravanda (Prof.) holds a Ph.D. in Philosophy from the University of South Africa (UNISA). He is an Associate Professor of Philosophy in the Department of Philosophy and Religious Studies (Great Zimbabwe University) and a Research Associate at the Ali Mazrui Centre for Higher Education Studies (University of Johannesburg). He has published several scholarly articles and book chapters in African epistemology, higher education, critical thinking and indigenous knowledge systems. He has co-edited two books, namely *African Higher Education in the 21st century: Epistemological, Ontological and Ethical Perspectives*, (Brill/Sense, 2021) and *Mediating Learning in Higher Education in Africa: From Critical Thinking to Social Justice Pedagogies*, (Brill/Sense, 2021).

Gift Gwindingwe (Ph.D.) is a Media and Cultural Studies Lecturer at Great Zimbabwe University, Mashava Campus. He holds a Ph.D. in Communication from the University of Fort Hare, South Africa. He is a former member of the Research Committee and currently a member of the Great Zimbabwe University International Relations Committee. He has published papers in local (South African) accredited journals. His research interests are in the following areas: cultural studies, postcolonialism, politics and the pervasive nature of digital media in shaping today's communication terrain.

Anesu Ingwani holds a Bachelor of Laws (LL.Bs.) from the University of Zimbabwe. She is currently pursuing Master of Science in Gender and Policy Studies at Great Zimbabwe University.

Jeffrey Kurebwa (Ph.D.) is a Senior Lecturer in the Department of Peace and Governance at Bindura University of Science Education, Zimbabwe. He holds a Ph.D. in Public Administration from Nelson Mandela University, South Africa. He teaches at both undergraduate and graduate levels. He has supervised and examined dissertations at undergraduate, masters and doctoral level. He has examined Ph.D. theses for Women's University in Africa (Zimbabwe), Durban University of Technology (South Africa), University of KwaZulu-Natal (South Africa), Zimbabwe Open University and Bindura University of Science Education (Zimbabwe). He has also externally examined Masters Dissertations for Africa University and Durban University of Technology. He has over 70 publications in the areas of gender, local governance, natural resource governance, cyber security and public policy. He has edited two books on *Participation of Young People in Governance Processes in Africa* (2019), and *Understanding Gender in the African Context in the 21st Century* (2020). He is a Programme Peer Reviewer for the Zimbabwe Council for Higher Education (ZIMCHE). He has also peer reviewed programmes for UNICAF, University of Zimbabwe, Arrupe Jesuit University, Great Zimbabwe University and Midlands State University.

Malvin Nyengeterai Kwaramba attained a Master of Science Degree in International Relations as well as a Bachelor of Science Honours in Political Science, both from the University of Zimbabwe.

Tendai Makaripe is a an award winning Zimbabwean journalist with over 7 years of writing experience, part of which have been spent as news editor for a number of online news sites. He is a passionate political scientist with a bias towards governance, human rights and international relations issues. He is a Reporter at Mased Media Inc. Harare, Zimbabwe. He holds a Diploma in Journalism and Communication, a B.Sc. Hons. Political Science and a M.Sc. Politics and International Relations.

Esther Mavengano is a Lecturer who teaches Linguistics and Literature in the Department of English and Media Studies, Faculty of Arts at Great Zimbabwe University in Masvingo, Zimbabwe. She holds a Ph.D. in Linguistics and Literary Studies obtained from the University of North West in South Africa. Her research areas maintain the interface of linguistics and poetics. She has interests in language policy and planning, sociolinguistics, languages use in media and political discourses, translingual practices in fictional writings, identity issues in contemporary transnational Anglophone/African literature, religion and gender, stylistics and language education in "multi" contexts. She has published in reputable international journals including *Cogent Arts and Humanities*, *African Identities, Literator, Journal of Multicultural Discourses*, among others. She is a Research Fellow at the Research Institute for Theology and Religion, College of Human Sciences, UNISA, in South Africa. She is currently a Humboldt Postdoctoral Fellow at TU (Techische Universistat) Dresden's Institute of English and American Studies, Department of English, Germany. She is a Co-Editor of *Zimbabwe in the Post-COVID-19 Era: Reflections, Lessons and the Future of Public Health*. Routledge Publisher—https://www.routledge.com/Zimbabwe-in-the-Post-COVID-19-Era-Reflections-Lessons-and-the-Future-of/Mavengano-Marevesa-Jakaza/p/book/9781032487748.

Lillian Mhuru is a Zimbabwean, born in Mhondoro Ngezi, Kadoma. She is based in Harare, Zimbabwe, where she is a Law Lecturer at Zimbabwe Open University. She has a passion for teaching and undertaking research in human rights and humanitarian fields.

Isaac Mhute (Prof.) is an Associate Professor with Midlands State University's Department of Language, Literature and Culture Studies. He is a chief examiner for language and literature with an international examining board, professional editor and translator/ back translator (English and Shona). He graduated with a Doctor of Literature and Philosophy in African Languages from the University of South Africa whose focus was on the morphological, syntactic and semantic representation of grammatical relations. His research interests are in both theoretical and applied linguistic areas such as language policy and development, syntax and semantics, onomastics as well as language and strategic communication issues in education, among others.

Thamsanqa Moyo (Ph.D.) is a Senior Lecturer in the Department of English and Media Studies at Great Zimbabwe University. He holds a Ph.D. in English from the University of South Africa. His research interests are in indigenous knowledge systems, communication and life-writing, particularly in the Zimbabwean context and African literature.

Andrew Mutingwende is a Lecturer in the Department of English and Communication at Midlands State University. His research interests are in discourse analysis, language and politics, religion and language use. He has published in these areas.

Gift Mwonzora (Ph.D.) is a Zimbabwean Scholar and is a holder of a Ph.D. in Political Sociology from Rhodes University in South Africa. He has worked as a Research Fellow at Rhodes University in the Department of Sociology and in the Department of Law at the Northwest University in South Africa. He is currently a Research Fellow in the Institute of Institutional Change and Social Justice at the University of Free State (UFS) in South Africa. He has published on areas that include democracy, democratisation, transitional justice, elections, social media, human rights, social movements and political violence.

Theophilus Tinashe Nenjerama is a graduate student at Columbia Theological Seminary, Decatur, United States. He holds a Master of Arts in Divinity and Master of Arts in Practical Theology. He is the Youth Director at Snellville United Methodist Church. His experience spans from being a High School Teacher in Zimbabwe to a Youth Worker and Arts Workshop facilitator in Ireland and being a Teaching Assistant in the United States. His most recent article is on practical theology and social movements in Zimbabwe. He is currently working on a project exploring civil religion in post-Mugabe Zimbabwe. His research trajectory intersect religion and public life.

Pedzisai Ruhanya (Ph.D.) is a Lecturer in the Department of Creative Media and Communication at the University of Zimbabwe. He is also a Founder and Director of the Zimbabwe Democracy Institute. He holds a Doctor of Philosophy in Media and Democracy. He has many publications on transition politics in Zimbabwe. His research interest is on the role of media in democratic transitions.

Collen Sabao (Prof.) is an Associate Professor of Linguistics, Literature and Communication in the Languages and Literature Department at the University of Namibia. As a Lecturer and Researcher, his research interests lie in the areas of phonetics and phonology, political discourse, media discourse, pan Africanism, afrocentricity, appraisal theory, argumentation, world literatures and rhetoric. He has published extensively in these areas, having published 31 (thirty-one) articles and several chapters in internationally refereed publications. He also holds a Bachelor of Arts Honours Degree in English and Communication and a Master of Philosophy in Theoretical Linguistics from universities in Zimbabwe and a Ph.D. in African Languages (Applied Linguistics) from Stellenbosch University (South Africa). He is also an American Council of Learned Societies Fellow'14 and an African Humanities Fellow '14. He is also an amateur footballer and an Elder Elect of Records in the House of Nyabhinghi Rastafari.

Lazarus Sauti holds an M.A. in Media and Communication Studies (with specialisation in Media and Communication) from the University of Zimbabwe and a M.Sc. in International Relations from Bindura University of Science Education. He also holds a B.A. (Special Honours) in Communication and Media Studies, a B.A. in Media Studies, as well as Certificates and Diplomas in Journalism and Communication, Public Relations, Business Promotion, and Library and Information Science. He has published book chapters and research papers. His research interests focus on media, conflict resolution and transformation; digital media cultures; political communication; and cultural productions, human rights, peace, democracy and governance.

Sibiziwe Shumba (Ph.D.) holds a doctorate degree from the University of South Africa. She is a Senior Lecturer in the Department of Languages and Humanities at Joshua Mqabuko Nkomo Polytechnic College in

Bulawayo, Zimbabwe. Shumba is her family name. She is also a Lecturer at Midlands University, Gweru, Zimbabwe. She moved from the college which she initially indicated in her biography. She is a Part-Time Lecturer with the Catholic University of Zimbabwe and Zimbabwe Open University. She has also served as a lecturer at several theological colleges. She is a Research Fellow at the Research Institute for Theology and Religion, UNISA. Her research interests lie in cross-disciplinary issues such as religion and gender, African Traditional Religion, theology and world religions among others. She is a peer reviewer with Studia Historiae Ecclesiasticae.

Eunitah Viriri (Ph.D.) holds a Doctor of Philosophy in Languages, Linguistics and Literature from the University of South Africa. She is a Teacher Educator at Great Zimbabwe University and has published and presented papers in language, culture and educational issues. She is currently a Postdoctoral fellow at the University of KwaZulu-Natal, Pietermaritzburg in South Africa.

Maradze Viriri (Ph.D.) holds a doctoral degree in Onomastics from the University of KwaZulu-Natal. He has published several publications in referred journals and has also presented conference papers in a number of international conferences. He is currently a Lecturer in the Department of Teacher Development at Great Zimbabwe University. His main research interests are in onomastics, gender, language policy and indigenous knowledge systems.

Takavafira Masarira Zhou (Ph.D.) holds a doctorate in Environmental History from the University of Zimbabwe. He is an environmental historian, a Lemba, trade unionist and Human Rights defender. He has lectured at Mutare Teachers College, Africa University and Great Zimbabwe University (2004–2008) where he helped to transform the history subject area into the Department of History and Development Studies. He has presented various papers at conferences in Zimbabwe, Africa, Europe and Asia. He has also published on African agriculture; white settler farming; the environmental impact of mining in Zimbabwe; peace and security in Africa; history curricula changes in Zimbabwe; post-2016 Africa's development; teacher education; poverty, natural resources curse, underdevelopment, and sustainable development in Africa; poverty, conflict, and vulnerability in Africa; Climate Change and Environment in 21st Century Africa; indigenous knowledge systems; and general history and politics of Zimbabwe.

List of Figures

Fig. 2.1	Zimbabwe Electoral Commission should enhance public awareness of the participation of women with disabilities in electoral reforms	35
Fig. 15.1	News article where a ZANU PF official was telling CCC to campaign on social media	268
Fig. 15.2	Old grannies at mutare rally	277
Fig. 15.3	Old woman dancing to CCC songs	278
Fig. 15.4	Chamisa chatting to an elderly man	278
Fig. 15.5	Chamisa mingling with the public at the Workers' Day commemorations	280
Fig. 21.1	Elite dis-cohesion vs. electoral impregnability (*Source* Author's analysis of ZEC election statistics in Appendices 1.2 and 1.3)	400
Fig. 21.2	How traditional leaders facilitate accessibility of the rural constituency	408

List of Tables

Table 2.1	Age of the participants	28
Table 2.2	Educational level of the participants	28
Table 2.3	Marital status of the participants	28
Table 2.4	Descriptive statistics on the level of participation for women with disabilities	29
Table 2.5	Challenges faced by women with disabilities in electoral participation	31
Table 4.1	Buhera South ZANU PF cell structure	61
Table 21.1	Percentage changes in economic growth Vs rural impregnability	401
Table 21.2	Political economy of dependency	411

CHAPTER 1

Introduction: The Nexus Between Gender, Religion and the Media in Zimbabwean Electoral Politics

Sophia Chirongoma and Esther Mavengano

INTRODUCTION

The chapters in this volume deliberate on how electoral politics in Zimbabwe is impacted by three foci. The first segment reflects on how gender dynamics have a bearing on men and women's participation in

---

S. Chirongoma (✉)
Midlands State University, Zvishavane, Zimbabwe
e-mail: sochirongoma@gmail.com

E. Mavengano
Department of English and Media Studies, Faculty of Arts,
Great Zimbabwe University, Masvingo, Zimbabwe

Research Institute for Theology and Religion, College of Human Sciences,
UNISA, Pretoria, South Africa

Alexander von Humboldt Postdoctoral Research Fellow at TU, Institute of English and American Studies, Faculty of Linguistics, Literature and Cultural Studies, Department of English, Technische Universitat Dresden, Dresden, Germany

© The Author(s), under exclusive license to Springer Nature
Switzerland AG 2023
E. Mavengano and S. Chirongoma (eds.), *Electoral Politics in Zimbabwe, Vol II*, https://doi.org/10.1007/978-3-031-33796-3_1

politics and how this inadvertently influences their role in the electoral processes. The second part explores the impact of the media on the electorate's values, beliefs and practices, and the third part discusses the role of traditional leaders in the political arena, particularly how the traditional leaders influence the electorate's voting patterns. These three parts are not disjointed entities; rather, they feed into each other. Below, we briefly unpack the thrust of each of the three parts.

Gender and Electoral Politics in Zimbabwe

The contributors in this part foreground how religion and culture shape society's gender constructs. The eight chapters in this segment bemoan how the inherent gender disparities in different sectors of life in Zimbabwe are also manifested in the political arena. In concurrence with Kaulem (2011), Katongole (2017) and Chirongoma (2020, 2022), the authors of the chapters in this part offer a concise critique of the deeply entrenched patriarchal values espoused in both the church and their community, which consequently push women to the periphery when it comes to political participation. This peripherization includes their participation in elections as candidates as well as in their capacity as the electorate. The authors in this segment also echo the painful reality that a culture of violence targeted towards women presents a major barricade to their participation in electoral politics. Citing the officially available statistics revealing women's minority status in key political leadership and decision-making forums, the contributors to this volume concur on the importance of making resolute efforts in flattening the curve of gender inequality in all political structures in Zimbabwe.

For instance, Kudzai Bingisai, in Chapter 2 titled, "Electoral Participation as a Fundamental Right for Women with Disabilities in Zimbabwe," pays particular attention to the challenges endured by women with disability not only when it comes to participating in politics, but more so, the barriers they often have to contend with in an endeavour to exercise their constitutional right to vote. In the same light, Chapter 8, by the title, "Post-Independence Election Violence: Rethinking the Marginalisation of Women in Zimbabwean Politics," authored by Kudzai Biri reverberates the unpalatable truism about the unholy alliance of religio-cultural and socio-economic injustices which confine many Zimbabwean women to a subaltern status. She further argues that this secondary status makes it difficult for most women to take up key leadership and decision-making positions in all sectors of life, including the political realm. In concurrence with Manyonganise (2015), Biri emphasizes the urgent need for empowering female politicians to equip them with skills to shun some negative and retrogressive malestream behaviour and transform to become effective and relevant voices of the countless voiceless women looking up to them. Hence, the overarching theme running through this first segment of the volume is an emphasis on the pertinent need to redress multifaceted factors which are exacerbating women's exclusion from political participation.

Another key factor influencing women's second-class status leading to their marginalization in the political sphere is the role of the media. The role of the media in Zimbabwe's electoral politics is the second theme covered in this volume. It is to this theme that we turn below.

Media and Electoral Politics in Zimbabwe

In this second part, comprising of six chapters, the contributors deliberate on the role of the media in disseminating information regarding politics and governance. They articulate how the media can serve as both friend and foe when circulating information on politics, especially when it comes to information pertaining the electoral processes. The contributors in this part also examine the power and shortcomings of both mainstream media and social media, particularly within the context of electoral politics. In concurrence with Sabao and Chingwaramusee (2017), and Sabao and Chikara (2018, 2020), in Chapter 10 titled, "Pollytricking or Political Contestation? The Digital Space as Alternative Public Sphere in the Run Up to the 2023 Public Election in Zimbabwe," Collen Sabao and Theophilus Tinashe Nenjerama discuss the use of social media as an alternative and effective channel for disseminating news, including politically related information. Similarly, in Chapter 12, titled, "Melancholia and Polysemanticism in Winky D's Sonic Retentions: Subverting Expressive Barricades and Voicing the Electoral Process Through Performance," Esther Mavengano illustrates how artists like Winky D make use of music, which is widely circulated via social media and other electronic platforms to unpack some of the people's deeply felt needs amidst the volatile election fever pitch era.

The media has also been utilized by both the ruling ZANU PF party and the main opposition, CCC, to reach out to the gatekeepers of the electorate, particularly, the traditional leadership in the rural and commercial farming communities. Below, we turn to discuss how the traditional leaders utilize various ways of communicating with their constituencies to ensure that they "vote wisely."

Traditional Leaders and Electoral Politics in Zimbabwe

The third segment consists of eight chapters. The contributors in this part discuss the role of Zimbabwean traditional leaders in the political structures. With a specific focus on the pivotal role of traditional leaders in the rural areas where the bulk of the Zimbabwean population resides, the chapters in this part illustrate how the two main contenders, the ruling party ZANU PF and the main opposition party, the CCC, are making concerted efforts to draw the traditional leadership on their side so as to ensure that they garner as much support from the rural electorate as possible. Acknowledging that the Zimbabwean constitution clearly stipulates that traditional leaders should be non-partisan, the authors cite several instances where some traditional leaders have been on record for openly expressing their allegiance to the ruling ZANU PF party whilst only a few have been vocal regarding the importance of remaining neutral as traditional leaders when it comes to political parties' campaigns.

Having briefly outlined the three parts covered in this volume, the upcoming section presents a summary of the chapters.

Part I: Gender and Electoral Politics in Zimbabwe (2–9)

As has been noted above, the chapters in this part deliberate on the interface of gender constructs and electoral politics in Zimbabwe. In Chapter 2 titled, "Electoral Participation as a Fundamental Right for Women with Disabilities in Zimbabwe," Kudzai Bingisai buttresses the fact that Zimbabwean women with disabilities have a fundamental right to participate in electoral politics. It is Bingisai's contention that whilst there are entrenched gender disparities which push women to the peripheries of electoral politics, women with disability suffer double oppression based on gender as well as their status of living with disability. Bingisai also articulates that rural women with disability also endure a third layer of being disadvantaged because of limited access to information and the physical barriers which make it difficult for them to access the polling stations. The chapter also highlights the fact that women with disabilities are more prone to violence than their counterparts without disabilities and they do not get adequate support from family and society towards electoral participation. The chapter concludes by propounding that women with disabilities should break the glass ceiling towards electoral participation by exercising the right to vote and hold political office. The study also recommends that the society should change its mind set and support women with disabilities so that they won't have to suffer from any sort of social exclusion wrought by systematic marginalization and stigmatization.

Thamsanqa Moyo is the author of Chapter 3 titled, "Unpacking the Issue of Gender and Electoral Violence in Christopher Mlalazi's *They Are Coming*." In this chapter, Moyo explicates how the Zimbabwean elections and the electoral processes have been an arena of violence and contestation since 1980. Reflecting on how the war of liberation and its legacies were rooted in the militarization of political spaces that produced violent patriarchal tendencies, the chapter contends that under the current Mnangagwa regime, Zimbabwe is still a patriarchal and militaristic society where outright victory and annihilation of the opponent is the guiding philosophy. Engaging in a literary and critical analysis of Christopher Mlalazi's novel, *They Are Coming*, Moyo illustrates how Zimbabwean men control the electoral discourses and practices in the country. Analysing the characters in the text, the chapter bemoans how women who dare to join these political spaces must sheepishly commit to being recruited and conscripted into ideologies that perpetuate and legitimize these patriarchal, militaristic and hegemonic identities.

Chapter 4, entitled "Women and Grassroots Politics in Zimbabwe: Prospects for the 2023 General Elections," is authored by Maradze Viriri and Euritah Viriri. The chapter traces the history of Shona women's participation in local politics in the ZANU PF political party in Buhera South. Lamenting how women have been perpetually under-represented in all the leadership structures, the authors attempt to proffer possible reasons for such a gender-skewed trend. They note that top among the key factors barricading women from participating and taking up key leadership and decision-making positions are the entrenched religio-cultural beliefs and practices, tainted by hegemonic patriarchal values as well as the fear of violence which is spewed especially during the election periods.

The chapter concludes by recommending that concerted efforts must be made to increase women's participation in the political realm. This includes adopting a women quarter system which must start at the grassroots level, conscientizing women to break the barriers and to create a conducive environment so that women can freely participate in politics without fearing violence, intimidation, sexual abuse, labelling and marginalization.

"Critical Thinking, Gender and Electoral Politics in Zimbabwe" is the title for Chapter 5, authored by Ephraim Gwaravanda. Herein, Gwaravanda asserts that the often hostile and polarized political environment in Zimbabwe poses a major hindrance for meaningful gender balance in the political train. Gwaravanda singles out three mistaken assumptions that tend to disadvantage aspiring female politicians from joining the political bandwagon. The first one being the tendency to resort to political violence as a tool for attaining a preconceived electoral outcome. According to the author, this discourages women to take up posts for political representation especially in opposition politics. The second one is the polarized political environment in Zimbabwe which has inadvertently created a false dichotomy whereby participants are categorized as belonging to either the ruling party or opposition politics. According to Gwaravanda, this reduces democratic space and it stifles freedom of political association and freedom of political expression. This dichotomy resultantly disadvantages female participants both as representatives and as voters resulting in gender imbalances in political representation. Lastly, Gwaravanda critiques the tendency to use prejudicial and hasty moral judgements against female politicians in Zimbabwe. He reaches the conclusion that this apparent political intolerance intimidates women such that only few women find the courage to stand insults in the attempt to be candidates for political representation thereby causing gender imbalances right from grassroots levels. The author recommends that critical thinking should be an important component of citizenship education so as to inculcate informed political participation and to create an enabling environment for female candidates and voters.

In sync with the issues raised by Gwaravanda in Chapter 5, Andrew Mutingwende in Chapter 6 writes on the topic, "Of Pains, Regrets and Suppressed Desires: Gendered Politics and Women Activism in Zimbabwean Electoral Politics." Mutingwende restates the fact that women's political activism within the polarized Southern African region entails major personal sacrifice, particularly because this terrain is riddled with violence, intimidation and the otherization of female politicians. Advocating for women to enter into a violence-free and fair political playing field, the author adopts the Critical Discourse Analysis (CDA) framework to analyse selected incidences where some aspiring female politicians were exposed to undue politically motivated violence. Hence, the chapter analyses selected articles published in the private-owned Guardian and the state-owned Herald online newspaper reporting on popular female electoral experiences between 2018 and 2022. Based on the major findings of his study, Mutingwende concludes that male politicians and state-controlled journalists only work to perpetuate the plight of women as both do not constitute the female embodiment. He therefore recommends that for more women to feel safe and secure to join active politics, there is need to create a conducive environment whereby political contenders engage in reasoned political debates without resorting to any form of violence.

In Chapter 7, titled "Rhetoric or Reality? Assessing the Efficacy of Policy and Legislative Interventions in Enhancing Women Political Participation in Zimbabwe," Anesu Ingwani and Malvin Nyengeterai Kwaramba concur with the views raised by the authors in the preceding chapters. They reiterate the fact that the vice of male domination in political spaces is not unique to Zimbabwe. Ingwani and Kwaramba undertake an analysis of the legislations as well as the practical steps taken by the government of Zimbabwe to increase women's political participation since its independence in 1980 up to the current time (February 2023). Hence, they take a closer look at the policies and legislative interventions that have been implemented to encourage women political participation in electoral processes from the advent of the universal suffrage to the Constitution of Zimbabwe 2013. Citing major challenges encountered by women candidates in electoral politics which include lack of funding, hostility faced due to the patriarchal nature of society and the gendered disadvantages of the simple majority electoral system among other factors, the authors of this chapter conclude that the measures taken to increase women's political participation appear to be mere rhetoric as far as practical results in this area are concerned. They recommend that more practical steps need to be taken to optimize the full involvement of women in electoral politics.

In concurrence with the foregoing chapters in this segment, in Chapter 8, entitled, "Post-Independence Election Violence: Rethinking the Marginalisation of Women in Zimbabwean Politics," Kudzai Biri describes the violence perpetrated against women in politics in Zimbabwe as institutional. She contends that the different forms of violence targeted towards women in politics are fuelled by cultural socializations and "religiously bound patriarchy" which manifest in deficient and rigid patriarchal theologies on gender relations. She also argues that the inherent economic disempowerment of women, coupled with the ingrained religio-cultural traditions have together produced toxic masculinities and repressed femininities, making it difficult for many women aspiring to actively participate in politics and occupy leadership posts in politics. Hence, Biri challenges both religious and political leaders to revisit their patriarchal worldview in an endeavour to remove all that which denies women and girls an opportunity for equal political participation, including their being able to freely contest for leadership posts. The chapter recommends the need for investing in socio-economic empowerment of women so that they can be fully equipped to rise and actively participate in politics. Biri challenges academic and activist movements such as the Circle of Concerned African Women Theologians to develop a robust political theology of hope, healing and restoration for women who have been wounded by acts of violence, intimidation and marginalization peddled within the political spaces. She also proposes a theology of responsibility and accountability to deter violence and cut the cord of recurring gender-based inequities which are prevalent within the political sphere.

Lilian Mhuru's chapter (9) concludes this part. Titled, "Voter Rights and Gender: An Analysis of the Importance of Voter Education in Zimbabwe," this chapter emphasizes the pivotal role of voter education in electoral politics. She explicates that for an election to be successful and democratic, voters must understand their rights and responsibilities, and they must be sufficiently knowledgeable and well informed to cast ballots that are legally valid and to participate meaningfully in the voting process. According to Mhuru, some of the problems experienced in Zimbabwe's electoral politics emanate from a lack of voter education. She concludes the chapter by recommending that the government of Zimbabwe must avail adequate resources to the Zimbabwe Electoral Commission (ZEC) so that it can conduct rigorous voter education in all the provinces. She proffers that with adequate voter education, the electorate will make informed electoral choices, and this will also reduce voter apathy, consequently propelling mass political participation.

The ensuing part discusses the role of the media in Zimbabwe's electoral politics. It emphasizes the fact that the media is a main source of information pertaining to electoral politics. Below, we turn to that.

Part II: Media and Electoral Politics in Zimbabwe (10–15)

The six chapters in this segment discuss the pros and cons of both mainstream and social media as purveyors of information on political matters, particularly electoral politics. Acknowledging the fundamental importance of the media in disseminating information, Collen Sabao and Theophilus Tinashe Nenjerama authored Chapter 10 by the title, "Pollytricking or Political Contestation? The Digital Space as Alternative Public Sphere in the Run Up to the 2023 Public Election in Zimbabwe." The chapter examines how web-based social media platforms have been extensively used as spaces for political campaigning and contestation in Zimbabwe, especially in the run up to the 2023 harmonized general elections. Asserting that the hegemonic ZANU PF-led government has continuously stifled any political dissent, the authors of this chapter foreground the power and significance of social media as alternative digital public spheres. The chapter also contends that the criminalization of internet-based protests viewed to be hostile to ZANU PF hegemony, through the recent enactment of the Cyber and Data Protection Act of 2021, is testament to the levels to which the political party will go to maintain a hold on power. The chapter concludes by noting that the political actors in Zimbabwe have come to realize the efficacy of social media-based platforms as avenues to provide counternarratives in a political space that limits their activities within the mainstream public mass media, which is highly regulated by the ZANU PF government.

Chapter 11, authored by Lazarus Sauti, Tendai Makaripe and Wellington Gadzikwa goes by the title "Music, Deceit, and Representation of Political Actors: Navigating the Connection of Chief Hwenje's Songs with Propaganda in Zimbabwe's Politicised Space." Analysing musical pieces, this chapter argues that Chief Hwenje uses the white propaganda form in his music to try to convince Zimbabweans that President Mnangagwa and the Zimbabwe African National Union-Patriotic Front (ZANU PF) party are the right actors to govern Zimbabwe. According to the authors of this chapter, Chief Hwenje resorts to the bandwagon, name-calling, glittering generalities and transfer propaganda techniques to win a heartfelt battle over President Emerson Dambudzo Mnangagwa and ZANU PF and consolidate their power in the Zimbabwean political arena. The chapter concludes by asserting that the use of propaganda in Chief Hwenje's music is inflaming the conflict between the Citizens Coalition for Change (CCC) and ZANU PF in the country. Hence, the chapter recommends that musicians should use their creativity to promote peace and unity instead of inflaming conflict.

Similarly, in Chapter 12, Esther Mavengano discusses how music can be used as an avenue for communicating people's socio-economic and political views. The chapter is entitled "Melancholia and Polysemanticism in Winky D's Sonic Retentions: Subverting Expressive Barricades and Voicing the Electoral Process Through Performance." Focusing on Winky D's two songs, "Parliament" released in 2018 and "Ibotso," a 2023 production, Mavengano reflects upon the representation of socio-economic and religio-political polemics. The chapter also contends that through music, the artists do not only articulate existential struggles endured by the common citizens in Zimbabwe's "Ghetto" space, but they also offer modes of resistance by speaking truth to power in the context of the 2023 electoral politics. According to Mavengano, the two songs analysed herein confound the claim that Zimdancehall music lacks semantic relevance to the Zimbabwean society. Hence, she concludes that this music genre conveys a reluctance to grant the artists freedom of speech, a characteristic that reveals the main tenets of an autocratic political culture and it opens avenues for re-imagining a progressive and democratic future.

Chapter 13, by the title, "The Morbidity of Zimbabwe's Transformational Politics: Hope or Doom in the Post-Coup Era?" is authored by Gift Gwindingwe. The chapter juxtaposes the campaign proclamations by Emmerson Mnangagwa on the one side and those by Nelson Chamisa on the other. The main thrust of this chapter is to illustrate the fact that both Mnangagwa and Chamisa have opted for populist politics which has led them to neglect the general welfare of the general populace. Gwindingwe builds his argument upon the data which was gathered through a selection of key purposive texts drawn from the two contenders' campaign manifestos. After analysing these manifestos, the author concludes that their vagueness blindfolded the electorate. Another conclusion reached in this chapter is that the two main political opponents' failure to find common ground is testimony of their political insincerity as the public continues to suffer whilst the leadership trade accusations and counter-accusations to score a political agenda. Furthermore, the author points out that the endless debate on whether corruption or sanctions are the causes of Zimbabwe's economic woes is a stark signal of political polarization. Gwindigwe leaves the reader with a fundamental and troubling question of whether the pending 2023 harmonized elections will bear fruits of peace, development and democracy.

Authored by Esther Mavengano and Thamsanqa Moyo, the title for Chapter 14 is "The Rhetoric of Onoma: The Intersection of Memory and Power Dynamics in Naming and Name-Calling in Zimbabwe's Electoral Politics." The authors of this chapter bring into conversation the current politics of names and naming practices in contemporary Zimbabwe's electoral discourses. They interrogate the rhetoric of Onoma as part of anti-opposition politics in Zimbabwe today. The chapter's focus is on the renewed name-calling and misnaming in the context of the formation of the new main opposition party, the Citizens Coalition for Change (CCC). The authors conclude that names and naming of the parties and central political personalities of the splinter groups are not mere labels of identification or reference artefacts, but they are also part of the complex political pragmatism which serve as tropes of national memory, nostalgia or an attempt to influence voting trajectories in the forthcoming 2023 elections. They also recommend that academic inquiry of names/naming should aim to generate deep insights into the dialectics of Onoma, power and the politics of elections in the country.

"The Effectiveness of Social Media in Mitigating Unfair Mainstream Media Electoral Coverage in Zimbabwe," is the title for Chapter 15, authored by Lucia Chingwena and Isaac Mhute. Herein, Chingwena and Mhute chronicle how more than four decades after attaining political independence, Zimbabwe, once famed as the breadbasket for Southern Africa, has been reduced to a basket case status, under the ZANU PF leadership. Chingwena and Mhute therefore focus their discussion on how social media has been adopted by the main opposition party, Citizens Coalition for Change (CCC), as a mitigatory measure against the backdrop of being denied access to the necessary coverage of the parties by the mainstream media. The chapter foregrounds that, as the CCC strategically positions itself for winning the 2023 harmonized elections, social media is the way to settle scores with the ruling parties that take advantage of their positions to cling to power through unfairly monopolizing the mainstream media.

The third segment of this volume discusses the role of traditional leaders in Zimbabwe's governance and electoral politics dynamics. Below, we turn to discuss this theme.

Part III: Traditional Leaders and Electoral Politics in Zimbabwe (16–21)

The six chapters in this segment concur that whilst the Zimbabwean constitution clearly spells out that traditional leaders must be non-partisan, it is apparent that the bulk of Zimbabwe's traditional leaders have aligned themselves to the revolutionary party, ZANU PF. Chapter 16, authored by Gift Mwonzora, is titled "Traditional Leaders as Vote Brokers and King Makers in Zimbabwe's Elections." It examines how and why Zimbabwean traditional leaders manipulate and coerce the vulnerable community members to vote in a particular way. Drawing on the clientelism literature, Mwonzora engages with the empirical and theoretical debates on vote brokers to analyse how and why traditional leaders act as intermediaries who deliver votes to the incumbent during and off election seasons. According to Mwonzora, this analysis is necessitated by the fact that it helps to shed light on how and whether the traditional leaders' actions undermine, disable or enable electoral and participatory democracy within polities. The chapter concludes by emphasizing the importance for other studies to continue adding to the existing policy and academic literature by offering a deeper theorization of state-citizen relations and patron-client relationships witnessed in the dispensing of patronage by African political elites during election cycles.

Jeffrey Kurebwa is the author of Chapter 17, entitled, "The Institution of Traditional Leadership and Partisan Politics in Zimbabwe." Kurebwa commences this chapter by asserting that the conduct of traditional leaders has raised a lot of concerns and constitutional questions in Zimbabwe. According to Kurebwa, the traditional leaders' partisan nature and perceived alignment with the ruling party, ZANU PF has ignited a lot of criticism over their relevance in the twenty-first century. It is this chapter's contention that the institution of traditional leadership in Zimbabwe has been captured by political parties especially ZANU PF for political survival. The chapter also critiques how some traditional leaders have been actively involved in political campaigns, particularly for the ruling party (ZANU PF), threatening known or suspected opposition supporters with eviction from their territories, or ordering opposition supporters facing threats of eviction to pay a fine of an ox in order to be forgiven. The chapter concludes by restating that the partisan nature of traditional leaders is in total breach of Section 281 of the Constitution of Zimbabwe (2013). It recommends that traditional leaders should act in a non-partisan manner and abide by the Constitution of Zimbabwe which prohibits them from participating in politics.

Chapter 18, titled, "The Role of Traditional Leaders and Culture in Zimbabwean Elections," is authored by Tavafira Masarira Zhou. The crux of this chapter is to examine the role of traditional leaders in Zimbabwean elections in the period 1980 to the present. Whilst acknowledging that some traditional leaders have continued to judiciously execute their responsibilities as custodians of traditions, culture and customs and treat their subjects impartially, irrespective of their political affinity, the chapter argues that most traditional leaders have largely become the ruling party's lackeys, cronies and puppets that could be counted on for rural votes during elections. The chapter also argues that Mugabe and his successor Mnangagwa have systematically pursued the politics of expediency by winning the allegiance of traditional rulers to curb the advancement of opposition and ensure election victory in the rural areas. The chapter concludes that traditional leaders have undermined democracy during elections in Zimbabwe and recommends that they must respect constitutional dictates as non-partisan custodians of customs and culture, with a keen interest in socio-political and economic matters affecting their people. The author also proffers that the traditional institution must entrench the African heritage of democratic governance that could help in the revitalization and consolidation of the democratic ferment in Zimbabwe.

Authored by Sibiziwe Shumba, Chapter 19 is entitled, "A Critique of the Responsibility of Traditional Leaders in the Electoral Process: A Zimbabwean Experience." In this chapter, Shumba argues that traditional leaders in the contemporary Zimbabwean context are fully engaged in the electoral and political processes in their respective communities. She notes how they always follow the dictates of the ruling regime in the governance process. According to Shumba, the traditional leaders assist the sitting government either by design, default or coercion. Hence, the thrust of this chapter is to critique the role of Zimbabwean traditional leaders in the election and electoral processes. Shumba also tenders that some traditional leaders in Zimbabwe find it difficult to remain apolitical during the elections and electoral processes because the government is their paymaster. Hence, they are weary of biting the proverbial hand that feeds them. The chapter therefore concludes by proposing that the laws of the country must be aligned with the 2013 Constitution. Furthermore, Shumba recommends that Section 49 of the Traditional Leaders Act 1998 should be accordingly amended to inhibit possible political abuse and a monitoring instrument for traditional leaders should be put into place.

In concurrence with the foregoing chapters in this part, Edmore Dube authored Chapter 20, by the title, "Abusing the Traditional Sceptre: Chiefs and Electoral Collusion in Zimbabwe." In this chapter, Dube argues that indigenous religio-political leaders' electoral innuendos have generally been at tangent with their mandates. He, however, notes that contrarily, ever since the indigenous leaders ceased to be appointed by their communities, their allegiances have shifted from communal to statutory. The chapter further argues that these external forces have generally been self-interested and at loggerheads with the freedom of expression by communities. For instance, Dube notes how being on the government's payroll has clouded the electoral perceptions of indigenous leadership from colonial times to date. He laments the sad reality that instead of championing local development as required by their mandates, indigenous leaders have tended to collude with central government, the appointing and paying authority. Embarking on a historical journey, Dube explores allegations of chiefs sacrificing indigenous sceptres as central government rigging machinery since colonial times—using their sceptred positions to legitimize regimes not in tandem with community aspirations. The chapter concludes by emphasizing the importance of assessing to what extend the chiefs, headmen and village heads chose to stand with their communities since the introduction of government payroll.

Pedzisai Ruhanya and Bekezela Gumbo offer the closing rendition of this part with Chapter 21, entitled "Leaders, Electoral Politics and Impregnability of the Rural Constituency in Zimbabwe." The chapter examines the role of traditional leaders in the electoral impregnability of the rural constituency in Zimbabwe. According to Ruhanya and Gumbo, Zimbabwe's transition has been hindered by electoral impregnability of the rural constituency where traditional leaders exercise their influence. The thrust of this chapter is that traditional leaders are key elites in the rural constituency; hence, their interaction with politicians and the political system is very critical to understanding the challenges, gaps and opportunities for a democratic breakthrough in the rural constituency. The chapter concludes by stating that, when it comes to electoral politics, traditional leaders exist in a complex system of capture and patronage which is historical and institutional that has created and maintained impregnability of the rural constituency.

Conclusion

As this introductory chapter draws to a close, it seems befitting for us to regurgitate the clarion call by Mavengano and Marevesa (2022) in their advocacy for adopting a multi-sector approach to deconstruct hegemonic and degenerative masculinities and to reclaim positive, empowering, life-giving and life-affirming femininities which will serve as fecund ground for developing a new gender complementarity political philosophy. In the same light, we aver with Gaidzanwa (2004), who vociferously calls for the urgent need to revisit some myths coined to disempower and to exclude women from political participation. One of such myths is the perpetration of the belief that only married women possess the requisite moral integrity to contest for leadership positions; otherwise, those who are unmarried commoditize their bodies to climb up the power hierarchies and their success in breaking the glass ceiling is perceived as an anomaly. Cognizant of the pivotal role of both mainstream media and social media, we proffer that political actors as well as the electorate should fairly and responsibly utilize these invaluable communication channels for the betterment of Zimbabwe and the rest of the African continent. As has been noted by the contributors under the section on traditional leaders and electoral politics, the traditional leaders are the cogs that hold rural communities together. The partisan stance adopted by many traditional leaders and the propensity of the ruling government to unseat and threaten traditional leaders who choose to remain neutral has become a cancerous worm which needs urgent expunging. It is our sincere hope and prayer that this volume, together with volume one in this series, provides useful resource material for transforming the political environment in the formative 2023 Zimbabwe's harmonized elections and beyond.

References

Chirongoma, S. (2020). Women as agents of peace in the midlands province, Zimbabwe: Towards sustainable peace and development. In A. Chitando (Ed.), *Women and peacebuilding in Africa* (pp. 108–123). Routledge.

Chirongoma, S. (2022). Young Christian women as agents of sustainable development in Zimbabwe: A case study of Murinye district, Masvingo. In E. Chitando, S. Chirongoma, & K. Biri (Eds.), *Women and religion in Zimbabwe strides and struggles* (pp. 266–286). Lexington Publishers (ISBN 978-1-66690-331-7).

Gaidzanwa, R. (2004). *Gender, women and electoral politics in Zimbabwe* (EISA research report 8).

Katongole, E. (2017). *Born from lament the theology and politics of Hope in Africa*. Grand Rapids.

Kaulem, D. (2011). *Ending Violence in Zimbabwe*. AFCAST.

Manyonganise, M. (2015). Oppressive and liberative: An Zimbabwean woman's reflection of Ubuntu. *Verbum et Ecclessia, 36*(2), 1–7.

Mavengano, E., & Marevesa, T. (2022). Re-conceptualising womanhood and development in post-colonial Zimbabwe: A social conflict perspective. In E. Chitando & E. Kamaara (Eds.), *Values, identity, and sustainable development in Africa. Sustainable development goals series*. Palgrave Macmillan. https://doi.org/10.1007/978-3-031-12938-4_15

Sabao, C., & Chingwaramusee, V. R. (2017). Citizen journalism on Facebook and the challenges of media regulation in Zimbabwe. In N. A. Mhiripiri & T. Chari (Eds.), *Media law, ethics, and policy in the digital age* (pp. 193–206). IGI Global. https://doi.org/10.4018/978-1-5225-2095-5.ch011

Sabao, C., & Chikara, T. O. (2018). Social media as alternative public sphere for citizen participation and protest in national politics in Zimbabwe: The case of #thisflag. In F. P. C. Endong (Ed.), *Exploring the role of social media in transnational advocacy* (pp. 17–35). IGI Global. https://doi.org/10.4018/978-1-5225-2854-8.ch002

Sabao, C., & Chikara, T. O. (2020). Social media as alternative public sphere for citizen participation and protest in national politics in Zimbabwe: The case of #thisflag. In *African studies: Breakthroughs in research and practice* (pp. 772–786). IGI Global.

PART I

Gender and Electoral Politics in Zimbabwe

CHAPTER 2

Electoral Participation as a Fundamental Right for Women with Disabilities in Zimbabwe

Catherine Kudzai Bingisai

Introduction

This study sought to unravel the reasons behind the limited electoral participation of women with disabilities in Zimbabwe. Regional human rights mechanisms in favour of women have gradually evolved around the world. The ratification of the Universal Declaration of Human Rights by the United Nations (UN) General Assembly on December 10, 1948, was a huge milestone to recognize the rights of people including those with physical or mental disabilities. The United Nations has called for greater support for women's participation in all aspects of the electoral process at International Conferences on Women as highlighted in Mexico (1975), Copenhagen (1980), Nairobi (1985), Beijing (1995), and the 23rd Special Session of the General Assembly in Beijing (2000). According to Matfess et al. (2022), women have been unable to increase

C. K. Bingisai (✉)
Babeș-Bolyai University, Cluj-Napoca, Romania

their political representation at all levels regardless of constitutional provisions due to the threat of political violence. Neither have they been able to increase their access to positions of power and decision-making.

While women's participation in politics already has a passive voice, there seems to be an orthodox convention that contends that women with disabilities are not competent to exercise the right to participate in elections both as voters and as candidates. The United Nations designated the International Day for Persons with Disabilities on June 3, 1992, as a day to honour the skills of people with disabilities all over the world; yet, the level of engagement of women in politics and decision-making positions remains a major concern. Article 6 of the United Nations General Assembly asserts that states must recognize that women and girls with disabilities face various degrees of discrimination; hence, states must take steps to ensure their full and equal enjoyment of all human rights and fundamental freedoms.

The researcher made use of the social constructivist theory to determine factors limiting women with disabilities in electoral participation. To obtain data, the study used both questionnaires and interviews. The study revealed participants' diverse perspectives on the interpretation of electoral participation as a fundamental right of women with disabilities in Zimbabwe.

Global Representation of Women in the Electoral Process

Women have historically been under-represented in political leadership positions around the world. Horst et al. (2022, p. 3) state that equality in political empowerment and political office is still not achieved. Major political parties have deliberately implemented quotas that require women to take up a particular percentage of the candidates they propose for elections (International Institute for Democracy and Electoral Assistance, 2006). Because of quotas, countries such as Rwanda and South Africa have seen significant increases in female political leadership. Countries such as Qatar endorsed women's participation in the national parliament for the first time in 2017; however, in the 2021 elections, no women were elected in the office (Uberoi et al., 2022, p. 25).

Evidence shows that there are regional variations in the parliamentary participation of women, which is sadly low despite international efforts to promote the political participation of women. Few countries in the world have had a female leader such that having a woman with a disability is not guaranteed soon. Some women such as Vigdis Finnbogadottir the first female President in the World from Iceland in 1980–1996, Slyvie Kiningi; the first female President in Africa from Burundi from October 1993 to February 1994; Joice Runaida Mujuru who held the Vice President's position in Zimbabwe from 2004 to 2014; Joyce Hilda Banda who served as President of Malawi from 2012 to 2014; Catherine Samba, Acting President of the Central African Republic from January 2014 to March 2016; and Sahle-Work Zewde, Ethiopian President from October 2018 to current at the time of writing this chapter have penetrated the glass ceiling and held electoral office in the presence of males in their respective countries.

According to Atkinson et al. (2017), disability inclusive election observation allows for the removal of barriers to political involvement and the empowerment of men and women with disabilities to act in leadership capacities. People with disabilities face exclusion, abuse and violence, a lack of medical services, work opportunities, education, income, social support, and civic participation (Mandipa & Manyatera, 2014), and they are more prone to face several deprivations than their non-disabled counterparts (Mitra et al., 2014). However, due to the limited availability of data showing statistics of women with disability in electoral participation, such is the motivation of this chapter to analyse the participation of women with disabilities in politics.

Electoral Participation of Women with Disabilities in Zimbabwe

Women with disabilities in Zimbabwe across all communities suffer several forms of discrimination and marginalization daily, yet there is a lack of empirical study. The goal of this study was to investigate electoral participation as an essential right of women with disabilities in Zimbabwe to establish a gendered approach to human rights in the aspect of disability.

Women constitute about 52% of the total population in Zimbabwe yet they are under-represented in societal structure (Dube, 2013). Women, by their numbers ought, to be equally represented in political spaces; however, that is not the case as the political space is largely driven by men. Explanations for variations in women's representation reflect on the country's cultural and socio-economic setting, as well as its election setup and party system characteristics. The effect of electoral regulations on women's representation is dependent on the historic environment in which elections are held (Holli & Wass, 2009; Valdini, 2013).

According to Manatsa (2015), Zimbabwe was the first country in the Southern African region to enact the Disability Persons Act (DPA) in 1992. The Act was ratified to help persons with disabilities in Zimbabwe, but it has failed to help them access fundamental necessities and services such as education, employment, and other critical possibilities. This Act, however, was not followed by the required and tangible administrative actions to ensure its successful implementation (Lang & Charowa, 2007). Many Zimbabweans regard the Disability Persons Act as merely cosmetic law in terms of individuals with disabilities' access to fundamental needs and services (Khupe, 2010; Mandipa, 2013).

The Zimbabwe Constitution of 2013 states that women shall have equal chances as men in all areas, including political engagement. The 2013 Constitution was founded on fundamental human rights and freedoms, as well as gender equality. Section 17 of Zimbabwe's Constitution says that the state must promote full gender balance in Zimbabwean society and in particular (a) the state must promote the full participation of women in all spheres of Zimbabwean society based on equality with men and (b) the state must take all measures, including legislative measures needed to ensure that (ii) women constitute at least half the membership of all Commissions and other elective and approved bodies established by or under this Constitution or any Act of Parliament. Section 22 of the Zimbabwe Constitution also guarantees the rights of people with disabilities to equitable access to public resources. The Constitution does not exclude women with disabilities from political involvement, but rather includes all women in an equal position with males in electoral participation.

While Section 80 of the Zimbabwe Constitution states that every woman has the same dignity as men, including equal opportunities in political, economic, and social activities, Section 85, on the other hand, strengthens the courts' enforcement of fundamental human rights and freedoms, as well as the provision of appropriate remedies and compensation when those rights are violated. Section 245 mandates the formation of the Gender Commission, whose goal is to ensure gender equality, investigate infractions, and take appropriate action. Section 246 directs the Gender Commission to conduct research on gender and social justice issues and to suggest reforms to laws and practices that lead to gender discrimination. Recognizing that women and girls are frequently victims of socio-economic and political inequality, legal frameworks and policies needed to be developed to provide their protection. The Zimbabwe Constitution went further to direct the re-alignment of laws including the electoral statutes to the Constitution. The Zimbabwean government has made attempts to advance women's rights; nevertheless, to what extent have initiatives to increase the political involvement of women with disabilities been adequately implemented across all societies?

The Zimbabwe Electoral Support Network (ZESN) (2018) acknowledges that in 2013, two senators with disabilities, Senator Nyamayabo Mashavakure (male) and Anna Shiri (female), were voted for to represent disability interests. The Commonwealth report (2018, p. 31) states that:

> In September 2017, Senator Nyamayabo Mashavakure, who served as the representative for people living with disabilities, appealed to the Zimbabwe Electoral Commission (ZEC) to employ sign language, and braille voter education and polling materials. However, in May 2018, the High Court dismissed an application seeking to compel the ZEC to make these provisions available and to print braille ballot papers for visually impaired voters, on the basis that ZEC had already made provision for this through the use of assisted voting.

The rights of people with disabilities ought to be promoted towards achieving sustainable development growth and also promote inclusivity in all the political processes across the globe. Zimbabwe had by-elections in March 2022 with only 15% female candidates, a decline that can be linked to political parties' failure to have more women in their political arenas, although their party constitutions and election manifestos call for gender equality. According to the ZESN (2018), only 14% of women managed to contest in July 2018 for the National Assembly elections. According to the ZESN (2022), approximately 21.4% of females obtained National Assembly seats, compared to 78.6% of males in by-elections held on March 26, 2022, indicating a significant disparity in seats between males and females. The statistics show a lack of inclusiveness in elections, yet women's participation in elections is worrying considering that the country has been actively advocating for disability-specific laws and policies. However, minimal research has been undertaken to establish political participation as a paramount right of women with disabilities in Zimbabwe. The national population census of 2012 did not delve deeper into features such as forms of disability and gendered disability information (Mandipa, 2013), and the 2022 census did not take impairments into account. Against this backdrop, the study examines electoral participation as a fundamental right of women with disabilities in Zimbabwe.

Social Constructive Theory

The study examined political participation as a fundamental right of women with disabilities using the social constructive theory. According to the social constructivist concept, the reality is socially produced through interaction. The concept that the human experience of the world is always filtered by socially inherited meanings that actors deliberately impose on it is central to this theoretical assumption (Alexandratos, 2021). Disability, for the sake of this study, symbolizes the society's construction and image of its relationships with persons who are physically different. That is, disability does not exist outside of specific social and cultural constructs. Disability is defined by societal references and constructions (Stiker, 2019). In this situation, the way disability is perceived by mainstream society and by people with disabilities is essentially a product of socially created subjective realities about what certain impairments can and cannot do or achieve in specific social and economic environments. The social constructivist theory culminates in what is usually referred to as the social model of disability in disability literature. To comprehend women with disabilities and electoral participation, it is necessary to first understand the framework in which disability is seen by society. Using the social constructivist theory helps in understanding that the reality of disability is created through perception. Thus, social interaction can therefore create opportunities or barriers for electoral participation for women with disabilities.

The Medical Model of Disability

The medical model of disability views people with disabilities as having something wrong with them and hence locates the problem in the person who is disabled. According to the medical model, disability is primarily defined by physical, sensory, or intellectual deficiencies. As a result, the cure or rehabilitation for any ailment is curative or rehabilitative. The medical model of disability has been criticized primarily by academics who have disabilities; they regard it as the underlying cause of poverty and unfavourable perceptions towards people with disabilities. According to Bunbury (2019, p. 28), the medical model of disability posits that the disabled person's sovereignty is limited owing to the impairment; thus, if medical practitioners are unable to cure or rehabilitate the individual, she or he is regarded as having a limited ability to engage in society.

Jackson (1990, p. 22) argues that 'in both Shona and Ndebele cultures in Zimbabwe, misfortunes, ill-health and disability convey natural and supernatural cause.' In terms of societal problems, catastrophes normally happen with one individual in particular rather than the next. According to Chataika (2007), the medical paradigm views disability as a predicament; this strategy not only medicalizes disability but also individualizes and privatizes what is fundamentally a social and political issue (Oliver, 1990). The medical model assumes that impairment is a medical issue that an individual is born with. It was therefore critical for this study to investigate barriers faced by women with disabilities concerning electoral participation taking into consideration the medical model of disability.

The Social Model of Disability

The social model of disability was first coined by Oliver Mike in the 1980s. According to Munsaka (2012), the Union of the Physically Impaired against Segregation (UPIAS), 1976, acts as the genesis of the social model of disability. UPIAS (1976) states that:

> In our view, it is society that disables physically impaired people. Disability is something imposed on top of our impairments by the way we are unnecessarily isolated and excluded from full participation in society. (UPIAS 1976, p. 14)

According to Munsaka (2012, p. 26), the social model of disability was founded on the concept of societal oppression. The ability to understand disability in communities is determined by society. Shakespeare and Watson (1997) noted that the main proponents of the social model of disability did not intend to blame all challenges faced by people with disabilities on external factors, but rather to provide an alternative explanation of how society appears to contribute to the problems faced by people with impairments. Swepston (2006, p. 14) contends that if people with disabilities are entitled to equal rights, the state must fulfil that right. The disability social model acknowledges the misery associated with disabled lifestyles and attributes the major cause to a lack of medical services.

It is here contended that the medical model of disability and social model of disability share a lot in common, such that society ought to remove barriers that prevent the effective participation of women with disability in the social order. Remarkably, the models help in investigating the factors limiting women with disabilities from electoral participation. This study, therefore, adopts these models to analyse women with disabilities' participation in elections.

Methodology

According to Saunders et al. (2016), the research design is concerned with the overall plan for one's research. It also provides guidelines on how evidence will be collected and analysed to answer questions posed in the study. The study used the mixed methods approach which synchronizes both qualitative and quantitative methodologies to strengthen the results. The study used questionnaires and interviews to collect data which then unravelled the motives that drive the electoral participation of women with disabilities in Zimbabwe. Using mixed methods also ensured the results were acceptable to both qualitative and quantitative enthusiasts; this ensured that the results and recommendations were credible and generally acceptable. Data was collected from women with and without disabilities. The researcher managed to conduct twelve interviews with women with disabilities and without disabilities. Interview discussions were conducted with five women with disabilities and seven women without disabilities. The researcher included women with disabilities to get a deeper understanding of the challenges faced by women with disabilities in electoral participation. The researcher managed to send twenty questionnaires using Google forms from which eighteen were filled and returned. The participants were selected using purposive sampling based on availability and willingness to contribute to the study. Quantitative data was analysed using Statistical Package for Social Sciences (SPSS) version 12 while qualitative data was analysed using thematic and content analysis. Frequency tables and descriptive statistics were used to generalize the responses of the participants concerning the political involvement of women with disabilities. Data was presented in the form of tables, graphs and texts.

Ethical considerations were observed in the study. The researcher first sought informed consent and permission from the participants and clarified the aims of the research, why they were chosen, and also that their participation was entirely voluntary, and that they had the right to leave at any moment. The researcher also explained that the study was not aligned with any political party but that it was solely for academic purposes.

Discussion of Findings

Interview discussions were conducted on women with disabilities and without disabilities who either participated in the electoral processes or who did not. Their education levels ranged from none to tertiary education. It can be gleaned that the participants' responses were clear and relevant because most of the respondents were educated and understood the topic under study. However, introductions and explanations were made for clarity purposes so that the respondents understand the research area. Participants came from a variety of religious backgrounds, including African Traditional, Catholic, Apostolic, and Methodist groups. As a result, participants had a mix of religious and cultural practices. Regarding marital status, some were married, divorced, or widowed, while others had never married before.

To safeguard anonymity, the participants were referred to as respondents throughout the findings and valuable quotes acquired from the interviews. This procedure was required since it was critical for the participants' details to remain anonymous. It also gave them the confidence to speak freely since they knew that the information they offered could not be linked back to them.

The researcher distributed 20 questionnaires from which 18 were completed, filled, and returned. The study had a 90% response rate which implies that the research findings were adequate to help the researcher to determine the electoral participation of women with disabilities (Tables 2.1, 2.2, and 2.3).

Most of the participants were above 47 years, while the least were below 25 years. Out of the 18 participants, only one participant had never been to school. According to Section 83 of the Zimbabwe Constitution, the state must take adequate efforts, well within the limitations of its resources, to ensure that persons with disabilities have special educational facilities and receive paid education and training as needed. In terms of

Table 2.1 Age of the participants

		Frequency	Percent	Valid percent	Cumulative percent
Valid	Below 25	2	11.1	11.1	11.1
	26 to 36	3	16.7	16.7	27.8
	37 to 47	5	27.8	27.8	55.6
	Above 47	8	44.4	44.4	100.0
	Total	18	100.0	100.0	

Table 2.2 Educational level of the participants

		Frequency	Percent	Valid percent	Cumulative percent
Valid	Never been to school	1	5.6	5.6	5.6
	Primary level	4	22.2	22.2	27.8
	Secondary level	11	61.1	61.1	88.9
	Tertiary level	2	11.1	11.1	100.0
	Total	18	100.0	100.0	

Table 2.3 Marital status of the participants

		Frequency	Percent	Valid percent	Cumulative percent
Valid	Single	10	55.6	55.6	55.6
	Married	6	33.3	33.3	88.9
	Divorced	2	11.1	11.1	100.0
	Total	18	100.0	100.0	

marital status, most of the participants were single (55.6%) and few participants (11.1%) were divorced. Interview discussions revealed that the ones who are married and those in the 'never been married' status have different perceptions concerning electoral participation. Wolfinger and Wolfinger (2008) state that married women tend to be more politically active than those who have never been married before. This concurs with another respondent who expressed that there is a social understanding and conception that married women tend to participate in political activities more than those who are not married (Table 2.4).

Table 2.4 Descriptive statistics on the level of participation for women with disabilities

	N	Minimum	Maximum	Mean	Std. deviation
Have you ever participated in political activities?	18	1	5	2.44	1.688
Are you aware of the provisions of people with disabilities in Zimbabwe?	18	2	4	2.72	0.826
Are you aware of Zimbabwe 2023 elections?	18	2	5	3.56	1.042
Do you know your councilor in your ward?	18	1	4	2.00	1.455
Do you have a desire to fight for the rights of women with disabilities in political participation and representation?	18	3	5	4.50	0.707
Valid N (listwise)	18				

Responses from both questionnaires and interview discussions indicated that women with disabilities are not fully involved in electoral participation due to several factors. Most of the participants expressed that they do not know their councillors; this was reflected by the mean score of 2.00 which is closer to disagreeing. On the other hand, a mean score of 3.56 which is closer to agreement indicates that an average number of participants were aware of Zimbabwe's forthcoming 2023 elections. The study presents that most of the participants were not aware of the provisions for disabled women with a mean score of 2.72 which is closer to neutral. The researcher noted that the level of political participation of women with disabilities is not satisfactory. However, the participants expressed their desire to fight for the rights of women with disabilities with a mean score of 4.50 which is closer to agreeing. In the light of this, the National Democratic Institute (2017) stipulates that as girls, women frequently experience challenges to political participation which might even affect their leadership qualities later in life. Phiri et al. (2022) state that women's invisibility in political participation is a concerning issue in Zimbabwe. Hence, discrimination against women and girls with disabilities based on their impairment is not adequately addressed in legislation and policies.

The interview discussions revealed that both women without disabilities and women with disabilities are not fully participating in the electoral processes. The research findings indicated that in the 2022 Zimbabwean by-elections, not even one woman with a disability contested for a seat. The research findings imply that there is a gap that needs to be filled in an endeavour to address gender imbalances in Zimbabwe's electoral field. Respondent 10 expressed that most of the women with disabilities are not financially stable and they are not fully capable to solicit financial aid to participate in electoral activities on their own. Statutory Instrument (SI) 144 by ZEC presented new fees for electoral participation from which a proportional representation candidate has to pay a total of 200 American dollars, an increase from 100 American dollars. The exorbitant prices were not welcomed and condemned by politicians and academia since ZEC failed to consider that the country is facing economic challenges and most of the youth are employed in the informal sector. Professor Madhuku commented in Harris (2022) that the new prices disenfranchise citizens' political rights which are guaranteed by the Zimbabwe Constitution. According to the World Bank and the World Health Organization's World Report on Disability (2011), women with disabilities are secluded and have limited opportunities to contribute to their communities due to a lack of awareness and information. The study found that women with disabilities are not only faced with discrimination and social barriers but they are also economically disadvantaged as citizens.

The study findings also revealed that some women with disabilities generally do not have any political interests. Respondent 11 expressed that, often it is pointless to participate in elections because we (women with disabilities) are the minority, and there is a conflict between majority and minority rights. The participant further expresses that people with disabilities often send their concerns to politicians and members of parliament more than people without disabilities; it is just that it takes forever for them to respond and implement their queries and requests. The research findings also indicated that there is no consistency in organizations that try to advocate for the rights of women with disabilities due to corruption. The study also found that a lack of political interest can be attributed to insufficient voter education. ZEC is responsible for providing foreknowledge regarding all relevant electoral information for citizens in order to participate as candidates or voters. Hence, without sufficient knowledge, it is not possible to have vibrant political participation of citizens especially women with disabilities (Table 2.5).

Research findings revealed that women with disabilities face several challenges in electoral participation. The question of whether women

Table 2.5 Challenges faced by women with disabilities in electoral participation

	N	Minimum	Maximum	Mean	Std. deviation
Husbands and family members do not allow political participation	18	1	5	3.39	1.335
Women with disabilities do not get adequate access to education	18	1	5	3.72	1.320
Women are their own enemies	18	1	5	3.89	1.132
Women with disabilities do not have equal access to health care	18	2	5	4.00	1.188
Women with disabilities get adequate funding to participate in political arena	18	2	5	4.06	1.056
Women with disabilities are more prone to violence that counterparts without disabilities	18	2	5	4.28	0.958
Valid N (listwise)	18				

with disabilities are more prone to violence than their counterparts without disabilities had the highest mean score of 4.28 which is closer to agreeing. Furthermore, the question regarding whether husbands and family members allow women to participate in politics had a mean score of 3.39 which is closer to agreeing. Another key theme emerging from this study is gender-based violence targeted against women with disabilities. Guzman (2021) concurs with this study and states that barriers to women's political engagement range from structural or institutional barriers to cultural behaviours that limit the potential of women with disabilities to electoral participation. Women with disabilities face additional hurdles, such as legal, political, and cultural constraints that prevent them from taking part in political activities. Maphosa et al. (2019) contend that even though there were disability electoral booths in the 2018 elections, people living with disability encounter several challenges that include a lack of access to medical health care and education. Furthermore, the disability electoral booths were not sufficiently dotted across the country. The study noted that women with disabilities do not only suffer political marginalization but also cultural constraints. People with disabilities and in this case, women are often unable to exercise their right to vote; hence, women with disabilities do not effectively participate in the whole electoral process.

Electoral Violence

All the interview discussions revealed that women with disabilities are more prone to experiencing electoral violence than women without disabilities. Respondent 7 explained that the Zimbabwean election period has never been free from violence and that is the reason why women with disabilities do not want to involve themselves in such dramatic scenes. The participant further expressed that violence does not necessarily mean that women with disabilities will be beaten in the streets, it can be emotional neglect or economical abuse. The data emerging from the study also revealed that there is political violence against women with disabilities, even against the backdrop that there is a law, and the Zimbabwe Constitution Section 156 stipulates that the Zimbabwe Electoral Commission ought to eliminate electoral violence and other electoral malpractices. According to Bartha (2019), women with disabilities, especially those with cognitive and psycho-social challenges, are more vulnerable to electoral violence and gender-based abuse. However, Respondent 6 appreciated efforts by Senator Ana Mashiri in representing women with disabilities in parliament. The participants noted that there should be an increasing number of women with disabilities taking up such positions in the parliament and other political spaces.

Limited Access to Education

Research findings indicated that women with disabilities do not get equal access to education as compared to women without disabilities. Respondent 5 acknowledges that less than 10% of people with disabilities have access to education which limits electoral understanding and participation. The research findings concur with the literature as Choruma (2007, p. 12) expresses that 'literacy levels of people with disabilities are generally lower than the rest of the population, while persons with disabilities are much less likely to be engaged in economic activity than the rest of the population'.

It is sad to note that the research findings revealed that women with disabilities are being looked down upon by fellow women living without disabilities. Respondent 7 expressed that women living with disabilities feel like they are being mocked when women with disabilities try to participate in electoral activities and influence political operations and systems. Respondent 9 contended that women are their own enemies, even before men come into play. The research findings indicated that these participants do not have enough confidence on their own as they think that they are being looked down upon. Interview discussions with women without disabilities revealed that women without disabilities face same challenges as their counterparts in the political field. Participants expressed that voter education is an important stage in the political process as it brings an understanding of the importance of participation and making their vote count. The research findings further foregrounded that the voter registration process is an important stage in the electoral process, such that women with disabilities should not be excluded or left behind.

Nevertheless, participants praised the participation of women without disabilities in the 2022 by-elections in March. Zimbabwean women have participated in the March 2022 by-elections naming a few such as Zalerah Hazvineyi Makari, Mavis Gumbo and Masarira Linda Tsungirirai. Nevertheless, the ZESN (2022, p. 14) states that in the March 2022 by-elections:

> In total, there were 120 candidates across the 28 contested National Assembly seats. Of the 120, only 16 were female, representing 13% percent. Out of 28 National Assembly seats, female candidates contested in 13 constituencies. When combined with the number of female candidates who contested in the local authority by-elections across the 122 wards, the percentage rises to a paltry 15%.

The Zimbabwean political and electoral field remains silent on women with disabilities. Efforts still need to be projected towards promoting the electoral participation for both women with disabilities and those without disabilities. Without the effective participation of the women with disabilities in politics and elections, achieving gender balance will remain a far-fetched dream. Sustainable development and regional peace require inclusive equal participation of citizens despite gender discrimination.

Electoral Participation of Women with Disabilities

The study sought to understand if women with disabilities have played any part in solving challenges they face in electoral participation. Participants acknowledge that efforts have been made by the Zimbabwe government towards full and effective participation and gender equality in the appointment of senators representing disability in parliament. According to the Commonwealth report (2018, p. 46), 'In September 2017, Senator Nyamayabo Mashavakure, who served as the representative for people with disabilities, appealed to ZEC to employ sign language, and braille voter education and polling materials.' Similarly, Oliver (2013) propounds that social structures ought to promote people living with disabilities instead of exclusion in social structures.

Respondent 11 gives credit to the work done by the late Senator Rejoice Timire in representing and advocating for the rights of women and girls with disabilities. Conversely, Respondent 12 argues that women with disabilities cannot fully advocate for their rights due to financial constraints. The research findings concur with the literature as Mtetwa (2011) states that disabled persons' organizations have financial challenges that limit their full potential to promote the disability emancipation agenda. Mtetwa (2011) states that women cannot fully participate in the electoral process due to limited political findings. Yet, the Zimbabwean Constitution provides that gender equality ought to be respected without any discrimination.

Participants were also asked to indicate their level of agreement that the Zimbabwe Electoral Commission should enhance public awareness of the involvement of women with disabilities in electoral reforms. Figure 2.1 depicts the results.

According to the statistics presented in Fig. 2.1, 22.22% of the participants agree that the Zimbabwe Electoral Commission should enhance public awareness of the inclusion of women with disabilities in electoral reforms. Furthermore, 77.78% of the participants strongly agree that the Zimbabwe Electoral Commission should enhance public awareness of the participation of women with disabilities in electoral reforms. All the participants expressed that the Zimbabwe Electoral Commission should enhance public awareness of the involvement of women with disabilities in electoral reforms so as to counter the challenges faced by women with disabilities in electoral participation. Society should not see a disability beyond gender as a limiting factor to electoral participation.

Recommendations

It is important to note that challenges faced by women with disabilities can best be resolved by effective collaboration from society and political parties in cooperation with disability rights organizations. There is an

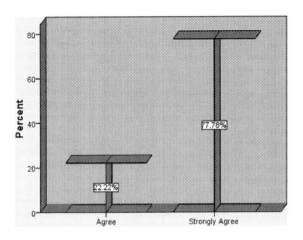

Fig. 2.1 Zimbabwe Electoral Commission should enhance public awareness of the participation of women with disabilities in electoral reforms

urgent need to promote and include women with disabilities in electoral participation before the 2023 elections. The Zimbabwe Commission on Gender should ensure 50:50 equal representation of women with disabilities and women without disabilities at legislative and political parties' levels. Women with disabilities have to continue to strive to fight to break the glass ceiling and enhance electoral legitimacy.

The study recommends that the Government of Zimbabwe and all its laws, legislations and policies such as the United Nations Sustainable Development Cooperation Framework 2022–2026 in Zimbabwe should work towards a mandate in the gender mainstreaming approach targeting women and girls with disabilities. The government should have updated statistics of women living with disabilities by age, gender, place of birth, religion, and educational level. While a national census was conducted from April 21 to April 30, 2022, statistics have to build on women living with disability and non-disabled.

Civil Society Organisations that advocate for equal rights for people living with disability should escalate their activities towards the inclusion of the rights of women with disabilities and exercising their political rights. The Zimbabwe Government should be designated with a monitoring and evaluation or track-accomplish system to achieve milestones and the United Nations Entity for Gender Equality and the Empowerment of Women (UN-Women) Strategic Plan 2022–2025.

In addition, the Zimbabwe Electoral Commission should put in place visible sound laws that protect women against violence in the pre-electoral period, election and post-electoral period. The laws should be majoring in electoral conduct and promoting women with disabilities' participation in elections. To eliminate prejudices and misconceptions regarding women with disabilities, communities and civil society organizations should adopt disability inclusion and gender awareness programmes.

In the same way that the Zimbabwean Government has been promoting inclusive education, likewise, inclusivity should be promoted in political participation. The Zimbabwe Broad-Casting Cooperation should ensure that all the programmes on electoral activities come along with subtitles and sign language to ensure equal access to information. This will also help to promote voter education during the electoral period.

Women's rights organizations should work in diverse communities and societies to establish a secure environment for women with disabilities to freely discuss political engagement experiences and obstacles that hinder effective electoral participation. The motivation and support towards electoral support should begin at a family level. Women with disabilities should be assisted in getting national documentation which will make it possible for them to register to vote.

Political parties should explicitly seek to integrate women with disabilities as party members and guarantee that their voices are heard. The Government of Zimbabwe must continue to uphold and protect the rights of women with disabilities to participate in policy-making decisions. The Zimbabwe Government should also have a collaborative approach with non-governmental organizations and civil societies towards promoting electoral participation for women with disabilities. In addition, the state should set a budget specifically responsible to assist women with disabilities in political participation. The budget should be responsible for ensuring all necessary resources such as disability electoral booths are sufficiently distributed across all provinces.

Conclusions

This study can be used as a tool in promoting the electoral participation of women with disabilities in the Zimbabwe 2023 elections and beyond. The researcher noted that disabilities do not limit or affect one's electoral participation. The study concludes that the electoral participation of women with disabilities is extremely invisible; yet, they are equally capable enough to participate in politics. This shows how principles of democracy (such as citizen participation, human rights, and media) are not fully promoted. The study concludes that the equal representation of women with disabilities is a necessary factor that must not be left behind in the aim of promoting inclusiveness in elections.

The study admits that the adoption of the United Nations Convention on the Rights of Persons with Disabilities has contributed to, promoted, and safeguarded the rights of people with disabilities, including women and girls. However, much effort still needs to be done in promoting the effective political participation of women with disabilities. Society acknowledges that women with disabilities are subject to discrimination; however, not enough efforts have been made towards ensuring the empowerment of women with disabilities. The study also concludes that women with disabilities do not have equal access to health care, education, disability-related services, and electoral participation despite the existence of legal documents that give them equal rights as fellows living without disabilities.

References

Alexandratos, F. S. (2021). "The structure of human action as a criterion for social analysis". Pragmatist ethics: Theory and practice. *European Journal of Pragmatism and American Philosophy, XIII*(2). https://doi.org/10.4000/ejpap.2553

Atkinson, V., Aaberg, R., & Darnolf, S. (2017). Disability rights and election observation: Increasing access to the political process. *Nordic Journal of Human Rights, 35*(4), 375–391.

Bartha, O. (2019). *Making the SDGs count for women and girls with disabilities data challenges and opportunity*. Commission on the Status of Women, Sixty Third Session on Women's empowerment and the link to sustainable development. Interactive Expert Panel.

Bunbury, S. (2019). Unconscious bias and the medical model: How the social model may hold the key to transformative thinking about disability discrimination. *International Journal of Discrimination and the Law, 19*(1), 26–47.

Chataika, T. (2007). *Inclusion of disabled students in higher education in Zimbabwe: From idealism to reality*—A social ecosystem perspectives (Thesis submitted in Fulfillment of the requirements for the degree of Doctor of Philosophy (PhD) in special educational needs). The School of Education, the University of Sheffield.

Choruma, T. (2007). *The forgotten tribe: People with disabilities in Zimbabwe.* Progression.

Commonwealth Observer Group. (2018, July 30). *Zimbabwe harmonised elections.* VERITAS.

Constitution of Zimbabwe Amendment (No. 20) Act of 2013.

Disabled Persons Act [Chapter 17:01]. 1992. Harare: Parliament of Zimbabwe.

Dube, T. (2013). Engendering politics and parliamentary representation in Zimbabwe. *Journal of African Studies and Development, 5*(8), 200–207.

Guzman, K. F. (2021). *The intersectional perspective on women and Girls with disabilities: A comparative analysis.* CUNY Academic Works.

Harris, L. B. (2022, August 22). *ZEC has no legal mandate to impose nomination fees: Madhuku.* ZimElections2023. CITE. https://cite.org.zw/zec-has-no-legal-mandate-to-impose-nomination-fees-madhuku/

Holli, A., & Wass, H. (2009). Gender-based voting in the parliamentary elections of 2007 in Finland. *European Journal of Political Research, 49*(5), 598–630.

Horst, G. P., Dao, S., Rahman, S., & Tucker, M. (2022). *More representation but not influence: Women in the European Parliament* (Policy paper 2). The German Marshall Fund of the United States.

International Institute for Democracy and Electoral Assistance. (2006). *Electoral management design: The international IDEA handbook.* International IDEA.

Jackson, H. (1990). Attitude to disability in Zimbabwe. In F. J. Brunn & B. Ingastad (Eds.), *Disability in a cross-cultural perspective* (Working Paper No. 4). University of Norway.

Khupe, W. (2010). *Disabled peoples rights where does Zimbabwe stand?* The Zimbabwean (Online). http://www.thezimbabwean.co/2010/04/disabled-peoples-rights-where-does-zimbabwe-stand/. Accessed 31 May 2022.

Lang, R., & Charowa, G. (2007). *DFID scoping study: Disability issues in Zimbabwe.* http://www.ucl.ac.uk/lc-ccr/downloads/scopingstudies/dfid_zimbabwereport. Accessed 31 May 2022.

Manatsa, P. (2015). Are disability laws in Zimbabwe compatible with the provisions of the United Nations Convention on the Rights of Persons with Disabilities (CRPD)? *International Journal of Humanities and Social Science Invention, 4*(4), 24–34.

Mandipa, E. (2013). *A critical analysis of the legal and institutional frameworks for the realization of the rights of persons with disabilities in Zimbabwe, in*

African Disability Rights Yearbook (C. Ngwena, I. Grobelaar-du Plessis, H. Combrick & S. D. Kamga, Eds.). Pretoria University Law Press.

Mandipa, E., & Manyatera, G. (2014). Zimbabwe. In C. Ngwena, P. I. Grobelaar-du, H. Combrick, & S. D. Kamga (Eds.), *African disability rights yearbook* (pp. 287–308). Pretoria University Law Press.

Maphosa, N., Moyo, C. G., & Moyo, B. (2019). Left in the periphery: An analysis of voting rights for persons with disabilities in Zimbabwe. In *7 African disability rights yearbook* (pp. 112–139).

Matfess, H., Kishi, R., & Berry, M. E. (2022). No safety in numbers: Political representation and political violence targeting women in Kenya. *International Feminist Journal of Politics*. https://doi.org/10.1080/14616742.2022.2045618

Mitra, S., Posarac, A., & Vick, B. (2014). Disability and poverty in developing countries: A multidimensional study. *World Development, 41*, 1–18. https://doi.org/10.1016/j.worlddev.2012.05.024

Mtetwa, E. (2011). Policy dimensions of exclusion disability as charity and not right in Zimbabwe. *Indian Journal of Social Work, 72*, 381–398.

Munsaka, E. (2012). *Including a disability agenda in development: Myth or reality? A case study of Binga district in Zimbabwe* (Thesis submitted for the degree of Doctor of Philosophy, Department of Applied Social Sciences). Durham University.

National Democratic Institute. (2017). *Youth political participation programming guide*. https://www.ndi.org/publications/youth-political-participation-programming-guide

Oliver, M. (1990). *The politics of disablement*. Macmillan Education Limited.

Oliver, M. (2013). The social model of disability. *Thirty Years on Disability & Society, 28*(7), 1024–1026.

Phiri, K., Ndlovu, S., Khumalo, S., Ncube, S. B., & Nyathi, D. (2022). Multiplying faces and amplifying voices: Do women's lives matter in local governance politics in Gwanda, Zimbabwe? *Journal of Asian and African Studies*, 24–40.

Saunders, M., Lewis, P., & Thornhill, A. (2016). *Research methods for business students* (7th ed.). Pearson.

Shakespeare, T., & Watson, N. (1997). Defending the social model. In B. Barton & M. Oliver (Eds.), *Disability studies: Past present and future* (pp. 263–273). The Disability Press.

SI 2022-144 Electoral (Nomination of Candidates) (Amendment) Regulations, 2022 (No. 1).

Stiker, H. J. (2019). *A history of disability*. University of Michigan Press.

Swepston, L. (2006) *Employment of people with disabilities, moving towards human rights approach in ILO: Employment of people with disabilities. A human rights approach (Asia)*. *Report of a tripartite technical consultation.* Bangkok, ILO skill and Employability Department.

Uberoi, E., Burton, M., Danechi, S., & Bolton, P. (2022). *Women in politics and public life* (House of Commons Library. Briefing Paper 01250). https://researchbriefings.files.parliament.uk/documents/SN01250/SN01250.pdf

Union of the Physically Impalred Agalnst Segregation. (1976). *Fundamental principles of disability.* UPIAS.

United Nations. (2006, December 13). *Convention on the rights of persons with disabilities.*

Valdini, M. (2013). Electoral institutions and the manifestation of bias: The effect of the personal vote on the representation of women. *Politics & Gender, 9*(1), 76–92.

Wolfinger, N. H., & Wolfinger, R. E. (2008). Family structure and voter turnout. *Social Forces, 86*(4), 1513–1528.

World Bank and World Health Organization World Report on Disability. (2011). http://www.who.int/disabilities/world_report/2011/en/index.html.

Zimbabwe Electoral Act, Section 136(1).

Zimbabwe Electoral Support Network (ZESN). (2018). *Final report of the 2018 voters' roll audit.* Zimbabwe Electoral Support Network. www.zesn.org.zw/wp-content/uploads/2018/10/Voters-Roll-Audit-Report-2018.pdf

Zimbabwe Electoral Support Network. (2022). *Promoting democratic elections in Zimbabwe. Report on the 26 March 2022 by-elections.* Zimbabwe Election Support Network. www.zesn.org.zw

CHAPTER 3

Unpacking the Issue of Gender and Electoral Violence in Christopher Mlalazi's *They Are Coming*

Thamsanqa Moyo

INTRODUCTION

Zimbabwe is preparing for elections in the coming months of 2023. The country has periodically held elections since the attainment of independence in 1980. While these elections are supposed to be a yardstick on the performance of those elected in office, they have generally been a routine "endorsement" of the ruling elites who are, by and large, male. They (the elections) therefore become a reflection of thin democracy in the country. Referring to Africa in general, but with major relevance to Zimbabwe, Motsamai (2010, p. 1) has characterised elections as a "curse." This is because electoral politics in Zimbabwe tends to bring out the worst in both men and women. The attitudes towards elections are such that there was never a yesterday nor will there ever be a tomorrow. All energies become canalised on winning the election by whatever method gives

T. Moyo (✉)
English and Media Studies, Great Zimbabwe University, Masvingo, Zimbabwe
e-mail: thamsmoyo@gmail.com

© The Author(s), under exclusive license to Springer Nature Switzerland AG 2023
E. Mavengano and S. Chirongoma (eds.), *Electoral Politics in Zimbabwe, Vol II*, https://doi.org/10.1007/978-3-031-33796-3_3

one an advantage. The competitive authoritarianism comes with the patriarchisation and militarisation of the political sphere. While elections are a site for the staging of hegemonic masculinities upon both subordinate masculinities and femininities, women are always on the receiving end. This is because in the "postcolony, power dons the face of virility" (Mbembe, 2001, p. 115) and that it also evinces "phallocentric metaphors of state power" (Musila, 2012, p. 154).

Thus, for women to gain access to the hallowed political spaces reserved for men, they have to assume socially constructed male identities that celebrate discourses and practices of dodaism or, as Robert Mugabe put it, *amadoda sibili* (real tough men) even if this does not work in their own interests as females. The chapter argues that electoral politics by political parties in Zimbabwe share an unmistakable patriarchal ideology that has always " (re)produced, enacted, authorised and left behind a gendered script and a highly masculinised socio-political terrain that goads us into looking deeply....at the issues of gender, sexuality, power, and nationhood" (Mawere, 2019, p. 16). This must be understood in the social construction of the liberation war teleology, agency and heroism as essentially male-centred. The specificity of women's struggles was subordinated to the overarching anticolonial prism that constructed their quests as incidental, peripheral and unimportant. Women were imagined as a group only needed to augment voices; they were ranged against the racial character of colonialism. In this way, nationalism was a means through which male nationalists performed their masculinity. Bhatasara and Chiweshe (2021, p. 221) argue that:

> ....the war of liberation-with the deeply militarised dimension to it-was profoundly patriarchal in both discourse and practice in depicting men as agents of heroic political change.

This philosophy was performed by Robert Mugabe (former President until he was deposed through a military-assisted power takeover) and was copied—even perfected some would say—by his protégé, Emmerson Mnangagwa. The approach is how elections are viewed by political contenders in Zimbabwe; they are a war where defeat cannot be countenanced. This attitude to electoral politics sanctions the annihilation and scattering of the political other, whether male or female.

There is no reason to be optimistic that the 2023 elections are going to be different from the previous disputed ones because the "electoral framework is problematic mainly because the electoral environment is patriarchal" (ibid.) for most political parties in Zimbabwe. This patriarchal, militarist and sexist arrangement is exclusionary but "into which deserving women may gain entry and therefore qualify as heroes too" (ibid.). You can only do that if you do not threaten to destabilise the patriarchal structures. Joice Mujuru's experiences as Vice President lends credence to this; once she fell out of favour with Mugabe and Grace, all the liberation war heroism that had festooned her was ignominiously taken away from her. So, the selected few women that serve as decoys can only enter electoral and apportioned spaces "…as praise-singers and ardent party supporters with little, if any, decision-making capacity within their parties" (Zigomo, 2022, p. 528). I read Mujuru's incumbency in the Presidium as no more than simply making up numbers. McClintock (1995) corroborates this view by stating that the electoral terrain captured above can only afford the political space to advance the agendas of their male counterparts. They are appointed by men as some form of tokenism, are policed and placed under the surveillance of men. In the end, the women normalise the view that politics is the domain of males; that their fate is to be their supporters even against women electoral contenders for public office; or that they should generally retire into the domestic sphere as care-givers. I therefore argue that to the extent that women normalise such a status quo, they become complicit in the perpetuation of their subordination and the institutionalisation of violence during election periods. The chapter therefore calls for the "destabilizing of powerfully established structures of mental authoritarianism" (Kaarsholm, 2005, p. 4).

The discourses of the threat of violence or actual violence do not affect women in the ruling party only; they also implicate the opposition parties whose gender ideologies replicate patriarchal militarism. Elections in Zimbabwe are a site for violence across the gender divide (Khadiagala, 2009; Koko, 2009). Toxic masculinities in both the ruling and the main opposition parties impose their hegemony through violence. The "enemy" is first stereotyped as a precursor to their commonsensical violation and annihilation (Steuter & Willy, 2009, p. 19). Once the political contender is stigmatised as a "sell-out," an intruder or a "mafikizolo" (Jonnie-come-lately), their outsideness is ameliorated in order to justify purging in various ways. This often results in retaliatory violence which spirals out of control and consumes both males and females during election periods. Already, at the time of writing this chapter (January 2023), the political rhetoric of bellicosity, threats, intimidation, arrests and banning of opposition gatherings had become regular as elections beckoned. The many degrees in violence are already being operationalised. The "New Dispensation" becomes irredeemably parasitic to the Mugabeist "Old Dispensation" with its gendered forms of violence. Since politics is constructed as dirty and dangerous, most women and subordinate masculinities tend to refrain from participating in the bustle and tumble of electioneering, leading to ennui, paralysis and apathy. This makes them by-standers in national processes that affect their future. Even if the forthcoming elections become "miraculously" violence-free, the "harvest of fear" (Zamchiya, 2013) will have done its part. This harvest of fear denotes the cultural and political implantation of the miasma of fear through remembrance of previous violent elections. Hence, Gallagher (2001, p. 28) talks of "the unspoken threat of violent reprisals, underwritten by memories of the violence of (past) elections." In the case of the impending elections, the chorus seems to be that people should remember elections of 2008 when the ruling party unleashed an orgy of violence using the military and the party militia in a campaign dubbed "Operation Man'uqonde" (Operation Vote Well). The next section situates the study within its context.

Theoretical Grounding

The chapter is grounded in Gramsci's (1977) notion of hegemony, consent and the related idea of ideology. It draws upon Bates' (1995, p. 351) unpacking of Gramsci "that man is not ruled by force alone, but also by ideas." I argue that hegemony is "a technique of political rule" (Riley, 2011, n.p.) where coercion plays a decisive part but is always aided by an array of cultural, political, economic and other tools that have the effect of making the subjugated view the self through the eyes of the dominant group. This manufactures consent and submission in ways that can be conscious or unconscious. Theorists of gender have found Gramsci's theory to be reductionist and have sought to deepen and expand it so that it offers a much more complex picture of how politics and patriarchy mutually reinforce each other to manufacture and normalise male discourses. According to Eagleton (1991, p. 112):

Gramsci…uses the word hegemony to mean the ways in which a governing power wins consent to its rule from those it subjugates-though it is true that he occasionally uses the term to cover both consent and coercion together.

The theory works through a complex mental process that normalises and naturalises the values and ideology of the dominant groups in society. Hegemony achieves its aims in a "conception of the world which belongs to the rulers" (Fiori, 1990, p. 238).

Thus, the theory posits the view that in an attempt to construct a particular social order as logical and commonsensical, narratives are yarned to buttress that worldview which has the effect of being "regimes of truth" (Foucault, 1972). The regimes of truth produced in the Zimbabwean electoral politics are: that ZANU-PF is an impregnable monolithic entity that cannot be dislodged from power through voting. Secondly, that it was seasoned through the crucible of liberation war violence and therefore that the space of violence is its hunting ground. Thirdly, its patriarchal militarism is unchangeable. Fourthly, that those who aspire to political office have to transform themselves in order to fit and adapt to its violent political identity and even then, as subordinates. This view disrupts the notion of changing ZANU-PF from within—a view held by opportunists wishing to join the gravy-train. Lastly, that heroism is male and ZANU-PF, and therefore, people vote for their "safety by voting a party that guarantees their physical security" (Mwonzora & Mandikwaza, 2019, p. 1135). The discourse that the liberation war was male tends to persuade women to view politics as male domain and that they have to be beholden upon men to perforate that space. The verbalisation that the gun is more powerful than the ballot ousts the democratic function of elections and often leads to paralysis, apathy and fatalism that dissuade people from voting. Hence, some voters consent to the militarised patriarchal structure as a permanent feature of politics. I view this theory as apposite in unpacking the ruling party's use of violence and the cultural intellectualisation of the asymmetries of power during elections. In peering into the 2023 harmonised elections, one cannot help but hazard the pessimistic view that, like most previous elections, this one will follow the same trajectory. In the next section, I examine the text *They Are Coming* in order to bring out the intersections of gender and electoral politics in Zimbabwe.

Gendered Violence?

The novel *They Are Coming* introduces us to electoral violence through the foreboding words from Mr Nkani, a male aspiring parliamentary candidate for the opposition Movement for Democratic Change (MDC) party. The words that portend violence and possible death are: they're coming! (Bayeza!). Whoever they are, we are given the impression that they are known and are regular trouble for the people of Lobengula because the sweeping women immediately disappear into their houses. This has become their routinised response to the performance of power during election time. Nkani, whose name in Ndebele means the brave one, the recalcitrant one, the stubborn one, aspires to power in a terrain dominated by the party of entitlement, the liberation party, ZANU-PF. It has generally brooked no opposition to its hold on power. In Ndebele worldview, a person with "inkani" often meets his comeuppance and Nkani's surname implies that he will meet his demise for deigning to challenge the dangerous ruling party. The book is set in 2004 when Zimbabwe is preparing for elections. We are told that Ambition, the child narrator, "sees blood flowing down the left side of his face. It's stained his shirt as if someone has sprayed him with raspberry juice" (p. 2). We are also told that Nkani and the group that he leads engage in retaliatory violence. Nkani therefore becomes the embodiment of masculine values of bravery, risk-taking, counter-violence and potential leadership. But why has Nkani been chosen as a parliamentary candidate? Is Mlalazi constructing running for political office in Zimbabwe as remarkably male? I invoke Mawere's (2019, p. 33) argument that "…Zimbabwe's electoral structures and systems remain male-dominated and controlled by a militant party-state." But the fact that he is an opposition candidate goes to show that patriarchy permeates and contaminates political and social structures across the party divide. Agency is imagined as masculine and this explains why Mr Nkala is selected during primary elections to face the beast (ZANU-PF) because, according to Ambition, "politics is a dangerous game…. And everyone knew that you didn't play around with ZANU-PF" (p. 11).

The construction of politics as dangerous and dirty is a buffering strategy meant to exclude other subjectivities deemed weak, fragile and vulnerable while hemming in others. In patriarchal discourses, women are figured as weak, motherly and fit only for nurturing roles. This culturally and politically banishes them from the spaces of campaigning which are viewed as aggressive, abrasive and therefore macho. In the novel, the prominent political protagonists chosen for public offices are expectedly male; there is mention of Robert Mugabe running for presidency in ZANU-PF, and then, there is the leader of MDC, presumably Morgan Tsvangirai and Mr Nkani. This reflects the masculinisation of power in the Zimbabwean body politic. Mawere (2019, p. 29) rightly points out that "the political centre in Zimbabwe is rendered a male space with buffers to prevent the political dominance of women regarded as taboo and out of line with Zimbabwe's nation-craft." The case of Grace Mugabe's rather brash and uncritical ambition for power corroborates this view of politics. Militarised masculinities, able to mutually dish out violence, have always been the bane of electoral politics in the country. Cock (1989, p. 30) refers to this "curse" when he points out that:

> …adoration of military masculinities leads to war being valued and legitimised in a manner that naturalises violence as a solution to conflict and makes militarism a foundation of society.

This was Mugabe's view of elections and politics in particular and, sadly, as the 2018 elections confirmed, this has been adopted and perfected by Mnangagwa's "Second Republic." It has dissuaded women from aspiring for possible office in the respective political parties. Zigomo (2022) admits that patriarchal norms influence selection processes of primaries.

But that Nkani is beaten and eventually killed makes essentialising violence as directed at women only difficult. When the ruling party constructs opponents as sellouts and puppets, the issue of gender does not arise. Once constructed as an enemy during elections, the violence does not don any particular gender although it is not often perpetrated by men. The discourse of sellouts and puppets is a political strategy to justify violence, the magnitude of which is contingent upon the threat posed by the opposition. It reflects that the greater the threat, then the greater the violence. This is why Nkani is killed to send a message to the would-be challengers of the ruling party. It is a message that politics is indeed a dangerous, life-and-death affair. But Mr Nkani also represents subordinate masculinities while Robert Mugabe is a metonym of hegemonic and even toxic masculinities. Robert Mugabe's masculinity lords it over other masculinities in an attempt to maintain stranglehold on power. Viewed in such a light, it would be remiss to imagine electoral violence in Zimbabwe in narrowly gender terms. Ironically, Nkani is constructed in ways that render him effeminate, as if to foreshadow his eventual demise. He is referred to as the "weak-bodied teacher..." (p. 10) who was "...not known for his bravery" (p. 11). This feminisation is further reinforced by the fact that he is beaten by Magumbo and suffers the ignominy of showing a clean pair of heels—an unmanly and scandalous act in Zimbabwe's masculinist society. In support of this, I draw upon Floss' (2008, p. 4) contention that "a society's political culture is gauged by the character of its institutions, practices and rationalities (and discourses and) is one of the most critical (sites) through which political cultures, values, and practices are instilled among citizens." One gets the distinct impression that Mr Nkani, though male, cannot match the violent masculinities embodied by Mugabe and his ilk.

Representations of Femininities in Electoral Politics

There is no denying the fact that men control the electoral space in Zimbabwe. For women to enter these spaces, they have to be recruited and conscripted into ideologies that prop up and legitimate patriarchal and militarised identities. Magumbo symbolises this kind of rationality. That she is a war veteran in this scheme of things means that the ideology that she endorses is nationalist which, in the Zimbabwean iconography, is masculinist. It is a nationalism that is "gendered, sexist, masculinist, militarist and violent" and diminishes the "social freedoms of those whose gendered and sexed identities (are) regarded as inferior..." (Mawere, 2019, p. 16). The problem is that in her attempt to dramatise the liberation war identity, she fails to appreciate that she is a pawn used to advance the interests of men during election times. She comes across as complicit in the marginalisation of herself and other women. She is constructed as a bully who sadistically takes every opportunity to discipline the students and opposition supporters. Her bullying habits reflect the way her party has bullied and continue to bully citizens, especially if they are in the opposition. This is reflected in the way in which opposition supporters like Sikhala have languished in prison for over a year without any trial. Sikhala is a member of the opposition Citizens Coalition for Change who was arrested for allegedly inciting his supporters to engage in violent protests over the murder of Moreblessing Ali, an assumed member of the opposition. He has been in prison for over seven months now, having been denied bail on several occasions. The trial has recently commenced. This is meant to instil fear and pain in order to disable the opposition and the voting public.

Mrs Gumbo is unwittingly quite enamoured of the tokenism that she represents. She does not wield much power within the system, though she claims to be a member of the Central Intelligence Organisation (CIO) reporting to the Chief of Police, presumably a man. Magumbo does not seem to worry about these asymmetrical gender relations, and she does not question her marginality. Reporting minor incidents of minor political skirmishes with minor political players within the school does not make her a significant party cadre; it is the men at the top of the political hierarchy who make decisions which she is expected to implement. For example, the ideologies that she has swallowed hook, line and sinker and which she imparts of the Green Bombers are personal thoughts of the President, Mugabe who is male. Geisler (1995, p. 546) destabilises women like Magumbo's exuberance over their position in the party because they "are given little or no space to influence policy formulation, not even policies directly relevant to them." She represents the kind of femininities that are heroic yet peripherised in the sense that she fought the liberation war together with men but she cannot penetrate the real spaces of power. Paradoxically, she embraces the discourses of violent electoral politics that frame the opposition as a cancer that has to be excised from the body politic. The position that she occupies in the party has been given to her by males and the socio-political structures she fights to maintain advance the interests of men. In this way, Magumbo does not in any way threaten the status quo; if anything, she is a useful tool in its reinforcement. The beating that she administers on Mr Nkani is an attempt to appropriate and approximate masculinist, military identities that allow her to be part of the "Boys Club." She tries to appropriate the image of real men (amadoda sibili). By characterising Mr Nkani as a coward, she scaffolds the self as hyper masculine. In other words, she wilfully consents to male hegemony. In discoursing about the size of Mr Nkani's penis, she seeks to withdraw him from those hallowed male spaces from which Zimbabweans who seek alternative imaginaries of the nation are exempted from. After all, cultural beliefs impose on men certain levels of independence which Mr Nkani and his kind, in Zimbabwean political discourses, do not possess because they are framed as stooges that advance the interests of whites. That she is a stooge for male dominance does not seem apparent to her.

Then, there is Mrs Nkani. Her identity is defined by her relationship to the husband. She cannot take the bull by its horns to compete for public office because of the many barriers that women face in a male-centred political space. She contents herself with being a domestic wife and a catalyst to her husband's campaign trail. Mrs Nkani is in the shadow of her husband. Gaidzanwa (2004) contends that women are invariably consigned to the political margins like the women's wings of the party which do not make substantive decisions. Even then, they are often under the gaze and surveillance of men. Mrs Nkani's role is selling party cards and arranging meetings for the opposition with fellow women and she finds this role uplifting. Her situation is not unlike the positions that Joice Mujuru and Grace Mugabe whose political identities depended upon their male husbands without whom they became nobodies. One can logically surmise that after the murder of Mr Nkani, the wife's political visibility and activity pales into insignificance. The electoral violence through the elimination of the husband will also traumatise her into resigned silence. This is because violence by its nature is meant "to paralyse their (individual's) will to resist and make them acquiesce in the new reality" (Humphrey, 2002, p. 25).

Senzeni and her association with the Green Bombers is an example of catching the females young so that they internalise the elections are war. She is a victim of epistemic and epistemological violence and indoctrination. Her name means what have we done? in Ndebele, and she is a synecdoche of the family as a nation. The name is a plea for patriarchy to unlearn the habits of marginalising women at both family and national levels. The family is run by Ngwenya, a father-figure whose authority is unquestioned. In a similar way, the national family is presided over by father-figures who brook no challenge to their authority as evidenced by the murder of Mr Nkani and mobilisation and deployment of the youth militia. Now, when Senzeni says: "I have a new family..." (p. 71), she dramatises Gramsci's notion of consent and submission. The new family is a family of violent masculinities, hell-bent on winning elections at any cost to preserve their interests. But Senzeni seems to be youthfully unaware of these manoeuvres and this is why she says: "My future is all but confirmed" (p. 71) and "we're going to win the elections and when I come back; I will be having a good job" (p. 134). She has been brainwashed to believe that she has a stake in the patriarchal militarist system that is masochistic and delights in dead bodies and charred houses. The elections that she is confident are going to be won are a parading of vulgar power and not an expression of people's will. Schedler (2012, p. 103) accordingly argues that:

> Authoritarian incumbents contaminate electoral contests....They stand for elections not to lose power but to legitimate their continuity in office; they commonly try to distort and control the electoral process in order to minimise the risk of defeat.

Through spreading the cultural structures of fear, elections become an endorsement of the extant asymmetries of power. Ironically, this happens with the full participation of both female and male youths whose futures should be of utmost importance to them. In Zimbabwean electoral politics, youths and women are the two constituencies fought and agonised over and yet the most easily weaponised by both the ruling party and the opposition. One has to take into account the opposition discourses about generational consensus that sought to galvanise the youths to negate the ruling gerontocrats in ZANU-PF. In the ruling party, the youths are promised land, money for projects and a quota of seats in parliament. The same goes for women whose attendance at rallies is only equalled by that of churches. Sadly, the two constituencies are the most prone to hoodwinking during election times. They are used as fodder to portray the ruling party as invincible during election times. The recent beating of Citizens Coalition for Change members in Hwedza attests to the manipulation of youths. The elderly people were beaten in January 2023 as a punishment for attending a meeting for the opposition. They were attacked with logs by ZANU-PF youths. The violence, captured on camera, was perpetrated by both male and female militias to ensure that no meetings of the opposition take place and therefore foreclose the possibility of an opposition win. In the text, Senzeni sneaks behind the bushes and boulders recording the speeches and attendees of the meeting that Mrs Nkani has called. As a female, one would expect that she identifies with the interests of fellow women. One of the greatest tragedies in the Zimbabwean electoral terrain is the ways in which women pull others down to fortify patriarchy. That Senzeni is always hoisting the Zimbabwean flag whenever they are carrying out their green bomber activities is symbolic of state-sanctioned violence against a section of the citizenry excluded from the national imaginary. When a state, which has an inordinate monopoly of force and can mobilise resources for its campaign, creates an uneven electoral space, then democracy suffers and periodic elections become a routinised sham to sanitise authoritarianism.

Conclusion

Peering into the 2023 harmonised elections, the prospects of a violence-free plebiscite appear gloomy. This is because the intersections between gender and electoral violence are not as clear-cut as is often imagined. Women advertently or inadvertently participate in actions and cultural discourses that render them marginal while perpetuating male hegemonic rule. The tokenist political spaces they inhabit are afforded them by men to prop up patriarchal militarist structures. In participating in such gendered spaces, they become complicit in their own marginalisation. But men are also victims of electoral violence by hegemonic masculinities who believe that participation in the liberation war entitles them to determine electoral outcomes in their favour. The "New Dispensation" inherited systemic structures of violence during periods of elections. The Mnangagwa regime seems to have perfected the art of constricting the electoral space so that only ZANU-PF is able to campaign freely. While the deployment of electoral violence may lead to resistance and alternative imaginations of elections, often it achieves the aim of submission cynically captured in the cliché that "if you cannot beat them, then join them." I argue that the prospects of a (re)configured electoral terrain in 2023 dims if one looks at the conscription of both genders into the structures of violence that accentuate militarism, patriarchy and political entitlement. The 2018 August shootings that killed both men and women was a declaration that the ruling party had not and may not change its electoral modus operandi.

References

Bates, T. R. (1995). Gramsci and the theory of hegemony. *Journal of the History of Ideas, 36*(2), 351–366.

Bhatasara, S., & Chiweshe, M. K. (2021). Women in Zimbabwean politics post-November 2017. *Journal of Asian and African Studies, 56*(2), 218–233.

Cock, J. (1989). Keeping the fires burning: Militarisation and the politics of gender in South Africa. *Review of African Political Economy, 16*(45/46), 50–64.

Eagleton, T. (1991). *Ideology*. Verso.

Fiori, G. (1990). *Antonio Gramsci: Life of a revolutionary.* Verso.
Foucault, M. (1972). *The archaeology of knowledge.* Tavistok.
Gaidzanwa, R (2004). *Gender, women, and electoral politics in Zimbabwe.* ISA.
Gallagher, M. (2001). *Gender setting: New agendas for media monitoring and advocacy.* Zed Books.
Geisler, G. (1995). Troubled sisterhood: Women and politics in Southern Africa: Case studies from Zambia, Zimbabwe and Botswana. *African Affairs, 94*(377), 545–578.
Humphrey, M. (2002). *The politics of atrocity and reconciliation. From terror to Trauma.* Routldge.
Kaarsholm, P. (2005). Coming to terms with violence: Literature and the development of a public sphere in Zimbabwe. In R. Muponde & R. Primorac (Eds.), *Versions of Zimbabwe. New approaches to literature and culture* (pp.1–3). Weaver Press.
Khadiagala, G. (2009, November 17–18). *Reflections on the course of election violence in Africa.* Paper presented at EISA fourth annual symposium, Johannesburg.
Koko, S. (2009). Understanding election related violence in Africa: Patterns, causes, consequences and framework for preventive action. *Journal of African Elections, 12*(3), 51–88.
Mawere, T. (2019). *Gender and sexual imaginations. The 2018 Zimbabwean E(r)ections and the Aftermath.* Centre for Sexualisation, AIDS and Gender. University of Pretoria.
Mbembe, A. (2001). *On the postcolony.* University of California Press.
McClintock, A. (1995). *Imperial leather: Race, gender, and sexuality in the colonial contest.* Routledge.
Mlalazi, C. (2014). *They are coming.* Weaver Press.
Motsamai, D. (2010). *When elections become a curse: Redressing electoral violence in Africa.* ISA Policy Briefing No. 1. EISA.
Musila, G. (2012). Violent masculinities and the phallocentric aesthetics of power in Kenya. In S. O. Opondo & M. J. Shapiro (Eds.), *The new violent cartography: Geo-analysis after the Aesthetic turn* (pp. 151–170). Routledge.
Mwonzora, G., & Mandikwaza, E. (2019). The menu of electoral manipulation in Zimbabwe: Food handouts, violence, memory, and fear in case of Mwenezi East and Bikita West 2017 bye-elections. *Journal of Asian and African Studies, 54*(8), 1114–1128.
Riley, D. J. (2011). Hegemony, democracy, and passive revolution in Gramsci's prison notebooks. *California Italian Studies, 2*(2). http://scholarship.org/uc/item/5x48fomz
Schedler, A. (2012). Elections without democracy: The menu of manipulation. *Journal of Democracy, 13*(2), 36–50.

Steuter, E., & Willy, D. (2009). Discourse of dehumanisation: Enemy construction and Canadian media complicity in the framing of the war in Iraq. *Global Media Journal-Canadian Edition, 2*(2), 7–24.

Zamchiya, P. (2013). The MDC- T's (un) seeing eye in Zimbabwe's 2013 harmonised elections: A technical knockout. *Journal of Southern African Studies, 39*(4), 955–962.

Zigomo, K. (2022). Virtue, motherhood and femininity: Women's political legitimacy in Zimbabwe. *Journal of Southern African Studies, 48*(3), 527–544.

CHAPTER 4

Shona Women and Grassroots Politics in Zimbabwe: Prospects for the 2023 General Elections

Maradze Viriri and Eunitah Viriri

INTRODUCTION AND BACKGROUND TO THE STUDY

A common trend in Zimbabwean politics is the under-representation of women in most political structures, and grassroots politics is no exception. Shona women form the largest group of Bantu-speaking people living in Buhera South which is constituted by groupings which include the Zezuru, Karanga, Manyika, Tonga, Korekore, and Ndau. Of these groupings which form the Shona, Buhera South is mainly inhabited by the Manyika, Ndau, and, to a lesser extent, Zezuru. These Shona-speaking people are identified by their unique culture which is characterized by their patriarchal belief which confines women to motherly roles which are usually restricted to the kitchen. It is against this background that women's participation in public domains like politics is usually much

M. Viriri (✉) · E. Viriri
Department of Teacher Development, Great Zimbabwe University, Masvingo, Zimbabwe
e-mail: mviriri@gzu.ac.zw

© The Author(s), under exclusive license to Springer Nature Switzerland AG 2023
E. Mavengano and S. Chirongoma (eds.), *Electoral Politics in Zimbabwe, Vol II*, https://doi.org/10.1007/978-3-031-33796-3_4

lower when compared to their male counterparts. Ford (2002, p. 5) believes that the starting point to understand the position of women in relation to politics will be to define politics beyond the traditional scope of electoral, party, or institutional behaviour, which will give a more complete examination of women's political behaviour. Politics is defined by Shafritz (1988) as, "The art and science of governance; the means by which the will of the community is arrived at and implemented; the activities of government, politician, or political party." History has it that worldwide, until at least 1920, women had been legally excluded from many conventional forms of participation in politics. Motebang (1997) opined that if we use an insider's definition of politics, focusing exclusively on political party activity, voting, campaigning, seeking office, or making direct contact with public officials, this will not prove very useful in examining women's activism prior to suffrage or in understanding the complexity of women's politics today.

Since long back, it seems women were indirectly involved in politics in one way or the other, but the fact still stands that their numbers were low when compared to that of males. Although in the past women were seen as outsiders prior to suffrage, the range of activities they undertook, the tactics they employed, and the issues they cared about were indeed political. The fact that only 32 out of 54 African countries had signed the Protocol on Women's rights in Africa by the end of 2012 is indicative of the challenges that continue to block progress towards the goal of social transformation, especially with regard to giving political space to women. Getting progressive policies adopted is but one step in a broader process since legislation on its own does not necessarily translate into broader gender equality, nor has it really transformed the political involvement of many African women. Lamprianou (2013) has it that political participation pertains to the quintessential act of democratic citizenship. According to Arstein (1969), there are levels of participation ranging from manipulation at the bottom of the ladder, consultation in the middle of the ladder, to citizen control at the apex. Buttod (1999) observes that there are different types of participation, and this research is aimed at the participation of women in grassroots political structures in Buhera South. Functional participation advocates for more women to participate in politics, yet the situation on the ground seems to point to poor participation of women in grassroots political structures. The government of Zimbabwe tried to boost the representation of women in parliament by introducing the quota system in 2013. The same move was expected to cascade to grassroots political structures. This quota system was supposed to end in 2023 but has since been extended after Constitutional Amendment Number Two sailed through parliament.

This research aims at assessing the level of participation of Shona women in the Zimbabwe African National Union Patriotic Front party (ZANU PF) grassroots cell structures in Buhera South. The constitution provides a system where 60 women are elected to the National Assembly through proportional representation. Through this amendment, 30% of seats in local authorities will now be reserved for women. Despite these calls, the representation of women remains very low compared to their male counterparts. According to the Gender Audit report of 2018, currently in Zimbabwe, women in parliament hold 31.9% seats, and the percentage goes further down in grassroots structures. Ochwada (1997) says that worldwide, women's representation in parliament and party politics remains low. Very few women in Buhera South hold meaningful posts in grassroots political structures. Several reasons were given for such low representation. The participation of women in politics in Zimbabwe has been very low since the attainment of independence in 1980 despite the fact the government of Zimbabwe has been on record declaring that women and men have full political rights—the right to vote and to hold office at all levels in the decision-making process. Ochwada (1997) has observed that there are several reasons which are often advanced to explain women's absence or under-representation in party politics, and some of these reasons may also explain the poor representation of women in grassroots structures in Buhera South. These range from women's illiteracy, lack of economic resources, lack of time, few role models, socialization and culture, and the most dangerous of all, "women's reluctance to vote for other women." The main concern in this chapter is to look into the history of women's participation in grassroots politics, focusing on the composition of the cell political structures in Buhera South, with the aim of providing the reasons for the low participation. Hamandishe (2018) says that women constitute more than half the world's population, yet their participation in electoral and governance processes—where decisions regarding their lives are made—remains peripheral in many countries. Zimbabwe is no exception to this global trend. Zimbabwe is a signatory to many declarations aimed at increasing women's leadership and decision-making, and the introduction of the progressive constitutional provision section 124 of the constitution provides for a quota of 60 seats for women as part of efforts to enhance women representation in parliament, and this is expected to be cascaded to grassroots structures. Even though Zimbabwe is signatory to several normative frameworks that seek the inclusion of women in major decision-making organs, the reality is still dire. According to the Gender Audit report of 2018, Zimbabwe has just 33.2% female representation in the National Assembly. Although the constitution requires all political parties to meet the constitutional provisions on gender parity and equal political opportunities, patriarchy remains widespread in Buhera South, and there seems to be a deliberate reluctance by political parties to appreciate the need for adopting affirmative measures towards gender parity. The political landscape in Zimbabwe remains a man's world as several obstacles perpetually work against women's participation in public institutions or politics. During elections, women's private lives are usually publicly scrutinized and demeaned, as misogyny and sexism take centre stage. Hamandishe (2018) concluded that it goes without saying that when the electoral environment is patriarchal and prejudiced, women are automatically marginalized.

Theoretical and Analytical Framework

This research is guided by two theories, namely the Feminist theory and the Africana Womanist theory as its lenses to guide this research. The feminist theory is "a branch of interdisciplinary enquiry which takes gender as a fundamental organizing category of experience" (Searing, 1985, p. 3). Hence, the feminist theory upholds the view that women's subordination must be questioned and challenged (Abbott & Wallace, 1993, p. 10). Feminists have bemoaned the fact that patriarchy tips the social scales in favour of the male child, creating a sub-human being in the female. It is a system that elevates one sex above another, creating inequality of sexes that feminism calls patriarchy (Butler, 2006). Feminism calls into question the public and private distinction and the condemnation of male-dominated mainstream politics and the state.

While feminism seems to be general, Africana Womanism is specific as it is an ideology created and designed for women of African descent. Hudson-Weems (2004) believes that this theory is grounded in African culture, and therefore, it necessarily focuses on the unique experiences, struggles, needs, and desires of African women. Thus, in view of the participation of women in politics, the Africana Womanist theory is of the view that since long back, women had their say in the politics of the day which was different to that of men. The Africana Womanism theory insists upon our own historical, political, social, and cultural matrix to interpret and translate our lives in order that our rich African legacy be presented correctly. In this research, concern is on the low participation of women in grassroots politics in Buhera South. Randall and Waylen (1998) noted that feminism is logical to the consequences of a more fundamental perception of male power as systematic and omnipresent, as encapsulated in the concept of "patriarchy." It concerns the political, social, cultural, and other forms of women and their social relations by patriarchy, a system of thought and social relations and privileges and empowers men, creates relationships between the genders that disenfranchise, disempower, and devalue women's experiences (Payne, 2005, p. 251). Feminism starts from the view that women are oppressed and that their oppression is primary. Rubaya and Viriri (2012) note that because of this feminist idea, women are fixed in a permanent state of dependency and estrangement within the gates of patriarchal structures. In other words, maleness in a patriarchal society of Buhera South becomes a signifier for superiority, for privilege, and for social importance. Femaleness, on the other hand, breeds subordination, passivity, and humility. This is why the political representation of members in the grassroots political structures in Buhera South is skewed towards men.

Thus, the feminist theory is relevant to this study because it is construed as a struggle to free the woman from the shackles of patriarchal grip that has disadvantaged her from participating equally with men on the political field. This study seeks to examine the number of women who are within the ruling ZANU PF cell structures with the aim of finding out if women are given equal opportunity to that of their male counterparts. The research has shown that women are under-represented in grassroots ZANU PF political structures. The few women who are in these structures are either given inferior posts or their ideas are never taken seriously during decision-making processes, resulting in men dominating much of the proceedings in these grassroots political structures.

Methodology

This research which is qualitative in nature used interviews and document analysis in gathering data. Ten participants were interviewed on the participation of women in grassroots politics. Of the ten, four were men and 6 women. These ten people were purposively assembled and interviewed on the participation of women in grassroots cell structures and politics in general in Buhera South. Among the ten people chosen, one was the chairperson of the Buhera South ZANUPF cell structure, and the other was the chairperson of the women's wing. The other four were members of the cell structure. The other two participants were just ZANU PF card-carrying members who attend political meetings very often. From the face-to-face interviews, the participants' views on the participation of women in grassroots politics were merged with documentary information on the statistics of women participation in grassroots political structures. The strength for purposively sampling participants who were within the political cell structures and those who were card-carrying members afforded the researcher room to judge particular people as suitable for the provision of the required information (Cohen et al., 2011). The study sample was seen to be large enough to provide the researchers with the necessary information required for the study. To ensure consistency in the interviews, one of the researchers was interviewing, and the other one was recording the proceedings of the interview sessions. Since participants were above the age of 18 years, the researchers sought their consent by requesting them to either fill in consent forms or to grant verbal consent. The participants were assured that the study was purely for academic purposes. This qualitative research was guided by the following research questions:

1. Do Shona women participate in grassroots political structures?
2. What are the reasons for low participation in grassroots politics?
3. What can be done to improve the political landscape in order to attract women so that they are free to participate in politics just like their male counterparts?

Findings and Discussion

This research has demonstrated a worrying trend in the participation of women in grassroots politics in Buhera South. Women are underrepresented in grassroots politics in postcolonial Zimbabwean politics. The few who are in the grassroots structures are usually not given enough platforms to express their views; thus, they are often regarded as puppets of their male counterparts. The ZANU PF cell executive committee structure of Buhera South bears testimony of the under-representation of women in grassroots politics.

The Table 4.1 shows the structure of the Buhera South ZANUPF cell structure. The cell comprises 50 members, and its structure is made of the main wing, the women's league, the youth league, and lastly, the non-executive members. On the main wing of Buhera South, the chairperson, treasurer, political commissar, security officer, and the two committee members are all men, and only the secretary is a woman. The women's league, as expected, comprises seven women. The youth league is dominated by males, with only three women being part of the youth league. The non-executive members' slot is made up of 29 members, and it has only 10 females, with the rest being males. Despite the fact that the Constitution of Zimbabwe makes a firm commitment to gender equality, the continued under-representation of women in politics is evidenced by the ZANU PF structures in Buhera South, which show that women are still far behind their male counterparts in politics. The Constitution calls for equal opportunities in political, economic, and social activities but what is obtaining on the ground is the opposite. The Gender Audit reports that in 2018, ZANU PF had a total number of 2178 candidates who contested 2168 seats. Women represented 15% of the candidates, and out of the 2178 total candidates for seats at the level of parliament and local council seats, there were 325 contesting women only and 1853 contesting men.

Information gathered by the researchers from the participants gives a worrisome picture with regard to the participation of women in grassroots politics in Buhera South. The following were responses of participants during interviews. The chairperson of the Buhera South ZANU PF cell structure had this to say on the participation of women in his area, "*Mumusangano medu tinopa mikanwa yakaenzerana pakati pevarume*

Table 4.1 Buhera South ZANU PF cell structure

Cell part	Female	Males
Main wing	1	6
Women's league	7	0
Youth league	4	5
Non-executive members	8	19
Total	20	30

nevakadzi kuti vatore zvigaro zvekutungamirira asi kuti chinoitika ndechekuti vakadzi vashoma vanoda kutora zvigaro izvi." (In our party, we give equal opportunities to both men and women to take up leadership positions but very few women are interested to take these positions.) On the same note, the chairlady of the women's wing said, "*Vamwe vangu havadi kupinda muzvigaro zveutungamiriri izvi vachipa zvikonzero zvakasiyana siyana saka nokudaro hatikwanisi kuvamanikidza tinozongogashira vashoma vanenge vabvuma ivavo.*" (My colleagues do not want to take up leadership positions citing different reasons, as such, we cannot coerce people, and as a result, we will work with the few who will be willing.) One male participant had this to say, "*Zvekupinda mune zvematongerwe enyika izvi zvinofanirwa kuitwa nevakadzi vasina varume nekuti kazhinji kunounganwa uye kumisangano kunoitwa zvinhu zvisina unhu.*" (Participating in politics must be left to single women because what transpires during political meetings is immoral.) Such sentiments seem to suggest the reason why there are few numbers of women in the cell structure of Buhera South.

Participant 3 had this to say, "*Dzimwe nguva panoitwa sarudzo yezvinzvimbo izvi panomboita mhirizhonga zvinova zvinoita kuti vanhukadzi varambe kupinda mazviri.*" (At times, elections to choose members into these cell structures are associated with violence, and this drives away women.) On the aspect of violence often associated with jostling for political posts, Hoeane (1984) argues that the political climate of most of the post-independence era which was dominated by physical violence prompted most women to retreat into the domestic sphere. Whatever little women's participation there had been was severely reduced after the experience of incidents of violence prior to and after every election. The same could have led to the current low participation of women in politics in Buhera South given the political violence witnessed during the previous elections, in particular the 2008 general election which left a lot of people maimed and even dead. Memories of what happened during that period can be a contributing factor to the present low participation of women in politics.

Participant 4 shared the following, "*Isu vanhukadzi hatidanani saka kazhinji pasarudzo vamwe vanhukadzi vanotovhotera vanhurume vachisiya vanhukadzi.*" (We women do not vote for each other, rather we vote for men.) Of the 4 female participants, 3 indicated that they would rather vote for male candidates to occupy influential positions in the grassroots party structures, citing the reason that their female counterparts usually forget those who vote for them once they are in power.

One of the female participants said, "*Dambudziko redu vanhukadzi ndere kuti tikaera tava pachigaro tinodadirana uye tinenge tongozvifunga tokanganwa vaya vakatisarudza.*" (The problem with us women is that once we are in power, we look down upon others, and we will concentrate on self-aggrandizement forgetting those who will have voted us into office.) In line with such sentiments is the myth that is often peddled, that lack of confidence in other women as leaders is another factor for low number of women in grassroots politics. In this scenario, women are depicted as being their own worst enemy, thus giving the impression that women are to blame, therefore, not much can be done. Ford (2002, p. 4) says, "Because women themselves hold different attitudes and opinions about their appropriate roles, their ability to effectively practice interest-group politics has been greatly diminished." If women could present a united front, their numbers alone would demand considerable respect and attention within politics. Due to the fact that women are unable to agree on unique sex and gender interests as women, and second, to disentangle gender interests from the powerful cross-pressures of class, marital status, motherhood, and sexuality, they often find their interests allied with multiple groups thereby reducing their chances of fully participating in politics. Randall and Waylen (1998) observed that in most of the cases, women do not enter politics, at whatever level, as a united force but often in conflict with one another.

Participant 5 said, "*Chivanhu chedu hachitenderi kuti vanhukadzi vawanikwe vachimira mberi kwevarume.*" (Our culture does not allow women to be seen to be above men.) Another participant had this to say, "*Vakadzi havana zvivindi zvekutungamirira saka nekudaro vanosarudza vanhurume kuti vatungamirire.*" (Women lack the courage to participate in political decision-making processes so they instead choose men to lead them.) Participant 7 had this to say, "*Kazhinji vakadzi vekuno havadi kutora zvinzvimbo zvematongerwe enyika.*" (Generally, women in Buhera are reluctant to take political posts.) Charlton et al. (1989) say, "Politics is the realm of public power, the sphere of justice, and systems of law ... Women are not part of politics per se, but provide, in their capacities in the private sphere, a refuge from public life for men when they share in the private sphere...." Randall and Waylen (1998) observed that radical feminists reject mainstream politics and the state because they view them as instrumental to, and an expression of, patriarchy, and because of this, they are viewed as infused with male assumptions, a male style of politics or political culture. One of ZANU PF MPs, Mavis Chidzonga is quoted as saying, "If nothing drastically changes at this national congress, women will continue to be window dressers. Women have always been recognized as those who mobilize votes, produce children and sing praise songs for the men." To further buttress men's chauvinistic attitudes towards women politicians, Chidzonga went on to say: "The men are very comfortable to have an all bull team. Their attitude since we made the resolution in Victoria Falls has been so bad. Even as we lobby them, some are getting extreme. They are used to a women's league that was passive and all it did was praise and sing for them."

What they forget is that according to de Beauvoir (1949, p. 295), "one is not born but becomes a woman." Thus, the perception that there are certain positions destined for men and women is just mere creation by men meant to keep them at the top, dominating women in most spheres of life including politics. Evans (2003, p. 57) observed that "all gendered behaviour is a matter of the internalization of social experiences." Maraisane in Walter (2009) says that since women are noticeable at many political rallies and in voting queues, their absence in high echelons of political parties can, therefore, not be ascribed to their lack of interest in political affairs; rather, it can be mainly attributed to the patriarchal nature of the Basotho, which bestows decision-making powers and headship on males. She goes on to say that historically, the entrenched gender stereotypes and expectations of the Basotho patriarchal society have always conferred decision-making processes in the hands of males. The same can also be said of women in Buhera South who seem to be bound by patriarchal beliefs and are always in their cocoons when it comes to politics. Culturally, the patriarchal status quo in Buhera South remains relatively unchanged and requires challenging and changing unequivocally and holistically.

Participant 8 said, "*Chechi yedu haitibvumiri kuti titore zvinzvimbo zvekumira pamberi pevarume tichivatungamiririra.*" (Our church does not allow us to take responsibilities of standing before men and leading them.) Another participant had this to say, "*Mazuvano kana tichisarudza vatungamiriri tinoda vanhu vakafunda zvino vakadzi vazhinji havana kuverenga.*" (These days when we choose political leaders, we need educated people. Unfortunately, most women do not have the required educational qualifications.) This response concurs with what the researchers observed with regard to the general level of education of women in Buhera South. A majority of the women in Buhera South did not go far with education, and some of them are primary school dropouts; hence, they lack the pre-requisites of holding office in the grassroots structures because when people choose someone for a political post, they do so with the hope that the individual will have the potential of rising to much better offices up the political ladder. A worrying trend was also observed by the researchers, which was that, of the few women who participated in the research, their level of education was very low compared to that of their male counterparts. Buhera South, by virtue of close proximity to Marange, has a lot of its people affiliated to the Johanne Marange Apostolic sect, which does not allow the girl child to pursue education beyond the primary school level. Given the low education standard of most women in the district, it will not be feasible to give such people leadership positions in the political structures. Geisler (2004) says, "If educated women have been missing from the leadership of the Women's league, so have the ex-combatants. With few prominent exceptions, alleged to have had 'top connections' women combatants kept a low profile in politics." Such sentiments seem to concur with Gillingham and Schneiders in Rubaya and Viriri (2012), who argue that even the devil can wrongly quote the Bible to achieve his aims. These scholars argue that gender roles are not divinely dictated but are socially orchestrated and determined, and the Bible has been misunderstood and abused as a tool to whip women into submission and suppress them. Butler (1999) argues that sexual difference is entirely constructed and that we construct our gendered selves through "performativity"—the "performance of socially established expectations of the masculine or the feminine." The researchers observed that those women affiliated to African Apostolic churches such as Johanne Marange, and Mwazha were the ones who were adamant in insisting that women must not take political posts in grassroots cell structures. Concurring with such sentiments is Ford (2002, p. 109) who argues that women are less likely than men to see themselves as politicians, let alone career politicians. She goes on to say that for a long time, women's primary path to elective office was in the wake of a male relative, usually a father or a husband. The research established that the few women who were in these structures were from the Roman Catholic, Reformed Church in Zimbabwe and some of the Pentecostal churches. These churches encourage women to take up leadership positions both in church and politics.

Participant 7 said, "*Kupinda mune zvematongerwe enyika izvi zvinoda mari kazhinji zvino ruzhinji rwevanhukadzi mari iyi tinenge tisina.*" (Being involved in politics entails some financial commitments, and yet most women do not have the financial muscle.) On the few women who are found in the ZANU PF cell structures, Randall and Waylen (1998) say that literature on women's political participation suggests that women find involvement in grassroots politics easier to negotiate because of its relative informality and nearness to home, but what is obtaining on the ground in Buhera South is different. Women in Buhera South only come to political rallies in numbers but when it comes to taking leadership positions in the party structures, their numbers go down dismally. Motebang (1997), in trying to justify the low participation of women in politics, suggests that conventional wisdom points to the fact that women have had a harder time than men in raising and spending money to get themselves elected to public office. She goes on to say that women are not equally represented in prestigious companies that have access to large single donations, nor any means to buttress their campaigns financially. Her argument seems to hold water, given the financial position of most women in Buhera South. Most of these women are not formerly employed; they depend on subsistence farming for food and income, yet Buhera South is a dry area which often experiences droughts. Holding leadership positions in these political cell structures comes with a lot of travelling, which requires money. The party occasionally meets the travelling expenses when members attend political meetings in Murambinda or Mutare, but when you are away from home there is always that need to have a substantial amount of money to cater for your personal welfare and the family which you will have left behind. In Latin America, they have decided to have localized and small meetings and some groups deliberately encouraging women to take on roles which challenged stereotypes, but of course they could not completely escape the influence of clientelism and caudillismo, but there was an attempt to develop new ways of "doing politics" which did facilitate women's participation.

The women's league, of late, has been the notable voice for women in the grassroots structures, but the problem with this wing is that most of the members did not go far with their education. The fact that they have lower educational qualifications hampers their participation in discussions pertaining the organization of the party, resulting in men dominating when it comes to decision-making. On the position of the women's league, Hove (1994, p. 35) has this to say, "The only political pain I have is to see the woman of my country in politics not as serious politicians, but as dancers, praise singers to the glory of the male politicians. They sing and dance, they kneel and make offerings in the manner of the traditional women of the village, paying homage to the glory of man...." Hove described the familiar sight at the airport, with women draped in party colours, welcoming dignitaries of the time, singing, apparently happy to be onlookers in their own destiny. His observations represent the stereotypical image of the ruling party's women's wing. This research, therefore, seeks to find out the reasons why women in Buhera South are few in the grassroots political structures. Geisler (2004) says that the ZANU (PF) election manifesto of 1980 had promised that "under the new government, women will enjoy equal rights with men in all spheres of political, economic, cultural and family life." Contrary to that promise, the then Secretary of the Women's League, Teurai Ropa Nhongo, complained at the 1984 conference that four years after independence, major areas of gender inequality had been left untouched. Geisler (2004) further observed that most political parties developed more particularistic goals which did not represent the aspirations of all citizens and often no longer included the concerns of women. Randall (1987) notes that in China, the rate of women's formal political participation is quite high, but this in no way ensures them political influence. The late former vice-president of Zimbabwe, Joshua Nkomo, was quoted by Jacobs (1998) exhorting the ZANU PF women's league saying, "the role of women in the party.... Is to fulfil the objectives of the party through the Women's league, but the Party would like women to take their role as mothers seriously.... [in order] to strengthen the nation" (Jirira, 1995, p. 12). Geisler (2004) says that many women politicians themselves have recognized the Women's League as a mere tank of canvassing women voters for the party where women themselves reinforce the supportive role assigned to them by fundraising, mobilizing, doing party propaganda, and participating in rallies, which men rather watch on the television. From the women's point of view, this wing is there to marginalize them more. As Hove (1990) aptly put it, "ten years of women in our national politics, ten years of singing and dancing, ten years of ululations." Moraisane in Deborah (2009) says that women are clearly visible at political rallies and other political activities in Lesotho, yet within political parties, women hardly ever ascend to higher positions in executive committees, which ultimately translates into fewer women in parliament and cabinet. The same scenario is found in Zimbabwe, where women are found in large numbers during ZANU PF political rallies but when it comes to influential positions in grassroots political structures, men will be dominating both in terms of numbers and leadership posts.

Chitsike (2015) argues that, while women are oppressed by culture, male attitudes, and behaviours as well as political structures and processes, they are also their own enemy. She (2015) notes that women suffer from a "pull her down syndrome" (PhD) in the sense that they do not support each other to hold leadership positions. She further posits that the reason why women sell each other out is seldom for their political affiliation but the "PhD" syndrome disguised as politics. Motebang (1997) says that historically, women have sought local office to solve a particular problem rather than to start a career in politics, and once the community problem is solved, many women choose to leave public service rather than seek higher office and by doing so, they will be limiting their numbers in the political pipeline.

Ochwada (1997) argues that "even some of the world's largest democracies at the end of 1991 such as the United States and the United Kingdom, could only boast 5.8 per cent and 6.4 per cent of the women's participation in political decision-making." In Africa, there have been very few women in politics even though women and men have full political rights—the right to vote and to hold offices at all levels in the decision-making process. Bryson (2007) has it that women's continuing under-representation in most national assemblies is itself a sign of women's collective subordination and lack of resources, including time. It means that important areas of human temporal experience arising from women's childbearing and their socially ascribed roles are excluded from the policy-making process. It is a fact that women are under-represented when it comes to grassroots political structures as was found out by this research, but we have to bear in mind the fact that even during the armed struggle, rural women in Buhera South just like other women scattered around the rural areas of Zimbabwe played a crucial role in the success of the struggle.

What is encouraging now is that the number of women in these grassroots political structures has improved over the past years, but it has not reached the desired number so that women could have equity, for instance, in the political proceedings of their district. Supporting the idea of having women in decision-making positions in politics, Ganzalez in Walter (2009) says, "Women are naturally more of caring, more inclusive and work more in a cooperative environment than men do." Ford (2002, p. 7) says, "When modern political campaigns began, women participated by performing duties consistent with their temperament by providing food, acting as hostesses and social organizers, and cleaning up afterward." Such works should not be taken for granted; rather, women exhibited a partisan fervour equal to that of men. This research has established that since the implementation of the quota system, the percentage of women in politics, especially the parliament and senate, have increased, but some quotas have argued that women elected through this system have no real political power as they have no constituency or access to Constituency Development Funds. Catherine Mhondiwa, a councillor for Ward 13 Mkoba in Gweru, who belongs to the Movement for the Democratic Change party, says although the quota system was created so that more women can be in top political positions, all they have are positions with no power. She went on to say that women put into power through this system do not contribute much in parliament as they have no constituency to speak on behalf of. She said that these women are not elected, hence if you are given something, you have no power to say no to the person who gave you that position. She said that it was not fair for women to be appointed a quota when they represented the larger population. She called on for a 50–50 representation as the solution to the under-representation of women in politics. This study has found out that although the nation has made significant inroads in terms of promoting women participation in politics through the women quota system, there is still more to be done to enhance this democratic process to enable women to enter into politics at grassroots level. There is need to strengthen the current legislation to protect women, especially from political violence and victimization during the electoral processes so that they can participate freely.

Conclusion

This study has shown that women participation in grassroots politics, just like in the mainstream politics, is still low, and patriarchal beliefs have been singled out as one of the major factors why women representation has remained low. Despite all the efforts, strategies and interventions by the government and other non-government organizations, representation of women is still very marginal, and one could describe it as tokenism. Thus, basing on the present results of this research, it seems that Zimbabwean women have, as predicted, "remained of politics, not in politics." This research has revealed that while there have been some moves towards gender equality, these have not resulted in gender equity. In addition to that, the existing efforts that attempt to bring gender equality, such as quota systems, are unlikely to have a sustainable impact on women's numerical representation in political processes, and in addition to that, women elected through this quota system have no real political power as they have no constituency or access to Constituency Development Funds (CDF). The dominance of men in grassroots political structures is but one of the key characteristics of a patriarchal state. The study also noted that although women might be under-represented in grassroots political cell structures, it does not mean that they are not involved in politics. Ford (2002) argues that although women were often relegated to support roles, they nonetheless participated in politics and acted politically long before they were awarded the franchise. A lot still needs to be done to enable women to participate on equal terms with men. In the light of the above, it is evident that political party mechanisms for advancing the status of women in grassroots political structures in Buhera South are inadequate. As we draw closer to the 2023 watershed general elections, we argue that more effort is needed to ensure that the environment is conducive for more women to participate in all levels of politics, from the grassroots structures up to the national level. To put it clearly and aptly, a radical unity in diversity, of rural and urban, old and young, educated and uneducated men and women, is needed to challenge the power of those traditions that still continue to hold many Zimbabwean women in virtual bondage, limiting them from participating fully in the politics that affects their lives.

References

Abbott, P., & Wallace, C. (1993). *The family and the new right*. Pluto Press.
Arstein, A. (1969, July). Ladder of citizen participation. *Journal of the American Planning Association, 35*(4), 216–224.
Bryson, V. (2007). *Gender and the politics of time*. The Poly Press.
Butler, J. (1999). *Gender trouble: Ferminism and the subversion of identity*. Routledge.
Butler, J. (2006). *Gender trouble: Ferminism and the subversion of identity*. Routledge.
Charlton, S. E. M., Everett, M., & Staudt, H. (Eds.). (1989). *Women, the state, and development*. State University of New York Press.

Chitsike, K. (2015). *Zim's new cabinet: An open letter to Mr R.G. Mugabe.* https://researchandaadvocacyunit.wordpress.com/tag/women/. Accessed on 7 February 2023.
Cohen, L., Manion, L., & Morrison, K. (2011). *Research methods in education* (7th ed.). Routledge.
De Beauvoir, S. (1949). *The second sex.* David Campbell.
Deborah, L. R. (2009). *Justice and gender: Sex discrimination and the law.* Havard University Press.
Evans, M. (2003). *Gender and social theory.* Open University Press.
Geisler, G. (2004). *Women and the Remaking of politics in Southern Africa: Negotiating autonomy, incorporation and representation.* Elanders Gotab AB.
Hamandishe, A. (2018). *Rethinking women's political participation in Zimbabwe's elections.* Harare: Africa Portal. South African Institute of International Affairs. info@africaportal.org
Hoeane, P. (1984). *Women and political participation: The case of Lesotho* (Unpublished Paper). Centre for Southern African Studies, York University.
Hove, C. (1990). *Bones.* Baobab Books.
Hove, C. (1994). *Shebeen tales: Messages from Harare.* Sage.
Hudson-Weems, C. (2004). *Africana womanist literary theory.* Africa World Press.
Jacobs, C. (1998). Institutional strengthening and technical co-operation: Developing a best practice model. *Journal of International Development, 10*(3), 397–406.
Jirira, K. O. (1995). Gender, politics and democracy. *SAFERE, 1*(2), 123–142.
Lamprianou, I. (2013). Contemporary political participation research: A critical assessment. *Jurnal Politik, 4*(2), 263–296.
Motebang, M. (1997). Women and politics: Prospects for the 1988 general elections. *Lesotho Social Review, 3*(2).
Ochwada, H. (1997). Politics and gender relations in Kenya: A historical perspective. *Africa Development, 22*(1), 123–139.
Payne, M. (2005). *Modern social work theory* (3rd ed.). Lyceum Books.
Randall, V. (1987). *Women and politics.* Macmillan.
Randall, V., & Waylen, G. (1998). *Gender, politics and the state.* Routledge.
Rubaya, C., & Viriri, E. (2012). *Breeding patriarchal patriots: The place of children within a patriarchal African home* (Occasional Paper, No. 67). Cape Town: Centre for Advanced Studies of African Society (CASAS).
Searing, S. E. (1985). *Introduction to library research in women's studies.* Westview.
Shafritz, M. (1988, July–August). Toward a Definition of Organizational Incompetence: A Negleted Variable in Organisation Theory, 54(4), 370–377.
Walter, D. (2009). Gender, diversity, elections and the media. *Gender and Media Diversity Journal, 6,* 33–39.

CHAPTER 5

Critical Thinking, Gender and Electoral Politics in Zimbabwe

Ephraim Taurai Gwaravanda

INTRODUCTION

Global trends in electoral politics tend to show gender imbalances in the participation of women as political representatives even though women tend to constitute the majority of voters numerically (Baoping, 2022; Jayachandran, 2015). This trend can also be found within the African continent at large. The main barriers that keep women out of politics are stereotypical views that are based on cultural, social, religious and economic assumptions about women's potentialities and capabilities. In this conceptual chapter, my aim is to examine the flawed reasoning that tends to keep many women outside the political representation space. I seek to show that mistaken thinking about one gender is responsible for gender imbalances in electoral politics in Zimbabwe, where male domination is seen in authority (Mavengano & Marevesa, 2022). This authority also includes political authority that is buttressed by entrenched cultural

E. T. Gwaravanda (✉)
Great Zimbabwe University, Masvingo, Zimbabwe
e-mail: egwaravanda@gzu.ac.zw

© The Author(s), under exclusive license to Springer Nature Switzerland AG 2023
E. Mavengano and S. Chirongoma (eds.), *Electoral Politics in Zimbabwe, Vol II*, https://doi.org/10.1007/978-3-031-33796-3_5

assumptions and concepts that tend to marginalise women who try to stand for political positions.

Recent literature about gender imbalances in Zimbabwean politics makes use of the lenses of gender studies (Ncube, 2020), political science (Manyeruke, 2018), political philosophy (Tendi, 2016) and media narratives (Mangena, 2022; Santos & Ndhlovu, 2016). However, the use of critical thinking as a component of logic to examine the reasoning behind such imbalances remains underexplored. The aim of critical analysis is to arrive at a reasonable position for the purpose of conceptual analysis and revision especially with reference to issues to do with women and politics as examined in this chapter. The chapter relies on philosophical analysis as a method to study the assumptions, premises and conclusions behind gender imbalances in Zimbabwean politics. I argue that politics simply enforces and endorses already held gender misconceptions about women as seen in other spheres such as culture and religion.

This chapter is made up of four main sections. The first section establishes the significance of critical thinking in the sphere of politics so as to move away from sophistry, rhetoric, propaganda and other forms of fallacious reasoning to allow credible and authentic rational disputation that provides respect to all political participants regardless of gender. The second section examines how mistaken thinking causes political violence that tends to discourage female participants in Zimbabwean electoral politics. The third section explores how political polarisation results in false dichotomies that impact negatively on female participants with the view of providing corrective measures. The last section constitutes a rebuttal of mistaken assumptions that lead to gender stereotypes about female politicians as expressed in negative moral judgements passed against women in politics.

Zimbabwean Electoral Politics and Critical Thinking

This section provides a brief background to the kind of discourse that is employed in Zimbabwean electoral politics so as to justify the relevance of critical thinking. I will begin by showing how the art of persuasion is used to support political claims. I will then proceed to examine how critical thinking can be used to correct mistaken claims.

Zimbabwean electoral politics involves the use of persuasive language that expresses approval or disapproval of political parties, individuals, manifestos, strategies among other elements. Terms such as 'criminals', 'sell outs', 'puppets', 'boot leakers' and 'satanists' are meant to disapprove certain political persuasions. In contrast, terms like 'democrats', 'human rights defenders' and 'progressivists' are meant to approve. When it comes to women in politics, the use of hate speech describes them as 'prostitutes' or 'husband snatchers' while those who are favoured may be described as 'mothers' or 'sisters'. Slurs such as 'prostitute' and 'husband snatcher' point to how women continue to be sexualised and objectified within Zimbabwean politics. The treatment of women in politics is no different from how they are regarded at home, in church and within African culture. This boils down to the fact that their competencies are often disregarded or unnoticed. Emphasis is placed rather on their bodies and sexualities rather than on their potentialities and actualities in terms of what they are likely to contribute in politics. The deliberate departure from the relevant aspects of likely contributions to the irrelevant descriptions of their bodies is characteristic of patriarchal society such as that of Zimbabwe.

In the few instances that women are accorded a space in politics, they are used as pawns in factional battles within political parties, as in the cases of Grace Mugabe, Sarah Mahoka and Mandiitawepi Chimene to mention a few. These women were used as political mouthpieces for male factional infights within the Zimbabwe African National Union-Patriotic Front (ZANU-PF) political party. When there were political differences between the late former President Robert Mugabe and the then Vice President Emmerson Mnangagwa, Mugabe did not publicly discredit his deputy, but women were used as mouthpieces to insult Mugabe's deputy. There are no corresponding descriptions done to the male counterparts within the Zimbabwean political sphere, and this demands the use of critical thinking to challenge such views. Critical thinking challenges the use of emotively charged language, and it places emphasis on analysis and rebuttal of assumptions, testing of factual claims and arriving at reasoned conclusions. Given the kind of language used in Zimbabwean electoral politics, it is important to engage critical thinking for a better position.

Critical thinking can be defined as the ability to provide a rational basis for beliefs and provide procedures for analysing, testing and evaluating claims about everyday situations (Rudinow & Barry, 2008). Analysis, as a dimension of critical thinking, involves the breaking down of components into parts to enable distinctions to be made. Analysis helps one to gain insights and determine whether given categories are related or mutually exclusive (Hurley, 2012; Warburton, 1996, 2013). The testing of beliefs involves a confirmation whether a belief is true or false by gathering the necessary evidence. This must be done objectively and independently (Boghossian, 2012; Iman, 2017). A lot of descriptions and re-descriptions of women in politics is done without any evidence. Empirical evidence is used to support claims that can be used to formulate rational arguments. Without the necessary evidence, one is likely to arrive at false conclusions (Copi, 2006; Copi et al., 2014; Forbes, 1994). Credible evidence should be based on a specific research, methods used, conclusions arrived at and recommendations made, and this becomes the foundation of irrefutable arguments (Gwaravanda, 2012, 2019). Evaluation is the systematic assessment and determination of the worth or merit of something. It involves measuring of effectiveness or suitability through weighing evidence in terms of strengths and weaknesses before arriving at a judgement. A sound judgement should, therefore, be informed by evidence.

Critical thinking enables one to assess the fields like politics where actions, norms and practices can be judged using objective reasoning criteria. Evaluation implies the use of established values based on introspection or self-reflection. The logical process of evaluation includes selection, assessment and adopting of known goods while avoiding far-fetched ideas and unsubstantiated claims. Critical thinking involves interrogation of beliefs that underlie one's culture for the purpose of seeking the truth. For Gwaravanda (2012), critical thinking helps to detect and avoid fallacies so that the conclusion follows from the given premises using the proper rules of inference.

Reflection is part of critical thinking in the sense that it enables one to closely examine evidence for the purpose of drawing accurate conclusions. As such, critical thinking goes against indoctrination and endorsement of societal assumptions without questioning. Critical thinking rises above one's culture by ability to seek justification for certain cultural norms and practices. According to Swafford and Rafferty (2016, p. 14), 'rather than accepting information at face value, critical thinkers are able to evaluate thoroughly the content of the issue'. This means that the critical thinker moves beyond the surface of things and seeks deeper evidence to justify claims.

Dismissing views or opinions is not what critical thinking entails, but it enables one to correct their own ideas and those of others. For one to be an effective thinker, they must be able to self-examine their own ideas through concepts such as self-correcting, self-examination and self-evaluation with the aim of avoiding misjudgements. Critical thinking avoids stereotypes, prejudices and negative attitudes that people harbour towards other people (Jones, 2005) and aims at problem-solving. Put in other words, critical thinking is introspection, retrospection and projection that an individual does based on the available information, facts and evidence (Beall & Restal, 2006; Hungwe, 2021). Therefore, what is significant about critical thinking is fundamentally the ability of an individual to interrogate the underlying assumptions, beliefs and value systems with an objective to improve or transform the status quo. Critical thinking, therefore, takes place within African culture in general and Ubuntu culture in particular (Metz, 2007, 2013a, 2013b; Ramose, 2002; Samkange & Samkange, 1980). This implies that critical thinking takes place within a particular context. Having explored the dimensions of critical thinking, the next section focuses on political violence as an obstacle to gender balance in Zimbabwean electoral politics.

Violence Against Zimbabwean Women in Politics

This section examines the concept of political violence and how it impacts on gender balance by discouraging women to participate in politics both as candidates for political parties and as voters. The section begins by defining political violence and then proceeds to show the forms of violence against women in politics. I then proceed to trace the root causes of violence against women, and I locate this in misconceptions and failure in reasoning.

Political violence can be defined as the deliberate use of power and force to achieve political goals (World Health Organization [WHO], 2023). Across the globe and in Zimbabwe, political violence is characterised by both physical and psychological acts aimed at injuring or intimidating populations. The WHO's definition of political violence is expanded to include deprivation, the deliberate denial of basic needs and human rights (WHO, 2023). Examples include obstruction related to freedom of speech and denial of access to food, education, sanitation and health care as seen in activists who are imprisoned.

Particularly when we look at dimensions of deprivation within political violence, it is clear that political violence is intimately related to structural violence: the ways that structures of society (e.g. educational, legal, cultural and health care) insidiously act as 'social machinery of oppression'

(Ackerly, 2008). Violence is often constructed along gendered notions of masculinity and femininity, including the binaries of man/woman, mate/opponent, conqueror/loser, strong/weak and public/private: the list goes on. Each of the binaries constructs one pole as superior to the other. The superior side carries essentialist notions of masculinity associated with men such as strong, winner, rational and smart (Ajei, 2007). The other carries simplistic notions of femininity associated with women: they are to be weak, emotional, losers, belonging to private space, etc. Such patriarchal—and homophobic—notions, thus, shape violence along gendered constructions, hence, the common use of violence against women in the Zimbabwean political environment.

The use of political violence against women, from the point of view of critical thinking, shows a failure of reasoning or rational disputation. It is a fallacy to resort to any form of political violence. Instead of appealing to force, it makes sense to use rational arguments and counter arguments within the political sphere. There is no reason to harm a political opponent physically or psychologically, but debates must be carried out instead. Each side must put forward their position and provide reasons for the arguments on the basis of facts.

While some of the misconceptions resulting in political violence against women can be corrected through voter education exercises, it can be argued that voter education in Zimbabwe is on the passive side because it does not allow critical engagement of voters. Instead, voter education is limited to the procedures to be taken in the actual voting process. Any form of critical engagement through voter education is construed as (de)campaigning for political parties. As long as voter education remains inadequate in terms of the critical thinking import, then it will be difficult to eradicate violence especially against women. Critical thinking is, therefore, a necessary and sufficient step to correct the thinking patterns of voters so as to eradicate political violence.

A central task of critical thinking is articulating what equality requires against this background of patriarchy within the contested political sphere. The primary task of critical thinking is to achieve the principle of procedural equality articulated by Aristotle that like cases should be treated alike and different cases differently in proportion to their differences. This procedural equality can be done independently of gender issues (Dotson, 2011). For some critical thinkers, this focus on procedural justice raises the question of whether there are differences between men and women that critical thinkers may justifiably take into account. It may be appropriate and justified to treat women differently in politics given that other fields such as law, economics and culture treat them differently. However, the different treatment should not constitute unfair treatment but rather some form of affirmative action. Having shown how political violence against women can be addressed using the resources of critical thinking, the next section examines how the myth of false dichotomy negatively impacts on women in Zimbabwean electoral politics.

False Dichotomies and Women in Zimbabwean Politics

This section focuses on the conceptual underpinnings of the fallacy of false dichotomy, and it shows how binary thinking leads to political polarisation, factionalism and power struggles that tend to victimise women participants in politics. I then draw from critical thinking to show how the faulty logic behind false dichotomies can be corrected.

To dichotomise is to divide individuals or things into two categories. Dichotomies can be legitimate or illegitimate (Allison, 2008). An example of a legitimate dichotomy is dividing human beings into tongue rollers and non-tongue rollers. Such a division is legitimate because it is based on facts, and it does not admit further divisions. An illegitimate dichotomy, also called false dichotomy, is a division of individuals or things into two categories yet there are always other possibilities (Hacking, 2001). An example of a false dichotomy that occurs in politics is the division of voters or political representatives as supporters belonging to party A or B. However, it is logically possible for one to belong to party C or even remain undecided among the existing parties. The false dichotomy is problematic in two ways; firstly, it ignores the existence of other political parties within the multiparty system. Secondly, it assumes that political parties are unified entities, yet there may be factions within them. These factions can be found at different levels starting from cell, ward, district, provincial and even national. This is evident in voting patterns where at one polling station, it is difficult to get the same number of votes for a particular party, for the different posts since voters may choose a parliamentary candidate for party A and choose a presidential candidate for party B even if the voters are perceived to be from the same political party.

The false dichotomy results in a highly polarised political environment that becomes hostile to women who are trapped in these dichotomies.

These dichotomies affect women political participants at different levels. At national level, dichotomies are made along the lines of the ruling party and the main opposition party. If a woman tries to form her own political party to challenge the ruling party as a presidential candidate, she is treated with hostility as seen in what happened to Joice Mujuru and Thokozani Khupe in the 2018 presidential race. For Nemukuyu (2018), genuine politics was perceived to be between male-governed parties such as ZANU-PF led by Emmerson Mnangagwa (2,460,463 or 50.8% of votes) and the then MDC Alliance led by Nelson Chamisa (2,147,437 or 44.3% of votes). Between these two political rivals, women participants were considered as nonentities that disturbed voters within the political space, and each of the female candidates obtained below 1% of the valid votes cast. Thokozani Khupe got a total of 45,573 votes nationally which is a mere 0.9% of total votes. Joice Teurai Ropa Mujuru obtained only 12,877 votes which translate to 0.3% of total votes (Nemukuyu, 2018). These voting statistics, though disputable in some instances, show how women candidates are lowly regarded within the Zimbabwean political sphere. However, the female presidential candidates accepted the outcome of the presidential race though they complained about harassment and intimidation from the electorate.

At provincial level, dichotomies form around powerful male figures who control provincial affairs of a given political party. Female candidates are not expected to take part in the provincial power wrestles, and their inclusion in such politics is to give support to the powerful male figures. Two male figures may be involved in factional fights thereby dividing other members of the executive especially women.

Factions at grassroots levels are often more difficult to handle since they cascade from the national level right down to the district. These wars follow the dichotomies that are found at higher levels including the national and provincial levels. At village level, for example, voters know each other by name and by political affiliation, and this makes the environment very hostile since individuals are divided along power wrangles that begin at primary elections within a given political party. The main contenders even at primary elections cause some false dichotomies that result in factions even if the overall winner is officially announced. Witch hunting to find out who voted for which candidate may follow, and this creates a hostile environment for women who are caught in between village power wrangles.

It can be argued that false dichotomies are a result of binary thinking that try to give only two alternatives in situations that have alternatives. Democratic practice actually gives alternatives for voters, but the creation of false dichotomies gives a hostile environment based on tensions that emanate from power struggles. The power fights result in women being caught in between or being used to fight male political power struggles as in the case of Sarah Mahoka who acted as Mugabe's mouthpiece to discredit Mnangagwa yet Mugabe himself remained silent and only made a written dismissal against his then deputy president. Critical thinking facilitates the dislodging of false dichotomies by demystifying them through rational argumentation so that voters and political representatives are allowed choices. Such choices, as enshrined in the constitution of Zimbabwe, enable political participants to exercise freedom of thought as well as political affiliations. Female political representatives should be accorded the chance to exercise their constitutional rights both as political representatives and as voters within a given constituency. An examination of the false dichotomy argument shows that the premise that contains the false dichotomy is misleading, and as a result, a false conclusion is obtained even if the rules of sound logical inference are followed. As such, a false dichotomy argument is unsound basing on the falsity of at least one of the premises contained in the argument. To avoid such a mistake, critical thinking exposes the falsity of the implied premise. Having shown how false dichotomies can be avoided, the next section explores how stereotypes and cultural assumptions are used to morally judge women in electoral politics in Zimbabwe.

Hasty Moral Judgements Against Zimbabwean Female Politicians

This section traces the formulation of moral judgements, identifies the types of moral judgements and how evidence is undermined in the judgements. I also examine the causes of such moral judgements against women in politics. I then proceed to show how the mindsets of citizens can be addressed so as to fight political gender imbalance in electoral politics in Zimbabwe.

Moral judgements can be defined as assessments that are used to evaluate behaviour or individuals. They are typically expressed in terms of positive aspects such as acceptable, permissible, obligatory and praiseworthy or in terms of negations such as bad, wrong, inappropriate, unacceptable and good or in a two-pronged expression such as right or wrong; good or bad; appropriate or inappropriate; and permissible or prohibited.

Moral evaluations are basically an assessment of whether behaviour is good or bad; right or wrong. Evaluations are basic human responses. In the political sphere in general and against women in politics in particular, such evaluations tend to take the negative side because they are based on already held mindsets that are based on cultural conditioning (Kim et al., 2020). This evaluative conditioning can be traced back to cultural and social assumptions since there is no morally significant evidence that has been gathered yet. In the political context of Zimbabwe, women in politics are often described as prostitutes. The rushed moral evaluation often lacks any grin of evidence, but the basis of such an evaluation is the cultural view that a good woman occupies domestic space and involvement in public space is considered a sign of loose morals. Such a label has been given to different women in politics such as Joice Mujuru, Grace Mugabe and Thokozani Khupe (Ncube, 2020). As such, these rushed evaluations do not constitute any genuine moral assessments, but they are based on faulty logic. These do not take any morally relevant facts into account. An examination of the implied argument shows that the premises are based on cultural assumptions while the conclusion is made up of an evaluative claim about the badness of an individual. Women in Zimbabwean politics are assumed to be prostitutes or witches, not because some evidence has been gathered but because there is such a culturally embedded belief.

Another type of judgement is called a norm judgement that determines whether something is permissible or not. While the first kind of moral judgement makes an attack on female political players, this kind of judgement makes an assessment on a practice, for example, politics is forbidden among women from a cultural point of view (Ncube, 2020). The field of politics, in this case, is judged to be morally inappropriate for a particular gender. In such a situation, the reasoning is based on established norms or traditions which classify certain areas as permissible (acceptable), prescribed (encouraged) or prohibited (forbidden). These established norms and traditions are then used to assess the suitability of politics, as a sphere that women can participate in (Catellani et al., 2004). Norm judgements are made before an action is made; for example, according to the said traditions, a married woman should not even think of joining politics. In other words, norm judgements are actually forms of instructions that order women to stay out of politics. Another difference is that while evaluations tend to make judgements based on the past and present, norm judgements appear to be future oriented.

The third category of moral judgements consists of wrongness judgements which are made up of violations. In this case, what is violated is the principle or standard set by society. For example, in the context of Zimbabwean politics, what is already set are standards of decency that are expected from women (Viriri & Viriri, 2018). Women are expected to come back home early, dress decently, respect their husbands and avoid associations with members of the opposite sex (except their husbands). Violations of such set standards, in the context of politics, consist of singing and dancing in public, dress in regalia that bears the face of another man and holding political meetings at night (while the husband and children are at home). The purpose of wrongness judgements is to preserve cultural moral standards which according to African culture, keep away women from indigenous politics.

The last category of moral judgements is blame judgements. In this type of judgement, one is considered morally blameworthy for intentionally and knowingly participating in something perceived to be morally wrong. The words intentionally and knowingly are important because they give responsibility to the individual involved in certain actions. Blame achieves these extensions by processing multiple sources of information, including the agent's causal contributions to the event, reasons and their potential justification, and counterfactuals about what the agent could have done differently (Cushman, 2008). Being sensitive to all this information enables blame to be a graded moral judgment and often expressed moral criticism of the norm violator. For example, a woman who is a Christian may be blamed for intentionally participating in political activities such as campaigning, name-calling, threatening and intimidating rival political opponents—actions that are seen as inconsistent with Christian principles. What this implies is that a young lady who joins politics for the sake of a profession is given less blame compared to a mature woman who is fully aware of the ills of politics. In this scenario, the blamed person is judged using motivational factors and reasons behind these actions to determine whether there is any moral justification to support the action. When unjustified, such actions will result in negative judgements (Monroe & Malle, 2017). The justifications in question must be accepted within a cultural or religious community, for example.

A moral judgement is an evaluation of someone as good or bad, and it is hasty when it is rushed and made on the basis of very little or even no evidence at all (Crockett, 2013). African culture gives the belief that a decent woman occupies the private domestic space of the home. Women who are involved in the public space of politics are judged as prostitutes, husband snatchers or witches. Logically, there is no contradiction between being a housewife and a political representative of a constituency at the same time. The use of hate speech and insulting language against women is a result of cultural assumptions that are endorsed without criticism. Various stereotypes have been used to undermine their capability to be active in politics analysts say (Mangena, 2022). When not deemed too weak to lead, women are often presented as having loose morals or as mercenaries for the governing party or opposition. Hasty moral judgements are made on the basis of gender, looks, backgrounds or political associations. Such judgements are made not on the basis of careful examination of evidence but on the basis of political intolerance, emotion or prejudice. It appears that hasty moral judgements tend to arrive at the same conclusion about different women involved in politics. Hasty moral judgements are basically non-rational, unreasoned, and they block insight and understanding.

A hasty moral judgement is a fallacy of weak induction where there is insufficient evidence to support the conclusion of an inductive argument. The premises give inadequate evidence to warrant the conclusion. The fallacies of weak induction occur not because the premises are logically irrelevant to the conclusion, as is the case with the fallacies of relevance, but because the connection between premises and conclusion is not strong enough to support the conclusion (Hawthorne, 2018). In each of the following fallacies, the premises provide at least a shred of evidence in support of the conclusion, but the evidence is not nearly good enough to cause a reasonable person to believe the conclusion. Like the fallacies of relevance, however, the fallacies of weak induction often involve emotional grounds for believing the conclusion.

This challenge of politically disadvantaged women can be solved through the 'dilemmas of difference' (Minow, 1991, p. 13). This occurs when a decision is based on unstated norms that presume the status quo as universal and inevitable when in fact these norms reflect a particular point of view. The structure of a difference dilemma is this: there is a difference, such as that only women are politically disadvantaged, and they may require affirmative action through the quota system. However, taking this difference into account also seems to instantiate unequal treatment, giving women special benefits (like reserving parliamentary or senate seats for women) men do not have. So, it seems there is no way to achieve equality in the face of differences such as these.

Countering a difference dilemma requires undermining the way the issue was initially formulated (more accurately, male-formulated). Feminist critics are of the view that political affirmative action, for example, points out that the only way these benefits can be judged special is if the norm against which they are being evaluated is male. If the standard was female, or even human, such benefits could not be considered special (or even unusual) since they are far more commonly needed than, say, benefits for a broken leg or prostate cancer (neither of which are considered special benefits). The underlying male standard is invisible because it is traditional for most workplaces, and political participation would require a change to these norms; but in the view of feminist critics, this underlying standard needs to be exposed as male because in fact it is not equal (Rhode, 1997). Once male norms are recognised as only that—male norms—the presumption of difference must be corrected. If the need for correction is taken seriously, then legal recognition of difference cannot by itself imply unequal treatment in politics. An assertion of difference is a factual assessment. Equality is a political (or moral) standard. One does not automatically follow from the other. Thus, formulation of the debate in terms of sameness or difference must be transcended by understanding equality (Smith, 2005) so that there is equal political participation without the negative judgements that women political candidates are facing. There is, therefore, need to deepen critical thinking and set aside all obstacles to critical thinking that hinder the attainment of political equality between men and women both as voters and as representatives of voters especially in the Zimbabwean context.

Conclusion

In this chapter, I have shown that obstacles to gender balance in Zimbabwean electoral politics tend to weigh down heavily on women resulting in limited political representation. It has been argued that traditional approaches to political (de)campaigns involve unwarranted assumptions and false claims about the place and role of the female gender in Zimbabwean electoral politics. The chapter has drawn from applied logic in general and critical thinking in particular to correct the flawed reasoning about women involved in Zimbabwean politics. I have argued that critical thinking should be part of voter education so that misconceptions about women in politics are corrected with the twin aim of respecting the rights of women in politics and placing politics on a rational platform to facilitate gender balance in Zimbabwean electoral politics. While this chapter has focused on the intersection between critical thinking and women in Zimbabwean politics, further research can still be done on ethical aspects as well as social-political issues surrounding women in politics within the Zimbabwean context.

References

Ackerly, B. (2008). *Universal human rights in a world of difference*. Cambridge University Press.
Ajei, M. (2007). *African development: The imperatives of indigenous knowledge and values* (Unpublished Phd Thesis). Pretoria: UNISA.
Allison, H. (2008). *Custom and reason in Hume*. Oxford University Press.
Baoping, S. (2022). *Tackling gender inequality: Definitions, trends, and policy designs* (International Monetary Fund Working Paper).
Beall, J. C., & Restal, G. (2006). *Logical pluralism*. Oxford University Press.
Boghossian, P. (2012). Critical thinking and constructivism: Mambo dog fish to the banana patch. *Journal of Philosophy of Education, 46*(1), 73–86.
Catellani, P., Alberici, A. I., & Milesi, P. (2004). Counterfactual thinking and stereotypes: The nonconformity effect. *European Journal of Social Psychology, 34*(4), 421–436.
Copi, I. (2006). *Symbolic logic*. Macmillan.
Copi, I. M., Cohen, C., & McMahon, K. (2014). *Introduction to logic* (14th ed.). Pearson.
Crockett, M. (2013). Models of morality. *Trends in Cognitive Science, 17*(8), 363–366.
Cushman, F. (2008). Crime and punishment: Distinguishing the roles of causal and intentional analyses in moral judgment. *Cognition, 108*(2), 353–380.
Dotson, K. (2011). Tracking epistemic violence, tracking patterns of silencing. *Hypatia, 26*(1), 236–257.
Forbes, G. (1994). *Modern logic*. Oxford University Press.
Gwaravanda, E. (2012). Shona indigenous knowledge systems and critical thinking: Lessons from selected Shona idioms. *Dzimbahwe: Journal of Humanities and Social Sciences, 1*(1), 78–102.
Gwaravanda, E. T. (2019). An epistemological critique of the African university education system. *Education systems around the world* (pp. 1–23). IntechOpen.

Hacking, I. (2001). *An introduction to probability and inductive logic.* Cambridge University Press.
Hawthorne, J. (2018). Inductive logic. In *The Stanford encyclopedia of philosophy* (Spring 2018 ed.). https://plato.stanford.edu/archives/spr2018/entries/logic-inductive/
Hungwe, J. (2021). The (in)compatible nexus between Ubuntu and critical thinking in African philosophy of education: Towards Ubuntu critical thinking in African higher education. In A. Ndofirepi & E. Gwaravanda (Eds.), *Mediating learning in higher education in Africa* (pp. 23–40). Brill and Sense.
Hurley, P. J. (2012). *A concise introduction to logic.* Wardsworth.
Iman, J. N. (2017). Debate instruction in EFL classroom: Impacts on the critical thinking and speaking skills. *International Journal of Instruction, 10*(4), 87–108.
Jayachandran, S. (2015). The roots of gender inequality in developing countries. *Annual Review of Economics, 7*(1), 63–88.
Jones, A. (2005). Culture and context: Critical thinking and student learning in introductory macroeconomics. *Studies in Higher Education, 30*(3), 339–354.
Kim, M., Park, B., & Young, L. (2020). The psychology of motivated versus rational impression updating. *Trends Cognitive Science, 24*(2), 101–111.
Mangena, T. (2022). Narratives of women in politics in Zimbabwe's recent past: The case of Joice Mujuru and Grace Mugabe. *Canadian Journal of African Studies, 56*(2), 407–425.
Manyeruke, C. (2018). A reflection on the women in Zimbabwean politics through gender lenses. *Journal of African Foreign Affairs, 5*(3), 119–136.
Mavengano, E., & Marevesa, T. (2022). Re-conceptualising womanhood and development in post-colonial Zimbabwe: A social conflict perspective. In E. Chitando & E. Kamaara (Eds.), *Values, identity, and sustainable development in Africa* (pp. 285–300). Palgrave Macmillan.
Metz, T. (2007). Towards an African moral theory. *Journal of Political Philosophy, 15*, 321–341.
Metz, T. (2013a). The western ethic of care or an Afro-communitarian ethic? Specifying the right relational morality. *Journal of Global Ethics, 9*, 77–92.
Metz, T. (2013b). Questioning African Attempts to Ground Ethics on Metaphysics. In T. Bewaji & E. Mafidon (Eds.), *Ontologised Ethics: New Essays in African Metaphysics* (pp. 189–204). Rowman and Littlefield.
Minow, M. (1991). *Making all the difference: Inclusion, exclusion & American law.* Harvard University Press.
Monroe, A. E., & Malle, B. F. (2017). Two paths to blame: Intentionality directs moral information processing along two distinct tracks. *Journal of Experimental Psychology, 146*(1), 123–133.
Ncube, G. (2020). Eternal mothers, whores or witches: The oddities of being a woman in politics in Zimbabwe. *Agenda, 34*(4), 25–33.

Nemukuyu, D. (2018, August 4). ZESN endorses ZEC results. *The Herald*.
Ramose, M. B. (2002). The ethics of Ubuntu. In A. P. J. Roux & P. H. Coetzee (Eds.), *Philosophy from Africa* (pp. 324–330). Oxford University Press.
Rhode, D. (1997). *Speaking of sex: The denial of gender inequality*. Harvard University Press.
Rudinow, J., & Barry, V. E. (2008). *Invitation to critical thinking* (6th ed.). Thomson Wadsworth.
Samkange, S., & Samkange, T. M. (1980). *Hunhuism or ubuntuism: A Zimbabwean indigenous political philosophy* (1st ed.). Graham Publishing.
Santos, P., & Ndhlovu, M. P. (2016). Media as political actors in times of political crisis. In L. Mukhongo & W. Macharia (Eds.), *In political influence of the media in developing countries* (pp. 23–45). IGI Global.
Smith, P. (2005). Four themes in feminist legal theory: Difference, dominance, domesticity & denial. In M. Golding & W. Edmundson (Eds.), *Philosophy of law and legal theory* (pp. 90–104). Blackwell.
Swafford, M., & Rafferty, E. (2016). Critical thinking skills in family and consumer sciences education. *JFCS Advancing FCS Learning, Programs, Practices and Policies, 108*(4), 13–19.
Tendi, B. (2016). State intelligence and the politics of Zimbabwe's presidential succession. *African Affairs, 115*(459), 203–224.
Viriri, E. N., & Viriri, M. (2018). The teaching of Unhu/Ubuntu through Shona novels in Zimbabwean secondary schools: A case for Masvingo urban district. *Journal of African Studies and Development, 10*(8), 101–114.
Warburton, N. (1996). *Thinking from A to Z*. Routledge.
Warburton, N. (2013). *Philosophy: The basics* (4th ed.). Routledge.
World Health Organization. (2023). *World report on violence and health*. WHO.

CHAPTER 6

Of Pains, Regrets and Suppressed Desires: Gendered Politics and Women Activism in Zimbabwean Electoral Politics

Andrew Mutingwende

Introduction

Zimbabwe, like elsewhere in the Southern African region, is replete with instances of state-sponsored gender-based election violence against women who have always been victims of a 'double displacement' between patriarchy and imperialism (Spivak, 1988). This has contributed to the glass ceiling concept on women who are already victims of sociocultural exclusion because they constitute a strange subculture or what Mavengano and Marevesa (2022, p. 235) interpret as men's 'conception of woman as second sex, or second class.' In the Zimbabwean political context, there is a narrowed media space that accommodates revolutionary women who choose to compete for leadership positions with men especially during elections. Such women have been crudely exposed

A. Mutingwende (✉)
English and Communication Department, Midlands State University, Gweru, Zimbabwe
e-mail: mutingwendea5@gmail.com

© The Author(s), under exclusive license to Springer Nature Switzerland AG 2023
E. Mavengano and S. Chirongoma (eds.), *Electoral Politics in Zimbabwe, Vol II*, https://doi.org/10.1007/978-3-031-33796-3_6

to state-sponsored gender-based violence since the state has come to label them as political stooges and prostitutes for opposition formations whose aim is to push for regime change agenda. Zimbabwe's pre- and post-election eras have harrowing incidences of state-sponsored election violence being unleashed on female activists whose attempt to push the feminist agenda has been criticised as transgendered macho activism antithetical to national development (Mavengano & Marevesa, 2022). Female victims exposed to state-sponsored election violence have been either coerced to remain silent or denied expressive space in the media (Acheson, 2008; Lahji, 2015). At worst, the media has offered vaster spaces to male politicians to comment on female activists' traumatic experiences during election violence than the victims themselves.

This research undertaking takes contrary positions that negate the status quo by arguing that male politicians' contrived advocacy to speak for women is wrongly positioned. It, therefore, interrogates the situatedness of such gender representation matrix since male politicians do not qualify to represent female consciousness as they constitute the female body's external world (Harding, 1993). There has been a paucity of research in this area which lacks a fair approach to media analysis to expose gendered (mis)representation. There is need to concentrate serious research around this delicate phenomenon since female activists continue to suffer gendered contrived assault in the media. Such media machinations existing as subterranean forms of gendered assault have locked women up from their attempt to climb to privileged decision-making positions equal to men (Mavengano & Marevesa, 2022).

This inward-looking research undertaking is on an analytical mission to linguistically deconstruct online media reports in order to unveil the gendered ideological subjectivities of both the reporters and male politicians in articulating the feminist discourse during electoral violence. To necessitate this, the article dwells on two theoretical frameworks: firstly, Harding's Feminist Standpoint Theory that permits the unlocking of female traumatic recounts and placing them *vis-a-vis* their male counterparts' misappropriated push for the feminist agenda. Secondly, the Critical Discourse Analysis (CDA) framework has been employed to offer analytical insights in the examination of textual and lexico-grammatical features of online media reports to unearth these gendered polarities. The corpus has been conscientiously picked from the private-owned Guardian and the state-owned Herald newspapers' online reports on popular female activists' electoral experiences between 2018 and 2022. The major findings are that a male politician only works to perpetuate the plight of women through media misrepresentation as the male figure is not the female embodiment.

Media Subjectivity-Objectivity Dialectics and Female Activism in Zimbabwean Election Period

The media coverage of revolutionary female activists exposed to state-sponsored violence during elections in the Southern African region has a long history of misrepresentations. Too much media focus has been paid on males' electoral exploits. This is so because gender ascriptions within the African sociocultural context with which males and females are raised up are based on rigid gendered dictations, women of virtue and men of valour. The transgression of these cisgendered boundaries by either sex has attracted attacks and labels as transgendered peculiarities (Szymansky et al., 2011). In particular, women who emit masculine characteristics such as political participation (as is the case with Zimbabwe) are often ostracised as either loose or domineering. As such, if political activism is reserved for males to shape a nation, as conceived within the conservative Zimbabwean patriarchal mindset, it therefore leaves female activists at the helms of victimhood. Indeed, this status populates the Zimbabwean media as an offshoot of journalistic ideological stance taking to defend the male agenda in which males are offered priority and privilege to speak for women. The problem with Zimbabwean politics lies in its evanescent dream for a utopian one-party state as manifested by the state's periscopic and panoptic surveillance on its citizens through the media and security apparatuses. The state has hailed silence more than even constructive criticisms and the culture of 'othering [i]s a permanent condition of political and cultural life where "difference" translates unproblematically into "foe"' (Muponde, 2004, p. 176).

The deep structures of these subjective media manifestations within the body politic of Zimbabwe trace back to the colonial period. A constricted media expressive space for opposition parties is both evidence of the state's disavowal for competition and a dream for one-party state. The birth of Zimbabwean independence in 1980 led to the immediate restructuration of the colonially based Argus Media Group press system that controlled the country's newspapers with a weaponry of media laws such as 'The Official Secrets Act (1970), the Law and Order (Maintenance) Act (1960)' (Willems, 2004, p. 5). As reiterated by Saunders (1999) as the indigenisation and compensatory move, in January 1981, the Zimbabwe Mass Media Trust (ZMMT) was introduced to carry out administrative roles of monitoring the operation of the Zimbabwean Newspapers Limited (Zimpapers) and the Zimbabwe Inter-Africa News Agency (ZIANA). From then on, the government-owned Manica Post, Kwayedza, Sunday News, Sunday Mail, The Herald and the Chronicle were run by Zimpapers. These state-owned newspapers ensured only the positive coverage of the ruling party and the state with a narrowed expressive space for the opposition whose 'editors and journalists were dismissed and others often threatened' (Willems, 2004, p. 5).

Civic societies, the labour unions and the general public began to question the way the Mugabe government ran the country. These disgruntlements led to the launch of the independent-owned newspapers in the 1990s like The Zimbabwe Independence, The Zimbabwean Mirror, The Standard and so forth which offered relaxed expressive space for opposition politics. This development ran contrary to the state's interest, and as a result, the state made 'death threats to and mounting assaults on reporters, charging editors and reporters with criminal defamation, and repeatedly suing newspapers for civil defamation, claiming large sums in damages' (Willems, 2004, p. 5).

In the late 1990s, the private-owned Daily News was officially introduced, and the paper invectively vilified state misgovernance and gave the opposition extensive positive publicity especially during and after the 2000 parliamentary elections. To muzzle it, the Daily News was mysteriously bombed in April 2000 and in January 2001 allegedly by secret state agents. The state further narrowed the expressive space for the opposition when the then Minister of Information and Publicity, Jonathan Moyo, propagated the imposition of stringent media laws like the Protection of Privacy Act (AIPPA), the Public Order and Security Act (POSA) and so forth which ensured that any information critical of government and the ruling party was censored. In particular, AIPPA enforced that independent news agencies should get registration and accreditation from the Commission of Media and Information. Alongside the persecution of journalists, subjective and biased reportage in favour of the state was promoted.

Since the formation of the Tsvangirai-led MDC in 1999 up to the military intervention that toppled the long-serving leader, Robert Mugabe, in November 2017, and his replacement by President Emmerson Mnangagwa, there has been a narrowed media expressive space particularly in state-owned press including the tight-fisted legislative laws that monitored the private media (McGregor & Chatiza, 2020, p. 2). President Mnangagwa's new republic set a dangerous precedent in the 2018 post-poll skirmishes between the military and the civilians on the 1st of August 2018 which saw the cold-blooded shootings in which six civilians died and thirty-five (35) of them injured. Subsequently, in early January 2019, a considerable number of peaceful protesters were also murdered by suspected ZANU-PF supporters. From then on, the Chamisa-led MDC-Alliance, under the machinations of the Mwonzora-led MDC-T, lost quite a huge number of its male and female councillors and MPs which were expelled in addition to the loss of property due to squabbles over the MDC-Alliance identity and leadership after the death of its founder Morgan Tsvangirai. As intimated earlier, this forced the MDC-Alliance to shed off its identity and rejuvenate itself into the CCC political party just at the eve of the 26 March 2022 by-elections to fill the council vacancies born out of the expulsions by the MDC-T leadership. To delegitimise the CCC party and legitimise ZANU-PF, all these political developments, which survived COVID-19 restrictions, received partisan coverage in the state media in favour of the state and ruling party.

Sometime in May 2020, to thwart dissent and to nip criticisms, three women activists from the then Chamisa-led MDC-Alliance party were abducted at a roadblock manned by the police and the military, held incommunicado for three days, tortured and later dumped by the roadside. The reason for such machinations on vocal female activists was their collective demonstration against the state's failure to provide COVID-19 facilities for the poor. However, as a ZANU-PF post-poll reflex action, the major crux of the arrest was a ploy to destabilise the MDC-Alliance party that had defiantly challenged the ruling party in the 2018 elections. Subsequently, other popular female activists like novelist Tsitsi Dangarembga and social media comedian, Gonyeti, were arrested and tortured to quell dissent.

As elsewhere in the Southern African region, there is a shrunken political and media space for women who continue to suffer from 'double displacement,' a prejudice in which they endure the repercussions of both patriarchy and imperialism (Spivak, 1988). Despite notable successes, the region proves its incapacitation to implement regional gender protocols stated in Part (4) Section 124 of the new May 2013 Zimbabwean Constitution which bears a clause for the appointment of other non-constituency female legislators as an attempt to uplift women in political decision-making (Zimbabwe Constitution Amendment Bill No. 20) (Ngoshi, 2013). The Zimbabwean government is a signatory of sundry regional and international gender protocols encapsulating the SADC Protocol on Gender and Development, the Maputo Protocol to the African Charter on Human and People's Rights on the Rights of Women in Africa, the Convention on the Elimination of All Forms of Discrimination Against Women (CEDAW), the Beijing Declaration and Platform for Action, among many.

However, against this perceived setback, the Zimbabwean government has shown a stride in implementing the SADC gender protocol that encourages the uplifting of more female representatives in leadership positions as espoused on section 120 (2) and 124 (1) (b) of the 2013 Constitution that is resonant with the 50/50 SADC gender parity blueprint (Ngoshi, 2013). To date, more women continue to assume leadership positions in politics such as those of permanent secretaries, directors, commissioners and so forth. The 2018 harmonised elections, since the country's 1980 independence, saw four (4) female candidates competing for the position of presidency. The Zimbabwean government has also influenced a change in media policies as it worked towards the elimination of negative portrayal of women in the media with some women promoted to senior positions and trained to be editors and journalists in popular media houses. Despite these significant strides by the Zimbabwean government, more female empowerment needs to be put into effect as stated in the recommendation section. The political elevation of Joyce Mujuru to Vice-President was in adherence to this legislative amendment. Her expulsion in 2014 from the position set a precedent for a mutating degenerating gender consciousness towards equity. This opened a vent for contrived electoral GBV against women as attested by the post-2018 and post-26 March 2022 by-elections swoop on revolutionary female activists. Such female activists who were subjected to electoral violence could not freely access the media to express their traumatic experiences during the state-sponsored gender-based violence which they were exposed to. Their recounts were either deemed as lies by the pro-ZANU-PF media and their political torture as 'political choreography,' 'Western-funded drama,' 'colonial mentality,' 'dirty tricks and lies' and as a ploy to 'turn domestic violence into a political issue' (Sunday Mail report, 24 May 2022). The objectivity-subjectivity dialectics of women activists' coverage in the media, especially the state-owned, remains an unsettling paradox due to the fluidity of the objectivity/neutrality condition of news reporting as stated above. Indeed, objectivity/neutrality is an elusive concept, far too hard to describe and define and subject to individual understandings of notions of 'truth,' 'fairness,' 'balance' and 'facticity'" (Sabao, 2013, p. 42). There are always loopholes for biases and ideological leanings in news reporting (Willems, 2004).

Feminist Standpoint Theory

Feminist Standpoint Theory is an extension of the Standpoint Theory which is a victim-centred theoretical framework that prioritises the subaltern groups to reclaim their positions in order to recount their individual experiences more than privileged groups (Harding, 1993). The leading proponents of the Standpoint Theory, Harding (1993) and Hartsock (1997), establish that the victims or marginalised social groups are strategically situated to give more knowledge and truth about themselves. Accordingly, Heath (1987) concurs that the framework works to reposition the underprivileged subaltern groups to articulate their lived experiences more than those who already occupy positions of social power and dominance. The main goal for this being to establish the truth value that is often misrepresented and overshadowed by the voice of dominant groups. The Feminist Standpoint Theory applies this concept to the polarised gender relations between males and females in which males occupy more privileged positions in society than their subaltern female counterparts. This subject-object situatedness within the feminist agenda has led to the subjugation and objectification of women by privileged men, and hence the Feminist Standpoint Theory places women in the right position to articulate their consciousness and experience from their own perspective. This is so because men are wrongly situated to speak for women because men already occupy a position of social power and influence (Heath, 1987). Accordingly, the subaltern female victims' representation by the socially privileged males only augments female prejudice (Gayatri Spivak, 1988). In general, the Feminist Standpoint Theory insists that males do not embody female consciousness and, for this reason, are not qualified to represent female consciousness and embodiment. This article places prejudiced revolutionary female voices who happen to be victims of state-sponsored election violence on the forefront because such females constitute what society has relegated as a gendered sub-class.

Critical Discourse Analysis (CDA)

Critical Discourse Analysis (CDA) is a linguistic framework that traces back to the work of Fairclough and Wodak (1997) and later adopted by van Dijk (1985), van Leeuwen (2015), Wodak (2001) and sundry in the recent years. CDA gives analytical insights into textual analysis interpreting language as a social semiotic communicative method that reflects the power dynamics existing within a social group. It effectively interprets the role of language 'in creating, maintaining, and legitimating inequality, injustice, and oppression in society' (van Leeuwen, 2015, p. 1). This means that there are hidden ideologies and power relations enshrined in language in any context. In CDA, a language analyst's major concern is to explore the power matrix that exists in language and adopt the necessary methodology to clarify the signs of power abuse that exists in society. At the centre of CDA is the situational context because it is through context that interactants' social relations, communication codes and communication channels, either written or spoken, are realised. This chapter analyses the experiences of popular female activists in state-sponsored election violence and the gendered articulation of such experiences by male politicians as projected in the media. This insider–outsider or subject-object dialectics poses a phallic hazard to the latter's body *habitus* and worsens the female plight and restrictions which perpetuate as undercurrents. As stipulated by the Feminist Standpoint Theory, female recounts of the victims are foregrounded for analysis to delve into the psyche and experiences of the female being when exposed to election violence.

Research Methods and Corpora

This chapter rests on two frameworks: the Feminist Standpoint Theory to reposition women's voice in a society where they are subaltern, and Critical Discourse Analysis to linguistically deconstruct media reports to unlock female consciousness and misrepresentations through a critical study of online media reports' textual and lexico-grammatical features. The corpus for this chapter has been conscientiously picked from two newspapers, the private-owned Guardian and state-owned Herald that covered state-sponsored election events in which popular female activists were victims between 2018 and 2022. The period was selected because it reserves heightened institutionalised election violence against women which polarised the media. From innumerable instances of state-sponsored gender-based violence against women during the election period, I draw my focus on the abduction and torture of the three women: Netsai Marova, Cecilia Chimbiri and Joana Mamombe in the post-2018 election era and the abduction, murder and mutilation of the Chitungwiza female activist, Moreblessing Ali. From both newspapers, I purposively selected two online reports based on their storyline and controversiality on state-sponsored election violence on popular female activists. Then, I used the random sampling criteria and chose one article per paper, reserving the other to serve as co-references. There is dearth of literature that focuses on the subterranean machinations against women because of state-sponsored election violence. Women are victims of male politicians and state-controlled reporters' wrongly situated contrived advocacy for them. I, therefore, posit that such journalists and male politicians are wrongly positioned to articulate female activists' election experiences because they do not embody female consciousness and body *habitus*. Their attempt to push the feminist agenda is only an instigation that perpetuates the female plight and an encumbrance that interlaces women's desire to acquire the same privileged and leadership positions equal to their male counterparts. In the analysis section, for convenience and quick reference, the data was coded as **WA1, WA2** for Woman Activist number one (**WA1**) and **JV1, JV2...JV5** for Journalistic Voice number one (**JV1**).

THEORETICAL GROUNDING

This article examines the media representation of revolutionary female activists during state-sponsored election violence in the context of Zimbabwe between 2018 and 2022. It advances the notion that male politicians who already possess privileged leadership positions within the nation's politics are given vaster media expressive space to comment on the lived experiences of female activists during election violence than the victims. Thus, through male feminism, contrived gendered assault has continued to surface in the media as subterranean forms of election GBV. I, therefore, argue that most journalists and male politicians are wrongly positioned to represent the female body's lived experience because they lack direct autonomy of the female consciousness. Contrarily, innumerable feminist scholars (Acheson, 2008; Bataille, 1986; Benedicta, 2011; Foucault, 2002; Lahji, 2015; Lorde, 1984; Marfudhotun & Wiyatmi, 2021; Parpart, 2019; Spivak, 1988 and more) observe that society has misconstrued a woman as constituting a gender subculture because 'the woman cannot control her body. She does not have any autonomy on her body' (Marfudhotun & Wiyatmi, 2021, p. 44). Mills (2005) and Lorde (1984) also argue that women have no access to their bodies as witnessed in their (women's) perceived silence when exposed to trauma. Lahji (2015) and Benedicta (2011) concur that a woman is metaphorically 'deaf and dumb' before her man while Bataille (1986) calls women's silence, 'silent violence.' This observation resonates with the Zimbabwe election scenario in which vocal female activists are victims of state-sponsored violent thrash to stifle dissent. In particular, Zimbabwe's 2018 and 2022 plebiscites are replete with cases of state-sponsored election violence unleashed on female activists. Mungwari (2019, p. 20398) opines that state media acted as the 'ZANU PF mouthpiece' to delegitimise the female election victims and legitimise the ruling party. A litany of feminist scholars (see Acheson, 2008; Lorde, 1984; Marfudhotun & Wiyatmi, 2021; Parpart, 2019)have promoted female oppression by conceptualising their 'silence' or, as Bataille (1986) chooses to call it 'silent violence,' as a form of revolution against patriarchal machinations and "as a potentially powerful form of expression and action" (Parpart, 2019, p. 317).

From this mainstream research chorus, I take a detour by arguing in line with Foucault (2002) that female silence is not voluntary but a product of patriarchal dictates and state-sponsored coercion to promote male dominance. These subject-object male-invented social relations need to be dismantled for gender restructuring to achieve equitable gender balance. For instance, Marfudhotun and Wiyatmi (2021, p. 43) argue that women's bodies are men's property and that the former do not have 'body autonomy' since 'from the subject-object position, the woman is the object.' They argue that virtually all female behaviours, appetite and dress are all male-dictated because a female reacts in relation to her male counterparts' social and sensual appetite. For this reason, males commodify the female body because they have autonomy over them (Lahji, 2015). This epistemological standpoint opens up a gap and needs to be reclaimed before this gendered status quo normalises into fixity. To address this lacuna, there is need to harmonise these binary gendered polar opposites through informed research undertakings like my own to come up with redeemable strategies that work towards restoring 'displaced' women back to their equitable gender positions. Couched in the Feminist Standpoint Theory and Critical Discourse Analysis frameworks, this chapter embarks on a fact-finding mission to gender (mis)representations in the popular media within the gendered discourse during both the pre and post-election period.

Analysis

This section explores female activists' traumatic experiences during state-sponsored election violence which transpired between the 2018 and 2022 election period drawing data from Zimbabwean national newspapers: The Guardian and The Herald online reports. The online newspaper reports contain undercurrents of gendered contrived assault on female election victims by male politicians and journalists which compete to articulate the narrative of these female victims. Their media comments are mired in subjectivities, and therefore, male politicians are wrongly situated to represent the female consciousness as their attempt to represent women worsens the female plight and restrictions. The section leans on the Feminist Standpoint Theory that allows the analysis of subaltern women's traumatic recounts. It also uses the Critical Discourse Analysis (CDA) framework to explore the online reports' textual and lexico-grammatical features to unveil these gendered polarities.

The deposing of the long-serving President Mugabe in November 2017 ushered in a new republic under President Emmerson Mnangagwa whose first term ran the controversial elections in 2018. The 2018 post-poll period witnessed the opening of live ammunition by the military in Harare urban on the 1 August 2018 to quell looming demonstrations which resulted in the killing of six (6) and injury of thirty-five (35) civilians. This incident received subjective coverage particularly in 'the state controlled and ZANU PF mouthpiece *Herald*' newspaper (Mungwari, 2019, p. 20398). These civilians-military skirmishes also resulted in the death of Silvia Maphosa, a female civilian 'aged 53 who was shot in [the] heart' (Mungwari, 2019, p. 20397). The recount given by the deceased's female relative, Miriam Chidamba, showed the insensitivity of the male medical practitioners at Parirenyatwa Group of Hospitals who attempted to subvert the autopsy results by forging 'a death certificate which listed the cause of death as stab wounds' instead of gunshot wounds (Mungwari, 2019, p. 20397). Miriam narrated that to cover up Silvia

Maphosa's cause of death, a doctor from Parirenyatwa Group of Hospitals 'was getting instructions from higher offices and [he] changed the death certificate and entered' a record that the victim had died of a stab wound (News Day, 18 October 2018). This gruesome recount by the female civilian was discredited as falsehood by state-owned press. The attempt by a male medical doctor in preparing a fake death certificate under the influence of politicians from high offices is a testament that male politicians are not qualified to represent the female consciousness and embodiment. Her male killers are so callous as to shoot her dead in the heart.

Other instances of election gender-based violence transpired in May 2020 which stood as an offshoot of the controversial 2018 harmonised elections. Having proved its efficacy in the 2018 harmonised elections, the then Chamisa-led MDC-Alliance continued to endure denial of free campaign spaces by the state due to the alleged COVID-19 restrictions. There were also corruption and embezzlement of COVID-19 allowances meant to procure protective equipment for the poor. Three female activists from the MDC-Alliance opposition party: Joana Mamombe, Cecilia Chimbiri and Netsai Marova staged a demonstration against the state's failure to provide COVID-19 facilities for the poor, and because of this, they were abducted on 13 May 2020 at a roadblock manned by both the army and the police. The three were later found dumped by the roadside sixty miles from Harare city with some unable to articulate their traumatic encounters. Netsai Marova recounted of her experiences during the abduction in an interview with police detectives while Cecilia Chimbiri and Joana Mamombe were interviewed later on 25 May 2020. The women were dragged before the court 'charged with publishing or communicating falsehoods,' according to the Herald report of 17 March 2022. This charge invites a lot of research interests as it begs a question around evidence of what determines falsehood. According to Foucault (2002), context offers open doors for CDA analysis, and the fact that the trio was 'abducted' by an identified vehicle at a roadblock manned by security law enforcers runs consonant with Cecilia Chimbiri's father, Henry Chimbiri, that the trio was abducted and tortured by 'state agents' who 'are killers' (The Guardian, 17 May 2020). The Herald is too pre-emptive of the actual experiences by the women as evidenced by its caustic and antithetical headline in **JV1** below.

JV1: 'We were never Abducted-CCC Activists'

In this Herald of 17 March 2022, the reporter quoted Mr Tapera Kazembe, the Postal and Telecommunications Regulatory Authority of Zimbabwe (Potraz) manager, who stood as state witness against the trio saying that by the time Cecilia Chimbiri and Joana Mamombe were saying that they had been held incommunicado by the Zimbabwean police, they were busy using social media to falsify their abductions as below:

JV2: **The two's mobile phone numbers were said to be active browsing on Internet, Facebook, Twitter, Snapchat and Instagram between 2:39 p.m. and 10p.m.**

As reported from the male perspective and in favour of the ruling party and the state, Mr Kazembe's suggestion is impassive and insensitive towards the female victims. This is so because the male politician does not embody the female body *habitus*, and his attempt to narrate or comment on the female traumatic experience only worsens the female plight and restrictions. The state witness wants to prove to the world that the three young female activists faked their abductions (see **JV1, JV2** and **JV3**).

JV3: **He said they have faked their abductions in May 2020**

The POTRAZ manager denies that the three had been abducted and tortured. The Herald reporter also tries to shield ZANU-PF by delegitimising the opposition and discrediting the three women's experiences of violence by alleging that the female victims faked their abductions to tarnish the image of the President. Paradoxically, the reporter reports that in these traumatic experiences unleashed on the trio, President Mnangagwa is the victim.

JV4: **President Mnangagwa who wears the torture scars**

The subjective statement in **JV4** is candidly ridiculous in its ironic twist of events to invite the audience to sympathise with the President in lieu of the disoriented female victims who bear the torture scars and traumatised psyche.

Contrarily, in the Guardian newspaper report of 17 May 2022 with the heading 'Zimbabwean MDC activists 'abducted and sexually assaulted,' the reporters Jason Burke and Nyasha Chingono quoted the three female recounts during their interview with police detectives on 17 and 25 May 2020. The newspaper quoted verbatim of the recounts as narrative evidence of torture through state-sponsored violence. While state-owned Herald reporters omitted these female recounts and included authoritative voices from the state and ZANU-PF officials to invectively comment on the three female victims' experiences of politically motivated violence, the Guardian newspaper reporter quoted the female recounts and implanted the pictures of the women's disoriented outlook while in hospital beds. Two segments of such female recounts appear in **WA1** by the victim Cecilia Chimbiri and **WA2** by Joana Mamombe.

WA1: 'They beat me on my back, all over the body using sticks. They used a gun to beat us, then molested me.'

WA2: 'They were pouring water on us. They beat us if we stopped. They made us drink each other's urine. They were fondling Cecilia.'

The above recounts are fractured with caesuras, and this tells more of the traumatised psychological state of the victims. Statement **W1** has a series of five action verbs while **W2** has six, and this evinces a series of reckless attacks on the victims' bodies using cold water, urine, guns and sticks as instruments to inflict pain. According to Cecilia, the women were stripped naked and exposed to physical, sexual and psychological abuse. In the Guardian report, the assailants spent the whole night sucking the women's breasts and sexually abusing them. In the same report, the Government's Information Secretary, Nick Mangwana was also sceptical that the three women were abducted and that if so, they should use the law enforcement agents to seek justice. This runs ironical in as far as the state uses the same law enforcers to swoop on civilians (Mungwari, 2019).

Despite an arsenal of machinations on the Chamisa-led CCC party from both the state and ZANU-PF as an abortive attempt to destabilise it, the party proved on the 26 March by-elections that it can withstand such seismic attacks. As intimated earlier, the plebiscite ensued to fill in the council vacancies that had been created as a result of the expulsions of councillors from the MDC-Alliance party by the Mwonzora-led MDC-T. Together with the confiscation of property and identity as explicated earlier, this move by the 'oscillating' MDC-T was interpreted as a ploy to swallow the MDC-Alliance into nought for ZANU-PF's political expediency. From the 26 March by-elections, there has been constant civic assault especially on the opposition supporters. One instance of this is the brazen and gruesome abduction and murder of the Nyatsime female activist in Chitungwiza, Moreblessing Ali on 24 May 2022. The Herald of 15 June 2022 published a report titled 'Opposition vultures 'feasting' on Ali's corpse;" the reporter, Fungi Kwaramba, pronounced that the then MDC-Alliance supporters were like greedy vultures tearing on Moreblessing Ali's corpse in order to tarnish the image of ZANU-PF and the state. Divergent views from the two warring parties, the ZANU-PF and the CCC emerged in the media. The Herald reporter shifts the murder blame on the CCC party while protecting ZANU-PF.

JV5: **Like vultures feasting on a buffalo carcass, the opposition CCC, its Western backers and lick-spittle civic society organisations are tearing on the corpse of Moreblessing Ali.**

Above, the CCC party is said to have staged the murder case on one of its supporters, in order to soil the image of the state and ZANU-PF ahead if the impending Commonwealth Heads of Government meeting in Rwanda to be held the following week from 24 May 2022. The simile in **JV5** is misappropriated as it compares the female victim to a 'buffalo carcass' to prove that the CCC supporters are bloodthirsty. On a female, so murdered and 'slaughtered like a chicken' and during the mourning week, the reporter should have opted for a meeker comparison than this. However, this stands as emotional evidence of the misrepresentation of female bodies by male voice.

Conclusion

The major aim of this chapter was to analyse the representation of female activists in both the state-owned and private-owned media during state-sponsored gender-based election violence. Through the theoretical lens of the Feminist Standpoint Theory and Critical Discourse Analysis on online media reports, it has been seen that state-owned media reporters are extensions of the ruling party ideology, and they cohabit with male politicians in the ruling party to assault female activists in the media. Women's activism for gender equality has been vilified as a regime change project instigated by opposition politics, and their voice about their election experience is shut out by the state media's constricted expressive space. Women's traumatic experiences and recounts have been interpreted by such male politicians and state-controlled journalists as 'political choreography,' 'Western-funded drama,' 'colonial mentality,' 'dirty tricks and lies' and a ploy to 'turn domestic violence into a political issue' (Sunday Mail report, 24 May 2022). Thus, state-controlled media is mired in reporter voice subjectivities as it gives media coverage more to ruling party male politicians to comment on female victims of state-sponsored election violence than female victims themselves as seen in the 'ZANU PF mouthpiece *Herald*' (Mungwari, 2019, p. 20398). The private-owned Guardian newspaper, however, provided spaces for women to share their traumatic experiences during violence against POSA and AIPPA media restrictions among others.

Way Forward and Recommendations

As a primary and immediate remedy to gender-based election violence, the Zimbabwean government must review its gender protocols stated in Part (4) Section 124 of the new May 2013 Zimbabwean Constitution which bears a clause for the appointment of other non-constituency female legislators to appoint women representatives in political decision-making processes (Zimbabwe Constitution Amendment Bill No. 20). It must not use the state security apparatuses to thrash on revolutionary female activists which are constitutionally struggling to push for equality and fair gender representation. Apart from the ruling party's need to accept constructive criticisms, it should also relax the politically constrained state press to create a permissive expressive space for women. Moreover, media reporters must report news as objectively as possible without fear of state torture and this means the Zimbabwean state must at all costs withdraw its policing and strict surveillance on the media in order to promote the existence of a free press system for national development.

References

Acheson, K. (2008). Silence as gesture: Rethinking the nature of communicative silences. *Communication Theory, 18*, 535–555.

Bataille, G. (1986). *Erotism*. City Lights.

Benedicta, G. D. (2011). Dinamika Otonomi Tubuh Perempuan: Antara Kuasa dan Negosiasi atas Tubuh. *Masyarakat Journal Sosiologi, 16*(2), 141–156.

Fairclough, N., & Wodak, R. (1997). Critical discourse analysis. In T. van Dijk (Ed.), *Discourse and social interaction—Discourse studies: A multidisciplinary introduction* (Vol. 2, pp. 258–284). Sage.

Foucault, M. (2002). *The archaeology of knowledge*. Routledge.

Harding, S. (1993). Rethinking standpoint epistemology: What is strong objectivity? In L. Alcoff & E. Potter (Eds.), *Feminist epistemologies*. Routledge (Print).

Hartsock, N. C. M. (1997). Comment on Hekman's "Truth and method: Feminist standpoint theory revisited". *Signs, 22*(2), 367–374 (Print).

Heath, S. (1987). Male feminism. In A. Jardine & P. Smith (Eds.), *Men in feminism*. Methuen, Inc. (Print).

Lahji, R. F. (2015). Objektifikasi Perempuan dan Tubuh: Wacana Tubuh Perempuan dalam Lirik Lagu Dangdut Populer Tahun 2000-2013. *Lakon, 4*(1), 103–130. https://e-journal.unair.ac.id/index.php/LAKON/article/download/1938/1444

Lorde, A. (1984). *Sister outsider*. Crossing Press.

Marfudhotun, I., & Wiyatmi, W. (2021). The body autonomy in the short story 'Wanita Muda di Sebuah Hotel Mewah' by Hamsad Rangkuti: The feminism discourse analysis of Sara Mills. *International Journal of Linguistics, Literature and Translation, 4*(10), 38–45. Published by Al-Kindi Center for Research and Development, London, United Kingdom. www.al-kindipublisher.com/index.php/ijllt

Mavengano, E., & Marevesa, T. (2022). Re-conceptualising womanhood and development in post-colonial Zimbabwe: A social conflict perspective. In E. Chitando & E. Kamaara (Eds.), *Values, identity, and sustainable development in Africa*. Sustainable Development Goals Series. Palgrave Macmillan.

McGregor, J., & Chatiza, K. (2020). *Geographies of urban dominance: The politics of Harare's periphery*. University of Manchester.

Mills, S. (2005). *Feminist stylistics*. Routledge.

Mungwari, T. (2019). Zimbabwe post election violence: Motlanthe commission of inquiry 2018. *International Journal of Contemporary Research and Review, 10*(2), 20392–20406.

Muponde, R. (2004). The worm and the hoe: Cultural politics and reconciliation after the Third Chimurenga. In B. Raftopoulos & T. Savage (Eds.), *Injustice and political reconciliation*. Institute for Justice and Reconciliation. www.ijr.org.za

Ngoshi, H. T. (2013). The female body and voice in audio-visual political propaganda jingles: The Mbare Chimurenga Choir women in Zimbabwe's contested political terrain. *Critical Arts: A Journal of Media Studies, 28*(2), 235–248.

Parpart, J. (2019). Rethinking silence, gender, and power in insecure sites: Implications for feminist security studies in a postcolonial world. *Review of International Studies, 46*(3), 315–324. https://doi.org/10.1017/S02602 1051900041X

Sabao, C. (2013). *The reporter voice and objectivity in cross-linguistic reporting of controversial news in Zimbabwean newspapers* (PhD thesis). Stellenbosch University. http://hdl.handle.net/10019.1/79939

Spivak, G. C. (1988). Can the subaltern speak? In C. Nelson & L. Grossberg (Eds.), *Marxism and the interpretation of culture* (pp. 271–313). Macmillan Education (Print).

Szymansky, D., et al. (2011). Sexual objectification of women: Advances to theory and research. *The Counseling Psychologist, 39*(1) 6–38. http://tcp.sag epub.com

van Dijk, T. A. (1985). *Handbook of discourse analysis: Discourse analysis in society 4*. Academic Press.

Van Leeuwen, T. (2015). Critical discourse analysis. *The International Encyclopedia of Language and Social Interaction*. https://doi.org/10.1002/978111 8611463/wbielsi174

Willems, W. (2004). Peasant demonstrators, violent invaders: Representations of land in the Zimbabwean press. *World Development, 32*(10), 1767–1783.

Wodak, R. (2001). What CDA is about—A summary of its history, important concepts and its developments. In R. Wodak & M. Meyer (Eds.), *Methods of critical discourse analysis* (pp. 1–13). Sage.

Zimbabwean Constitution Amendment (No. 20) Act. (2013). https://www.dpc orp.co.zw/assets/constitution-of-zimbabwe

CHAPTER 7

Rhetoric or Reality? Assessing the Efficacy of Policy and Legislative Interventions in Enhancing Women Political Participation in Zimbabwe

Anesu Ingwani and Malvin Nyengeterai Kwaramba

INTRODUCTION

The commitment to achieving meaningful Women Political Participation (WPP) is an issue that has been pronounced in Zimbabwe's political dialogues and has taken form through legislative interventions and through policies and formal assurances. The intention of the Zimbabwean government, civic organisations as well as concerned stakeholders to achieve gender equality in general and women involvement in electoral and political spaces in particular has been widely stated and reaffirmed. This chapter is written against the background of a host of numerous commitments to improving women political participation which is expressed through legislative and policy interventions since 1980

A. Ingwani (✉) · M. N. Kwaramba
Great Zimbabwe University, Masvingo, Zimbabwe
e-mail: anesuneneingwani@gmail.com

© The Author(s), under exclusive license to Springer Nature Switzerland AG 2023
E. Mavengano and S. Chirongoma (eds.), *Electoral Politics in Zimbabwe, Vol II*, https://doi.org/10.1007/978-3-031-33796-3_7

and depressingly little results 43 years later despite repeated commitments by government, civic groups and political parties. Notwithstanding the efforts to enhance women involvement in electoral politics, the field of politics remains male dominated even in the face of various legislative and policy interventions put in place to address this ill. With the 2023 Zimbabwe's harmonised elections looming, it is critical to revisit this issue in order to lobby for more reforms that have a practical effect when it comes to levelling the playing field for women politicians in Zimbabwe. In line with Sustainable Development Goal number 5 which seeks to promote gender equality and women empowerment, Zimbabwe has taken steps to achieve this seemingly mammoth feat to achieve gender equality on the political arena, to the appointment of the first female vice president, the introduction of the quota system and its subsequent extension, the National Development Strategy as well as constitutional provisions that guarantee gender equality in politics. According to the UNDP Report (2021) which assessed Zimbabwe's progress in implementing the Sustainable Development Goals, the Zimbabwean government has made positive progress towards achieving gender equality and women empowerment. In its report, it refers to the improvement namely that representation of women in decision-making bodies has generally increased. It makes reference to the constitutional provisions for a special quota system for women of 60 additional seats in the lower house of assembly and election to senate through proportional representation. The UNDP Report (2021) further notes that the representation of women in the Senate increased from 23.2% in 2012 to 47.5% in 2017 before declining to 43.75% in 2019. Representation of women in the National Assembly increased from 16% in 2012 to 31.85% in 2019 as noted by the same report. It is in the light of these statistics that the Report recommends that though there is an increase in women participation in electoral politics, there is need for more reforms to ensure participation and representation of women on a 50–50 basis.

The various domestic legal instruments and policies draw their inspiration from the international and regional instruments that advocate for meaningful women political participation such as the Beijing Declaration and Platform for Action, 1995, the Maputo Protocol to the Charter on Human and People's Rights on the Rights of Women and the Convention on the Elimination of all forms of Discrimination Against Women (CEDAW). With all the measures adopted, Zimbabwe is still a long way from enhancing women political participation as the statistics are staggeringly low when it comes to the number of women in local government, parliament, cabinet and positions of influence in political parties. According to the Africa Barometer (2021), this owes to structural and societal barriers that militate against the full enjoyment of political rights for women in a practical manner which may at times render the legal interventions theoretical and leave women bereft of any real political involvement despite the good intentions of parties involved.

Like so many countries who have heed the call to increase women political participation, Zimbabwe finds itself riddled with inbred barriers against gender equality in politics due to the patriarchal nature of its society as reflected in the institutions like religion, culture, education and the general resistance and unwillingness to move with the times (Hamandishe, 2018). Regrettably, these barriers have posed challenges to the enhancement of women political participation making the goal for gender equality in politics almost theoretical as very little progress has been registered despite commitments through policy and legislative interventions.

Theoretical Framework

Various theories can be used to explain and analyse the efficacy of legislative frameworks and policies in enhancing women's participation in politics. For this research, the liberal feminist theory is going to be utilised and a number of concepts will be used. The researchers will marry key aspects of several scholarly definitions of concepts and come up with definitions that will be utilised in this chapter. Liberal feminism remains a strong feminist political thought. Liberal feminism is mainly concerned about protecting and enhancing women's personal and political autonomy. Its main concept is largely about women's participation and freedom in decision-making and shaping the political direction in their respective communities. Thus, in simple terms, liberal feminism is espoused in the attainment of women's legal and political rights. According to Ackerly (2008), the liberal feminism idea of women's legal rights better explains the concept of universal suffrage in Zimbabwe, espoused in the Zimbabwean Electoral Act which accords women rights to make decisions as adults and to enjoy full civil and political rights which are critical tenets in the quest to achieve equality in electoral processes. The researchers therefore made use of the liberal feminist theory in order to ascertain whether these aspects of affording equal rights among men and women through legislative frameworks have resulted in effective women participation in electoral processes.

Liberal feminism further elaborates challenges that hinder women participation in electoral politics. Berlant and Prosser (2011) argues that one of the major impediments in women's participation in electoral politics is how they are viewed by society as only suitable for private spaces and therefore limited to the home and domestic work including that of rearing children. This then confines women to the periphery when it comes to decision-making from grassroots levels because of the nature of the society we live in which is patriarchal in nature. Thus, the research relied on liberal feminism to recognise challenges faced by women in politics which include but are not limited to deeply rooted patriarchy, gendered stereotypes and gendered stigma so as to assess whether the legal and policy frameworks put in place in Zimbabwe have been effective in increasing women's participation in electoral politics and contestations.

Research Methodology

This study made use of the qualitative research method. According to Bhandari (2020), research is a process of steps used to collect and analyse information in order to increase our understanding of a topic or issue. The qualitative research method has been defined by Bhandari (2020) as the studied use and collection of a variety of empirical materials. It involves methods of data collection and analysis that are non-quantitative. It is against this background that this chapter used published books, government reports, newspaper articles and legal documents to analyse legislative frameworks and policies put forward by the government in order to increase women's participation in electoral politics. The choice of this method was informed by the need to analyse these frameworks and policies which include among others, the Constitution of Zimbabwe (2013), the National Development Strategy 1 (2021–2025), the Electoral Act [*Chapter 2;13*]. These policies and legislative interventions were juxtaposed with the results of the number of women in parliament, government, political parties in order to come up with a determination on whether these policy and legislative interventions have had practical impact in enhancing women political participation or are merely theoretical.

Regional and International Frameworks for Gender Equality in Electoral Politics

The Zimbabwean policy and legislative framework for gender equality in electoral politics has been largely shaped by regional and international provisions that have set the tone for women political participation. While some of the policy and legislative provisions dealing with women and electoral politics are arguably home-grown, it is not surprising that much of the direction regarding this area has been stirred and moulded from regional and international conventions and declarations that agitate for women political participation. This is so because section 326 of the Constitution of Zimbabwe states that customary international law is part of Zimbabwean law to the extent that it is consistent with the Constitution and with Acts of Parliament. In terms of section 327 of the Constitution, international conventions, treaties and agreements are binding in Zimbabwe if they are domesticated and passed by parliament. Additionally, in interpreting the fundamental rights, any forum, body, court or tribunal is enjoined to take into account international law, treaties and conventions that Zimbabwe is a party to.

On an international level, the rights of women in electoral politics are enshrined in a number of conventions, policy documents and declarations. The Convention on the Elimination of all forms of Discrimination Against Women, which Zimbabwe is a party to, proscribes discrimination against women in all areas including in politics. In particular, Article 7 of the convention prohibits unequal treatment of women in political life and accords them an unconditional right to vote and to hold public office as well as participate in formulation of policy at every level of government. At the regional stage, the Maputo Protocol to the African Charter on Human and Peoples' Rights on the Rights of Women in Africa, which Zimbabwe is a signatory to, outlines the rights of women to participate in electoral politics on the same level as men. The Protocol, in clear and elegant language in its ninth article, outlines the rights of women in the following manner:

> 1. States Parties shall take specific positive action to promote participative governance and the equal participation of women in the political life of their countries through affirmative action, enabling national legislation and other measures to ensure that:
>   a) Women participate without any discrimination in all elections;

b) Women are represented equally at all levels with men in all electoral processes;
c) Women are equal partners with men at all levels of development and implementation of State policies and development programmes.
2. States Parties shall ensure increased and effective representation and participation of women at all levels of decision-making.

These regional and international instruments have formed a solid foundation for the domestic provisions in Zimbabwe aimed at increasing women's political participation.

National Policy and Legislative Framework for Gender Equality in Electoral Politics

The quest for women's political participation in Zimbabwe cannot be fully narrated without referring to the adoption of the universal suffrage during the 1980 elections where women particularly black Zimbabwean women were afforded the right to vote and to participate in the electoral processes unconditionally. Although the number of women in government was very low, this was the beginning of the actual involvement of women in electoral politics. The Passage of the Legal Age of Majority Act (1982) reaffirmed the Zimbabwean government's pledge to enhance rights of women by conferring majority status on all women above the age of 18 years, giving them rights to participate even as political candidates. These landmark legislative and policy interventions set the bedrock for women's political participation and paved the road to the involvement of women in electoral politics. Indeed, section 67(3) of the Constitution of Zimbabwe (2013) reflects this position as every Zimbabwean over the age of 18 years is eligible to vote or to be voted for.

The coming into force of the Constitution of Zimbabwe (2013) ushered in provisions that promote the involvement of women in politics. While one of the major constitutional milestones in electoral politics is the quota system, it would be remiss to omit some pertinent provisions which deal with the involvement of women in politics. These are:

Section 56(2) of the Zimbabwean Constitution prohibits discrimination of women in all spheres including politics and makes it mandatory for women to be given equal opportunities in politics. It provides that:

Women and men have the right to equal treatment, including the right to equal opportunities in political, economic, cultural and social spheres.

The same right is echoed in section 80 of the Constitution which provides that:

Every woman has full and equal dignity of the person with men, and this includes equal opportunities in political, economic and social activities.

This right to equality in political opportunities is expressed in section 3(a) of the Electoral Act [*Chapter 2.13*] which states the following:

Subject to the Constitution and this Act, every election shall be conducted in a way that is consistent with the following principles:

> a) the authority to govern derives from the will of the people demonstrated through elections that are conducted efficiently, freely, fairly, transparently, and properly on the basis of universal and equal suffrage exercised through a secret ballot.

These provisions place women and men on an equal footing when it comes to accessing political opportunities.

The Constitution of Zimbabwe further provides for Special Temporary Measures to advance the participation of women in electoral politics in order to compensate for the historical imbalances which have resulted in women being politically marginalised. This, it does through the "quota system" which finds expression in sections 120 and 124 of the Constitution and elaborated in section 45 of the Electoral Act. The centrality of the quota system to the themes discussed in this chapter necessitates dedicating a whole passage as detailed below.

Quota System

In order to effectively improve and encourage women's participation in electoral processes, the government of Zimbabwe adopted a constitution in 2013 which provides for a system that allows the reservation of seats for women in the National Assembly for two terms. In terms of section 124 of the Constitution, the National Assembly of Zimbabwe is made up of 210 members voted from the 210 constituencies in the country and an additional 60 women elected through a system of Proportional Representation from the ten provinces of the country, based on the number of votes cast for political parties in the provinces. Furthermore, as provided by section 120 of the Constitution, 60 senators are elected through Proportional Representation in which male and female candidates are listed alternatively with every list being headed by a female candidate. This was a welcome break-through in increasing the overall number of women participating in electoral politics in Zimbabwe.

Although the women's quota was a Temporary Special Measure meant only to subsist for 2 parliamentary terms ending in 2023, the measure has been extended through Constitutional Amendment No 2 of 2021 to run for a further 2 terms translating to 10 more years from 2023 to 2033. In the same Constitutional Amendment 2 of 2021, the women's political involvement in electoral processes was further enhanced with regard to local authority elections where section 277 of the Constitution was amended by the addition of subsection 4 which mandates that women constitute at least 30% of the seats for local authorities.

While the quota system has played a critical role in increasing women participation in electoral processes, the absence of remedies and sanctions in the 2013 Constitution with regard to non-compliance on the issue of parity in candidates' lists for senate and provincial lists draws back the steps taken in ensuring women's participation in electoral politics. Moreover, even though there has been an increase in women's participation, women's visibility as leaders is at times dented by the very quota system that ought to improve the plight of women. Tshuma (2018) avers that this special temporary measure has resulted in spaces being closed for women to challenge for other 210 constituencies as political parties encourage women to opt for the quota system, hence, resulting in a decrease in the number of women-led constituencies. It is not clear whether the electoral governing body in Zimbabwe, namely the Zimbabwe Electoral Commission (ZEC), will disregard lists with gender disparities in an endeavour to encourage strict adherence to legislative frameworks and policies espoused in the Constitution so as to increase women's participation in electoral politics.

National Development Strategy 1 (2021–2025)

As part of its policy to enhance female political participation, the Zimbabwean government adopted the National Development Strategy which has an overall goal of transforming Zimbabwe into an upper-middle-income economy. According to the ZIMSTAT (2021), the government aims to embark on a meaningful gender mainstreaming agenda in order to, among other goals, achieve gender equality, catapult women into positions of influence, advance women political representation and fully operationalise the Zimbabwean Gender Commission to spearhead the gender agenda. While the inclusion of women's political issues in the National Development Strategy is a commendable step in the right direction, Hamandishe (2018) avers that it remains mere rhetoric if these theoretical commitments are not translated into meaningful and tangible results. In the absence of real and practical action to enhance electoral politics for women, the policy laid down in the strategy may become a white elephant and of no real consequence to the need to improve women political participation in practical terms.

Assessment of the Sex Disaggregated Data for Women in Electoral Politics

It is worth noting that no real or competent assessment of the efficacy of the legislative and policy interventions towards enhancing women political participation can be done without outlining the statistics regarding women in the field of electoral politics. Women remain underrepresented in party political posts, parliament and in the cabinet despite efforts to achieve the 50/50 representation in politics, according to the Election Watch 9 (2023). Zimbabwe's 2022 March 26 parliamentary by-elections recorded no movement in the number of women participating in political contests as the figures remained at a stubborn 15% as was the situation in the 2018 elections. As of 5 September 2018, when the members of parliament for the 9th Zimbabwean Parliament were sworn in, there were 121 female members of parliament out of a total of 350 members translating to 34.57% and this figure includes the reserved seats already set aside for women,(Election Watch 9, 2023).

To paint a vivid image of the figures, it may be crucial to outline the composition of parliament and the number of seats. There are 350 seats for the members of parliament which are broken down as follows:

- 210 directly elected National Assembly members,
- 60 party list Female Members of the National Assembly,
- 60 party list Senators,
- 18 Senator Chiefs and
- 2 Senators representing people living with disability.

It is important to note that of the 121 female members of parliament, very few were elected on a First Past. The Post which in its simplest form can be defined as a plurality voting system in which a candidate with majority votes wins the election. Out of the 47 political parties that fielded candidates for the legislative assembly, only 27 fielded at least a woman candidate. In essence, approximately 15% (243 out of (1652) were female contestants, thus highlighting the lack of political will from political parties in implementing legislative frameworks formulated to enhance more women participation in electoral politics (Gaidzwana, 2020).

Currently, 31% of the seats in the Zimbabwean Parliament are held by women which is a commendable increase from the 14% of women in parliament as at 1995 (Hamandishe, 2018). However, though significant gains have been noted, there is work that needs to be done to ensure more women participate in electoral processes and achieve 50% representation as is the case in other leading countries like Rwanda which have 60% of women in parliament and Namibia here in southern Africa has a commendable representation of 47%.

Role of Political Parties in Ensuring Women's Participation in Electoral Politics

Political parties in Zimbabwe, namely the ruling ZANU PF party and the opposition parties like the Citizens Coalition for Change, have repeatedly committed themselves to advance women political participation, but the evidence on the ground shows that there is still a long way to go. Political parties are a vital cog when it comes to solving the women's participation in electoral politics because they are the ones who groom leaders and put them up for nomination starting from grassroots structures up to the upper echelons of party positions. As the cornerstone to women's quest for political inclusion, political parties are critical in ensuring that more women take part in electoral processes through training and mentorship programmes and through changing the general outlook of the party towards women leaders.

Though the Constitution provides and requires political parties to meet the provisions of equal representation and parity among men and women, according to Hamandishe (2018), there seem to be some reluctance among political parties to appreciate the need for more women participation in order to attain gender parity in electoral processes. The low percentage of women either nominated or directly elected in election is a clear testament of political parties' hypocrisy and unwillingness to wholly work towards gender parity in electoral processes. According to Hamandishe (2018), the composition of the candidates for the 2018 general election clearly paints the true picture of the political parties' reluctance towards women's participation in electoral processes as political parties largely ignored the clarion call and previous commitments to attaining gender parity.

Despite the government coming up with legislative frameworks and policies to enhance women's participation in electoral processes, political parties continue to negate and fail to implement them as they allow other political considerations to take precedence in fielding the candidates.

Deeply Rooted Patriarchy

Patriarchy is arguably at the centre of Zimbabwe's body politic. For political parties, patriarchy is embodied in the manner and process in which primary elections are conducted to choose leaders during elections. Acts of violence against women aimed at intimidating and silencing women participation in electoral politics epitomise the problems espoused in the attainment of gender parity and women's participation in electoral politics. Women are faced with a hostile and prejudiced environment where abuse, gender-based invectives and campaign slurs are common (Wanzala, 1995). A good example is that of Thokozani Khupe, the former deputy prime minister of Zimbabwe during the government of National Unity era (2009–2013) who suffered serious abuse in the run up to the 2018 general election. After the death of the opposition leader Morgan Tsvangirai in February 2018, opposition members opposed her ascension to the leadership position labelling her a prostitute and threatened to burn her in a hut during the funeral of their late leader in order to bar her from leading the party (https://wwwvoazimbabwe. com/2018/02/20/MDC-TVPThokozaniKhupeBeatenUp,NearlySet onFireinHamletAtTsvangiraiFuneral).

These gender-based acts of violence are perpetrated against women candidates or women who take interest in policies and politics and are further perpetuated by the government and political parties' inaction when it comes to these abuses. This has created a toxic environment for politicians in general and for women politicians in particular as most women are discouraged from having active political views or putting their names up for nomination as candidates due to the toxicity that is fostered and painfully endured by women. Due to this noxious environment, many women who deem themselves to be "self-respecting" have shied away from running for political office as they bear the burden of being mothers, wives and daughters who have to possess a certain status in society which is inconsistent with the character assassination associated with the Zimbabwean electoral politics. Joice Mujuru, the first Zimbabwean woman to rise to be appointed as the Vice President of the ZANU PF party, suffered the consequences of deeply rooted patriarchy in our politics as during the ZANU PF Congress of 2014, youths sang derogatory songs targeted towards her saying they did not want to be led by a woman. Phrases like *"tipeiwo commander asina mazamu"* which, loosely, translates to "give us a leader with no breasts" were carelessly thrown around and danced to in songs. This resulted in her being booted out of the presidium and subsequently replaced by a male, the now President of Zimbabwe, Emmerson Dambudzo Mnangagwa. Thus, one can argue that the efficacy of legislative frameworks and policies aimed at increasing women's participation in politics are just but in name, not in character, as deeply rooted patriarchy results in parties' reluctance to implement these policies. This confirms the argument put forward by Nyakudya (2000), asserting that when the electoral environment is patriarchal and prejudiced, women are automatically marginalised.

Political Clientelism

Political clientelism in its simplest form is defined as giving material goods in return for electoral support, that is, the exchange of goods and services for political support in a *quid pro quo* manner. Hilgers (2011) defines politics as who gets what, when and how, and given that Zimbabwean politics is deeply rooted in this asymmetric relationship between politicians and voters, the efficacy of legislative frameworks and policies aimed at increasing women's participation in electoral politics is gravely undermined. In Zimbabwe, voters expect gifts and tokens for them to generally vote for a candidate as evident in these popular statements by the general voting populace saying "*tofanira kukunwa, tokuputa, tokudya kuti tikuvhotere*" which is loosely translated as "we have to drink, smoke and eat at your expense if we are to vote for you" (https://www.herald.co.zw/2018/12/24/patron-clientpoliticsnotgoodfordemocracy). It is against this background that the system of political clientelism adversely impact the gospel of women participation in electoral politics as they lack necessary funding to compete with their male counterparts given that most women have no financial capacity due to economic and historical scales unfairly tipped against them. Money plays a huge role in politics in Zimbabwe, and given the historical economic imbalances where most women do not own or control the means of production, it is difficult for them to compete on a level playing field, thereby decreasing women's participation in electoral processes and politics.

Gendered Stereotypes

Generally, women suffer from gendered stereotypes in the political arena. According to Chimhandamba (1999), gendered stereotype is a generalised view or preconception about attributes or characteristics that ought to be possessed by women and men or the roles that are or should be performed by men and women. It is against this background that women fail to participate in electoral politics as they tend to suffer from these gendered stereotypes. These stereotypes start from grassroots level where gender inequalities are rife within families, together with the inequitable division of labour within households. These gender stereotypes are further rubberstamped by cultural attitudes towards women which further subjugate them, hence, limiting their participation in political processes. A good example is that of women in politics often being associated and seen as loose and immoral as evidenced by the utterances of most social media users in Zimbabwe who refer to female politicians like Fadzai Mahere and Linda Masarira as "*mahure*" (prostitutes) just because they are vocal and engrossed in national politics (https://www.nehandaradio.com/2022/07/06/maherethreatenstosueKudzayioverdefamatoryadulteryallegations). These stereotypes are further perpetuated by religion which is generally an opium for subjugation of women and inequality. Dykes (2019) argues that religion plays a pivotal role in gender discrimination, most of them support women's exclusion from the public sector. For instance, according to the Bible which is the manual for Christians, women are expected to submit to their husbands (Ephesians 5:22). This therefore informs the written and unwritten rules adopted from religion which most societies use as tools for confining women to the private space as they are made to occupy positions of subordination and not leadership in line with their religious teachings. Dykes (2019) further connotes that religion has assigned women to the status of helpmates, too rational to lead and too intellectually limited for public dimensions of life. It is against this background that legislative frameworks and policies have little success as these gendered stereotypes drawback women's participation in electoral politics.

Gender Stigma

Since Zimbabwe is largely and deeply a conservative country, gender stigma is highly prevalent, and it accounts for lesser women participation in electoral politics. Norris and Lovenduski (1994) attest to the fact that gender stigma contributes to women apathy in participation in electoral processes as there is close to a general consensus in conservative societies that women are generally unprepared for leadership roles. It is against this background that women in politics are often appointed to peripheral and token positions. These stigmas are perpetuated by political parties which are supposed to be at the forefront in encouraging women's participation in politics. The recently held ZANU PF congress in October 2022 is a clear testament to these gender stigmas as the politburo composition leaves a lot to be desired with regard to tokenism and women's positions in politics. Only one woman was appointed in the top 7 posts that is the position of Chairperson which is currently held by Oppah Muchinguri Kashiri. The rest of the women were allocated peripheral positions in the all-powerful organ of the party, with the majority of women deputising their male counterparts (https://www.herald.co.zw/2022/12/23/PresidentappointsnewPolitburo).

However, it's not all doom and gloom as the Second Republic has made strides in trying to enhance women's participation in electoral politics by reducing these deeply rooted gendered stigmas through appointing more women in government top positions in an attempt to redress the scourge of prevalent tokenisms. The President of Zimbabwe appointed 5 women to be provincial ministers, namely Judith Mukwanda (Bulawayo Metropolitan), Ellen Gwaradzimba (Manicaland), Monica Mavhunga (Mashonaland Central), Apollonia Munzverengwi (Mashonaland East), Mary Mliswa (Mashonaland West), and in that aspect achieving gender parity. Furthermore, for the first time in Zimbabwean politics, the influential ministry of defence is headed by a female, namely Oppah Muchinguri Kashiri (http://chronicle.co.zw/2018/09/08/lea nercabinetnamed…FirstfemaleDefenceMinisterappointed). This therefore shows that though the quest for women political participation has not yet come full circle, positive and meaningful steps are being taken in implementing legislative frameworks and policies aimed at increasing women's participation in electoral politics.

The Negative Impact of the Electoral System to Women's Political Participation

It is critical to note that the degree of female political participation largely relies on the electoral system used in a given country or place (Dziva, 2018). According to the Women's Political Participation (African Barometer, 2021), more women political representation is most likely to be achieved where the electoral system in place is the Proportional Representation system also known as the "list system" as opposed to the First Past the Post system. In fact, women constitute 34% of parliamentarians and 30% of councillors in African countries with the Proportional Representation system. The lowest representation of women (17% at both local and national levels) is in First Past the Post countries with no quotas. What this entails is that more women are likely to be elected into political seats in a Proportional Representation system than in the First Past the Post system. This owes to the nature and characteristics associated with each electoral system as will be briefly discussed below.

In Zimbabwe, the electoral system that is in place is the First Past the Post system which is also referred to as the "Constituency based system," where candidates campaign and are voted for as individuals who may or may not belong to specific parties. This is the subsisting electoral system except for elections of senators in terms of section 120 which provides for Proportional Representation using party lists as well as section 124 which provides for a quota for women in the National Assembly.

This electoral system that is the First Past the Post system registers very low female candidates owing to various factors. Chief among the factors is that campaigning is financially taxing to candidates who have to fund themselves if they have no money injected into their campaigns by well-wishers. Due to historical imbalances that exist, many Zimbabwean women usually find themselves bereft of any financial aid which discourages them from even thinking of placing their names as candidates or dooms them to fail if they so decide to participate. To add on, the First Past the Post system invariably focuses on the candidate as an individual as opposed to the Proportional Representation List system which focuses on the party instead and its policies. The candidate-centred nature of the First Past the Post system has therefore regrettably become a breeding ground for toxic and harmful gender biased mud-slinging and character assassination of women which discourages women from participating or dwindles their prospects of success if they do participate in the elections. As a consequence of the operative electoral system in Zimbabwe, women inclusion in politics remains at depressingly low levels.

Conclusion

In summation, and in view of the foregoing, it is apparent that despite the efforts made towards enhancing women political participation, Zimbabwe is still a long way from realising practical results for women in electoral politics. This owes to a host of factors that work against the full enjoyment of the policies and legislative interventions aimed at increasing opportunities for women in electoral politics. The sticky issue that perhaps needs mentioning is that perhaps the legislative and policy provisions set out are inadequate in as far as gender parity in electoral politics is concerned. This is because the solutions advanced to improve women's political participation pale in the face of the negative factors militating against a wholesome enjoyment of the political rights of women. Perhaps it is time that government goes an extra mile and invest in programmes that change the attitudes of the electorate, the political parties, men and women themselves as opposed to merely putting down theoretical solutions through rhetoric and continued commitments to achieve gender parity in electoral politics.

The quest for women participation in electoral politics requires a complete overhaul of the attitudes which pose structural and systemic barriers for women to enable them to participate at the grassroots level up to the presidium. The idea of female leaders and especially of a woman president is still a distant dream because of the many obstacles in the path to effective and holistic political participation. Little wonder therefore why this chapter has dedicated very little time to the idea of a woman president as those few women that have dared to compete in the presidential election have been deemed too insignificant to talk about with the highest post being the lieutenant and deputy and never the ultimate price of being president. When all is said and done, this chapter acknowledges the progress made towards achieving women participation in electoral politics but notes with regret that the progress is quite minimal as more needs to be done to achieve gender parity in electoral politics.

References

Ackerly, B., & True, J. (2008). *Reflexivity in Practice: Power and Ethics in Feminist Research on International Relations, 10*(4), 693–707. Oxford Univeristy Press

Adhiambo-Odoul, J. (2013). *The women in the New Political Dispensation: A false Start in challenges and opportunities.* Journal of the Institute of Certified Public Secretaries of Kenya. Nairobi.

Africa Barometer. (2021). *Women's political participation.* International Institute for Democracy and Electoral Assistance. Accessed 10 January 2023.

Arendt, C. (2018). Unpacking the political conditions behind gender quotas in Africa. *Politics and Gender, 14*(3), 295–322.

Ballington, J. (2012). *Empowering women for stronger political parties: A guidebook to promote women's political participation.* UNDP and NDI

Berlant, L., & Prosser, J. (2011). *Life writing and intimate publics: A conversation with Laurent Berlant* (Vol. 34). University of Hawai Press

Bhandari, P. (2020). *What Is Qualitative Research? Methods & Examples.* https://www.scribr.com

Chikwanha, A., Sithole, T., & Bratton, M. (2004). *The power of propaganda, public opinion in Zimbabwe* (Afrobarometer Report No 42).

Chimhandamba J. (1999). *SADC women raise their voices in Parliament.* Renaissance, p 9. 90

Constitution of Zimbabwe (2013).

Constitutional Amendment No 2 (2021).

Dziva, C. (2018). The 2013 constitutional reform and the protection of Women's rights in Zimbabwe. *East Africa Social Science Research Review, 34*(2), 21–35.

Dykes, D. L. (2019). *Faith and reason.* faithandreason.org Accessed on 28 January 2023.

Election Watch 9. (2023). *Women's Political Participation in Zimbabwe*.veritaszim.net

Electoral Act [*Chapter 2:13*].

Hamandishe, A. (2018). *Rethinking women's political participation in Zimbabwe's elections*. African Portal. Published 27 July 2018.

https://www.herald.co.zw/ 2018/12/24/patron-client politics not good for democracy/. Accessed on 9 January 2023.

https://www.nehandaradio.com/2022/07/06/mahere threatens to sue Kudzai over defamatory adultery allegations. Accessed on 28 January 2023.

https://www.herald.co.zw/2022/12/23/President appoints new Politburo. Accessed on 28 January 2023.

https://www.sundaytimes.co.zw/ 2020/10/04/Quota system: The key towards active participation of women in Zimbabwean politics. Accessed on 28 January 2023.

http//chronicle.co.zw//2018/09/08/leaner cabinet named...First female Defence Minister appointed. Accessed on 28 January 2023.

Hilgers, T. (2011). *Clientelism and conceptual stretching: Differentiating among concepts and among analytical levels*. Theory and Society, 40(5), 567–588.

Gaidzanwa, R. (2020). The political culture of Zimbabwe: Continuities and discontinuities. In S. L. Ndlovu-Gatsheni & P. Ruhanya (Eds.), *The history and political transition of Zimbabwe: From Mugabe to Mnangagwa* (pp. 25–50). Springer Nature.

Krook, M., & Childs, S. (2010). *Women, gender, politics*. Oxford Press.

Lande, H. C. (2014). *Political clientelism and comparative perspectives*. Sage.

Legal Age of Majority Act (1982).

Makumbe, J. M., & Campagnon, D (2000). *Behind the smokescreen, politics of Zimbabwe's 1995 general elections*. University of Zimbabwe Publications.

Mlambo, C. (2019). *Factors influencing women political participation: The case of SADC region*. Accessed on 28 January 2023.

Molokomme, A. (2000). *Building inclusiveness in SADC's democratic systems*: The case of women's representation in leadership positions, in Southern African Elections Forum Conference Report: In Pursuit of Electoral Norms and Standards, Windhoek.

Norris, P., & Lovenduski, J. (1994). *Gender and Party politics*. Sage Publications

Nyakudya, M. (2000, July 11). *Zimbabwe election update 2000*, (3), 6.

Panahi, M. H. (2007). *Sociology of women's political participation*. Allameh Tbataii Publication.

Philipps, A. (1998). *Feminism and politics*. Oxford University Press.

Rai, M. S. (2010). *International perspective on gender and governance*. Macmillan Press.

Research and Advocacy Unit. (2010). *Women politics and the Zimbabwean Crisis*. Institute of Democracy in Africa (IDASA).

Tshuma, D. (2018). *Looking Beyond 2023 what next after Zimbabwe's parliamentary Quota system.* Accord.org

Wanzala, W. L. (1995). *Women and elections in Namibia after five years of independence.* SAFRE 1(2) Sept/Oct 1995.

ZIMSTAT 2021

CHAPTER 8

Post-independence Election Violence: Re-thinking the Marginalisation of Women in Zimbabwean Politics

Kudzai Biri

Introduction

> Kudzi, the world is not ready for female leadership, it is not only in Africa but the whole world, it is what it is.

The words came from a pastor in 2013, as we were having a conversation at the Desmond Tutu Conference Centre in Nairobi at the All Africa Conference of Churches. We were discussing issues to do with the church, politics, and violence against women. After reflecting on the statement cited above, it came to my realisation that if the world is not ready for female leadership, as the pastor claimed, then Africa is worse given the cultural beliefs and practices and theological rigidity on gender relations that are espoused by the church. More so, if the religious leaders 'endorse'

K. Biri (✉)
University of Zimbabwe, Harare, Zimbabwe
e-mail: kudzibiri@gmail.com

© The Author(s), under exclusive license to Springer Nature Switzerland AG 2023
E. Mavengano and S. Chirongoma (eds.), *Electoral Politics in Zimbabwe, Vol II*, https://doi.org/10.1007/978-3-031-33796-3_8

the status quo without an attempt to challenge forces that fight and deter the acceptance of female leadership, then gender equity will remain a pipe dream in Africa, particularly because religion commands such a huge following in Africa, and most religious adherents do not critique the patriarchal values espoused in their faith communities. However, I understood the pastor's position because in the church, female leadership has remained a contention. Hence, it mirrors the situation in the political corridors of power: the marginalisation, exclusion, and cycle of violence against women in politics, whether it is participation or occupation of key political leadership positions. Methodologically, the study uses the socio-historical approach as its theoretical grounding and intersectionality as a tool of analysis to unravel, expose, and analyse the deficiencies and shortcomings of Zimbabwean politics and the weak position of the church. The church is used in generic terms that transcend denominational boundaries. Despite some individual clergymen/women that have spoken against the violence against women, the church has not unanimously come out in full force against the violence endured by women in the political space.

Chitsike (2011, p. 59) notes that:

> In the early post-independence period between 1980 and 1985, Zimbabwe had government introducing protecting women's rights through legislation such as the Legal Age of the majority Act. However, there is little respect for women's rights in Zimbabwe as discrimination and violence are justified through cultural and religious arguments.

The observations from Chitsike (2011) summarise aptly the environment of women as far as participation in politics and occupation of leadership positions in politics is concerned. The intersectionality of cultural factors and theology culminates in discrimination, marginalisation, and exclusion of women in the electoral process, and participation and occupation of leadership positions remain a domain dominated by men because women are scared off through violence. Zimbabwe has a deep-rooted culture of violence in politics, but this violence has also spread in the church (Kaulem, 2011). The constitution is violated. It is unimaginable if both powerful institutions combine to unleash violence against women despite the freedoms and rights of women enshrined in the constitution of Zimbabwe; they continue to be trampled in the political arena. A chronology of some key developments and incidents that violate women's rights in Zimbabwe are important to unravel how the state has been complicit in the face of violence against women, and especially those in top positions in different sectors and have a bearing on politics. Utilising the example of violence in Congo, Katongole (2017) provides insights useful for the Zimbabwean context. There are multiple dislocations in the socio-economic and fabric of the nation that make women lose hope and think they are fighting a losing battle.

The policing of women's bodies has been challenged, and another wave of recurrence of sexual violence is the order of the day, especially during election periods. The political arena in Zimbabwe provides a landscape of lament, displacement of women, and sexual violence. Sexual violence of women especially by the army does not only reflect disorder and military structural fragility, but also represent 'a new pathology' (Katongole, 2017, p. 15). Katongole cites an example of a group of teenage boys raping an 80-year-old woman during the Congolese crisis. In my opinion, the rape of the 80-year-old during political upheavals in Congo is comparable to many incidents in Zimbabwe, ranging from the liberation struggle, post-independence political unrests during the Gukurahundi atrocities, Mashurugwi,[1] where women's bodies have been taken advantage of and women and girls are raped. Worse, in situations where the rapists continue to live among those that they have raped, and justice has not been granted to the victims. Hence, transgenerational trauma from the Gukurahundi carnages, the liberation struggle, and post-independence era have created perceptions that need to be dismantled to allow women to be effective citizens in terms of their participation. The failure of the state to effectively deal with sexual violence of women gives the impression that it is not a serious crime to rape women and take advantage of political instability. Actually, it is justified, and theology has remained silent, and, in some instances, the theology of forgiveness and reconciliation has been popularised. This in turn fuels violence against women because they are always told to forgive, and it is my contention that this is a big promoter of violence against women. The theology of forgiveness is mediated through several ways.

---

[1] This is a group of machete wielding artisanal miners infamously known for a reign of terror which started in the Shurugwi mining community in the Midlands province, Zimbabwe. Their criminal activities include murder, rape, physical fights, and various other crimes.

Language and Perception of Masculinity

The section below documents different forms of violence against women and provide specific examples.

Language is a powerful tool for effective communication. Pongweni (1983) makes the point clear that there is power in naming. A popular mechanism and tool to silence women, apart from sexual violence is verbal violence and the naming system. The name-calling of prominent women to degrade and insult them is common. Most women who actively participate in politics are given names that insult and degrade them. For example, they are called prostitutes or whores (*mahure*). The perception is that women cannot work their way up to the top, but they engage in sexual relations with their male leaders in order to make it to the top. The name carries derogatory and shame innuendos as it refers to one who avails sex without restraint to different men. This scares away women from political participation because many are afraid of being labelled such because it usurps their dignity and integrity. While name technique illuminates experience, joy, pain, and aspirations of the participants during the Second liberation struggle (Chitsike, 2011), the naming technique for women in politics in post-colonial Zimbabwe is largely negative. In fact, there is little if any that captures their strengths and achievements except to bash them. The idea behind is that no woman should participate in politics, especially attaining a leadership position for it is space reserved for men. Stepping into the domain becomes a violation of societal and cultural boundaries. Hence, the women must be punished. Attacking women by giving them those derogatory names is confined not only to the grassroots levels but to the highest powers, and being a woman is attacked and degraded. Rutoro (2012) has examined masculinities among the Shona, and she points out that the Shona embody masculinities that encourage men to be domineering in all endeavours. There is a strong relationship between language and culture among the Shona, and this relationship mirrors cultural perceptions of masculinities. The masculinities and language both reinforce patriarchy, and they provide the blueprint for violence against women who aspire to be political leaders or actively participate in politics.

Degrading Womanhood

The former President Robert Mugabe, one honoured as an icon of the revolution and champion of women's empowerment, castigated his Vice President Joyce Mujuru for aspiring to be President. He reinforced the popular and deep-seated idea that a woman will not rule Zimbabwe. Thus, setting pace in the corridors of power to deter any attempt by a woman to contest against a man. His statement was '...and the person who wants to take over from me is a woman for that matter' (Manyonganise, 2015, p. 4). As pointed out by Manyonganise, such aspiring women are labelled as lacking *ubuntu*, an ethic that defines the individual's Africanness. However, *ubuntu* is used in politics as an oppressive tool to deter women from politics by drawing a line that says that any woman who dares into the political space has no dignity because she wants to be like men or compete with men. This is contradictory since women fought side by side with men to bring independence in 1980. Years later, the Nigerian President, Buhari, on his visit to Germany in 2018, reiterated the idea during an interview with Angela Merkel and said that the place for his wife is the kitchen. The role of women as mothers in the home deters them from participating in politics or aspiring for top leadership positions. The aspiring of women to serve is because of the burdens they carry. People occupying high office reinforce negative cultural perceptions through what they say, especially if the words come from a President. The degrading of womanhood has taken different dimensions in Zimbabwe. The use of thugs or so-called green bombers to physically assault members from the opposition or within the party to control show the magnitude of state-sponsored violence. This confirms Chitsike's observation that violence intensifies during election times, and women's bodies are often used as battlefields. The governments' failure to uphold the women's rights as full and equal citizens despite legislations and signing and ratifications of regional and international legislation sends a clear message to the community that women's lives are less precious and that violence and discrimination against them are tolerable. Beatrice Mutetwa is one of the prominent human rights lawyers who has represented members of the opposition and journalists who are unjustly arrested, tortured, and persecuted. One male police officer was recorded verbally shouting at her at the court, calling her '*voetsek*', revealing disorder and lawlessness. She has consistently been abused by the police officers (Tsunga, 2009). The consistent abuse of Mtetwa and the act by security personnel that shout at her without any form of justice that follow is continuation of cases that set precedence on violence against powerful and prominent women.

Women from alternative political movements have suffered the more. Two members of the Movement for Democratic Change (now Citizens Coalition for Change), the major opposition party, Joanna Mamombe and Cecilia Chimbiri, and friend Netsai Marova were abducted and tortured and sexually assaulted by state agents in 2020. The deficiency of politics in Zimbabwe is that it is seen as a control game, fame, and status and not to serve. Thus, women remain victims of this political deluge, firstly as most victims of violence and secondly, of failure to deliver services because of the role that women have that burdens them with responsibility in the families. The will to arise in the public domain is submerged by 'the will to survive' because they fear for their lives and what remains of their children. One of the local Zimbabwean newspapers, Zim Eye, reports a recent case (31 January 2023), the murder of a female teacher in Harare, Magdalene Mandiveyi, who reportedly had refused to attend the 'Teachers for ED' event. These are forced gatherings orchestrated by supporters of ED[2] before elections because of dwindling political support. The teacher complained of poor remuneration and refused to attend the meeting. Thereafter, she reportedly shared some information with those close to her, revealing that some unidentified men were following her, and she reportedly received some threats on her mobile phone. After having been reported as a missing person, she was found dead after a few days. This is an example of violence that scares away women. For instance, the deceased teacher left behind a three-month-old baby, a reality which frightens many women who worry about the welfare of their families in the event of their untimely demise.

The Portrayal and Depiction of Women in Politics

Male political leaders suffuse the narratives of the liberation struggle with the abuse of women. The war was gendered as the masculinities of soldiers who commanded the warriors, and those who fought in Zimbabwe were the most dominant (Gaidzanwa, 2015). Any woman that rises to the top at work is assumed to have had sexual relations with men for promotion. When courageous women try to cross the boundaries in the domain

---

[2] Emmerson Dambudzo Mnangagwa, the incumbent President of Zimbabwe and the presidential candidate in the forthcoming 2023 harmonised elections.

reserved for men, they are stigmatised. This is worsened by the fact that most women have accepted the notions of masculinity prescribed by society. Hence, they also accept and perpetuate disempowering femininities (Biri, 2016). The presence of a woman in a male-dominated space is often presumed as pre-supposing that she will avail sex to men around her and if she refuses, violence against her can be justified.

The public slapping of Thokozani Khupe at the Harare International Conference Centre is one of the incidents of violence at the highest level. According to Gambakwe media, 24 January 2022, Tapiwa Chiyangwa, a supporter of Douglas Mwonzora, slapped Khupe against the backdrop of alleging that she was a captured political clown. The silence of both men and women in power is a template that seems to have authenticated and justified violence against prominent women aspiring to participate in politics. This explains why not only in Zimbabwe there are few women who are nodal power points, in not only politics, but also those who are indirectly involved in politics related issues. For example, Jestina Mukoko a human rights and gender activist suffered torture under the leadership of Mugabe as she was abducted and tortured in 2008 (Mukoko, 2016). Critics see Mugabe as the author of dangerous and violent masculinities in Zimbabwean politics. As pointed by Mkodzonge (2020), with reference to the violence unleashed by Mashurugwi, but generalisable in most cases of either state-sponsored violence or violence justified by political heavyweights, lack of police intervention confirms the belief that the perpetrators have a close connection with some powerful politicians. The cases of Mtetwa and Mukoko are a pointer to the intersectionality of human rights activism and politics and that any woman who dares to enter politics or anything that infringes with politics should be a courageous woman. Hence, the empowerment of women should have a holistic approach to empower them in all facets of life that will make their entry and participation into politics safe.

Women in the corridors of power have not done enough to promote the participation of other women. This is compounded by the fact that on the level of social activism, most of them have not been forthcoming to interact and serve the needs of women and girls. Hence, most women are not confident to vote for women whom they feel betray them when they step into and enter the corridors of power. All this has promoted gender disparities and widened the gender gap in political participation and occupation of top posts. The most feared form of violence is sexual violence, for the history of Zimbabwean politics from the colonial era to post-independence Zimbabwe is tainted by sexual violence against women. Therefore, it deserves attention.

Sexual Violence: A Persistent Pathology

The corridors of power, be it religious or political are suffused with violence. My analysis is that systematic and structural violence against women can be effectively dealt with if the male leaders are serious with eradicating violence. However, the masculinist politics in post-colonial Zimbabwe answers why there are no stiff penalties for rapists to discourage them or any meaningful action from the top to deal with violence. A combination of sexual violence and other forms of violence scares away women from politics. Violence as a tool to silence and disempower women continues without being challenged effectively by institutions, especially the church. The sexual violence and murder of Moreblessing Ali of the opposition party, CCC in 2022, is a befitting example to show how violence is condoned through compromising the arm of the law. The brutal murder of Moreblessing Ali represents what Katongole (2017) calls a 'new pathology' in the matrix of violence.

During the peak of the COVID-19 era, the three women from the opposition (see above) were sexually violated, and supporters of the ruling regime defended and justified the violence in the state press, *The Herald*, Facebook, and Twitter. The significance of these forms of justifying state-sponsored violence to silence or eliminate opposition members breeds a fertile ground for rapists who target women in general, highlighting the serious breakdown of the moral fabric and lawlessness. The youths are used in committing crimes of abduction and violence. Hence, they are socialised and nurtured into a culture of violence against women even outside the domain of politics. The rise of Mashurugwi (machete militia) has witnessed violence against women, resulting in countless women being raped and beaten, and to date, justice has not been done.

Moreover, seeing women as sexual objects means that they put themselves on a pedestal in every facet of life, hence they cannot tolerate the leadership of women or their ascendency to high positions where they can lead, command authority, and embody power. Chiroro et al. (2001) make a valid observation and comment: Zimbabwean male psyche is characterised by an internalised insatiable self-centred desire for sex with multiple partners coupled with an intolerant attitude who are perceived primarily as objects of sexual gratification and childbearing. Men are conditioned to dominate and dictate. This study identifies violence as the most hindrance to participation in politics. This violence is fuelled by masculinities that are nurtured in culture and in theologies that bolster patriarchy. Hence, any meaningful change, transformation, and the realisation of many women participating in politics hinges on transformed masculinities. The study therefore challenges Zimbabwean men to deal with their ego and accept that women are equal partners and can compete, lead, and execute political duties and responsibilities.

The Role of the Church in Curbing Violence Against Women

In a nation that aspires to develop and rebuild the nation, the question of gender equality and equal participation in politics are key to realise the full potential of women and promoting sustainable development. Women need redemption from oppressive masculinities that manifest in politics through violence of all forms. The church is a powerful institution in Zimbabwe, and it is strategically positioned to take a mediating role and in denouncing violence against women. However, Kaulem (2011) points out that there is violence in the church, and this violence mostly affects women because they are the most victims.

Chitsike (2011) emphasises the need for reconciliation. However, this reconciliation does not seem to work in Zimbabwe mainly because of two reasons. First, the church has preached reconciliation, initiated by politicians who would have committed acts of violence. It means that the church is co-opted by the state. The state directs the church on what to do and say. Second, the cycle of violence continues to be accompanied with the same messages of forgiveness and reconciliation. I have argued that there must be a theology of responsibility and accountability to deter violence and cut the cord of recurrence. The nation needs a commission of inquiry, accountability, and justice meted out for perpetrators because the current status quo creates fertile ground for perpetrators to continue. Radford Ruether (1998, p. 1) talks of women and redemption, and gender equality in the first Jesus Movement. She traces history to show that women and men should be equal because Christ redeemed both men and women and that there is no male or female, because there is inclusive, universal redemption. However, in African countries that were colonised, the legacies of discrimination of women continue to persist and manifest as they became anchored in the fertile patriarchal setting. In addition, Radford Ruether (1998, p. 255) notes that the higher education extended to an African male elite was usually assumed to be beyond African woman's reach. Thus, colonialism compounded aspects that discriminate women and reshaped the internal gender relations in ways that dismantled women from political participation by reinforcing that the place of a woman is in the home after having been trained to work in the kitchen and become a housemaid in the European manner. The need for de-coloniality is key because these aspects of colonialism tap into indigenous oppressive traits and together create a thwarting environment for women to demonstrate their capabilities in political participation and occupation of leadership positions. When women are confined to their homes or burdened with household chores, they cannot be equal competitors with men in politics. Hence, postcolonial Zimbabwe has structures and sociocultural tenets that prevent women from full participation in politics.

CRITIQUING THE ROLE OF WOMEN IN KEY LEADERSHIP POSITIONS

The measuring rod for the success of women in politics is to examine the perceived small things that are cherished by women and how they have responded. Women and girls have pressed for sanitary ware in schools and hospitals for mothers. Little effort has been made by women in political positions to pressure the government to factor subsidies for women's basic needs. Apart from these basic things required by women, women constitute the majority in our nation, and the logical move was to mobilise, voice out, and force the government to descend on oppression and against cases such as Mashurugwi. The girls dying in shrines is another example that suffices to show that women have let down themselves in our nation. Girls are often forced to get married at a fragile age, and several of them die at shrines giving birth. The churches do not allow them to go to hospitals. Babies have died in major hospitals in incubators due to negligence, and women in political and religious positions have not been forthcoming to stand in the gap when crises occur. This chapter upholds the assertion that most female political leaders in Zimbabwe have been a huge disappointment. Their presence in the corridors of power gave hope to women at grassroots level. However, little efforts have been made by women to challenge men and oppressive structures. In fact, we have witnessed divisions among women and or total silence on key issues that require their input. For example, the dying of women and babies in hospitals, the need for sanitary ware for girls and women, and promoting accessibility of drugs to women with HIV and Aids, and issues of sexual violence have not yet received adequate attention from female politicians in the high echelons of power.

The Women's Coalition of Zimbabwe was born in 1999, and it comprises of women's groups and women's rights activists, clubs, associations, and political parties. Their role is to provide activism for rights of girls and women (Chitsike, 2011, p. 173). The important question is to probe how effective the women's organisations have been in terms of activism of representing girls and women and activism against violence. In addition, Zimbabwe adheres to the SADC Protocol on Gender and development. They have not been forthcoming in dealing with and addressing issues that are important in the lives of women and girls. Critically, we need to consider why most of them have been ineffective. Manyonganise (2015, p. 4) correctly observes that female politicians have not been effective. Why do women become ineffective when they occupy leadership positions? Women in political circles have turned deaf ears to the cries and needs of women at grassroots level, and many wonder why they become so detached from the realities and egalitarian struggles of women. The study identifies two basic reasons for the ineffectiveness of women. First, political positions are seen as opportunities to amass wealth; hence, they join the race of looting, and the promises to serve disappear. Second, the women who cross the restricted line into the political space cease to be women. Biologically, they are women, but they seem to feel that they have made it by entering a male domain, hence they 'have become men'. The Shona say, *uyu murume chaiye* (this woman is a man) if a woman does things reserved for men or outstanding achievement. In this sense, they become men in that those are positions reserved for men culturally; thus, they no longer associate with women in terms of understanding their needs and aspirations. They submerge themselves into the pool of men, and they begin to identify with malestream behaviour. In my critique, I have argued that they then pick patriarchal traits. While most ordinary women continue to see them as women who are supposed to represent them and wonder why they do not, they fail to realise that transitioning into political power has many connotations because of an intersectionality of sociocultural challenges that are engendered by patriarchy. Thus, no meaningful transformation is initiated by most of them.

Also, they become weak to challenge masculinist politics because they identify with the agenda of men more than women. Generally, it is unacceptable and cannot be justified because, despite the reasons above, they should embody a sense of responsibility and accountability to the needs of girls and women.

The Role of the Circle of Concerned African Woman Theologians (Circle) in Zimbabwe: Re-Engaging Society on Political Violence

The Circle in Zimbabwe must be forthcoming in not only research and writing but effectively engaging the communities through seminars, workshops, and outreaches to empower women, for example, conducting seminars and workshops not only in the urban centres as has been the tradition but to penetrate villages. Issues of masculinities and femininities are key in shaping perspectives and approaches in gender relations, especially concerning politics. There is no more urgent female theological task to provide hope and challenge women to rise up given the endless cycles of violence in the political space. It entails arguing and wrestling against all forms of violence against women. In addition, the Circle should develop a robust political theology of hope for women since many have got scars and press for accountability and responsibility. Katongole (2017, p. xii) points out that there is need to provide the much needed theological critique and interruption of the politics of violence that wantonly sacrifice millions in Africa. In the case of Zimbabwe, the Circle must organise workshops to empower female religious leaders to rise up and challenge gender-based and sexual violence against girls and women, and in particular, in politics. In addition, male religious leaders in liaison with ordinary men of faith should be brought to the dialogue table in workshops and seminars in order to push for theologies of responsibility and accountability. The platforms will also challenge different masculinities that feed, fuel, and unleash violence. The research and published material by Circle members unravel inequalities within the patriarchal cultures and churches. A practical engagement with all stakeholders ensures that the nation is mobilised to hate and shun violence, and few people who are nodal power points in the corridors of power are rendered powerless to incite violence. Most acts of violence in Zimbabwe are committed by the youths. The implication is that any meaningful quest to preserve peace has to rope in the youths and educate them on the futility of violence in their lives. The nexus of violence, absence of safety in the church and in the political space can be the focus of the workshops and seminars.

Generally, the Circle members are active in their circles and large gatherings comprise of their group. The challenge they should take is to collaborate with male theologians, engage different key stakeholders in the fight against gender-based violence. This also entails advancing political theologies that pursue a head-on confrontation with all political sectors to influence peace in the political arena in Zimbabwe. In other words, the Circle has the mandate to reconstruct political theology in Zimbabwe. Concentrating on Circle activities that confine within their circles cannot produce the desired results. Most Circle activities have helped to unravel cultural and theological bias and the gender inequalities. The issues of violence are among the works of the Circle as they endeavour to transform spaces into safe spaces. Inclusiveness is an authentic biblical truth, hence the Circle through seminars and workshops with outsiders should begin, continue, and intensify because simply writing and publishing is not enough. Silence is not an option in the context of repeated violence against women in politics. The voice of the Circle should be louder, recruit and mentor more members against violence through social activism. The church's response to both domestic and political violence is weak because violence against women is also happening in the church, and this has ethical and theological implications. The church has espoused a weak political theology that does not challenge violence. A collective effort of the Circle, female religious leaders, and other stakeholders will inevitably empower women to carry their egalitarian struggles. It will signal a serious approach to dismantle violence and promote justice, peace, and development in all the structures. An important factor for the empowerment of women to rise up is to educate them on the cherished femininities that are not docile and a collective cry and demand for justice against violence.

The composition of the Circle transcends geographical and tribal boundaries. This composition is strategic, and it serves as an example in challenging violent politics that thrive on fronting tribalism and geographical locations as tools of exclusion, marginalisation, and violence. It entails a unanimous move to a culture of violence against the women who do not belong to a particular political group and tribalism and promote non-violent alternatives amid a volatile political climate. The Circle should challenge the unjustified thesis purporting that rape is a weapon of war. The argument does not hold water because a spree on raping innocent women is simply a mark of misguided masculinities that seek sexual gratification through force and violence. If left unchallenged, it will continue to be normalised every time there is a crisis. The trauma of brutal murders and sexual violence that include gang rape continue to linger in the minds of victims. Hence, it can be a lifelong or generational trauma and threat to women and deter them to participate in politics.

Women need to take a collective active role in politics, not only to articulate their experiences. They need to dismantle the patriarchal mindset of relegating leadership positions to men and develop themselves so that they qualify to occupy positions, not only in politics but also in other social and economic structures. Some of the key leadership positions make them powerful to influence political decisions and to make powerful voices that can be heard and challenge inequalities and press for gender justice. Most women are economically disempowered, and worse, the traditional culture of relegating the home as the confine of a woman is a great deterrent for the full participation of women in politics. Some women who have gone through the university or college cannot go to work or participate in public activities because they do not have permission from the husband. I have counselled female students at the University, who after finishing their first degrees are not allowed to proceed to postgraduate studies. This is a strong cultural weapon that feeds into political disempowerment of women and deters them from participating and attaining top leadership posts. Because there is an intersectionality of challenges in Zimbabwe that all feed into disadvantaging women politically, a serious confrontation of the vicissitudes is key. In such cases, it is key to conduct workshops with men to deal with dangerous masculinities that are oppressive and exploitative.

I have consistently castigated the gender card in occupying leadership positions. While it was noble and a means to close the gender gap in early post-independence Zimbabwe, the historical developments and reality on the ground show that it can negatively be used as a tool to perpetuate stereotypes and oppress women as they are often reminded that they did not qualify, but instead, they came through the gender card. They are hired on gender card and not on merit; hence, the women are forever silenced because they are often reminded that they did not qualify, and certain individuals in positions of power have ground to either silence or abuse them. Therefore, women must fight hard to develop themselves and compete for positions so that they close doors of potential abuse and violence and be in a position to promote the welfare of women. 'Mothers are the roots of the nation' is in tandem with the traditional *musha mukadzi*. There is no meaningful development that factor in the pressing needs of the nation when women are sidelined, oppressed, and exploited. A total force to expunge patriarchy in politics require concerted effort by female leaders in all sectors of life. Female religious and political leaders are key in leading to dismantle patriarchy, promote the unity of women, and fight against violence. But the Circle ought to take the initiative of making them know of the struggles and what should be done. The biggest challenge is that some female political and religious leaders are abused; hence, they are powerless to deal with abuse. There remains a mammoth task for women, and the solution is to collaborate with men to deal with violence.

My contention is that the challenges of political participation and occupation of leadership positions should not be approached from a surface level. An intersectionality of challenges, religion, cultural, social, and economic has badly impacted on the well-being and welfare of women in Zimbabwe. Any meaningful quest to dismantle the negative tradition of political violence against them requires a focus on the issues that feed into the political culture of violence, discrimination, and marginalisation of women. It should also entail understanding the intersectionality and overcoming the violence of extreme feminised poverty and its impact on gender relations. The main challenge is that a combination of men who have sexually abused women, plus those with an entrenched patriarchal mindset within the corridors of power, has dismantled efforts to effectively deal with violence against women. Instead, they normalise violence against women who dare into politics. Hence, the task is to cultivate a spirit of solidarity to fight against violence against women and promote gender justice and free political space.

Conclusion

The cycle of violence against women in Zimbabwe's political arena cannot be debated. In this post-independence period, women's organisations seem to have barely scratched the surface to deal with violence such that the few courageous women become more vulnerable. The intersectionality of challenges feeds and promotes violence against women in politics. The Circle, female religious leaders, and other stakeholders have the mandate to unanimously act and challenge different forms of violence against women and more so, in politics.

Bibliography

Biri, K. (2016). Proverbs 31 Woman: Pentecostalism and disempowering femininities and oppressive masculinities in Zimbabwe. In J. Hunter & J. Kuegler (Eds.), *The Bible and violence in Africa* (pp. 223–238). Bamberg University Press.

Chiroro, P., et.al. (2001). *The Zimbabwean male psyche: With respect to reproductive health, HIV, AIDS and gender issues.* University of Zimbabwe.

Chitsike, K. (2011). The role of women in Zimbabwe's transition. In T. Murithi & A. Mawadza (Eds.), *Zimbabwe transition: A view from within. International Journal of Religion,* 159–190.

Gaidzanwa, R. (2015). Grappling with Mugabe's masculinist politics. In S. J. Ndhlovu-Gatsheni (Ed.), *Mugabeism?: History, power and politics in Zimbabwe (African histories and modernities)* (pp. 157–179). Palgrave Macmillan.

Gambakwe Media, 24-01-20222.

Katongole, E. (2017). *Born from Lament the theology and politics of hope in Africa.* Grand Rapids.

Kaulem, D. (2011). *Ending violence in Zimbabwe.* AFCAST.

Makaudze, G., & Gudhlanga, E. (2015). Shona writers' vision of the liberation struggle: A name centred approach. *Open Access Library Journal, 2*(7), 1–8.

Manyonganise, M. (2015). Oppressive and liberative: An Zimbabwean woman's reflection of Ubuntu. *Verbum Et Ecclessia, 36*(2), 1–7.

Mkodzonge, G. (2020). The rise of Mashurugwi machete gangs and violent conflicts in Zimbabwe's artisanal and small-scale gold mining sector. *ELSEVIER, 7*(4), 1480–1489.

Mukoko, J. (2016). *The abduction and trial of Jestina Mukoko: The fight for human rights in Zimbabwe.* KMM Review Publishing.

Radford Ruether, R. (1998). *Women ad redemption: A theological history.* SCM Press.

Pongweni, A. J. C. (1983). *What's in a name: A study of Shona nomenclature.* Mambo Press.

Rutoro, E. (2012). Gender transformation and leadership: On teaching gender in Shona culture. In H. Jurgens et al. (Eds.), *Men in the pulpit, women in the pew, addressing gender inequality in Africa* (pp. 159–169). Thomas Nelson.

Tsungo, A. (2009). The professional trajectory of a human rights lawyer in Zimbabwe from 2000–2008. *Journal of Southern African Studies, 35*(4), 977–991.

CHAPTER 9

Voter Rights and Gender: An Analysis of the Importance of Voter Education in Zimbabwe

Lillian Mhuru

INTRODUCTION

The procedures used to choose candidates for positions in the government or political office are called elections (Zembere, 2020). They serve as the cornerstone of representative democracy and one of the legitimate methods for choosing presidents in a democratic country (Mapuva, 2019), and therefore, voter education is of paramount importance. Voter education, according to IDEA International Standards for Voter Education (2014), provides potential voters with the necessary information to make an informed choice in the voting booth. Voter education is therefore a crucial prerequisite for voters to express or shape their will because elections serve as the foundation upon which democratic improvements can be established. Therefore, well-run, impartial educational campaigns and the unrestricted spread of political party literature

---

L. Mhuru (✉)
Zimbabwe Open University, Harare, Zimbabwe
e-mail: leecalf@gmail.com

© The Author(s), under exclusive license to Springer Nature Switzerland AG 2023
E. Mavengano and S. Chirongoma (eds.), *Electoral Politics in Zimbabwe, Vol II*, https://doi.org/10.1007/978-3-031-33796-3_9

are necessary components of actual elections. In addition, it is argued by Moehler (2010) and Finkel and Smith (2011) that "voter knowledge and education are essential components in fostering public trust in any real democratic nation". Further, Moehler (2010) and Finkel and Smith (2011) all agree that a major obstacle to voter education efforts is establishing and maintaining public confidence in the electoral process. According to Kassilly and Onkware (2010), the aim of voter education is to make information available and approachable to all constituencies. Kramon (2016) asserts that in order to accomplish this effectively, it is necessary to engage both marginalized groups and mainstream voters. Voter education, for instance, ought to consider things like high electoral illiteracy rates or the translation of all voter education materials from English into 16 official languages in Zimbabwe.

According to Lieberman et al. (2014, pp. 69–80), "more work needs to be done to make voter education materials understandable for voters who are blind, illiterate, or only partially sighted". Voter education is viewed as an activity that increases public understanding of the election process, as well as the prerequisites and guidelines for voter registration, voting, and other electoral process components. Last but not least, voter information is frequently implemented as brief programmes that focus on certain electoral facts, providing voters with timely access to relevant factual information on a particular electoral process (International IDEA, 2016, p. 67). Making information visible and accessible to all people is the aim of voter education, according to Human Rights Watch (2018). Therefore, voter education initiatives should aim for complete coverage of the electorate, and in order to accomplish this successfully, it is necessary to include both disadvantaged populations and mainstream voters. Thus, special attention should be paid to minority populations, internally displaced people, and other marginalized societal groups. Publicity urging people to vote should be included in voter education programmes Human Rights Watch (2018). According to Human Rights Watch (2018), voter education should explicitly target women as well as men. It should emphasize that everyone has the right to vote and work to foster a culture where women are welcomed and encouraged to engage in politics.

Section 67(3) (a) of the Constitution of Zimbabwe Act 20 of 2013), declares that "every Zimbabwean citizen has the right to vote in all elections". Zimbabwe has also ratified international agreements including the Universal Declaration of Human Rights (1943) and the International

Covenant on Civil and Political Rights (1966) all of which firmly establish the democratic right to vote in elections. However, the most potent combination in Zimbabwean politics is made up of citizens who decide not to vote and electoral no-shows. Uneven voter education availability and high levels of electoral illiteracy, particularly among rural residents, contribute to the problem. Human Rights Watch (2018) contends that due to inadequate voter education and registration drives, elections in Africa, and particularly Zimbabwe, are frequently determined long before the actual voting takes place on the Election Day. Additionally, he claims that while "voter registration" has received more attention, "voter education", which offers unbiased, non-partisan information about the candidates and the issues at stake, about voting options, the fairness of the electoral process, and the value and significance of casting a ballot, has received disproportionately less attention (Human Rights Watch, 2018, p. 325). This study, therefore, seeks to show how voter education is important in Zimbabwe. It argues that some of the problems experienced in Zimbabwe and the low turnout of citizens during voting can be directly linked to the lack of voter education as well as the high level of electoral illiteracy specifically for people in rural areas. The researcher, however, acknowledges that Zimbabwe's literacy rate is at almost 96%, which is higher than that of other African countries, but the lack of knowledge about the electoral process makes it difficult for Zimbabweans to make informed decisions (Mapuva, 2013). Therefore, the present role of the Zimbabwe Electoral Commission is to ensure that rigorous voter education is done in all the provinces in Zimbabwe for mass political participation and the maintenance of sustainable social order in terms of Section 40B of the Electoral Act and 239(h) of the Constitution of Zimbabwe, respectively.

The study explores the role of the Zimbabwean Electoral Commission and the voting rights enshrined in the constitution that are being undermined by the lack of voter education. The author has chosen Zimbabwe as this is her country of origin. She is familiar with the political problems experienced in the country, most of which are caused by the lack of rigorous voter education. This has had a negative impact on the civil values and the full enjoyment of the voting rights and obligations of the people in Zimbabwe.

Theoretical Framework

The chapter is informed by the theory of participation in elections. According to the theory of election participation put forth by Feddersen and Sandroni (2006, pp. 1271–1282), "voting behavior under the plurality rule is largely compatible with the results of strategic voting". The theory claims that turnout is influenced by information levels (Howlett et al., 2010). The theory's main principle is the recognition that voters are driven by a feeling of civic duty, with the weight of the election placed on voters' preferences for the winner in relation to the costs of voting. Additionally, truthful, thorough, and intelligent account of current events in a context that gives them meaning should be provided by the media; it should act as a forum for the exchange of comments and criticism; it should present a representative image of the constituent groups in society; and it is the press' duty to present and make clear the society's concerns. In order to prepare the Zimbabwean populace for the general elections in 2023, voter education should be conducted rigorously to raise awareness among the people across all the 10 provinces of Zimbabwe. By making the media aware of its crucial role in preparing potential voters for active political engagement, the theory aids in the promotion of the democratic process of voting. The theory is thus, grounded as a method of studying the phenomenon of voter education, making it appropriate for this study as it emphasizes on increasing voter education and upholding democratic ideals.

Voter Rights and Elections in Zimbabwe

In Zimbabwe, citizens have the fundamental civic right to vote, which is an essential component of elections (Constitution of 2013's Section 67 (3) (a)). In addition, everyone has the right to participate in the government of their country, either directly or through freely chosen representations, according to Article 21 of the United Nations Charter on Human Rights. Therefore, this implies that the people's will should be the foundation of the authority of the government; this should be expressed in regular, legitimate elections, which should be by universal and equal suffrage and shall be conducted by secret ballot or by comparable free voting processes. In Zimbabwe, every Zimbabwean citizen over the age of eighteen (18) has the constitutional right to vote. This right is enshrined in the Zimbabwean Constitution of 2013, Universal Declaration of Human Rights as well as the entire body of international human rights law. Most countries accept these rights in theory, and they are at the foundation of several national constitutions. Voting is a formal expression of choice for a candidate for a specific office or for a proposed resolution to an issue affecting a single state or country and is one of the most important ways for individuals to influence government decision-making (Human Rights Watch, 2018, p. 324).

The United Nations General Assembly unanimously adopted the Universal Declaration of Human Rights in 1948, recognizing the critical role that transparent and open elections play in ensuring the fundamental right to participatory government. The International Covenant on Civil and Political Rights, the European Convention for the Protection of Human Rights, the Charter of the Organization of American States, the African (Banjul) Charter on Human and People's Rights, and several other international human rights documents all recognize the importance of periodic, free, and credible elections in ensuring political rights respect. The right to vote is widely acknowledged as a fundamental human right, but it is not fully enforced for millions of people worldwide, and Zimbabwe is not an exception. Article 25 of the International Covenant on Civil and Political Rights (ICCPR) is the most basic and fundamental international guarantee of voting rights and free elections, but it is closely related to other provisions especially Article 2, paragraph one which states, "....each state party to the present Covenant undertakes to respect and to ensure to all individuals within the territory and subject to its jurisdiction the right recognized in the covenant, without distinction of any kind, such as race, color, sex, language, religion, political or other opinion, national or social origin, property, birth or other status", and Article 25 states that:

> Every citizen shall have the right and opportunity, without any of the distinctions mentioned in Article 2 and without unreasonable restrictions;
>
> (a) To take part in the conduct of public affairs, directly or through freely chosen representatives;
> (b) To vote and to be elected at genuine periodic election which shall be by universal and equal suffrage and shall be held by secret ballot, guaranteeing the free expression of the will of the elections;
> (c) To have access, on general terms of equality, to public service in the country (ICCPR).

Zimbabwe is a signatory to Article 21 and a member of the UN. These provisions, which are codified in Article 2 of the ICCPR, state that "voting and participating in elections are fundamental freedoms that should not be restricted based on one's "status". Deeply flawed electoral systems result in the systematic and unintentional disenfranchisement of some people in Zimbabwe and around the world. For instance, Zimbabwe gained independence in 1980, and most of the elections are contested by the opposition parties questioning the credibility of the national elections citing a number of electoral fraud schemes that denied a number of voters the opportunity to support the candidate of their choice. This denial of voter rights, according to Solidarity Peace Trust (2018), can be seen in the 2018 election results which were highly contested. It goes further to say that "the opposition parties in Zimbabwe claimed that the elections had serious flaws and were marred by violence and vote rigging in some parts of the nation". As a result, the Solidarity Peace Trust (2018, para. 4) argues that "the process in no way reflects on the people of Zimbabwe's ability to plan and conduct successful elections" (2018). According to the analysis by Solidarity Peace Trust (2018), one comes to a conclusion that unjust electoral procedures constitute a systematic method or means of depriving voters of their rights.

As a result, Solidarity Peace Trust contends that "when voters realize that their voting rights cannot be protected or guaranteed, this usually results in voter apathy during elections". Thus, the majority of Zimbabweans are said to have no faith in their government, their democratic institutions, or their nation's ability to maintain a democratic trajectory going forward. This study therefore emphasizes the fact that voter rights are essential for any credible elections. Additionally, it is on the basis of this that the catchphrases "one man, one vote" and "votes must count" become a crucial component of electorate sensitization in Zimbabwe. Hence, this chapter was motivated by ZEC's failure to provide Zimbabwean voters with a thorough voter education programme.

Electoral Act of Zimbabwe: An Analysis

In accordance with Section 40B of the Electoral Act of Zimbabwe [Chapter 2:13], ZEC must provide "sufficient, accurate, and unbiased voter education". Section 40B(1)(b) requires ZEC to guarantee that voter education delivered by others is adequate, correct, and objective, in addition to confirming that other actors are permitted to deliver voter education while being supervised by ZEC. According to clause 40B (3), ZEC "may permit any person to assist it in conducting voter education". This suggests that ZEC may appoint representatives to assist it in providing voter education. However, ZEC in the process of appointing these representatives, it is accused of appointing partisan organizations or bodies: those that are aligned to the ruling party ZANU-PF. There are strict requirements for those who provide voter education: those who wish to do so must meet local identification requirements. Furthermore, participants must be "domiciled in Zimbabwe", either personally or through associations. This effectively excludes Zimbabweans living abroad. Companies must also seek ZEC's permission to ensure that their courses and materials are not deceptive or biased in favour of any political party. The instructors of voter education must be Zimbabweans, and ZEC must have their personal information. Additionally, local funding is required. ZEC must be informed of any proposed voter education initiatives' methods and funding sources. Foreign investment must be channelled through ZEC. Section 40E states that ZEC "may allocate" foreign funding to the service provider, implying that this decision is theirs. ZEC may choose to keep the money instead of distributing it, or if it does, it may choose to do so in a limited fashion. These clauses are simply too restrictive in addition to that. Section 40E requires ZEC to start a voter education programme a week after the election dates are announced. Although this does not prevent ZEC from carrying out its obligation to provide voter education at other times, in practice, ZEC has only begun programmes after the announcement of election dates. This shows that there is a small and ineffective window for voter education. Section 40E requires ZEC to supervise any voter education provided by third parties. If a provider does not follow ZEC's rules, ZEC has the power to stop them, and violations have repercussions. The accused provider of voter education, however, has a chance to be heard thanks to the law. Even though the Constitution's framework for voter education is adaptable and permissive, the Electoral Act's provisions are generally excessively intrusive and restrictive.

THE ROLE OF THE ZIMBABWE ELECTORAL COMMISSION

The Zimbabwe Electoral Commission is created by Section 238 of Zimbabwe's 2013 Constitution (ZEC). Additionally, Section 239 (a) of the Constitution outlines ZEC's constitutional duties, which include "preparing for, conducting, and supervising elections" (Constitution of Zimbabwe 2013). According to Section 239(b), ZEC is tasked with ensuring that elections are held "efficiently, freely, fairly, and transparently in accordance with the law". The ZEC, according to the Constitution, is "responsible for overseeing both voter registration and the compilation of voters' rolls". Since the Zimbabwe Electoral Commission is also in charge of voter education, including informing citizens of where and how to register to vote as well as other related issues, it is required by the Constitution to "report on the results of every election to Parliament". Further, the Zimbabwe's Constitution grants ZEC the "authority it needs to carry out these duties successfully". Therefore, voter education typically provides "information about the electoral process and why voting is significant" according to the ACE Project (2012). This means that "impartial and objective information is disseminated on what voters need to know in order to exercise their right to vote, such as what time the polls open and on what day, the offices that are being contested for and how to mark a valid ballot" (ACE Project, 2012, para. 5). It makes the point that an environment where free and fair elections cannot take place is created by a lack of voter education.

Voters must, therefore, be aware of their constitutional and election law-related rights and obligations in order to fulfil their duties in a responsible manner. According to Tuccinard (2014, p. 3), "voter education should nurture competent and responsible involvement". In his analysis, he goes on to say that "such involvement entails more than just trying to influence public policy". He emphasizes that "the basis of competent and responsible participation must be moral consideration, knowledge, and careful consideration". Additionally, Tuccinard (2014) contends that poorly designed or non-existent voter education programmes can cause integrity issues. In his opinion, voter education is expected to neutrally and factually inform voters so they can participate in elections with knowledge. Numerous researchers also address the significance of voter education. For instance, after it was discovered that only Shona and English were the preferred languages in Zimbabwe, the Zimbabwe Election Support Network (ZESN) (2022) expressed concern over the failure to use other ethnic languages in voter education and awareness campaigns. There are 16 official languages in the nation according to s6 of the Constitution of Zimbabwe, which include English, Chewa, Chibarwe, Kalanga, Khoisan, Nambya, Ndau, Ndebele, Shangani, Shona, sign language, Sotho, Tonga, Tswana, Venda, and

Xhosa. However, it also makes it clear that even in co-circumstances where Ndebele is the primary language, voter education messages were primarily conveyed through Shona and English. As a result, it believes that voter education and awareness campaigns in Zimbabwe are biased.

In their article, Rusinga (2021) point out that "the Zimbabwean harmonized general elections in 2008, 2013 and 2018 were marred by voting irregularities and primarily voter apathy". Furthermore, they contend that "there were heated political debates surrounding the practice of direct, formal, as well as indirect and informal voter education among various stakeholders" (Rusinga, 2021, p. 46). To resolve the issues, Rusinga (2021) suggested in their article that "ZEC and other stakeholders, such as Civil Society Organizations (CSOs) should develop a coordinated voter education programme". Additionally, Gumbo (2020), who was attempting to understand the role of Civil Society Organizations (CSOs) in the electoral process and the impact of CSOs on the electoral process and voter turnout, emphasizes the "significance of voter education" in her article titled *"A Critical Analysis of the Role of Civil Society in Zimbabwe's 2018 Harmonized Elections"*. Furthermore, she draws the conclusion from her research that "CSO participation in pre-, during-, and post-election interventions in Zimbabwe helped to improve the electoral process and increase voter turnout" (Gumbo, 2020, p. 327). The 2018 research that was carried out by Human Rights Watch highlights the "significance of voter education in Zimbabwe". It stresses the "necessity of full citizen participation in the political process, freedom of association, tolerance, equal access to the state media for all political parties, independence of the judiciary, independence of the media, impartiality of the electoral institutions, and voter education given that Zimbabwe is a signatory to the Southern African Development Community (SADC) Principles and Guidelines Governing Democratic Elections" (Human Rights Watch, 2018, para.10). Therefore, according to Transparency International, 2017, "voters' list, and how to deal with irregularities in voter information should be a defining characteristic of free and fair elections in Zimbabwe" (Transparency International, 2017, para. 3).

The Electoral Act's provisions that place restrictions on "who can provide voter education to the public were among the challenging restrictions on voter education in Zimbabwe" that were mentioned in the article that Southern Africa Litigation Centre published. According to Sections 40C (1) (g) and 40C (2) of the Electoral Act, the Zimbabwe

Electoral Commission must provide or approve all voter education materials (ZEC). Political parties, which are partisan by definition, are exempt from this requirement. Aside from that, Sections 40C (1) (h) and 40F forbid the use of foreign funds for voter education. However, as part of the plan, ZEC is permitted to accept donations from abroad for the purpose of voter education and then distribute those funds to outside organizations. In the case of Veritas v. Zimbabwe Electoral Commission & 2 Others, HC 11749/17. 10 MAH 2018, these provisions were contested. Veritas (2018, para. 8) claimed that "these restrictions violate the fundamental right to freedom of expression because they effectively give the state a monopoly on speech and amount to unjustified prior restraint". Additionally, Veritas (2018) contends that "even though the right to free speech is not unqualified, these limitations are inadmissible in a democratic society". Furthermore, Veritas (2018) claims that "the provisions in this case violate the rights of the general public to equality, free and fair elections, access to information and ideas, and the freedom to make informed electoral decisions". Therefore, the Zimbabwean Parliament passed the Electoral Amendment Act 2018, in May 2018 in response to this legal challenge, repealing section 40F of the Electoral Act but leaving in place section 40C (1) (h). As a result, 40C (1) (h) became "meaningless" because s40F was repealed. Given the current gap in the law, the Applicant, as well as the Second and Third Respondents, concurred at the hearing that "the Court should strike down 40C (1) (h)". However, the government persisted in defending the restrictions set forth in sections 40C (1) (g) and 40C (2), and on 27 June 2018, the case was dismissed without consideration of the merits by the court. Due to Veritas' lack of *loca standi* to bring the case before the court, the court dismissed the application.

The Role of Civil Society Organizations in Voter Education

In accordance with Section 40B (3) of the Zimbabwean Constitution, ZEC "may enable any person to assist it in conducting voter education". This implies that ZEC "may choose representatives to assist it in offering voter education". These agents are primarily "groups with an electoral focus" in accordance with Section 40B (3). These participants in terms of Section 40B (3) are "part of a number of CSOs in Zimbabwe that come under various aegis, including the Crisis in Zimbabwe Coalition, the Zimbabwe Election Support Network, and churches". To support credible, inclusive, and transparent elections, the CSOs operating under their aegis take part in voter education and the electoral process. The Electoral Commission in Zimbabwe, however, has the ultimate responsibility for the CSO's provision of voter education. Therefore, with ZEC's approval, civil society organizations can offer voter education. According to Gumbo's (2020) research, CSOs help to increase voter registration by disseminating information about the Biometric Voter Registration (BVR) activity across the nation. To qualify for voter education, "these CSOs must be locally supported and reveal their financial sources to ZEC" according to Gumbo (2020, p. 327). This makes their participation in voter education problematic. Furthermore, ZEC "may allocate" the foreign funds to the service provider at its "discretion" in accordance with section 40E of the constitution, which results in the exclusion of a number of CSOs. This ultimately makes it more difficult for voter education to spread across the entire nation as Gumbo (2020) puts it.

CREDIBLE ELECTIONS AND ELECTORAL ILLITERACY IN ZIMBABWE: THE NEED FOR RIGOROUS VOTER EDUCATION

Citizens have the right and duty to decide who should rule them and how they should be governed. "Voter education" therefore according to Denver and Hands (1990, pp. 263–279), is "crucial" when people are making decisions of this nature. In other words, Denver and Hands (1990, pp. 263–279) contend that "electoral literacy" is the "knowledge of fundamental ideas and details required to understand the topics covered in public discourse". Therefore, "setting goals for self-government, understanding global dynamics, and becoming informed about voting processes and procedures are all necessary for citizens" (Denver & Hands, 1990, pp. 263–279). The goal of electoral literacy is to "enable informed electoral participation and decision-making". According to Denver and Hands' (1990, pp. 263–279) observations, the electorate in the majority of Third World nations, particularly those in Africa, lacks the necessary electoral literacy. As a result, ZEC needs to "invest more of its resources in voter education" according to Gumbo (2020). She further argues that "the inability of voters to comprehend the full significance of their participation in elections is referred to as electoral illiteracy" (Gumbo, 2020, p. 325). Additionally, she stresses that "the inability of voters (the electorate) to challenge the electoral process in the event of electoral irregularities is another manifestation of electoral illiteracy" (Gumbo, 2020, p. 325). Therefore, electoral illiteracy becomes apparent if voters' rights are violated during an election and can be used as leverage, undermining the validity of the results, according to Gumbo (2020, p. 326). In addition to making it more difficult for people to vote on Election Day, electoral illiteracy also makes it more difficult for them to engage with the issue, comprehend the mechanisms at work, and have faith in the fairness of the electoral system as Gumbo (2020) concurs with Human Rights Watch (2018, para. 4). Therefore, "levels of participation" will remain low when people are "unfamiliar with the electoral process and unable to become familiar with it". Additionally, there will be a large number of votes that are cast "improperly" or a "lack of confidence" in the fairness of the elections or the validity of the results (UJAH Volume 21, No.1, 2020, p. 35).

Furthermore, despite the fact that parties in Zimbabwe are permitted to employ polling agents to staff polling places, "most of the agents in the 2008, 2013 and 2018 elections" were simply chosen for the position without any "formal education" or "training" based on their "loyalty" to their respective political parties, meaning that according to Veritas (2018), "they had no idea what they were expected to do". Further, Norris (2014) broadens the definition of electoral illiteracy to include "voters' inability to challenge electoral procedures when there are anomalies". Additionally, "sham elections are always the result of widespread electoral manipulation in situations where voters lack knowledge of their electoral systems" as Norris (2014) asserts. For instance, Gumbo (2020, p. 325) concurs with Norris (2014, p. 260) as they contend that "traditional chiefs, headmen, and kraal heads in Zimbabwe use their influence to persuade the majority of rural voters to support the ruling party, Zimbabwe African Union - Patriotic Front". In the elections of 2008 and 2018, according to Gumbo (2020, p. 324), "traditional chiefs intimidated registered voters by ordering residents in their constituencies to bring the serial numbers of the ballots they used to the local traditional leadership for a potential follow-up on who they would have voted for". Therefore, "due to their lack of electoral literacy, citizens were intimidated and harassed, according to Zembere" (2021). Zembere (2021) further assets that "about 40% of voters in rural areas gave their respective traditional leaders the serial numbers of their ballot papers". Therefore, Zembere

(2020, p. 60) argues that "it can be inferred that the majority of Zimbabwe's rural population cast ballots out of concern that their votes would be tracked down and, therefore, for candidates they did not prefer". A good example is the incident that was reported in Kubatana (2022), where Presiding Officer Nokuthula Sibanda was observed assisting a 90-year-old male voter in the March 2022 by-elections at Mhlali Primary School in Magwegwe. Voter intimidation, politically motivated violence, and the partisanship of the army and police, who are supposed to be impartial, have all been common in Zimbabwe's elections despite the presence of international observers (Zembere, 2020).

Kubatana (2022) also expressed concern about "Zimbabwe's poor voter education". Taking into consideration that the number of people who were turned away from various polling stations in Bulawayo during the March 26, 2022 by-elections, Kubatana (2022) claims that "it was evident that little was done to educate voters". Most people, according to Kubatana (2022), "were turned away for having copies of their national identity cards (IDs), while others had their driver's licenses with them and some were not even listed as voters on the voters' list". An example was given by Kubatana (2022) of a Pumula resident who had actually brought in their card as a war veteran. According to Kubatana (2020), "the Zimbabwean Electoral Commission (ZEC), political parties, and community organizations failed to effectively conduct voter education campaigns to lower the number of people turned away for lacking proper identification". These factors, according to observers who took part in a CITE Twitter and Facebook space during the time of the elections, "show that voter education lacked in Zimbabwe, demonstrating the need for more civic education in communities so that people are aware of the conditions necessary to be able to vote" Kubatana (2022). The people on these social sites argued that "the commission should regularly conduct voter education campaigns as part of civic education instead of waiting until the very last minute, particularly as the nation prepares for national elections in 2023".

Conclusion and Recommendations

Lack of voter education and electoral illiteracy have been identified in this study as two key reasons for Zimbabwe's electoral challenges. Citizens with limited electoral knowledge are more susceptible to overt electoral manipulation, rendering democratic rights useless. ZEC must therefore begin creating a voter education curriculum that will be made accessible in each of Zimbabwe's provinces. Initiatives to educate voters can therefore assist those who lack electoral literacy. As a result, the voters and citizens will gain self-confidence and be better equipped to handle big life changes and challenges like bullying, discrimination, and electoral fraud. People will thus have a voice and be able to positively impact society as a whole. The voter education being promoted include some crucial components like:

- Knowledge and Understanding: Voters and citizens must have a basic understanding of concepts like democracy, justice, equality, freedom, authority, and the rule of law. They also have knowledge of laws and rules, the democratic process, the media, human rights, diversity, money and the economy, and sustainable development.
- Skills and aptitude: Critical thinking skills include problem-solving, issue analysis, objective opinion expression, active participation in discourse and debate, negotiation, conflict resolution, and electoral and social action.
- Values and dispositions: Respect for justice, democracy, and the rule of law; openness; tolerance; the courage to stand up for one's beliefs; and the willingness to pay attention to, collaborate with, and support others (International Journal of Humanities and Social, 2011). The Voter Education Curriculum will also make voter education active, interactive, relevant, critical, collaborative, and participatory, bringing out the best in every citizen as a moral agent of transformation endowed with the qualities to fulfil humanity's purpose on earth with regards to democracy, politics, and elections. Additionally, it is advised that ZEC provide adequate information regarding voting procedures, particularly regarding the confidentiality of the vote.
- Political parties and CSOs may take part in voter education under the Electoral Act with the ZEC's approval. The ZEC's outreach materials are used by a small number of CSOs, though. In rare instances, some CSOs employ their own resources and ZEC-approved methods. A number of interested parties claim that they were deterred from taking part because they found the current Electoral Act provisions on voter education to be overly restrictive. The Zimbabwe Election Support Network's Policy Brief from 2017

states that ZEC needs to permit a larger number of voter education providers in order to increase voter education participation. The following are the three options presented to ZEC in this brief:

- to conduct voter education on its own,
- to conduct voter education with specially selected assisting organizations, and
- to open up voter education to a broader group of independent voter education providers.

As a result, ZEC will use its position as a supervisor to encourage rather than prevent other groups from educating voters. In order to strengthen ZEC's ability to conduct thorough voter education, it is advised that CSO involvement in voter education be increased in Zimbabwe.

References

ACE Project. (2012). *Civic and voter education*. The Electoral Knowledge Network.
Denver, D., & Hands, G, (1990, April). Does studying politics make a difference? The political knowledge, attitudes and perceptions of school students. *British Journal of Political Science, 20*(2), 263–279. Cambridge University Press.
Dewa, D. (2014). The voter education "ghost" in Zimbabwean harmonised elections of 2008 and 2013: What can be done? Case of Midlands, Gweru District. *International Journal of Research in Humanities and Social Studies, 5*(2), 20–40.
Electoral Act of Zimbabwe [Chapter 2:13].
Feddersen, T., & Sandroni, A. (2006, September). A theory of participation in elections. *The American Economic Review, 96*(4), 1271–1282.
Finkel, S. E., & Smith, A. E. (2011). Civic education, political discussion and the social transmission of democratic knowledge and values in a new democracy: Kenya 2002. *American Journal of Political Science, 55*(2), 417–435.
Giroux, H. A. (2015). *Theory and resistance in education: A pedagogy for the opposition*. Bergin & Garvey.
Gumbo, O. (2020). A critical analysis of the role of civil society in Zimbabwe's 2018 harmonized elections. *Open Journal of Electoral Science, 10*(2).
Heater, D. (2017). *Citizenship: The civic ideal in world history, politics and education*. Manchester University Press.
Howlett, M., Craft, J., & Zibrik, L. (2010). Government communication and democratic governance: Electoral and policy-related information campaigns in Canada. *Policy and Society, 29*(1), 13–22.

Human Rights and Elections. (2017). *United Nations handbook on the legal, technical and human rights aspects of elections.*

International Covenant on the Civil and Electoral, adopted by the General Assembly Resolution 2200A (XXI) of 16 December 1966.

International IDEA. (2016). *Electoral management design: The international IDEA handbook.* International IDEA.

International IDEA. (2020). *Engaging the electorate: Initiatives to promote voter turnout from around the world.* International IDEA.

Kassilly, B. J. N., & Onkware, K. (2010). Struggles and success in engendering the African public sphere: Kenyan women in politics. *Kenya Studies Review, 3*(3), 71–83.

Kramon, E. (2016). Electoral handouts as information: Explaining unmonitored vote buying. *World Politics, 68*(3), 454–498.

Kubatana. (2022, March 26). *Concern over low voter education.* Available at https://kubatana.net/2022/03/26/concern-over-low-voter-education/. Last accessed 7 June 2023.

Lieberman, E. S., Posner, D. N., & Tsai, L. L. (2014). Does information lead to more active citizenship? Evidence from an education intervention in rural Kenya. *World Development, 60,* 69–83.

Mapuva, J. (2013). Enhamcing citizen participation through civic action, 1997–2010. *International NGO Journal, 8*(6), 117–130.

Mapuva, J. (2018). Militarization of public Institutions, flawed electoral processes and curtailed citizen participation. *Journal of Legislative Studies, 16*(4), 460–475.

Mapuva, J., & Miti, G. P. (2019). Exploring the uncharted territory of devolution in Zimbabwe. *Africanus: Journal of Development Studies, 49*(1), 10–25.

Masunungure, E. (2016). The 'menu of manipulation' and the 2013 Zimbabwe elections: Towards explaining the 'technical knockout'. *Journal of Elections, 21*(1), 20–40.

Moehler, D. C. (2010). Democracy, governance, and randomized development assistance. *The ANNALS of the American Academy of Political and Social Science, 628*(1), 30–46.

Moore, H. M. (2013). *Public value governance: Moving beyond traditional public administration and the new public management.* Routledge.

Norris, P. (2014). *Why electoral integrity matters.* Cambridge University Press.

Norris, P. (2019). *Why electoral integrity matters.* Cambridge University Press.

Raftopoulos, B. (2018). The 2018 elections in Zimbabwe: The end of an era. *Journal of Southern African Studies, 39*(4), 15–39.

Research Advocacy Unit. (2016, February). *A valedictory for civil society in Zimbabwe.* Research & Advocacy.

Research Advocacy Unit. (2016, February). *Are former liberation movements inherently violent as governments?* Research & Advocacy Unit.
Rusinga, R. (2021). Zimbabwe's 2018 harmonised elections an assessment of credibility. *Journal of African Elections, 20*, 90. https://doi.org/10.20940/JAE/2021/v20i1a5
Somin, I. (2017). *Democracy and electoral ignorance.* Cato Unbound. Constitution of Zimbabwe of 2013.
Tuccinard, D. (2014). *International obligations for elections: Guidelines for legal framework.* Stockholm, International IDEA.
Universal Declaration of Human Rights, adopted by the United Nations General Assembly on 10 December 1948.
Zembere, M. (2018). *Democratic citizenship education in Zimbabwe and its implications for teaching and learning.* Sun Scolar. Stellenbosch University.
Zembere, M. (2020). Electoral illiteracy and democratic citizenship in Zimbabwe. *Unizik Journal of Arts and Humanities, 21*(1), 54–70.
Zembere, M. (2021). Reconceptualisation of democratic citizenship education against social inequalities and electoral violence in Zimbabwe. *International Journal of Curriculum Development and Learning Measurement, 2*(2), 1–9.
Zimbabwe Electoral Support Network. (2016). *ZESN condemns vote buying and intimidation in Chimanimani West.* Harare.
Zimbabwe Electoral Support Network. (2017). *Enhancing citizen participation in electoral processes through voter education.* Zimbabwe.
Zimbabwe Election Support Network (ZESN). (2022, July 26). *Press statement.* Available at https://www.zesn.org.zw/zimbabwe-election-support-network-ballot-newsletter-elections-bulletin/pressstatement/5875/38/38/09/26/07/2022/ashley/. Last accessed 7 June 2023.

Internet Sources

Human Rights Watch. (2018, June 7). *Zimbabwe: Lack of reform risks credible elections.* Available at https://www.hrw.org/news/2018/06/07. Last accessed 7 June 2023.
International IDEA, Civic and Voter Education. Available at https://www.veritaszim.net/sites/veritas_d/files/IDEA%20International%20Standards%20for%20Voter%20Education%202014.pdf. Last accessed 8 February 2023.
Kubatana. Zimbabwe By-Elections March 2022. Available at https://www.kubatana.net/news/2022/003/22/zimbabwe-by-election-March-2022. Last accessed 8 February 2023.
Solidarity Peace Trust Zimbabwe. (2018). *The 2018 elections and their aftermath.* Available at http://www.solidaritypeacetrust.org/cgi-bin/dada/mail.cgi/archive/mailings/20180930192638/. Last accessed 7 February 2023.
Veritas, In the High court of Zimbabwe case no. hc/17 held at Harare available at. Last accessed 8 February 2023.

PART II

Media and Electoral Politics in Zimbabwe

CHAPTER 10

Polytricking or Political Contestation? The Digital Space as Alternative Public Sphere in the Run up to the 2023 Public Elections in Zimbabwe

Collen Sabao and Theophilus Tinashe Nenjerama

INTRODUCTION

The growth of social media in the digital space over the last two decades has allowed for the proliferation of a multiplicity of platforms where contestations on almost all facets of human existence are debated and interrogated. Within an environment in which in most countries, fundamental freedoms such as the freedom of expression and freedom of the media are gagged, these platforms have emerged as an alternative form of what Jürgen Habermas (1991) theorises as public sphere—the

C. Sabao (✉)
Department of Humanities and Arts, University of Namibia,
Windhoek, Namibia
e-mail: csabao@unam.na

T. T. Nenjerama
Columbia Theological Seminary, Decatur, GA, USA

alternative digital public sphere (Mpofu, n.d.; Sabao & Chikara, 2020; Sabao & Chingwaramusee, 2017). This sphere allows for the expression of political/ideological expressions, dissent and protestations to proliferate—away and free from the gaze of law enforcement, while at the same time providing users with the security of anonymity, if they so choose or need it. These social networking sites "have also become quite central as alternative public spheres, breaking stories before the mainstream official media does. The impact that such social networks have on contemporary society as platforms for group social interactions and news outlets should not be undermined" (Sabao & Chikara, 2018, p. 20). They have thus, become alternative sources of news and platforms for unrestricted and uncensored debate on all aspects of life. The chapter examines the divergent discourses surrounding the challenges faced by opposition political parties and actors, such as the Nelson Chamisa-led opposition political party, Citizens Coalition for Change (CCC) (potentially the current biggest threat to the existing ZANU PF hegemony) in campaign communication in mainstream media as the nation heads towards the 2023 plebiscite. Social media threads on Twitter evince a proliferation of discourses that ideologically promote and denigrate the CCC and opposition politics alike, and of interest, as representing the plurality of voices, are individual accounts of persons such as Fadzai Mahere, Hopewell Chin'ono, ZANU PF Patriots, Nick Mangwana, Jonathan Moyo, Saviour Kasukuwere and many others. These present interesting evidence of political contestations that would otherwise not proliferate in the absence of the alternative digital sphere of social media because of the stringent and tilted political playfield that Zimbabwean politics represents.

The Zimbabwean Political Space in the Last Few Decades

Zimbabwean governance politics in the last four decades have been characterised by the quashing of any form of opposition to the ruling Zimbabwe African National Union Patriotic Front (ZANU PF), even through the use of the military. Zimbabwe became independent from her British colonial masters on 18 April 1980. This was after two notably protracted armed guerrilla wars fought against the erstwhile former coloniser—the First Chimurenga and the Second Chimurenga. On the official day of independence, Robert Gabriel Mugabe (then leader of

ZANU PF) was inaugurated as the Prime Minister of the newly independent Zimbabwe. Since independence from British settler rule in 1980 up to the late 1990s, Zimbabwe had predominantly been a one-party state under ZANU PF rule. The former and now late president, Robert Gabriel Mugabe, until his ousting through what has been dubbed a "soft coup" or "smart military coup" in November 2017, was Zimbabwe's authoritarian leader for nearly 40 years. His tenure was characterised, until the early 2000s, by little, if any, meaningful opposition and calculated quashing, even through military means, of any threats to his and ZANU PF political hegemony.

Political violence, repression, electoral theft and deceit have characterised the political space in Zimbabwe for quite some time. This has largely evinced itself through the calculated silencing of opposition political forces—including the banning of their advertisements on public owned media, banning political rallies and general stifling of the political space (Chibuwe, 2017; Makumbe, 2002). This toxic political culture still thrives in the post-Mugabe era. The major excuse for ZANU PF's autocratic desire for the elimination of all opposition forces has been the 'preservation of the gains of the liberation struggles'—and all opposition politics and political actors were, in ZANU PF discourses, labelled as "western puppets and harbouring a regime change agenda in Zimbabwe" (Sabao, 2013). This narrative is arguably meant for self-preservation and to de-legitimise other political contenders (Moyo & Mavengano, 2021; Muchemwa, 2010; Ndlovu-Gatsheni, 2009; Ndlovu-Gatsheni & Ruhanya, 2020). The birth of the Movement for Democratic Change (MDC) in 1999, which represented the fiercest opposition against Mugabe and ZANU PF since independence, has continued to haunt ZANU PF. The political inroads made by the then newly formed MDC in the 2000 plebiscite, in which it won a resounding historic 57 of the possible 120 seats in parliament, represented a serious political threat that managed to shake the ZANU PF political hegemony. To date, such a feat is still unmatched in Zimbabwean politics by the MDC or any other political party. Through the machinations of ZANU PF operatives, the MDC has over the years suffered from serious infiltration, resulting in divisions fanned by factionalism. These, however, can also to some extent be accounted for by internal power struggles within the opposition party ranks.

Since the successes of the MDC on the Zimbabwe political scene, national politics participation has been tempting and inviting for other political actors, and as such, the last decade has borne witness to the birth of several new political parties as well as breakaway factions from the mainstream political parties—especially within the opposition ranks (Chibuwe, 2017; Makumbe, 2002). The ZANU PF government has, however, always found strategies and ways to quash any dissenting voices—especially by denying them the public communicative space for their voices to be heard. Through this process, ZANU PF has been able to sustain a troubling state monologic narrative that militates against what, in Bakhtinian formulation of dialogic discourse, is imagined as the creation of polyphonic political space, which is aligned with democratic political practices. The ZANU PF government has over the years tactfully always ensured that opposition political parties would not make inroads in communicating with the electorate through the traditional means of mass communication such as public broadcasters, public newspapers and public political campaigns. Political rallies in Zimbabwe require prior police clearance, and opposition political parties have always historically been denied such clearance. Resultantly, they have failed to launch successful political campaigns. Furthermore, because the ZANU PF government was, for the longest time, the sole operator of radio and television in Zimbabwe, the opposition parties were never granted access to flight advertisements on these public media platforms. These mechanisms of political silencing thus, necessitated a rethinking of methods of raising dissent and political communication. Social media, thus, became an avenue for the dissemination of political messages that the government would have otherwise censored in, and culled out from mainstream public media. While a new phenomenon to Zimbabwe and Zimbabwean politics, the impact and communicative potential of social media as an alternative public sphere has been well embraced (Sabao & Chikara, 2018). However, the joys of this freedom might not last for long, especially considering the recent promulgation by the ZANU PF government, of two news laws in Zimbabwe, the Cyber and Data Protection Act of 2021 (which monitors and restricts usage of the cyber-space) and the Patriotic Act of 2023 (which criminalises any criticism of the government on any platform).

The desire by the ZANU PF government to gag information flow and the proliferation of the plurality of opinions in Zimbabwe is largely hinged on their desire to shield the spread of narratives of its mismanagement of the country from the world public gaze. The last two and half decades have witnessed a collapse in both the nation and national affairs. Evidence of such is observed from the unstable political and socio-economic environments, characterised by economic meltdown, the maiming of all those politically opposed to the ZANU PF hegemony and incessant droughts (Sabao, 2016). The observed general collapse of state affairs in Zimbabwe was a culmination from a diverse number of factors, chief among them despotic political tendencies by the ZANU PF government, disregard of the rule of law, hyperinflation, political intolerance as well as the violent land grabs of 1999 (Matondi & Rutherford, 2021; Mkodzongi, 2018; Mlambo, 2005; Sabao & Chikara, 2018). The combination of these factors resulted in a complete political and economic meltdown. The economic sanctions from the European Union (EU) and the United States of America (USA) in 2008 further complicated the political and economic landscapes in Zimbabwe (Mlambo, 2005; Sabao, 2018).

Confronted with a runaway economy and a plethora of problems that pointed towards the collapse of the economy—signalling the dismal incompetence of the ZANU PF government—a host of mechanisms were put in place to gag the reporting of the 'reality on the ground'. Instead, ZANU PF went on a campaign to sell some political rhetoric that would project them in a good light (Southall, 2013). So highly pronounced was the victim disposition through which ZANU PF blamed the dysfunctionality of the nation state on factors external to it, such as the EU and US imposed sanctions. In the process, ZANU PF has sought to blame opposition political parties for conniving with the West to promote regime change agendas. In this false context, ZANU PF has sought to expunge any opposition activities, through for example, stifling all mass communication attempts by opposition political parties and actors through traditional mass media channels. Such a volatile political and economic state of affairs opened up the political scene and demanded aggressive political strategies for survival. The major political parties needed to gear up and rethink political strategies. Campaign strategies had to be rethought and revisited. New forms of political ideological tools had to be invented—and the digital space became the immediate choice. However, as demonstrated in later sections, the ZANU PF government still found ways to quash this through the promulgation of draconian and restrictive laws such as the Cyber and Data Protection Act of 2021 and the Patriotic Act of 2023 which criminalise the sharing of online content deemed to be seditious and anti-government.

The (Mis)Regulation of the Mass Media in Zimbabwe: Election Coverage and Challenges

A sizeable amount of critical scholarship currently exists which seeks to examine and analyse the (mis)regulation of the Zimbabwean media in reporting political, socio-political and economic issues—especially in the wake of the political dynamics that emerged from the year 2000, when the MDC emerged as a remarkable opposition political party. The birth of the MDC and its attendant victories in the 2000 national plebiscite hogged the media's attention to political issues. The MDC provided Zimbabweans with an alternative to the traditionally ZANU PF one-party state governance. Through the use of mass public media platforms, the MDC managed to sell itself well, drawing the attention and editorial sympathy of the private-owned mass media. Inevitably, this resulted in the 'worst' form of media plurality the country had/has ever witnessed after the attainment of independence (Mano, 2005; Sabao, 2013, 2016) in which the public and private media reported at parallels. However, the bulk of this scholarship has been historically observed to have taken the form of watchdog reports of the media representations published periodically. While some have attempted to be critical to some extent, the majority of such studies have evinced themselves as more confined to mere content analyses of the Zimbabwean public media and its plurality along political ideological lines (Chibuwe, 2017; Mutsvairo, 2015; Sabao, 2013). One major concern that such scholarship has extensively covered is the issue of 'voices' in news reporting. The concept examines the sections of society that are represented in the media. In our case, we assess the political actors and parties whose voices have been incorporated in some of this critical scholarship, as well as in the media. The majority of this corpus has, however, failed to do this with such detail as to reveal the dialectic nature of media discourse, that is, to show how such media representations affect the reading positions assumed by the readership as well as how such representations are an ideological tool for agenda-setting. In other words, they fail to evince how the journalistic ideological biases in newspapers affect the reading positions of the electorate.

The advent of web-based platforms, imagined in this paper as the alternative digital public sphere, has provided Zimbabweans with "an avenue to discuss a taboo subject in Zimbabwe without fear or being reprimanded by the secretive and authoritarian state" (Sabao & Chikara, 2018). As far as this is concerned, the 'tabooed' issues in this context refer to issues that the ZANU PF-led government does not want to discuss in public like the government's ineptitude, election rigging/theft, electoral malpractice, corruption, the ailing economy and state of medical facilities in Zimbabwe or the levels of unemployment and state-sponsored corruption, just to mention a few. We thus, here in this chapter, discuss the manners in which the internet has challenged these ZANU PF elitist-dominated domestic public spheres and created a sphere where ordinary citizens interact among themselves and those in power (Mpofu, n.d.). Moyo (2007), reflecting on this condition and how it birthed the rise of a communal reliance on the digital alternative media in Zimbabwe, opines that:

> Restricted democratic space has spawned a multiplicity of alternative public spheres that enable groups and individuals to continue to participate and engage in the wider debate on the mutating crisis gripping the country since the turn of the century… the diaspora are creatively exploiting new media to resist state propaganda churned out through the mainstream media. (p. 81)

Following the challenge to such a one-party hegemony by the Movement for Democratic Change (MDC) in 1999, the ZANU PF government realised the need to hold on to power by all means necessary. Part of such measures was a stringent gag on the free flow of information, especially within the traditional media of broadcast and print news sources (within which, ironically, the state had a huge controlling state—being the sole television and radio broadcaster and owning one of the largest circulating national daily newspapers). The ZANU PF government thus ensured that the flow of information within the country and outside was highly regulated and constricted. This resulted in the deliberate targeting of organisations and persons thought to be spreading anti-ZANU PF rhetoric and ensuring that the bulk of the news in circulation was largely, more than often, bordering on government propaganda. In order to guarantee that there would be no counterbalancing of the propagandistic news in circulation, the ZANU PF government initiated "measures that made it extremely impossible to register news reporting mediums such as newspapers and radio stations. Such restrictive media laws included the Access to Information and Protection of Privacy Act (AIPPA) and the Public Order and Security Act (POSA) which were promulgated and were used together with previously existing laws such as the Official Secrets Act (OSA) and the Broadcasting Services Act (BSA)" (Sabao & Chikara, 2018, p. 24).

This invariably gave birth to the rise of a largely web-based wave of protest movements. The desire to formulate and freely circulate counternarratives to the propagandised news proliferated by the 'despotic' ZANU PF government birthed the need to (re)formulate innovative ways of communicating counteractive information to the general public in order to give them a semblance of balance in the news. As such,

> A broad range of activities by the populace under the banner citizen journalism has also been deployed to counter the state metanarrative and of course in some cases to affirm it. Thus, citizen journalism has played an important role in shaping political attitudes, altering the boundaries of political interaction and bringing into existence new methods and channels for resistance since the build up to the 2008 elections and 2013 elections. (Mujere & Mwatwara, 2015, p. 216)

The power of the mass media, imagined as the fourth pillar of the state in shaping public opinion, and by extension changes that could occur within any given society within the political, socio-economic and social spaces should never be downplayed. Undemocratic governments are always awake to this potential power of the media and are always keen on controlling the flow of information—both the channels through which the information flows and the content of such. As Sabao and Chikara (2018, p. 24) observe, "[t]he high proliferation of a diversity of free speech and opinions is anathema to the sustenance of despotic political hegemonies". As such, faced with a credibly serious threat in the shape of the MDC opposition, the ZANU PF government was quick to realise that the control of the media was paramount to its continued existence. Inevitably, it followed that draconian media regulating measures in the form of laws such as the Access to Information and Protection of Privacy Act (AIPPA) and the Public Order and Security Act (POSA) were promulgated. In the years to come, the Cyber and Data Protection Act of 2021 and the Patriotic Act of 2023 will certainly be the go-to laws for ZANU PF for such media gagging practices.

Such stringent laws, which are additions to the previously existing laws such as the Official Secrets Act (OSA) and the Broadcasting Services Act (BSA) made it further impossible for the proliferation of freedom of expression in Zimbabwe. Many Zimbabweans thus begun seeking for alternative news from web-based channels, especially those on social media platforms. These seemed to offer more diverse reportage of news from, about and in Zimbabwe. The embrace of these alternative digital web-based alternative spaces/providers of news can largely be credited to being the major influence for how, in part, Zimbabweans embraced the 'new' trend of citizen or participatory journalism. Mujere and Mwatwara (2015, p. 216) opine in this regard that,

> ...Zimbabweans have reacted to the narrowing of the democratic space by resorting to subterranean methods. Thus...a narrow media in Zimbabwe incubated the rise of citizen journalism'. It became clearer that the majority of Zimbabweans began to use the internet not only as consumers but rather as 'prosumers' of information. 'Their status as 'prosumers' gives them freedom, power and a voice to speak up to authority and generate content.

For most Zimbabweans during this period and beyond, the internet offered an alternative digital public sphere where ordinary citizens could "meet" (virtually, of course) and discuss issues they are not typically able to discuss within the ZANU PF government-controlled public spheres. This is due to the promulgation and existence of regimes of control which make it impossible to have open discussion on topics of governance, maladministration, the economy as well as political participation which have been tabooed (Moyo, 2007; Mpofu, n.d.). In addition, the fact that the Zimbabwean public media, which was largely government controlled, was stifling vibrant debate that speaks against state programmes meant that people were technically, perpetually in the dark. As a measure to circumvent this, the internet has emerged as "a forum for power, voice and self-expression, and has made it possible for debate and tensions between the elite and ordinary people to be experienced in a typical Habermasian public sphere fashion online" (Mpofu, n.d., p. 7). This was especially so in the aftermath of the 2013 harmonised elections—marred by the biggest clampdown on opposition political parties and the haunting and taunting of the general electorate by the ZANU PF machinery.

The Post-2013 Zimbabwean Crisis and Protest Actions

In Zimbabwe, the post-2013 harmonised elections period was characterised by the re-emergence of challenges and problems akin to those that had previously led to what has come to be regarded as the 'Zimbabwean crisis' (Raftopoulos, 2006), whose peak was ideally in the year 2008. This period, dubbed the 'Zimbabwean crisis' spanning between 1999 and 2008, represents some of the darkest times that Zimbabwe as a country has gone through. It was a period characterised by a runaway economy, hyperinflation, political intolerance and maiming, the breakdown of international relations between Zimbabwe and 'the world', high levels of unemployment and many other challenges—all of which coalesced to reflect a very serious level of corruption and misgovernance (Ndlovu-Gatsheni, 2009; Ndlovu-Gatsheni & Ruhanya, 2020; Rusvingo, 2014). The period thus witnessed "the emergence and engagement of labour movement, activist groups, and the MDC as alternatives challenging the excesses of ZANU-PF" (Nenjerama & Sabao, n.d.).

The Zimbabwean national environment, characterised by poor governance, political intolerance and the refusal to implement electoral reforms that could level the political playing field, despotic tendencies in all matters of national governance, the bungled land grabs (propagandised as the Fast Track Land Reform programme) and the general violations of basic human rights among other things, provided fertile ground for the birth and growth of nationwide protest movements. These forms of protest, of course, trace their history to 1999 when an amalgamation of unions, civic organisations and activist white farmers, came together and established the MDC—a unified movement whose immediate goal was to challenge the ZANU PF despotic hegemony (Kasambala, 2016; Raftopoulos & Mlambo, 2009; Sachikonye, 2017). The MDC, other Civic Society Organisations (CSOs) and a sizeable number of Non-Governmental Organisations (NGOs) have since then, been at the forefront in challenging the ZANU PF hegemony. This was vividly evinced through the national constitutional referendum of 2000 in which the MDC successfully campaigned and won through the "NO" vote, and literally left the ZANU PF government with egg in face. The 2002 and 2008 harmonised elections were also wake up calls for the ZANU PF government as the MDC demonstrated its influence and power in challenging this hegemony by scoring substantive victories in parliament.

The inroads made by the MDC under the late Morgan Tsvangirai in both presidential and parliamentary elections seriously affronted the core of Mugabe's ZANU PF hegemony, and were to have severe repercussions on the opposition political party and the generality of Zimbabweans. The 2008 elections were especially telling, because, despite being conducted amid reports of a multiplicity of electoral anomalies such as the banning of international observers, the targeting of opposition leaders, the torture of opposition supporters, ZANU PF lost its parliamentary majority and the then Zimbabwean president and leader of ZANU PF, Robert Gabriel Mugabe, polled fewer votes when compared to his main opponent, Morgan Tsvangirai of the MDC-T (Sabao, 2013, 2016). The opposition leader, Tsvangirai and his party, claimed an outright win. However, the official results (which were unnecessarily delayed amid allegations of tampering) awarded him 47.9% of votes, which was below the 50% threshold required to avoid a run-off.

This resulted in a presidential election run-off which, in the wake of the electoral humiliation Mugabe and ZANU PF had suffered, was marred by violent retribution and intimidation of the electorate, especially within the MDC-T urban strongholds. The run-off which was supposedly pitting Mugabe and Tsvangirai was boycotted by the MDC-T, who sought to protect the electorate. Tsvangirai withdrew from the race last minute, allowing Mugabe to claim a 90% victory in the run-off (Sabao, 2018; Southall, 2017). The resultant impasse, which was critically castigated by various CSOs, NGOs, human rights activists and the Southern African Development Community (SADC), prompted SADC to propose the establishment of a Government of National Unity (GNU) as a compromise power-sharing deal between the three major political parties in the election—ZANU PF and the two MDC factions—MDC-T (led by Morgan Tsvangirai) and MDC-N (led by Arthur Mutambara). The then South African President, Thabo Mbeki, and a South African high-powered delegation (later dubbed as the 'mediators'), under the mandate and auspices of SADC, intervened and instituted an interim power-sharing agreement and a Government of National Unity (GNU) between ZANU PF and the two main opposition formations (Aeby, 2016; Chinyere, 2014; Moore, 2014; Oberdorf, 2017; Sabao, 2013, 2016). The GNU, whose tenure spanned between 2008 and 2013, raised the hopes of many Zimbabweans, who believed that such a move would ultimately expunge ZANU PF's despotic practices and perhaps hail the dawn of a gradual recovery of the country's political, economic and socio-political circumstances (Chinyere, 2014; Oberdorf, 2017; Sabao, 2013). During the tenure of the GNU, the Zimbabwean economy evinced promises of recovery—especially fanned by the significant recoveries observed within the immediacy of its setup (Southhall, 2017). Sadly, the ZANU PF section of the GNU was not prepared to cede power, and as such, throughout the tenure of the GNU, the balance of power continued to remain heavily skewed in favour of ZANU PF. As such, the institutional and political environment could not be decisively altered (Aeby, 2016). The GNU was to be dissolved by a general election in 2013.

ZANU PF's 2013 alleged "electoral win" ended the tenure of the GNU amid the MDC-T's insistence on irregularities and electoral fraud at the hands of Mugabe's ZANU PF party. The bulk of the accusations pointed towards "trickery, coercion, populism and the connivance of its regional peers" (Moore, 2014, p. 101). The electoral win gave ZANU PF a strong majority in parliament and extended Mugabe's presidential tenure (Chinyere, 2014). Neither did the GNU nor the 2013 election usher in democracy in Zimbabwe (Moore, 2014), as had been dictated in its formation—with the specific objectives of reform and policy implementation (Chirimambowa & Chimedza, 2014). The highly heralded 'resounding electoral victory for ZANU PF in the 2013 elections' marked seriously concerted efforts by the party to restore its hegemony by all means necessary—and this largely included machinations to ensure that the political party resumed power monopoly. However, imminent economic corrosion resulting in public dissatisfaction against the Mugabe administration and its intolerance of opposition activity ultimately sparked a rise in civic action and public demonstrations (Chinyere, 2014; Raftopoulos, 2013; Sabao, 2018; Southhall, 2017).

SOCIAL MEDIA: THE DIGITAL ALTERNATIVE PUBLIC SPHERE IN ZIMBABWE

In the wake of the 2013 elections, the Zimbabwean economic and political spheres evinced severe signs of deterioration and collapse. The post-2013 period bore witness to a massive industrial incapacitation and closures of high employing companies and organisations in especially the private sector, resulting in severe remuneration backlogs and gross job layoffs (Mawere, 2020). So alarming was the level of unemployment resulting from this that, for example, in 2016 unemployment was estimated at 90%, largely owing to the observed decline in activities in the manufacturing and agricultural sectors. Further to that, a generalised poverty of 70%, with over a million persons facing food and nutrition insecurity were also observed, with reports of female-headed households experiencing the highest levels of poverty among the rest (Mawere, 2020; Oberdorf, 2017). The period was thus, marked by the recurrence of a crisis that was comparable to the 2008 "Zimbabwean Crisis" and culminated in the birth and/or the reinvention of protesting and dissenting voices. These protests however, because of the restricted political and public opinion spaces were largely web-based. Women for the first time since independence were also observed to be taking centre-stage in challenging the hegemony of the ZANU PF government. For example, the predominantly women-led 'Beat the Pots' campaign in which women marched through urban areas in demonstration while banging pots and pans in show of protest and demonstration against poverty and precarious livelihoods, demanding for broad-based change (Sachikonye, 2017), is one such movement.

The economy took a downturn, fast approaching the levels of the pre- and post-2008 elections (Mawere, 2020) in which inflation alone ballooned to proportions of hyperinflation (Sabao, 2018). International economic participation was limited, thus negatively impacting the foreign currency flow in the country. The multi-currency system and general stability which had prevailed during the GNU, increasingly deteriorated, rendering ordinary people vulnerable (Mawere, 2013). This saw the government introduce a surrogate currency called the 'Bond Note' in 2016, aimed at addressing the liquidity crunch resulting from foreign currency shortages. Resultantly, the cash crisis intensified as the US dollar continued to disappear from the market, resulting in black market foreign exchange activities resurfacing—making international trade difficult for the informal market since it requires foreign currency.

Protest movements such as #thisflag led by Evan Mawarire and #Tajamuka/Sesijikile led by Promise Mkwananzi emerged in the context of the deterioration of the economy. The objectives of these movements varied—Mawarire's #this flag called for an address to poor governance marred by corrupt activities and nepotism, while the #Tajamuka/Sesijikile movement called for regime change (and vendors and unemployed graduates led their own movements in the conflictual context of 2016). These movements, in order to circumvent the stringent regulation of public debate and the stifling of political plurality in Zimbabwe, were largely organised and instituted through online platforms for ease of communication as well as to encourage the free participation of those interested in the fight for justice and equality, while able to protect their identities and thus safeguard themselves from physical harm and harassment by state agents.

With the #thisflag, Mawarire, an ordinary citizen donning the Zimbabwean flag, and through his verbalisations, managed to rally behind him a movement that largely emerged as an unplanned initiative as he had only used social media to vent out his grievance against the government. The movement, drawing strength from the realities of his speeches, emerged as a platform through which the larger part of the Zimbabwean population, frustrated by the political and economic status quo and also joined by civic groups, agitated for political and social change. Mawarire managed to draw sympathy from the populace by juxtaposing the social realities of ordinary Zimbabweans to the promises carried by the Zimbabwe national flag. The #thisflag movement emerged as a citizen-led movement to hold the government accountable for the status quo—it had political and economic demands, citing issues of poverty, corruption, economic crisis, the introduction of the bond note, political suppression and injustices bewildering Zimbabwe (Chinyere, 2014; McGrath, 2016; Sabao & Chikara, 2018). The #thisflag movement emerged through the cyber-space but later also utilised physical street protests.

Mawarire thus managed to mobilise the national sentiment and to speak of a nationalism contrary to that of the state (Mawere, 2020). As the video attained public support through social media, Mawarire established the #thisflag movement and encouraged all else interested to also make their own recording of protest and post them as an expression of their own grievances against the ZANU PF government's betrayal of the ideals the nation held dear as enshrined symbolically in the national flag. This was done in demonstration of one's love and patriotism for Zimbabwe and secondly, as one's protest against the country's leadership's failure and ignorance (Mawere, 2020). The movement eventually exploited both the cyber and physical worlds, and developed in phases— from a five-day campaign to a twenty-five-day campaign of citizen action demanding political and economic reforms (Gukurume, 2017; Oberdorf, 2017).

The successes of the movement, now complemented by other similar hashtag coded protest movements, were fully realised when a coalition of them successfully organised a nationwide strike action (dubbed 'stay-away protests') on 6 July 2016. The objective was to bring the government to attention as businesses and education came to standstill on the day. In seeming tacit acknowledgement of the power of the movement, Mawarire was arrested at the behest of the ZANU PF government on charges of fanning violence and disturbing the national peace. His arrest naturally aggravated the movement to a mass demonstration on 13 July 2016, when thousands of Zimbabwean citizens from all walks of life thronged the Rotten Row courtroom in his support (McGrath, 2016). To the pro-democratic front, Mawarire embodied the principles of citizen participation and empowerment, while to the state, ZANU PF and the then Zimbabwean President, Robert Mugabe, he emerged as a national threat under the tutelage of Western countries. The ZANU PF responses to this are embodied in Mnangagwa's inciting of the ZANU PF Youth League to also fight opposition discourses within the social media platforms. This gave birth to movements such as Varakashi 4ED and ZANU PF Patriots as active pages on most mainstream social media platforms (Mavengano & Marevesa, 2022; Moyo, 2019), created especially to provide counternarratives to opposition political discourses while at the same time popularising ZANU PF ideology and political propaganda.

Perspective: Towards the 2023 Harmonised General Election

As the Zimbabwean nation trudges towards the 2023 harmonised presidential and parliamentary elections slated for 23 August 2023, the political space in Zimbabwe is clear testimony to the old adage that "the more things change, the more they remain the same". Despite a change in governance in 2017 when the incumbent President Emmerson Dambudzo Mnangagwa was ushered into power through a military assisted "soft coup" (Moore, 2018), the ZANU PF political power play tactics have remained the same. In fact, it would be prudent to imagine that they have become even more draconian and desperate. The political playing field remains tilted in favour of sustaining the ZANU PF autocracy and hegemony as opposition political players still find themselves unable to campaign freely, and political activists continue to be arrested and detained for long periods that are rarely, if at all, legally justified

(Musarurwa, 2016). Even more so, the ZANU PF government has made moves to stifle even the web-based political activities which had remained the only avenue through which opposition political activism could thrive. This is largely through the promulgation of the draconian and restrictive laws such as the Cyber and Data Protection Act of 2021 and the Patriotic Act of 2023, which criminalise the sharing of online content deemed to be seditious and anti-government (Sabao & Chikara, 2018) as well as criminalise any criticisms of the ZANU PF government.

Political activists such as award winning journalist and filmmaker, Hopewell Chin'ono, have been, on several occasions, arrested for allegedly peddling or spreading falsehoods through their social media pages. What is interesting is that the alleged falsehoods often tend to be anything considered anti-ZANU PF such as exposing the corruption within ZANU PF ranks and government, exposing the deteriorating health infrastructure in state-owned hospitals and clinics, the deteriorating standards in the education system, the general collapse of the Zimbabwean economy and the attendant suffering and impoverishment of the general populace, as well as the waning of the local currency which has seen, for example, professionals such as university lecturers and medical doctors pocket a monthly net salary of a measly US$200. The arrest of web-based political activist Chin'ono is reminiscent of the torture and victimisation of Evan Mawarire of the #thisflag movement.

Formed under the leadership of a youthful clergyman, Evan Mawarire, for example, the #thisflag presented itself as a non-political movement with the main agenda as spelt out on both their Facebook and Twitter accounts as being "the citizens of Zimbabwe [who] have decided to speak and be heard" (Sabao & Chikara, 2018). Mawarire, whose protests are quickly identifiable by his draping of the Zimbabwean national flag, proclaims that he was not a politician but merely a citizen of Zimbabwe frustrated by the political and economic decay in Zimbabwe. He is quoted as having confessed that "[w]hen I look at this flag, it is not a reminder of pride and inspiration, it feels as if I want to belong to another country". His movement represents one of the major, if not the major, web-based protests in Zimbabwe. And his arrest and silencing signals the nascence of political descent on all those viewed as enemies of the ZANU PF government—as further demonstrated by the arrest of Chin'ono and others.

While the Mugabe-led ZANU PF government attempted to downplay the significance of the 'national' boycott through its state-funded news outlets the national daily newspapers, *The Herald* and the national broadcasters (Zimbabwe Broadcasting Corporation run *Zimbabwe Television* as well as radio stations), the significance of the nationwide boycott remained implanted in the minds of the Zimbabwean population. The impacts of the protest are also best evinced through the reactions of the ZANU PF-led government in the aftermath of the 6 July, 2016 mass protest. In the immediacy of the protest, Mawarire became a wanted person—charged with violence and disturbing the peace. On 12 July 2016, Mawarire handed himself over to the Zimbabwe Republic Police where he was formally charged with inciting violence and disturbing the peace, a charge later amended in court to 'attempting to overthrow a government'.

This new charge within the Zimbabwean legal system is tantamount to treason. This new charge of treason was, however, only read to the accused Mawarire in court, prompting the judge presiding to dismiss the charges and release Mawarire. This was not the first time that the National Prosecuting Authority in Zimbabwe has failed to convict such 'high' profile figures. Politically motivated charges were once pressed on opposition party leader Morgan Tsvangirai, who was also acquitted of such charges (Hudleston, 2005). Chin'ono has in the past also faced similar charges which were of course, as has become the pattern, later dropped. These kinds of charges, consistently brought by ZANU PF against any political actor(s) perceived to be a threat to their hegemony signify the desperation by the government to silence any dissenting voices seen to be in discord to their propagandistic agenda. Failing to prosecute Mawarire, the governments then resorted to its usual tactics of enacting draconian laws that inhibit any political processes perceived as opposition to ZANU PF to commence.

Political activists such as Job Sikhala and others have been maimed and incarcerated for crimes that members of the ruling ZANU PF party continuously commit daily such as sloganeering. The partial application of the law continues to proliferate in Zimbabwe with the denial of bail to most opposition activists for political crimes and yet in some instances, members of the ZANU PF party with more serious crimes such as alleged corruption roam scot-free in the country. The opposition political party the CCC has in the last few months leading towards the 2023 harmonised general elections, has been unable to campaign, as their applications to hold rallies have always been rejected by the Zimbabwe Republic Police, whose political allegiances have remained largely biased towards the ZANU PF government—their employer. In the first two weeks of February 2023, the Nelson Chamisal-led opposition political party, the CCC was denied the permission to hold two rallies in consecutive weeks. The incumbent president (Emmerson Dambudzo Mnangagwa) and his vice (Rtd General Constantine Guvheya Chiwenga) have not, in their political rhetoric, shied away from making declarative verbalisations that they are willing to even rope in the military to ensure the continued sustenance of the ZANU PF hegemony. This, they claim, is because of the historical relations between the military and ZANU PF spanning from the liberation war (Kriger, 2005; Tendi, 2020).

The alternative digital public sphere that web-based social platforms represent has in Zimbabwe also become a heavily restricted and monitored space. Political actors that are seen to peddle political messages that are seen to project the ruling ZANU PF party in a negative light have suffered the wrath of the law. The once alternative safe space has become a minefield in which political actors against the establishment risk arm and limb daily. The power that social media and digital platforms pose as an influence of political consciousness and ideas has also been realised and clandestinely embraced by the Mnangagwa-led ZANU PF government. The high levels of activity, for example, by ZANU PF functionaries such as the party's current spin doctor Nick Mangwana, Zanu PF Official, Zanu PF Patriots, Gondai Mutongi, Zanu PF Youth League among others, are a clear indication of their realisation of the potential that can be tapped from the web-based platforms. Nick Mangwana especially has been providing counterbalancing ZANU PF propagandistic rhetoric in clear attempts of levelling the political field on social media. Yet, painfully, the same government ensures an almost zero visibility of opposition political activity in the physical space.

Conclusion: Whither Way Forward?

The power of social media as alternative digital public sphere within which citizens are empowered can coordinate and popularise political ideological convictions, processes and campaigns both nationally and internationally, especially so on social media platforms. This was demonstrated in Zimbabwe by the ZANU PF governments' reactions to the proliferation of dissent on such platforms. ZANU PF's attempts to quash any political opposition manifesting through social media platforms, even through the creation of counter content and pages, clearly demonstrate this. In the aftermath of the 6th of July 2016 national protests in Zimbabwe, "the ZANU-PF led government's reactions were largely threats of arrest and imprisonment, threats of tracing of individuals responsible through the national cellular phone registration database etc. The use of the national flag in protests was criminalised" (Sabao & Chikara, 2018). It has been politically interesting though, that despite such a clampdown, Zimbabweans from across the spectrum have continued to defy such a criminalisation and continue to register protests and dissent through such platforms. The major opposition political party, CCC, has continued to officially campaign through these platforms as, in a country characterised by the militarisation of the political space, this continues to remain the only avenue through which such a political activity (election campaigning) can continue. The criminalisation of internet-based protest and the attendant arrest of political activists utilising these forums to speak truth to power do not come as a surprise in a nation "that has a history of passing laws restricting the free flow of information in an attempt to curtail political communication by people or organisations regarded as critical of the government or opposition political parties" (Sabao & Chikara, 2018, p. 32). As Sabao and Chingwaramusee (2017) observe, it has become commonplace within the Zimbabwean political sphere that the ZANU PF-led government has always resorted to promulgating draconian legislation militating against the proliferation of the plurality of speech in a bid to curtail opposition politics. For example, historically, "in the face of serious opposition from the MDC, ZANU PF realised that the control of the media was key to its continued survival. Stringent media regulating statutes such as the Access to Information and Protection of Privacy Act (AIPPA) and the Public Order and Security Act (POSA) were promulgated. Such laws, together with previously existing laws such as the Official Secrets Act (OSA) and the Broadcasting Services Act (BSA) made it nearly impossible for the freedom of expression to thrive" (Sabao & Chingwaramusee, 2017, p. 197). This was further compounded by enactments of the Cyber and Data Protection Act of 2021 and the Patriotic Act of 2023 as further arsenal for ZANU PF to use in quashing dissent.

References

Aeby, M. (2016). Making an impact from the margins? Civil society groups in Zimbabwe's interim power-sharing process. *Journal of Modern African Studies, 54*(4), 703–728.

Chibuwe, A. (2017). s*The nationalist discourses of an African ruling party: An exploration of Zanu-PF print media election advertisements for the July 2013 elections* (Doctoral dissertation). University of Johannesburg, South Africa.

Chinyere, P. (2014). Negotiated government in Zimbabwe-tool for peaceful co-existence or momentary suppression of inherent divisions? *Mediterranean Journal of Social Sciences, 5*(25), 73.

Chirimambowa, T. C., & Chimedza, T. L. (2014). Civil society's contested role in the 2013 elections in Zimbabwe—A historical perspective. *Journal of African Elections, 13*(2), 71–93.

Gukurume, S. (2017). #ThisFlag and #ThisGown cyber protests in Zimbabwe: Reclaiming political space. *African Journalism Studies, 38*(2), 49–70.

Habermas, J. (1991). *The structural transformation of the public sphere: An inquiry into a category of bourgeois society*. MIT press.

Hudleston, S. (2005). *Face of courage: A biography of Morgan Tsvangirai*. Juta and Company Ltd.

Kasambala, T. (2016). *"You will be thoroughly beaten": The brutal suppression of dissent in Zimbabwe* (Vol. 18, No. 10). Human Rights Watch.

Kriger, N. (2005). ZANU (PF) strategies in general elections, 1980–2000: Discourse and coercion. *African Affairs, 104*(414), 1–34.

Makumbe, J. M. (2002). Zimbabwe's hijacked election. *Journal of Democracy, 13*(4), 87–101.

Mano, W. (2005). Scheduling for rural and urban listeners on bilingual Radio Zimbabwe. *Radio Journal: International Studies in Broadcast & Audio Media, 3*(2), 93–106.

Matondi, P. B., & Rutherford, B. (2021). The politics of "land grabs" and development contradictions in Zimbabwe: The case of the Chisumbanje Ethanol project. In *The transnational land rush in Africa: A decade after the spike* (pp. 189–212). Springer.

Mavengano, E., & Marevesa, T. (2022). A critical discourse analysis of media landscape and political conflict in Zimbabwe. In I. Mhute, H. Mangeya, & E. Jakaza (Eds.), *Emerging trends in strategic communication in the Sub-Saharan Africa* (pp. 224–240). Routledge.

Mawere, M. (2013). Coping with poverty in rural communities of third world Africa: The case of Mukonoweshuro cooperative gardening in Gutu, Zimbabwe. *International Journal of Politics and Good Governance, 4*(4.3), 1–19.

Mawere, T. (2020). The politics and symbolism of the #ThisFlag in Zimbabwe. *Strategic Review for Southern Africa, 42*(1), 165–188.

McGrath, C. (2016). What everyone's getting wrong about Zimbabwe's #ThisFlag movement. https://foreignpolicy.com/2016/07/21/what-everyones-getting-wrong-about-zimbabwes-thisflag-movement/. Accessed on 12 July 2019.

Mkodzongi, G. (2018). Peasant agency in a changing agrarian situation in Central Zimbabwe: The case of Mhondoro Ngezi. *Agrarian South: Journal of Political Economy, 7*(2), 188–210.

Mlambo, A. S. (2005). 'Land grab' or 'taking back stolen land': The fast track land reform process in Zimbabwe in historical perspective. *History Compass, 3*(1), 1–21.

Moore, D. (2014). Death or dearth of democracy in Zimbabwe? *Africa Spectrum, 49*(1), 101–114.

Moore, D. (2018). A very Zimbabwean coup: November 13–24, 2017. *Transformation: Critical Perspectives on Southern Africa, 97*(1), 1–29.

Moyo, D. (2007). Alternative media, diasporas and the mediation of the Zimbabwe crisis. *Ecquid Novi, 28*(1–2), 81–105.

Moyo, C. (2019). Social media, civil resistance, the Varakashi factor and the shifting polemics of Zimbabwe's social media "war". *Global Media Journal-African Edition, 12*(1), 1–36.

Moyo, T., & Mavengano, E. (2021). A Déjàvu of Orwellian proportions: Re-reading animal farm in the context of Zimbabwean politics of change. In O. Nyambi, T. Mangena, & G. Ncube (Eds.), *Cultures of change in contemporary Zimbabwe: Socio-political transition from Mugabe to Mnangagwa* (pp. 171–184). Routledge.

Mpofu, S. (n.d.). *The power of citizen journalism in Zimbabwe* (Unpublished manuscript).

Muchemwa, K. Z. (2010). Galas, biras, state funerals and the necropolitan imagination in the re-construction of the Zimbabwean nation 1980–2008. *Social Dynamics: A Journal of African Studies, 36*(3), 504–514.

Mujere, J., & Mwatwara, W. (2015). Citizen journalism and national politics in Zimbabwe: The case of the 2008 and 2013 elections. In B. Mutsvairo (Ed.), *Participatory politics and citizen journalism in a networked Africa: A connected continent* (pp. 215–228). Palgrave Macmillan.

Musarurwa, H. J. (2016). The rise of youth activism and non-violent action in addressing Zimbabwe's crisis. *Conflict Trends, 2016*(3), 50–56.

Mutsvairo, B. (2015). Recapturing citizen journalism: Processes and patterns citizen journalism and national politics in Zimbabwe: The case of the 2008 and 2013 elections. In B. Mutsvairo (Ed.), *Participatory politics and citizen journalism in a networked Africa: A connected continent*. Palgrave Macmillan.

Nenjerama, T. T., & Sabao, C. (n.d). *The #thisflag movement—its decline and implications on the Zimbabwean political landscape*. Unpublished paper.

Ndlovu-Gatsheni, S. J. (2009). *Do Zimbabweans exist? Trajectories of nationalism, national identity formation and a crisis in postcolonial state*. Peter Lang.

Ndlovu-Gatsheni, S. J., & Ruhanya, P. (2020). *The history and political transition of Zimbabwe: From Mugabe to Mnangagwa*. African Histories and Modernities Series (AHAM). Palgrave Macmillan.

Oberdorf, J. P. R. A. (2017). *Inspiring the citizen to be bold: Framing theory and the rise and decline of the #ThisFlag-movement in Zimbabwe* (Master's thesis).
Raftopoulos, B. (2006). The Zimbabwean crisis and the challenges for the left. *Journal of Southern African Studies, 32*(2), 203–219.
Raftopoulos, B. (2013). The 2013 elections in Zimbabwe: The end of an era. *Journal of Southern African Studies, 39*(4), 971–988.
Raftopoulos, B., & Mlambo, A. (Eds.). (2009). *Becoming Zimbabwe. A history from the pre-colonial period to 2008*. African Books Collective.
Rusvingo, S. L. (2014). The Zimbabwe soaring unemployment rate of 85%: A ticking time bomb not only for Zimbabwe but the entire SADC region (2014). *Global Journal of Management and Business Research, 14*(B9), 1–8.
Sabao, C. (2013). *The reporter voice and objectivity in cross-linguistic reporting of controversial news in Zimbabwean newspapers: An appraisal approach* (Doctoral dissertation). Stellenbosch University, Stellenbosch.
Sabao, C. (2016). Shades of the GNU in Zimbabwe (2009–13): Linguistic discourse analyses of representations of transitional politics in Zimbabwean newspapers. In *Political discourse in emergent, fragile, and failed democracies* (pp. 306–327). IGI Global.
Sabao, C. (2018). Hegemonising Zimbabwe? The polity of Mbare Chimurenga lyrics in perpetuating Mugabe's and ZANU-PF's rule. *Muziki, 15*(1), 109–130.
Sabao, C., & Chikara, T. O. (2018). Social media as alternative public sphere for citizen participation and protest in national politics in Zimbabwe: The case of #thisflag. In F. P. C. Endong (Ed.), *Exploring the role of social media in transnational advocacy* (pp. 17–35). IGI Global. https://doi.org/10.4018/978-1-5225-2854-8.ch002
Sabao, C., & Chikara, T. O. (2020). Social media as alternative public sphere for citizen participation and protest in national politics in Zimbabwe: The case of #thisflag. In *African studies: Breakthroughs in research and practice* (pp. 772–786). IGI Global.
Sabao, C., & Chingwaramusee, V. R. (2017). Citizen journalism on Facebook and the challenges of media regulation in Zimbabwe. In N. A. Mhiripiri & T. Chari (Eds.), *Media law, ethics, and policy in the digital age* (pp. 193–206). IGI Global. https://doi.org/10.4018/978-1-5225-2095-5.ch011
Sachikonye, L. (2017). The protracted democratic transition in Zimbabwe. *Taiwan Journal of Democracy, 13*(1), 117–136.
Southall, R. (2013). How and why ZANU-PF won the 2013 Zimbabwe elections. *Strategic Review for Southern Africa, 35*(2), 135.
Southall, R. (2017). Bob's out, the croc is in: Continuity or change in Zimbabwe? *Africa Spectrum, 52*(3), 81–94.
Tendi, B. M. (2020). *The army and politics in Zimbabwe: Mujuru, the liberation fighter and kingmaker*. Cambridge University Press.

CHAPTER 11

Music, Deceit, and Representation of Political Actors: Navigating the Connection of Chief Hwenje's Songs with Propaganda in Zimbabwe's Politicised Space

Lazarus Sauti, Tendai Makaripe, and Wellington Gadzikwa

INTRODUCTION

Music permeates many aspects of human society, including the political sphere (Guzura & Ndimande, 2015; Mangena et al., 2016; Sawo, 2020). Together with political warfare, it has been used in various political spaces to deliver sociopolitical messages to specific target groups (Sawo,

---

L. Sauti · T. Makaripe
Department of Journalism and Communications, Christian College of Southern Africa, Harare, Zimbabwe

W. Gadzikwa (✉)
Department of Humanities, Journalism and Media Studies, Africa University, Mutare, Zimbabwe
e-mail: wmgadzikwa@gmail.com

© The Author(s), under exclusive license to Springer Nature Switzerland AG 2023
E. Mavengano and S. Chirongoma (eds.), *Electoral Politics in Zimbabwe, Vol II*, https://doi.org/10.1007/978-3-031-33796-3_11

2020). Political warfare usually refers to using political means to impose an enemy's will, using words, images, and ideas. Mano (2007) further states that 'music competes with other mainstream media platforms in articulating political and socio-economic realities in polarised countries such as Zimbabwe' (p. 61).

True to the edicts of Mano (2007), Munhuweyi (2022), and Sawo (2020), musicians use their creative power and that of the song as a cultural text to craft political messages that praise certain political figures while denigrating others. Some political songs contain propaganda aimed at entrenching political leaders. This places music at the centre of politics, defined by Street (1997) as 'the clash of ideas, identities, and interests' and how 'scarce resources are distributed' in society (p. 26). Guzura and Ndimande (2015) buttress this point by arguing that musicians are activists that politicians use to spread their ideological narratives. Brown (2008) argues that this makes music a combat zone for political ideas and expression. Music can also be used to express political turmoil among the ruled and challenge the weaknesses of the ruling elite (Ncube, 2022).

To that end, this chapter navigates the connection of music with propaganda in Zimbabwe's political space. It analyses how Chief Hwenje uses music to push the ideological and hegemonic narratives of the Zimbabwe African National Union-Patriotic Front (ZANU PF). The period under study is limited between 2017 and 2023. In 2017, Emmerson Mnangagwa, a former long-time ally of the late President Robert Gabriel Mugabe, replaced Mugabe as President of Zimbabwe (Chibuwe & Munoriyarwa, 2022). Mnangagwa's reign, described as the Second Republic, is supported by musicians such as Chief Hwenje, hence his selection in this study.

The chapter recognises that music was, and still is, central to Zimbabwe's political space and that musicians use their creativity and popularity to garner support or malign political actors. Its distinctive figuration lies in the link between music, deception, and propaganda in politicised spaces like Zimbabwe.

The chapter is organised as follows: this introduction is followed by a brief memoir of Chief Hwenje and a section on Herman and Chomsky's propaganda theory, which informs this chapter. This theory assumes that society's elites use the media, of which music is a part, for ideological and hegemonic purposes. In this way, music advocates for elite political actors more than for voiceless people. We, thus, use this theory to understand how Chief Hwenje uses music to manipulate Zimbabweans and convince them to support President Mnangagwa and ZANU PF.

After this, we conceptualise music and propaganda. The argument underlying this section is that music provides a memorable way to convey a desired political message to a particular audience (Guzura & Ndimande, 2015). Our contention here is that music is often seen as entertainment within and across Zimbabwe, so it can discreetly convey political messages.

In the next section, we describe the methodology we employ to analyse Chief Hwenje's songs as propaganda tools. This chapter employs qualitative content analysis to examine the nexus of Chief Hwenje's songs with propaganda. Two songs, namely 'Young Man' and 'Internet', were purposively sampled and analysed. After analysis, we provide conclusions and recommendations.

A Brief Memoir of Chief Hwenje

Chief Hwenje was born, Admire Sanyanga Sibanda, in 1987 in Victoria Falls. The Zimbabwean musician grew up in Chitungwiza but later relocated to Zvishavane (Muzari, 2018). Chief Hwenje stayed briefly in South Africa but returned to pursue farming in his home village of Zvishavane where he now lives.

He started his music career as a gospel musician in 2011 and recorded two albums *Munamato* and *Danaishe*. In 2014, he switched to Afrotraditional and Jiti music, which he calls 'Hwenje Music'. Politically, Chief Hwenje leans towards ZANU PF. He rose to prominence early in President Mnangagwa's administration, praising the ruling party while denigrating members of the opposition (Sithole, 2022).

Muzari (2018) claims that Chief Hwenje's music tells a story of liberation and triumph, and Sithole (2022) calls him a ZANU PF activist. He is the nephew of President Emmerson Mnangagwa (Muzari, 2018) and is famous for the song 'ED Pfee' (Chitumba, 2018; Khosa, 2020; Mabika, 2022; Madzimure, 2020).

Family ties are always stronger than other ties, so Chief Hwenje uses his music to strengthen family ties and strengthen the political influence of President Mnangagwa and ZANU PF. The artist might as well be using music to tighten his relations with President Mnangagwa rather than singing for love for ZANU PF. Accordingly, we select his songs as case analysis because he has connections to ZANU PF.

Theorising Media and Propaganda

For Mano (2007), music functions as a variation of journalism, expressing sociopolitical realities in its content and themes in specific contexts and historic moments. He further argues that music serves a normative function in entertaining, informing, and educating people on political and socio-economic issues. In post-colonial Zimbabwe, musicians have relied on subtle wordplay to promote tourism, agriculture, and land reform and to denounce human rights violations (Chinouriri, 2014; Guzura & Ndimande, 2015; Musiyiwa, 2008; Palmberg, 2004).

In this regard, this chapter examines how music can be used to manipulate populations, using the propaganda theory put forward by Herman and Chomsky (1988). Through the lens of Herman and Chomsky, this theory focuses on the performance of the media—of which music is a part—in society. It also describes how public consent to political and socio-economic policies is 'manufactured' by persuasion techniques used to influence opinion and appeal to emotions. The theory further assumes that media platforms are neither innocent nor neutral because they are always in the throes of political capital and power. Proponents of this theory, thus, explain that political actors use music as megaphones to spread hegemonic and ideological narratives.

Propaganda theory is relevant to this chapter as it helps to explain how music shapes the political and socio-economic attitudes of the mass consciousness. It serves as an effective way to illustrate how political actors use music to shape narratives of ideology and hegemony. It also shows how musicians can use their creativity to influence their listeners to support some political actors at the expense of others. The selection of propaganda theory was heavily influenced by the fact that musicians in a deeply divided country like Zimbabwe use their creativity to lure people into joining certain political figures or denigrating members of the opposition.

Conceptualising Music and Propaganda

Kaemmer (1993 cited in Matiure, 2019) captures the different meanings of music as perceived by different authors. He characterises music as 'fine arts', 'phonetic form', 'natural sounds', 'subcategory of ritual', and 'subdivision of entertainment' (Kaemmer, 1993, p. 59). Blanking's (1973 cited in Matiure, 2019) description of music captures all the dimensions presented in Kaemmer's (1993) definition and presents music as humanly organised sound. His comprehensive definition shows that music encompasses all aspects of human life. This means that it can also be used as a propaganda tool used by various actors to promote their interests.

Propaganda in the neutral sense means sharing a particular idea to gain sympathy and support from the target audience. For Jowett and O'Donnell (1999), propaganda is defined as 'a deliberate and systematic process of forming opinions, manipulating cognitions, and directing actions to obtain a response that furthers the propaganda's intentions' (p. 6). Velasco-Pufleau (2017) adds that propaganda is a political legitimisation tactic aimed at luring and swaying a particular group of people. Koppang (2009) also defines propaganda as the use of political power to induce people to submit to political views. He further affirms that propaganda is used by political actors to compel citizens to act and think in line with their philosophies and to support the 'manufactured' image they wish to represent. The same scholar asserts that propaganda manipulates acceptance by exploiting individual emotions such as anger, fear, grief, guilt, and revenge. Koppang (2009) further avows that 'us' and 'them' binaries support well-crafted messages and lure unsuspecting audiences.

Political actors use seven basic propaganda techniques to gain, maintain, and consolidate power (Cull, 2019; Hamdani, 2017). These are bandwagon, card stacking, glittering generality, name-calling, plain folk talk, testimonials, and transfer (Cull, 2019). Bandwagon is when propagandists attempt to persuade the target audiences to accept their views (Cull, 2019). Loosely translated as '*gundamusaira*' in ChiShona, the language spoken by about 77% of people in Zimbabwe (Mlambo, 2009), bandwagon tries to make the recipient of the message feel out of the way because they are not part of the train. Slogans such as '*ED Pfee*' (ED in office) and '*Chamisa Chete Chete*' (Chamisa only) are used to lure support for ZANU PF and CCC, respectively.

Card stacking is another propaganda technique in which facts are carefully chosen to build a compelling case that focuses on one side of an issue and intentionally hides the other (Lee & Lee, 1939). ZANU PF uses words such as 'ED for Economic Development' to build the profile of Emmerson Mnangagwa while CCC uses 'One People One Vision One Nation' as one of its slogans. Glittering generalities are a way of associating ideas with flattering abstractions like democracy, freedom, liberation, and justice (Hamdani, 2017). Glittering generality also alludes to presenting one's agenda in an obscure but captivating way. Here,

ZANU PF supporters portray President Mnangagwa as a liberation hero while CCC supporters frame Nelson Chamisa as a social democrat. Cull (2019) unpacks name-calling as tarring others with phrases or words intended to undermine their credibility and respect. Nelson Chamisa, the leader of the Citizens Coalition for Change (CCC), has been called 'young man', 'small boy', or 'sell-out' by ZANU PF supporters. CCC supporters are also called '*zvimbwasungata*' (Western puppets). Chamisa supporters sometimes call ZANU PF supporters '*varakashi*' (destroyers or killers), '*mhondi*' (thugs), and '*mbavha*' (thieves) (Sauti, 2022).

Lee and Lee (1939) postulate that plain folk talk is a technique used by politicians to identify with low-ranking members of society. Cull (2019) further argues that the propagandist connects familiar social values with positions expressed in folk wisdom. Another propaganda technique used by political actors is transfer. This includes associating products, ideas, or people with high/low credibility depending on the intent of the message. By using this device, propagandists unfairly tie their arguments to respected ideological categories like patriotism. Cull (2019) also defines testimonials as a propaganda technique, in which intermediaries are quoted or registered with a certain credibility to target groups to gain support and trust.

Jowett and O'Donnell (2012) classify propaganda into three forms: (i) white, (ii) black, and (iii) gray propaganda. They argue that white propaganda 'seeks to convince target groups that the sender is a "good guy" with the best political ideology' (p. 17). Such propaganda comes from precisely identified sources. The information in the message is probably correct as well. Jowett and O'Donnell (2012) also emphasise that individuals behind white propaganda messages are consciously identified and made known to the audience.

Jowett and O'Donnell (2012) refer to black propaganda as 'big lies' hewed to mislead audiences. They also point out that gray propaganda lies between white and black propaganda and serves to humiliate competitors or enemies. Sources of black and gray propaganda may or may not be correctly identified, and the accuracy of the information is uncertain.

Soules (2015) professes that propaganda is used to activate strong emotions in people, to attack opponents, and to appeal to the dreams, fears, and hopes of people. He further positions propaganda media as powerful and effective ideological institutions that activate strong emotions in the audience. Jowett and O'Donnell (1999, p. 6) add that the propaganda media tries to cover up the existence of unpleasant facts (white propaganda). Sometimes, it includes lies and half-truths (black propaganda). For instance, ZANU PF or CCC supporters use both white and black propaganda to attract supporters before, during, and after elections.

The danger of the propaganda media is to escalate political polarisation (Steuter & Wills, 2008) in fragile states like Zimbabwe. Propaganda techniques such as name-calling divide people instead of uniting them as evidenced in the 1994 Rwanda genocide where Tutsis were dehumanised and labelled cockroaches. This contributed to the massacre of more than 800,000 people in 100 days (Orgeret, 2016). Zimbabwe's Gukurahundi massacre, in which more than 20,000 civilians from Matabeleland province and parts of the Midlands were killed by security forces, is also proof that propaganda can have a devastating effect.

Connection of Music with Propaganda in Politicised Spaces

The interplay between music and propaganda in politicised spaces shows that music reflects politics, and politics influences music (Garratt, 2018; Street, 2003; Velasco-Pufleau, 2017). Politics intervenes in the production, distribution, and consumption of music, and music affirms the country's political and socio-economic realities. This means that music interacts with and reflects the politics of any nation.

Sawo (2020) associates praise songs with white propaganda. He argues that white propaganda glamorises national symbols and that music is intended to inflame a deep, passionate, and unreserved loyalty to political actors. True to this, musicians such as Andy Brown, Cde Chinx, Last 'Tambaoga' Chiangwa, Mbare Chimurenga Choir, Movement for Democratic Change (MDC) Choir, Paul Madzore, and Raymond Majongwe among others have promoted the political interests of politicians such as Robert Mugabe, Morgan Tsvangirai, and Nelson Chamisa in an organised mass persuasion way (see Chinouriri, 2014; Chiridza et al., 2015; Musiyiwa, 2008; Muyambo, 2022).

Onyebadi (2019) also examines the connection between music, propaganda, and politics in Africa. He investigated the role of music in elections in several African countries and found that political parties used music to publicise their election manifestos and also to mock opposition parties. The Mbare Chimurenga Choir used '*Jiti*' and '*Pfonda*' melodies to drum up support for former President Robert Mugabe and ZANU PF during the 2005, 2008, and 2013 elections. Jah Prayzah's song 'Kutonga kwaro' (hero's reign) was used by ZANU PF during the 2018 elections in Zimbabwe. The song was used at every ZANU PF gathering to prop up support for President Mnangagwa as the people's choice.

The use of musical galas that were a prominent feature during the Robert Mugabe tenure and carried into the Second Republic is a testament to the intertwining of music and politics. Musicians who are considered pro-ZANU PF and whose lyrics are deemed 'clean' and non-critical of the state are called to perform at galas and other ZANU PF events. Thus, the musical gala unfolds as a modern-day *pungwe* (night vigil), employing various propaganda techniques to consolidate ZANU PF's power in the country's political landscape.

For Velasco-Pufleau (2017), songs can have many meanings depending on the historical context of their composition and its reception, the political rituals in which they are performed, and the artistic and philosophical discourse surrounding them. For this reason, he argues that music plays an important role in representation, deception, or resistance to political ideas and actions. He sums up songs as propaganda tools due to their powerful, soothing, innocuous nature, and goodwill towards the targeted listener.

Nevertheless, Mano (2007) argues that music can be used to challenge the elite and give a voice to the marginalised. He adds that musicians such as Thomas Mapfumo, Leonard Zhakata, and Oliver Mtukudzi used music to criticise official corruption, human rights violations, and poor governance in Zimbabwe. The musicians debated, promoted, and provoked debate about political and socio-economic realities in the country through the power of their songs. Some of their works were 'banned' from radio for challenging the Zimbabwean state from 1999 until 2005 (Mano, 2007).

As also evidenced by Mano (2007) and Nyairo and Ogude (2005), music was used to challenge and unseat dictators, as well as to liberate the oppressed. In Kenya, music was used to challenge the autocratic regime of Arap Moi. Musicians used the power of songs, as cultural expressions, to ridicule Arap and his cronies until they were dethroned (Gecau, 1997). Music was also used in Cameroon to criticise economic decay, condemn social injustices, and slow development (Nyamnjoh, 2005). Musicians denounce the Cameroonian government's complicity and inaction in the face of corruption.

Methodology

In this chapter, we employ a qualitative content analysis to collect data and examine the connection of Chief Hwenje's music with propaganda in Zimbabwe. Two songs, namely 'Young Man' and 'Internet', were purposively sampled from YouTube and placed in historical settings that help to highlight their connection to propaganda. These songs were selected because they framed political actors and affairs in the country.

We selected the lyrics and verses that were relevant to this study. Attention was paid to the lyrical content and the historical period to which the lyrics respond, and the broader ideological influences embedded in them. Selected lyrics were translated from ChiShona to English for analysis.

Critical discourse analysis was used as an analytical technique to question the connection of Chief Hwenje's selected songs with propaganda. Jørgensen and Phillips (2002, p. 17) define discourse as 'a predetermined way of speaking about the world and its scope'. This, in the words of van Dijk (2003), shows the power of language use, the relationship between beliefs (cognition), and interactions in social situations in the meaning-making process.

We used Fairclough's (2000) critical discourse analysis, which is an integration of text analysis, analysis of production, distribution, and use of text process and sociocultural analysis of discourse event as a whole to interpret meanings from the analysed songs. Further, newspaper reports and journal articles were used to validate the study findings.

Presentation and Analysis of Selected Songs

This section focuses on the presentation and analysis of two purposively sampled songs: 'Young Man' and 'Internet'. Since music is a variation of journalism in its content and themes in specific contexts and historic moments (Mano, 2007), Chief Hwenje adopts a 'positioned' style of reporting that was 'located' in his compositions and propagated name-calling, hate speech, and propaganda to get support for President Mnangagwa and ZANU PF.

'Young Man': Infantilises Opposition Politics

The song 'Young Man' infantilises Nelson Chamisa, President of the Citizens Coalition for Change (CCC). The track refers to Chamisa as a 'young man' and a 'small boy'. This is shown when Chief Hwenje sings: '*Hona ari kuchemeiko* young man?' (Look! Why is the young man crying?); '*Arakashwa naVaMnangagwa*' (He lost to Mnangagwa); '*Ari kuchemeiko* small boy?' (Why is the small boy crying?); '*Arakashwa navaMnangagwa*' (He lost to Mnangagwa).

In the same song, Chief Hwenje also portrays Chamisa as an immature troublemaker, who is 'soiling honey' in Zimbabwe as reflected in his lyrics: '*Chigaba chehuchi hachidirwi mavhu*' (a tin of honey should not be soiled); '*Wakazvinyengera* young man' (You fooled yourself young man); '*Kuteya ngwena ne*necklace' (snaring a crocodile with a necklace); '*Wakazvinyengera* young man' (You fooled yourself, young man).

In the song 'Young Man', Chief Hwenje infantilises Chamisa and reduces his political relevance. He uses the name-calling propaganda technique to refer to Chamisa as a 'young man' and a 'small boy'. Cull (2019) defines name-calling as camouflaging opponents with phrases or words intended to lower their integrity. Portraying Chamisa as a 'young man' and a 'small boy' teases him for not being strong enough to challenge 'mature' and 'big boys' like ZANU PF's counterpart, President Mnangagwa. Tsarwe and Mare (2019, p. 10) characterise this as the 'infantilisation' or 'childrenisation' of opposition political actors. The song 'Young Man' thus gives the impression that young people are incapable of becoming political leaders, but global trends show that they can make socio-economic and political changes.

Chief Hwenje's narratives denigrate Chamisa and portray Mnangagwa as ripe to lead the country. In a 2018 interview with *The Herald* newspaper, Chief Hwenje said he composed 'Young Man' to remind Nelson Chamisa that he was still politically immature and a young man trying to join a club of mature men (Muzari, 2018). In his interview and song 'Young Man', Chief Hwenje belittles Chamisa as unripe to lead. He completely disregards the fact that Chamisa was a Minister of Information Communication Technology, Postal and Courier Services in the Government of National Unity (GNU) from February 2009 to July 2013.

In 'Young Man', Chief Hwenje uses the white propaganda form to make Zimbabweans believe that Chamisa was a political novice and politically naïve. This portrayal helps spread ZANU PF's dominant ideology. Sawo (2020) states that white propaganda glorifies political leaders and symbols. Chief Hwenje also deploys the bandwagon propaganda technique to get people to support ZANU PF when he popularises the slogan '*munhu wese ED pfee*' in the song. The fact that Chief Hwenje regularly attends national galas (Madzianike, 2019) further confirms that ZANU PF benefits from relationships with musicians.

'Internet': Opposition Politicians Portrayed as 'Suspects' and 'Sell-Outs'

Qualitative content analysis reveals that Chief Hwenje portrays opposition politicians as 'suspects' and 'sell-outs' or 'traitors'. In the song 'Internet', Chief Hwenje describes President Mnangagwa as a man of action. This is shown when he sings: '*Baba* (Father) Mnangagwa front man'; '*hona vari kungodanidzira* action' (look, he calls for action); '*iwe neni tikabatana*' (if we unite); '*hona tinounzaka budiriro*' (look, we develop our country).

The song also reminds listeners that ZANU PF defeated Britain during the liberation struggle as Chief Hwenje sings: '*hondo takairova*' (we fought the war); '*tisu takakunda ma*British' (we defeated the British). A constant mention of how ZANU PF helped gain independence is an indirect way of telling Zimbabweans that they owe something to the party, and other political groups whose leaders did not participate in the liberation war are not fit to lead. This promotes a 'one-party dictatorship', creates demigods, and violates people's political rights.

The song also portrays opposition politicians as 'sell-outs' as the lyrics attest: '*hona hatitambi nana* small boy' (look, we don't play with small boys); '*hona vanongoteverera vana* yes-man' (look, who follows the yes-man); '*hona taurirai* (look, tell) small boy'; '*hona nyika haitongwi pa*WhatsApp' (look, that the country is not ruled on WhatsApp); '*tauriraiwo* (tell) small boy'; '*hona nyika haitongwi pa*Facebook' (look, that the country is not ruled on Facebook); '*kuzadza manyepo pa*WhatsApp' (spreading lies on WhatsApp); '*nyika haitongwi pa*Internet' (the country is not ruled on the Internet).

In the same song, Chief Hwenje portrays Chamisa as politically void and an instigator of turmoil in Zimbabwe. This is backed by the lyrics: '*hauna shoko rebudiriro*' (no development message); '*kuronga musindo kufadza varungu*' (organising turmoil to please white people).

Additionally, the subject of sanctions was raised in the song as Chief Hwenje accuses CCC of seeking sanctions. He asserts that CCC officials are eating candy cakes with whites and encouraging them to impose economic sanctions on Zimbabwe to bring about regime change. He sings: '*munoswera muri* take take…*shure kwevarungu*' (you always follow the white man); '*maguta ma*candy cake…*modanidzira* sanction' (eating candy cakes and calling for sanctions).

Chief Hwenje also claims that CCC officials are suspects as evidenced when he sings: 'Tsungi *bata* (take your) cellphone'; '*hona timboraira ma*suspect' (look, we want to counsel the suspects). He constantly deploys the word '*hona*' (look) to direct people's attention to Mnangagwa as a man of action and CCC as a party of traitors. The word is deliberately used to urge people to open their eyes and support political actors who are committed to developing Zimbabwe.

Chief Hwenje employs the glittering generality propaganda technique when he frames President Mnangagwa as '*Baba*' (father) who is at the forefront of calling for unity and development in the country. He uses the word '*baba*' (father) to give Zimbabweans the impression that President Mnangagwa is the patriarch of Zimbabwe. The artist pampers the President and his party because he benefits from spreading ZANU PF's ideology. In one of his 2020 interviews with *ZimEye*, an online media outlet, Chief Hwenje said President Mnangagwa visited him on New Year's day and gave him a token of appreciation (ZimEye, 2020). This reinforces the claim that Chief Hwenje and ZANU PF benefit from each other.

The artist also uses the transfer propaganda technique in portraying President Mnangagwa as a 'nation-builder' and a patriot, who cares about his country. The transfer is a propaganda technique that associates products, ideas, or people with high/low credibility, depending on the intent of the message (Cull, 2019). By using this technique, propagandists falsely associate their arguments with ideas of respect such as nation-builders and patriots (Hamdani, 2017). Chief Hwenje also uses the name-calling propaganda technique in the same song, portraying Chamisa and CCC party as 'suspects' and 'sell-outs'. He accuses CCC officials and supporters of destroying Zimbabwe by spreading fake news using the Internet, WhatsApp, and Facebook.

The song 'Internet' also reminds Zimbabweans that ZANU PF brought independence to Zimbabwe. It celebrates the party as having stood up and defeated Britain during the liberation struggle. Chief Hwenje utilises the theme of liberation to express the dominant political ideas of ZANU PF, and this confirms that musicians use historical and philosophical discourses to make the dominant political ideologies more comprehensive (Velasco-Pufleau, 2017). Chief Hwenje also weaves historical and philosophical narratives in his song to make Zimbabweans realise that ZANU PF was a liberator and the only political party worthy of ruling the country.

Chief Hwenje continues to use the white form of propaganda to deceive Zimbabweans into believing that nothing good can come out of the CCC. He intends to preserve ZANU PF's hold on power. He tarnishes the image of Chamisa and CCC and absolves ZANU PF of domestic misconduct. In the song 'Internet', Chief Hwenje glorifies President Mnangagwa as a cult figure, and this is in sync with Guzura and Ndimande's (2015) assertion that one of the overriding themes used by Zimbabwean musicians is the creation of cult personalities to win the battle for the heart and mind. Fettering political leaders with praise is dangerous as it creates an indispensability syndrome and one-partyism (Guzura & Ndimande, 2015).

It is with no doubt that Chief Hwenje uses his art to mobilise support for ZANU PF and its officials. This supports the contention of Chinouriri (2014) and Musiyiwa (2008) that music is a powerful mass mobilisation tool that can be used for political gain. The two scholars argue that music was used as an ideological tool during and after the Zimbabwean liberation war, in the political mobilisation of Zimbabwe's land reform programme, and the quest for national unity. Chief Hwenje also uses the same tactic of using music to get support for President Emmerson Mnangagwa and ZANU PF ahead of the 2023 general elections.

Concluding Remarks and Recommendations

As shown in this chapter, Chief Hwenje uses the white propaganda form to convince Zimbabweans that President Mnangagwa and his ZANU PF party are the only proper actors to govern Zimbabwe. He deploys bandwagon, name-calling, glittering generalities, and transfer propaganda techniques to win the battle for heart and mind for President Mnangagwa and ZANU PF and to consolidate their power in the Zimbabwean political space. Chief Hwenje portrays President Mnangagwa as a father, a liberator, and a nation-builder, who is nationalistic and serves the dreams and hopes of Zimbabweans. He also denigrates Chamisa as a young man, a small boy, a suspect, and a sell-out, who should not be trusted with the levers of power in Zimbabwe. His songs are thus inflaming the conflict between the CCC and ZANU PF in the country. Consequently, this chapter recommends that musicians should use their creativity to promote peace and unity, especially in deeply divided countries like Zimbabwe.

References

Brown, C. (2008). *Politics in music: Music and political transformation from Beethoven to hip-hop*. Farsight Press.

Chibuwe, A., & Munoriyarwa, A. (2022). Repetition without change?: A critical discourse analysis of selected ZANU-PF advertisements for the July 2013 and July 2018 elections. *Discourse & Communication*, 1–25. https://doi.org/10.1177/17504813221132977

Chinouriri, B. (2014). *Singing 'the third Chimurenga': An investigation of the use of music as an ideological force in the political mobilisation of Zimbabwe's land reform 2000–2010* (Unpublished PhD thesis). University of Pretoria.

Chiridza, P., Chirambaguwa, W., & Mukungurutse, S. Y. (2015). Zimbabwe's politics of violence as shown in music from the liberation struggle to the post independence state. *Asian Journal of Humanities and Social Studies*, 3(4), 271–278.

Chitumba, P. (2018, December 7). Chief Shumba back with a new song. *The Herald*. https://www.herald.co.zw/chief-shumba-back-with-new-song/

Cull, N. J. (2019). Counter-propaganda: Cases from US public diplomacy and beyond. In M. Connelly, J. Fox, S. Goebel & U. Schmidt (Eds.), *Propaganda and conflict: War, media and shaping the twentieth century* (pp. 269–284). Bloomsbury Academic.

Fairclough, N. (2000). *Critical discourse analysis* (F. Shayeste et al., Trans.). Media Research Center.

Garratt, J. (2018). *Music and politics: A critical introduction*. Cambridge University Press.

Gecau, K. (1997). The 1980s background to the popular political songs of the early 1990s in Kenya. In R. Zhuwarara, K. Gecau, & M. Drag (Eds.), *Media, democratisation and identity* (pp. 149–176). University of Zimbabwe.

Guzura, T., & Ndimande, J. (2015). Music, political space and power in Zimbabwe: A critique. *International Journal of Politics and Good Governance*, VI(6.4), 1–19.

Hamdani, S. S. M. (2017). Techniques of online propaganda: A case study of Western Sahara Conflict. *International Journal of Media, Journalism and Mass Communications*, 3(2), 18–24.

Herman, E. S., & Chomsky, N. (1988). *Manufacturing consent: A political economy of the mass media*. Pantheon Books.

Jørgensen, M. W., & Phillips, L. J. (2002). *Discourse analysis as theory and method*. Sage.

Jowett, G. S., & O'Donnell, V. (1999). *Propaganda and persuasion* (3rd ed.). Sage.

Jowett, G. S., & O'Donnell, V. (2012). *Propaganda and persuasion* (5th ed.). Sage.

Khosa, T. (2020, October 12). *Chief Shumba collaborates with nine artists.* H-Metro. https://www.hmetro.co.zw/chief-shumba-collaborates-with-nine-artistes/

Koppang, H. (2009). Social influence by manipulation: A definition and case of propaganda. *Middle East Critique, 18*(2), 117–143.

Lee, A. M., & Lee, E. B. (Eds.). (1939). *The fine art of propaganda: A study of Father Coughlin's speeches.* Harcourt Brace and Co.

Mabika, C. (2022, October 24). Artistes ready for Anti-Sanctions gala. *The Herald.* https://www.herald.co.zw/artistes-ready-for-anti-sanctions-gala/

Madzianike, N. (2019, October 25). Musicians promise fireworks at gala. *The Herald.* https://www.herald.co.zw/musicians-promise-fireworks-at-gala/

Madzimure, J. (2020, November 16). Chief Hwenje releases nine-track album. *The Herald.* https://www.herald.co.zw/chief-hwenje-releases-nine-track-album/

Mangena, F., Chitando, E., & Muwati, I. (2016). Introduction: Navigating the interstices of music, identity and politics in Zimbabwe. In F. Mangena, E. Chitando, & I. Muwati (Eds.), *Sounds of life: Music, identity and politics in Zimbabwe* (pp. xi–xviii). Cambridge Scholars Publishing.

Mano, W. (2007). Popular music as journalism in Zimbabwe. *Journalism Studies, 8*(1), 61–78.

Matiure, P. (2019). Hegemony and music in the pre-colonial, colonial and post-colonial Zimbabwe. *Ethnomusicology Journal, 2*(1), 86–96.

Mlambo, M. (2009). A survey of the language situation in Zimbabwe. *English Today, 25*(2), 18–24.

Munhuweyi, K. T. (2022). Praising the croc, despising Nero: The politics of hero-worshipping leaders through music and speech in Zimbabwe. *Journal of Asian and African Studies,* 1–12. https://doi.org/10.1177/00219096221080195

Musiyiwa, M. (2008). The mobilisation of popular songs in the promotion of national unity in Zimbabwe. *Muziki: Journal of Music Research in Africa, 5*(1), 11–29.

Muyambo, T. (2022). 'Sandi bonde': An indigenous knowledge systems perspective on Oliver Mtukudzi's reconstruction music. In E. Chitando, P. Mateveke, M. Nyakudya, & B. Chinouriri (Eds.), *The life and music of Oliver Mtukudzi: Reconstruction and identity* (pp. 135–147). Springer Nature.

Muzari, G. (2018, August 25). The man behind 'ED Pfee' hit song. *The Herald.* https://www.herald.co.zw/the-man-behind-ed-pfee-hit-song/

Ncube, B. J. (2022). Musicians and political songs in the struggle for freedom in Zimbabwe. In U. Onyebadi (Ed.), *Political messaging in music and entertainment spaces across the globe* (pp. 183–206). Vernon Press.

Nyairo, J., & Ogude, J. (2005). Popular music, popular politics: Unbwogable and the idioms of freedom in Kenyan popular music. *African Affairs*, *104*(415), 225–249.

Nyamnjoh, F. (2005). *Africa's media, democracy and politics of belonging*. Zed Books and UNISA Press.

Onyebadi, U. T. (2019). *Music and messaging in the African political arena*. IGI Global.

Orgeret, K. S. (2016). Introduction—Conflict and post-conflict journalism: Worldwide perspectives. In K. S. Orgeret & W. Tayeebwa (Eds.), *Journalism in conflict and post-conflict conditions: Worldwide perspectives* (pp. 13–22). Nordicom.

Palmberg, M. (2004). Music in Zimbabwe's crisis. In S. Thorsen (Ed.), *Sounds of change: Social and political features of music in Africa* (pp. 18–46). Sida Studies.

Sauti, L. (2022). *Mediating political and electoral violence: An analysis of The Sunday Mail and The Standard newspapers' reportage of the 26 March 2022 by-elections in Zimbabwe* (Unpublished MA thesis). University of Zimbabwe.

Sawo, A. (2020). *Arts, propaganda and politics in contemporary Africa: The role of music and musicians in entrenching dictatorship in The Gambia during the Jammeh's Regime (1994–2016)* (Unpublished MSc thesis). Wageningen University.

Sithole, S. (2022, July 9). ZANU PF hires Mark Ngwazi. Bulawayo24 News. https://bulawayo24.com/index-id-news-sc-national-byo-221215.html

Soules, M. (2015). *Media, persuasion and propaganda*. Edinburgh University Press Ltd.

Steuter, E., & Wills, D. (2008). *At war with metaphor: Media, propaganda, and racism in the war on terror*. Lexington Books.

Street, J. (1997). *Politics and popular culture*. Temple University.

Street, J. (2003). 'Fight the power': The politics of music and the music of politics. *Government and Opposition*, *38*(1), 113–130.

Tsarwe, S., & Mare, A. (2019). Journalistic framing of electoral conflict in a politically fragile society: A comparative study of the Zimbabwean weekly press. *African Journalism Studies*, 1–18. https://doi.org/10.1080/23743670.2019.1570297

Van Dijk, T. (2003). *Studies in discourse analysis: From text structure to critical discourse* (P. Izadi, Trans.). Media Research Center.

Velasco-Pufleau, L. (2017). 'We are the world': Music and propaganda in democracy. Music, Sound and Conflict. https://msc.hypotheses.org/11.

ZimEye. (2020, January 21). *Mnangagwa visits musician who sold his only two cattle to record ED Pfee song*. ZimEye. https://www.zimeye.net/2020/01/21/mnangagwa-visits-musician-who-sold-his-only-two-cattle-to-record-ed-pfee-song/

CHAPTER 12

Melancholia and Polysemanticism in Winky D's Sonic Retentions: Subverting Expressive Barricades and Voicing the Electoral Process Through Performance

Esther Mavengano

INTRODUCTION

While it is generally agreed that musicians across the world have a propensity to address polemic issues in their immediate social environment, the advent of Zimbabwe dancehall music which is popularly known as

E. Mavengano (✉)
Department of English and Media Studies, Faculty of Arts,
Great Zimbabwe University, Masvingo, Zimbabwe
e-mail: emavengano@gzu.ac.zw

Research Institute for Theology and Religion, College of Human Sciences, UNISA, Pretoria, South Africa

Alexander von Humboldt Postdoctoral Research Fellow at TU, Institute of English and American Studies, Faculty of Linguistics, Literature and Cultural Studies, Department of English, Technische Universitat Dresden, Dresden, Germany

© The Author(s), under exclusive license to Springer Nature Switzerland AG 2023
E. Mavengano and S. Chirongoma (eds.), *Electoral Politics in Zimbabwe, Vol II*, https://doi.org/10.1007/978-3-031-33796-3_12

Zimdancehall in the early 2000s was scoffed at by many. Yet, Sabao (2018), referring to a growing popularity of the new music genres in Zimbabwe, contends that music, as popular culture, has the power to penetrate into audiences in which official modes of communication typically fail and also has the capacity to reach multitudes in ways such forms cannot. This chapter locates Winky D's two songs titled 'Parliament' on the Elders Riddim album and 'Ibotso' on the album titled Eureka within the context of electoral politics in present-day Zimbabwe. The purposively selected songs disrupt a tradition of silence in matters that are considered as socio-culturally and religio-politically forbidden in Zimbabwe, as well as talking back to power in bell hooks' (2015) vocabulary. The study draws insights from Cultural Linguistics (CL) and Achille Mbembe's (1992, 2001, 2003) theorisation of power which demonstrate a profound willingness to coerce its subjects, using munitions of domination in the postcolony. These conceptual frameworks are essential in probing sonic representation of haunting socio-economic and religio-political polemics in contemporary Zimbabwe. The textual analyses of the chosen lyrics in this study aim to convey complex seditious acts against stifling political milieu and entrench the semantic of commandment, conviviality and resistance which are intricately constructed in the selected sonic retentions. Allen (2004, p. 1) opines that 'music functions as a trenchant political site in Africa...' This view is true especially when one studies Zimdancehall as a site of controversial encounter between what Giorgio Agamben (1998) calls the sovereign power and Foucauldian subjects of power. This tension-filled terrain thereby generates salient vistas where socio-cultural and religio-political subjects interconnect to foreground an artistic voice and agency that also becomes a fundamental voice of the subaltern in Spivak's (1988) terminology. In the same vein, Sabao (2018, p. 113) posits that music represents a superstructural linguistic and semiotic tool through which power dynamics and relations are (re)established and (re)negotiated. Imperatively, the study shows how the songs offer important sites of engagement with transition discourses from which to interrogate the polemics of contemporary electoral politics in Zimbabwe and gain new perspectives in pursuit of socio-political and religious recovery. Within this unstable milieu, artists seek to recalibrate power and reconstruct alternative socio-political and religious modes replete with subversive semiotics which challenge us to re-consider existing political subjectivities. This nuanced dynamic of power is in line with Foucault's (1975/1995) argument that power can come from below; hence, the "microphysics" of power are varied and intricate. Central to the discussion in this chapter is a vexing question, how are the elect songs linguistically and semantically making a lurid call for decisive actions in shaping new vistas of becoming and suggest novel political rationalities in post-Mugabe Zimbabwe? The intention is to provide fresh acumens into key issues around the electoral process in Zimbabwe which has great impact on the state of affairs in the national space.

A Synergy of Cultural Linguistics and Mbembe's Modes of Rule in a Postcolony

Drawing its discursive frames from Farzad Sharifian's (2011) Cultural Linguistics perspective and Achille Mbembe's political thought in his formulation of the postcolony (Mbembe, 1992, 2001), this study is interdisciplinary in nature as it sits between the subfields of applied linguistics, sociolinguistics and political theory. This multifaceted conceptual terrain is appropriate for the interrogation of a nuanced subject that demands intricate analytical gaze in order to make productive debates. In addition, as Guzura and Ndimande (2015) rightly note, music, just like any other form of art, is informed by the socio-cultural and political context. Cultural Linguistics and Mbembe's theorisation of the postcolony serve as important conceptual paradigms that are used to bring into sharp focus the contextual dimensions of the studied songs. Sharifian (2017) underlines the semantic significance of both linguistic construction of discourse and the cultural context (a co-text) from which language is used. The term Cultural Linguistics (CL) denotes a lately established discipline with a multidisciplinary background that analyses the connection between language and cultural *conceptualisations or* cultural schemas (Sharifian, 2008, 2011). CL is concerned with linguistic structures that embedded with culturally fashioned conceptualisations including the entre scope of human experience in a particular socio-cultural, historical and political milieu (Palmer, 1996; Sharifian, 2017). Essentially, cultural cognition continues to be negotiated as it is shaped by evolving circumstances within the social world. This implies that even when considering linguistic stylisations of the purposively selected songs, the evolving urban linguistic ecology or metrolingualism, according to Pennycook and Otsuji (2015), becomes a significant analytical dimension that informs local language practices in this cultural contact space. This view takes us to Bakhtin's

(1981) concept of the outsideness of language which brings into conversation the importance of the socio-cultural world in human cognition of language and discourse. This also resonates with Ngugi wa Thiong'o's (1994) remarkable contention that the human language is a fundamental feature of cultural cognition since it functions as a communal memory bank of a particular cultural group. Thus, Cultural Linguistics provides both a hypothetical and an analytical outline for probing the cultural meanings that lie beneath the use of language (Palmer, 1996). Mbembe's notions of *commandment, conviviality* and vulgarity of power are applied together with CL in complementary ways in this study. Achille Mbembe's formulation of power in the postcolony compels us to re-explicate numerous premises that hitherto appeared undisputable. Mbembe (1992) envisions the African postcolony as subject to *commandment* a type of rule that re-enacts the violent authority with which colonial domination was prescribed and sustained. For Mbembe, the postcolony adopted colonial practices of power. The discussion is guided by the following vexing questions: How do the songs upset normative political framework set by agents of power to present an appealing account of those from below? How do these songs construct the perceived subjects as constitutive part of power dynamics in electoral politics in current Zimbabwe? In this regard, Mbembe's theorisation of power is put into dialogic interaction with Foucauldian conceptualisation to further appreciate a power convolution in Zimbabwe's electoral context. What deep yearnings from those on the margin are communicated through sonic performances?

ZIMDANCEHALL MUSIC GENRE: BORN OUT OF THE LOGIC OF DOMINATION AND OTHERISATION

The fundamental role of creative arts or cultural products such as literature, music, paintings and theatre among others, in shaping public opinion and behaviour, has long been established (Guzura & Ndimande, 2015; Mavengano, 2020; Ngugi wa Thiong'o, 1994; Palmer, 1996). In the context of Zimbabwe, the vexed entanglement of music and politics is traceable to precolonial history (Dube, 2016; Vambe, 2004). During the liberation struggle, the oppressed black Africans used songs and dance as sites for deep political expression and civic mobilisation. In other words, music was part of political ideological apparatuses in Althusser's (1971) language. The ruling party, Zimbabwe African National Union Patriotic Party (ZANU PF), is conscious of how music was instrumental in fighting the colonial government. It is then logical to argue that the state's disturbing desire to control not only the music industry but generally the entire creative arts is informed by this historical memory of those in the corridors of power.

Ndlovu-Gatsheni and Willems (2009) note how cultural performances and commemorations that is reference to biras and galas according to Muchemwa (2010) become vital part of the ruling party's anxious effort to generate nationalist politics based on affect, emotion and performance. The diplomatic tension between Zimbabwe and the Western countries especially America and Britain prompted the then Mugabe-led government to take drastic actions against its imagined or real political foes. The introduction of the 75% local content during early 2000 in Zimbabwe's public airwaves was one such radical stance to spite the West and reduce its perceived harmful influence on the local population (Dube, 2016). Jonathan Moyo who was then the Minister of Information and Publicity radically transformed the music landscape in Zimbabwe through the Broadcasting Services Act (BSA 2001), which demanded a 75% local content to be played on airwaves (Tendi, 2010). The Act, according to the government, was meant to promote national identity, character and paradoxically cultural diversity. Yet, the move was viewed by critics as the state's attempt to muffle dissenting voices and monopolise power through its interference with both the media content and creative arts (Tendi, 2010). It appears, the state's obsession with absolute control was meant to disregard what Chimamanda Ngozi Adichie (2009) calls the danger of single story telling or monological discourse according to Bakhtin (1981). Adichie (2009) poignantly cautions that single story telling (whatever the story is about) produces stereotypes and the story is perpetually imperfect in the absence of other competing narratives. Adichie offers a significant principle that could considerably transform political thinking and behaviour. Contrary to the state's claim that the shift to the 75% local content was also meant to empower local artists by creating more space for their music, Dube (2016) contends that the government blacklisted songs that were in contradiction of its policies. Dube (2016) further points out that the state also worked towards influencing and directing civic perceptions through music and public broadcasting by funding and supporting musicians whose songs supported the political elite. Thus, the present-day Zimdancehall music genre was born out of the logics of domination, quest to create a culture of patronage among artists, a bid to alienate ordinary Zimbabweans from other sensibilities and Otherisation of those whose views were not in agreement with the Mugabe regime, particularly the West. What is most worrisome is the evidence that the logic of political domination and state censorship still thrive in Zimbabwe. Their embeddedness in everyday socio-economic and political spheres cannot be refuted. The logic of domination can no longer be considered as a phenomenon that only arises during election times but rather has become part of practices of everyday life (de Certeau, 1984), in Zimbabwe, which is a disheartening national character.

Winky D's Track '*Ibotso*' Featuring Holly Ten on Eureka Album 2023

A popular Zimbabwean musician famously known as Winky D released his latest album Eureka, on the eve of 2023 welcoming the new year in style. The term Eureka is a Greek word, it evokes semantic ambiguities, and it qualifies as an interjection or a lexical item that can articulate deep emotions such as rage, delight, agony or astonishment https://learninge nglish.voanews.com/a/eurika-word-discovery/3510636.htm. Winky D's album Eureka has 14 tracks which are: Tears Ft. Anita Jaxson, Vafarisi Ft. Bazooker and Poptain, MuSpirit Ft. Dr Chaii, Shaker Ft. Enzo Ishall, Gonyera, Ft. Exq, High Grades Ft. Herman, Ibotso Ft. Holy Ten, Urere Ft. Killer T, Nherera Ft. Mwenje Mathole, Peter Friend Ft Nutty O, XYZ Ft. SaintFloew, Dzimba Dzemabwe Ft. Shingai and Chauruka Ft. Tocky Vibes. The release of this album sparked controversy around its political innuendoes which seem to have provoked those in power and their supporters. Winky D's music has been at the centre of controversy because of its inimitable thematisation of the prevailing political affairs in Zimbabwe. Kadzura (2023) remarks that the art as an outlet for expression is on track record as seriously affected by the tragedies of polarisation. Winky D's career peaked alongside the broadcast of his crucifixion as a troublemaker to national security. Instead of fleeing from his persecutors, he shields in mass *esprit de corps* as the voice of the voiceless. Currently, his new album Eureka sparked mixed reactions because of its distinctive allusions to the socio-economic and political affairs in current Zimbabwe. One of the young musicians, Holy Ten whose real name is Mukudzei Chitsama, collaborated with Winky D on the song Ibotso, but later denounced him publicly in a bid that is viewed by critics and fans as a desperate move to escape the wrath of Mnangagwa-led government.

The Translated 'Ibotso' Track on Eureka Album (2023)

Aiwa! Hoyo! (An interjection- an expression of contempt and perplexity)
Vanotora zvevapfupi nekureba! (The Tall Eat or take what is supposed to be for the Short)
Sekutamba sekuseka (banter or like mere joking)
Ibotso! Woriitei? (A cursed fate, what can one do about it?)
Vanonyepa vanonyepedzera! (They lie, they pretend)
Vanozesa vanozeza zera (They are scared of age/aging)
Vanospender vanotenga vanotenga-tenga (they spend, they purchase a lot)
Ibotso (It's a cursed fate)
Ini ndiri muimbi chete (I am just an artist)
No, pfumo no bakatwa! (With neither a spare nor a sword)
Musandikande pasi kunge hakatwa! (Don't throw me down like fortune telling bones)
Ibotso (It's a cursed fate)
Aiwa ini ndiri muimbi chete (No, I am only a mere artist)
No pfumo no bakatwa! (No spear, no sword!)
Saka ini musandikakata! (So, don't terrorise me)
Ndoda pekugara, ndinoda roof (I need a place to stay, I need a roof over my head)
Ndoda chekudya mumba mune hupfu (I need food, a house with mealie-meal)
Paghetto tirikuchema kunge rufu (In the ghetto space, we are grieving as if we are at a funeral)
Vamwe varikukwata varikuchemera muvhu (Some are scared, they hide or stifle their grief)
Vauya netsvimbo hanzi ndiani anoti bufu? (They came with rods / clubs asking, who have dared to speak?)
Vatengesi votengesa vopiwa mafufu (betrayers, name the dissenters and they are rewarded with only crumbs)
Torwisana tega (the poor fight each other)
MaHutu nemaTutsi (and re-enact the Rwandan Hutus and Tutsis genocide)
Aiwa hauzombozvida futi, futi (the unfolding scenario does not please anyone)
Zvimoko zvogaya kuti life iri mubeauty (young girls regard physical beauty as a means of survival)
Vobhaizwa nemadhara nemacooler boxes muboot (they are tricked by the old men with cooler boxes in their car boots)
Yobva yangorohwa raw sushi (the young girls engage in unprotected sex with these old men)

Pobarwa kamwe kayouth (and another youth is born)
Youth koshaya life irikunanga nekupi (the susceptible youth fails to comprehend the circumstances that define his life)
Koona magevha kotambidzwa pfuti (The youth meet criminals and is given guns)
Kopinda paghetto, koblinker neGucci (The youth get into the city and show off the newly purchased Gucci brand)
Vanotora zvevapfupi nekureba! (When the Tall eat or take what belongs to those who are Short)
Sekutamba sekuseka (as if they are joking)
Vanonyepa vanonyepedzera (They lie, they pretend
Vanozesa vanozesa zera (They are scared of age/ aging)
Ibotso Woriitei? (It's a cursed fate, what can be done about it?)
Ini ndiri muimbi chete! (I am just an artist)
No pfumo, no bakatwa! (With no spear, no sword)
Saka ini musandikakata! (So don't threaten me)
Ah, ghetto youth zvotimakisa (Ah! Urban youths we are considered as rebellious)
Zvokuvati boss chakadaro (When we criticise the boss about the ills around us)
Because posh yavanayo magetsi (Because the rich boss drives a posh car)
Parikubuda mazheti nemaziunhu (The boss has lots of money and some weird ethics)
Mwanasikana buda mumabedroom (the young girls get into the bedrooms of the rich)
Mwanasikana rinotambika botso iri (the young is enticed and her cursed fate is sealed)
Tone down usafirita photo iri (avoid filtered photos)
Unoerekana wazotsvakwaka nemagevha anotemera musaga (scoundrels will look for you)
Vamwe vedu takakurira munhamo too (some of us grew up in poverty also)
Asi takazviudza kuti mudhara go prove (But we told ourselves to go out there and prove our worth)
I will never go broke
Even if you show me zvinhu zvacho zvemumovie (Even if you lure me with fake things)
I will go no group, never, never! (I will never be influenced by peer pressure)
Pane zvakadhura but hapana aisevenza (some have expensive stuff but they have never been employed)
Pane akanyura but hapana airedza (some drowned but they were not fishing)

Vanotora zvevapfupi nekureba (The Tall take what belongs to the short
Sekutamba sekuseka (As if they are joking)
Ibotso Woriitei (It's a cursed fate, what can be done?)
Vanonyepa vanonyepedzera (They lie, they pretend)
Vanozesa vanozesa zera (they are scared of age/aging)
Vanospender vanotenga tenga (they spend, they acquire a lot)
Ini ndiri muimbi chete (I am only an artist)
No pfumo, no bakatwa! (No spear, no sword)
Musandikande pasi kunge hakata (don't throw me down like fortune telling bones)
Ibotso! (It's a cursed fate)

Winky D's Track Parliament on Elders Riddim Album (2018)

https://soundcloud.com/pdmd263/winky-d-parliament-elders

The single track was released in 2018 coinciding with Zimbabwe's elections.

Gaffer chete, chete chete (Gaffer only)
Hoyi! Vamwe vati ita independent candidate (Ah! Some advised me to become an independent candidate)
Mavotes unowana percentage 100 (They say I will get 100 percent votes)
Hapachada zvemapato apa paakuda sorosheni (It's no longer time for party politics but seeking a solution)
Vakomana musazononokera Colgate (peers don't delay)
Hapachada mafunny apa, pavakuda chiGaffer muparamende (No time for funnies, what is urgently needed is leadership in parliament)
Ndipei mukana ndinotungamira pakaboka muparamende (Give me an opportunity to lead in parliament)
SaMoses ndinotungamira huyai tiende mundosiya mandigadza muparamende (Like Moses I will lead, let us go for my inauguration)
Pavakuda chiGaffer muparamende (What is urgently needed is leadership in parliament)
Ndipei mukana ndinotungamira, huyai tiende mundosiya mandigadza (Give me an opportunity to lead, let us go for my inauguration)
Mr Speaker paghetto ndokumbira kuti dai masvika (Mr Speaker could you please come and see the Ghetto space)
Hapambodi zvekutimira, huyai mega muzvionere maGhetto youth akasticker (Don't send others, come and witness how the youths have succumbed to illicit drugs)

Nekuti kufa kwemayouth ndokufa kwenyika (Because there is no future of the country if the youth succumb to drugs)
Pachagarwa nani ipapo muchinge madzika (Who will be the future leaders?)
Handimbowithdrawer statement yangu (I will not withdraw my statement)
Itai serious imika (Be serious you people)
Hapachada mafunny apa, (No more funnies)
Pavakuda chiGaffer muparamende (Radical leadership in parliament is now urgently needed)
Ndipei mukana, SaMoses ndinotungamira (Give me an opportunity to lead, I will lead like Moses)
Paghetto tateketera panamadzudzo (In Ghetto we have suffered, there are so many problems)
Vazhinji vanenge Marechera Dambudzo (There are many who are like Marechera Dambudzo)
Yasvika zvino nguva yekuti tiyambuke (The time has come for us to cross)
Vakomana musazonetera zambuko (peers never tire when you are already at the bridge)
Tombomira kusimbisana pavakuda shanduko (Let us stop consoling each other, what is now needed is political change)
Kana mati pasi ratsamwa ndauya nepfuko (If you say the spiritual world is angry, I have brought a clay pot for appeasement)
Maronda ayo ari pazvanza (Wounds on my hands)
Ndadana mutupo (I have made a plea by saying a totem)
Hapachada mafunny apa (There is no time for funnies)
Paakuda chiGaffer (radical leadership is needed)
SaMoses ndinotungamira (Like Moses I will lead)
Huyai tiende mundosiya mandigadza muparamende (Come, let us go for my inauguration in parliament)

The Invigorated Artistic Contestation of Expressive Barricades in Zimbabwe

Wallace Chirumiko's music oeuvre (famously known as Winky D) is part of the contemporary youth's popular culture in Zimbabwe which should be located in evolving contexts of 'multi' that disrupt rigid dichotomies. Kufakurinani and Mwatwara (2017) remark that Zimdancehall arose in a peculiar socio-cultural and political metropolitan environment. Similarly, Raftopoulos (2009) also points out that from early 2000, the Mugabe government introduced deterring laws such as the Public Order and Security Act (POSA) and the Access to Information and Protection of

Privacy Act (AIPPA) which were intended to eradicate dissent and limit freedom of expression and instil widespread terror among ordinary citizens, human right activists and artists in Zimbabwe. The usually liberal and lashing tongue of the artist was then compelled to remain behind the teeth. Instead of effectively silencing the artistic voice, this despotic political culture augmented disillusionment and distrust of nationalist politics in Zimbabwe (Mavengano, 2020; Muchemwa, 2010). Several Zimbabwean artists demonstrated a propensity towards non-conformity creative art across the different genres of the art industry. For instance, radical music came even from the old generation of Zimbabwean musicians like Thomas Mapfumo and Oliver Mtukudzi among others. Fictional writers also challenged government efforts to rob them their creative liberties as evident in unguarded critique of the ruling party and its leaders in Jinga's *One Foreigner's Ordeal*, Brian Chikwava's *Harare North*, Valerie Tagwira's *The Uncertainty of Hope*, Tsitsi Dangarembga's *This Mournable Body*, Valerie Tagwira's *Trapped*, NoViolet Bulawayo's *We Need New Names*, and *Glory*, among many others. The writers of these cited works speak truth to power daring the Mugabe regime at the time. This radical artistic tradition still persists and apparently inspires some of the young generation of musicians in Zimbabwe like Winky D who are also frustrated by the visible inherited arrogance and retributive culture in the 'New Dispensation' after Mugabe's departure.

Singing Truth to Power and Polysemantic Allusions as Artistic Ammunitions

The songs 'Ibotso' and 'Parliament' invite numerous meanings due to their intertextual, polyglossic and interdisciplinary construction. The artist consciously and creatively constructed thought-provoking titles of his tracks. In the Zimbabwean context, the terms Ibotso and Parliament assume cultural and political significance, respectively. The word Ibotso from a cultural understanding refers to a bad omen or a curse from one's parents, especially an aggrieved mother who then curses the insolent child to suffer the consequences of impudence (Chigidi, 2009). Such a child is then required to appease not only the wronged parent but also the entire community by wearing rags and confessing the evil committed publicly (Tatira, 2014). The concept of botso in Zimbabwe is linked to African Traditional Religion (ATR). The parliament is where highly cherished individuals who politically represent the people debate issues, just like the traditional Council of Elders is known for. These are respected members of parliament (honourable MPs) whose level of moral standards should be unquestionable in their communities. They are elected to speak for the people. In this regard, Winky D envisions a competing nationalism which is different from the one constructed by the ruling class in Zimbabwe. By drawing from the African Traditional Religion's concept of Council of Elders, the MPs are, therefore, expected to uphold the political, economic and even the moral interests of their people. His songs delineate a reimagined nationalism as an undertaking of moral renewal which pursues to bring together the diverse elements of the nation including the traditional, religious and modern, as pertinent sources of life ethos.

It is this socio-cultural and political context that feeds into Winky D's music and suggests semantic possibilities of his songs. The titles of these two tracks thus serve as cultural and political metaphors which offer nuanced layers of meanings. The titles together with the messages in the songs create polysemantic illusions and ambiguities that demand contextual knowledge to uncover embedded meanings.

The angry tone in both songs conveys biting critique of the state of affairs in present-day Zimbabwe. The persona is irked by fragility and depressing existential circumstances that have reduced the ghetto people to the level of what Agamben (1998) theorises as bare life or the figure of homo sacer whose life is insignificant. Fragility and sentimentality are illustrated in a litany of the problems encountered by the people in the ghetto space including lack of accommodation and food. As Terry Eagleton (2008, p. 833) commenting on the subversive prowess of creative works concludes, artists are "trained to imagine alternatives to the actual." In this regard, 'Parliament' becomes an oxymoronic title that ridicules those in Zimbabwe's parliamentary positions who have let down the electorate and severely undermine the orderly functioning of the society. This oxymoronic juxtaposition is observed in the light of the fact that it is the MPs and other elderly people in this society, who are expected to act in the interest of the populace, whose egotistical socio-cultural and political behaviour is foregrounded. For example, the rich and powerful elderly men take youthful girls for paid sex.

Palmer (1996, p. 63) contends that "[i]t is likely that all native knowledge of language and culture belongs to cultural schemas and the living of culture and the speaking of language consist of schemas in action." The mixture of ATR, Christianity and popular culture in Winky D's selected tracks endorses the reading that the musician suggests embraces an ever evolving polycultural and multi-religious scope which, however, troubles the interpretive process. Winky D employs lexical and semantic items related to religio-cultural schemas to locate his music not only in Zimbabwe but in the region and even beyond. His music not only defies the 'barbed wire of rules' from the political domain but also challenges linguistic, cultural and religious boundary thinking that fractures humanity in the modern world. His music thus ridicules the elite discourse and imposed nationalism that misleadingly underlines notions of 'pure' and homogeneous 'Zimbabwean culture' or Zimbabweanness which is a contested term (Ndlovu-Gatsheni, 2009). For Muchemwa (2010), the ruling party in Zimbabwe has reconstructed a monological narrative about nationhood, culture and historiography to align with its political ideology. In other words, the introduction of the 75% local content policy was based on a fallacious political effort to isolate citizens from the rest of the world and also create false sensibilities about nationhood which can never be entirely divorced from the 'foreign influence' as erroneously argued by the state.

The persona in 'Parliament' track reiterates his message that "SaMoses ndinotungamira, huyai tiende mundosiya mandigadza muparamende" (like Moses I will lead, come, and let us go so that you will bestow me as a new leader in parliament). This clearly is a fusion of ATR and Christianity as the song makes a biblical allusion to Moses who led the Israelites and saved them from Pharaoh's vicious treatment. The biblical analogy evokes striking comparative that leaves us with a disturbing understanding of how bad the political situation is in Zimbabwe which then is comparable to the Israelites' experiences under Pharaoh. The persona is not only mobilising civic support against the uncanny leaders in the parliament, but rather also issuing a firm warning about the need for 'chiGaffer' that will bring change. According to the persona, only the 'chiGaffer' will transform a political context where party politics and independent candidates have failed to yield urgently needed results. The term gaffer is semantically laden as it implies a personal as well as collective identities. The prevailing political situation demands a strong gaffer, like a Moses, that is a leader to take the languishing citizens out of Pharaoh's Egypt (implicature). Yet the leader needs support of other gaffers (civic solidarity), to take a bold action 'chiGaffer chete, chete.' It is ironic that the moral decay of the nation is initiated by the elders called Ndichie in the context of Nigeria who are selected men of integrity, expected to be the custodian of morality (Ezenagu, 2014). This sad reversal foregrounds the youthful musician's critique of the political leadership in Zimbabwe. The belief that youthful musicians lack cultural consciousness and identity is strongly troubled in Winky D's music (Chari, 2009).

In the track Ibotso, it is those in positions of authority or the 'Tall' who snatch away from the 'Short' what they are entitled to get. "Vanotora zvevapfupi nekureba, Sekutamba sekuseka" (in some kind of a banter or like mere joking and yet, they are serious). The Shona idiomatic expressions and metaphorisation are employed to speak about abuse of power by those in authority who adopted egocentric culture that further impoverishes ordinary citizens (the Short). Winky D's music makes a relentless call to the urgent need for active citizenship. The postcolonial Zimbabwean story is a complex one, and citizens have an active role to play in demanding justice and parity (Mavengano, 2020; Moyo & Mavengano, 2021; Muchemwa, 2013; Ndlovu-Gatsheni & Ruhanya, 2020).

One of the critical elements of Winky D's music is its ability to refer to various themes and diverse associative experiences, envisioned transculturalism, syncretism and intertextuality that realistically project a complex socio-cultural and religio-political environment of the contemporary society (Kadzura, 2023). This is in line with Cultural Linguistics model which accounts for the localisation of English language through code-switching, code-mixing and translanguaging in Winky D's songs. For example, the use of words and phrases like muparamende (in the parliament), 'even if you show me zvinhu zvemumovie' (even if you try to entice me with fictionalised things), hapachada mafunny apa (no more time for funnies), further locates his music in local language practices especially in the city space where slang or metropolitan linguo, English and Zimbabwe's indigenous languages are used in a new semiotic code that disregards linguistic boundaries. Winky D also uses first person plural pronouns such as 'we' (Tivenga, 2018) and 'us' to buttress the idea that he identifies and speaks for the ghetto people whose living condition is a thorn in his flesh. Winky D's music also links the local with the regional and global as well as different historical times, spaces, creative traditions and genres. This is an incredible and compelling approach that also refutes canonisation of creative works and rigid dichotomisation in an increasingly globalised world.

If we understand these creative works as a depiction of the prevailing culture, then Winky D is successful in this respect as he locates his songs in the recognisable and convincing semiospheres in the semiotic cosmos of the Zimbabwean culture. He also identifies with the language of the people whom he speaks for, thereby presents biting and poignant socio-cultural and political commentary. Winky D also pays homage to Dambudzo Marechera perhaps to suggest continuation of his subversive creative tradition in his literary works. Flora Veit-Wild (1993a, 1993b, p. 262) observes that: Marechera's writing legacy is known for his open-mindedness and polyphonic stance. Veit-Wild (1993a, 1993b, pp. 260–261) notes that Marechera's literary oeuvre is counter-discursive, subversive and dynamic in the post-structuralist logic, as he quizzes and undermines "the notion of absolute and distinct reality." By alluding to Marechera, Winky D connects music and literature, a scenario theorised as intertextuality from linguistic and literary perspectives. Allen (2011) explains the term intertextuality by proposing that a network of prior texts or textual cross-fertilisation provides the context of possible meanings of the present text. Allen (2011) further argues that identifying intertexts is a case of interpretation. The mentioning of Marechera also creates semantic ambiguities since he was associated with drug abuse. The modern-day youth in Zimbabwe are also at risk due to a frustrating socio-economic and political environment. It is therefore appropriate to consider these possible meanings.

The tone of the songs is scornful and woven together with remarkable translingual practices which translate into a complicated semiotic assemblage reflective of the sociolinguistic and intercultural realities in present-day metropolitan space. Such language practices also envision a pluricentricity society and hybridity in socio-cultural and political identities. The youth in a cut-throat ghetto space are equally devious and 'young girls engage in prostitution with rich immoral adult men "mudhara,"' as a desperate means of survival. Young boys get into criminal activities using firearms. It is this dog-eat-dog milieu that also compel the youth to lose themselves to illicit drugs. Yet, it is important to note that it is this same zone of non-being, an 'arid region where an authentic upheaval can be born' as rightly hypothesised by Fanon (1963/1961, p. 2). The ghetto people who are severely incapacitated as captured in the statement "paghetto tiri kuchema kunge rufu." The ghetto people pose a threat to the autocratic leadership; hence, whenever they protest, those in authority use brutal force to silence them, "vauya netsvimbo hanzi ndiani anoti bufu?" (They came with rods/clubs asking, who has dared to speak?). It is this silencing that makes some scared citizens to stile their discontent (amwe vari kukwata vari kuchemera muvhu). The artist utilises metaphoric language 'kuchemera muvhu' to capture the aesthetics of muteness. The autocratic culture also survives on divide and rule mechanism where a certain part of the society strives to identify with the elite and in the process betrays a just cause 'Vatengesi votengesa, vopiwa mafufu' (betrayers, name the dissenters and they are rewarded with only crumbs). Mbembe (1992) views brutal performance of power as part of what he theorises as vulgarity of power. It is quite unnerving that it is the poor and marginalised who are made to fight each other and re-enact the Rwandan genocide between Hutus and Tutsis scenario. The historical allusion to the holocaust memory is more forceful as it highlights the danger of manipulative politics or divide and rule political thinking and warns about its threat to national security. The allusion to Rwanda is also an act of subversion as explicated by Valerie Wagner's (2002) notion of history's mortal remains. For Wagner, the living can exercise a claim to what remains after a violent destruction of life when the power that destroys life also obliges the bereft to forget the dead, rebuffing that compulsion to forget and recovering the mortal remains of the dead establish acts of resistance. Thus, the Zimbabwean story is interwoven with other sad stories of the postcolonial Africa. The artist as rightly observed by Ngugi wa Thiong'o (1994) resists the finality of enforced inertia and amnesia. Holocaust memory is a reminder of postcolonial Africa's complicated trajectory.

Mbembe (1992) explicates the postcolony not as a simple sequence of time, but as a timescape of entanglement where multiple traces of colonisation and its violence overlap in an interlocking of presents, pasts and futures that bear on and alter one another. Winky D's presentation of violence and undignified leaders is also articulated in his other songs on the album Eureka. For instance, in a track entitled 'Chauruka,' which features Tocky vibe, Winky D warns proud leaders that one day they will be humbled (remekedza vanodzika gomo paunorikwidza iwe nokuti paunenge woridzika vanogonha kunge ivo vorikwidza), Kutonhodzwa kwaChauruka vanorema vachareruka, and pacharira mupururu, mupururu, Pasi pano hapanzarwo, pakaturunura mikono, vamwe vachiti tisu vachenjeri vakabva kumabva zuva (This world has witnessed the fall of the mighty before. Some view themselves as the wise men from the East, but one of these days, such self-deception will bring your downfall and the poor will celebrate). This could be interpreted as reference to the recent historical event of 'a soft coup' that led to the demise of Robert Mugabe in Zimbabwe. The Mnangagwa government is warned about hubris and hamartia in Shakespearean language (human folly) which bring disgrace, a possible repeat of history in Zimbabwe.

THE COMPLICATIONS IN ZIMBABWEAN STORY AND ELECTORAL POLITICS: IBOTSO WORIITEI?

The examined songs in this study convey what Gilroy (1993) calls the postcolonial melancholia. For Winky D, music serves as a de-silencing strategy in a country where speaking truth against power is unpardonable (Bhebhe, 2023). The musician insists on his artist function which should be respected "Ini ndiri muimbi chete, no pfumo, bakatwa, musandikandire pasi hakata" (I am a mere artist, without a spear nor a sword, please don't persecute me). Winky D hints at the ongoing persecution of artists which has not stopped in the present post-Mugabe era. Examples of such cases include that of Tsitsi Dangarembga, a Zimdancehall musician Platinum whose real name Ian Makiwa got in trouble after his release of the song 'Ndoyacho Here President' translated to 'Is it so, Mr President,' which reminds Mnangagwa of his unfulfilled promises to the nation (Dziva, 2019). Samantha popularly known as Gonyeti is among this recent list; she was forced to drink sewage by suspected state security agents. During Mugabe's reign, Thomas Mapfumo and Chenjerai Hove fled the country. Thus, Winky D exposes semantic hollowness of the "new political dispensation" as has also been argued by a number scholars such as Mavengano and Hove (2019) and Ndlovu-Gatsheni and Ruhanya (2020). The audience are told that the politics of falsehood runs the nation 'Vanonyepa vanonyepedzera' (they lie, and they are pretentious). The repetition in Ibotso track of this message is meant to highlight how the leadership thrives on fairy tale and subterfuge. The persona in Ibotso laments deprivation and penury "ndoda chekudya mumba mune upfu" (I just want to get food, I want a house with mealie-meal) and "ndoda pekugara ndoda roof" (I want a shelter, I want a roof). This genuine plea invites the state's wrath as it is considered as undermining the sovereign power (Agamben, 1998), or despondency in Zimbabwe's political context where 'kuti bufu' (to speak) is indictable. The grievable condition of the poor is, however, juxtaposed with that of the ruling affluent who enjoy lavish lifestyle, "vano spender, vanotenga-tenga" (they spend, they buy a lot). It is sad reality that invites the song's foreground message 'Ibotso Woriitei?' (It's a cursed fate what can be done?). This rhetorical question underscores disenchantment and powerlessness of the fated populace.

The rhetorical question also suggests the need to question and investigate citizenry failure to resist the autocratic system.

Another theme that is articulated in Ibotso is that of conviviality, "vatengesi votengesa vopiwa mafufu" (naïve supporters or perverts, report to the powers and are given insignificant rewards). The political problems in Zimbabwe are not only generated by the power, but they also emanate from the ordinary people who have normalised the abnormalities and even participate in oppressive acts of power. Victims of state power take consolation in participating in orgy of violence against fellow citizens. Such uncritical patronage system is evident in a situation where some citizens act on behalf of the state and become "petty sovereign" (Agamben, 1998), that use coercive means and actualise the necropolitical power (Mbembe, 2001). This is not only a case of ordinary people fighting against each other, but even security agents act against the common citizenry. This is in line with Mbembe (2001)'s notions of conviviality and zombification. Such a disturbing scenario has significantly contributed to the current state of political stasis. Winky D makes a relentless call in the track Parliament about how the common people should question their political thinking and move away from party politics in order to break away from a toxic political culture "hapachada zvemapato apa." The victims of state engendered recurring scarcity, starvation and overall circumstances of precarity partake in "cheap imitations of power" (Mbembe, 2001). The "disciplined bodies" of these victims become coconspirators of the sovereign power that also subjugates them (Mavengano, 2020; Mbembe, 2001). This has augmented the failure of the post-independence nationalist project in Zimbabwe (Ndlovu-Gatsheni, 2009). However, Mhike (2014, p. 1) has revealed that Zimbabwean youth participation in political violence "has largely been involuntary because economic and social developments constrained them to cyclical poverty," and therefore, they become victims of state-engineered forms of violence and manipulation. The socio-political degeneration in Zimbabwe severely impact on the youth as the young females engage in romantic affairs with immoral aged men "mwanasikana ava kuenda nemagevha" Vobhaizwa nemadhara yobva yangorohwa raw, sushi, pobarwa kamwe kayouth.' The deployed vulgar "kurohwa raw sushi" (to have unprotected sex) provides impetus entry into the ghetto world which has certainly lost a sense of morality. This situation is a mockery of the government's claimed Afrocentric worldview. The elders, as Winky D implies, have generated conditions that compel their youth to be immoral. His songs bear the peculiarities of polysemantic lexical items and intriguing idiomaticity and metaphoricity that demand deeper reflection as part of the interpretive process. This is not surprising for an artist operating in a space where biopolitical elements are operative and confining freedom of expression. The present-day Zimbabwe is a society in which official views originating from political rulers are often distorted not only as the wish of the masses but also inaccurately proffered as the 'truth.' Winky D's music is laden with religio-cultural symbolism, imagery and its performance to create forceful evocations that suggest new meanings to the Zimbabwean political situation. His songs present different versions of the state narrative (Manase, 2011). The artist rewrites the story of the people he represents and risks direct confrontation with the power. Chitando and Tarusarira (2017) have remarked that in the Zimbabwean political context, songs are used often to emotionalise people. This is endorsed by an appeal to indigenous people's spirituality and the local cosmic order which is known to uphold peace (Chivasa & Mukono, 2017). This essential religious outlook on life continues to thrive in Zimbabwe even today. Through the cultural locality of the tracks, Parliament and Ibotso, it is arguable that these songs project a contaminated Shona cosmos vision and electoral violence as indicative of the corrosion of the peaceable tradition that is fast replaced by conceited socio-political culture. Chikerema and Chikunda (2014, p. 62) observe that "elections constitute one of the most important ingredients of democratic governance. They provide a space to assure political involvement of the citizens in the political system and the determination of national leadership. Ideally, therefore, elections are supposed to ensure the developing and consolidation of democratic governance and political stability." This is far from the reality of the electoral process in Zimbabwe. The election period is marked by violence and even loss of life. Mbembe (2001, p, 133) elaborates conviviality of power in this manner, "in their desire for a certain majesty, the masses join in the madness and clothe themselves in cheap imitations of power to reproduce its epistemology, and when power, in its own violent quest for grandeur, makes vulgarity and wrongdoing its main mode of existence." In Mbembe's theorisation of power in the postcolony, every member of this model of society is implicated in its vulgarity, domination and violence. His concept of commandment is about how power is negotiated blurring the demarcation line between the rulers and ruled. Furthermore, this exceedingly intricate relationship between the sovereign power and its subjects is problematic in Zimbabwe as the oppressed citizens struggle to identify themselves with the same autocratic system. In some cases, the masses appear to have been reduced to senseless objects of power who are largely manipulated to fight each other especially during elections. Sadly, they are thrown into the dust bin immediately after and only to be retrieved again during the next election. This cyclical Machiavellian political behaviour has generated a deep-seated problem not only in Zimbabwe but across Africa.

> In short, the public affirmation of the "postcolonial subject" is not necessarily found in acts of "opposition" or "resistance" to the commandement. What defines the postcolonized subject is the ability to engage in baroque practices fundamentally ambiguous, fluid, and modifiable even where there are clear, written, and precise rules… This is what makes postcolonial relations not only relations of conviviality and covering over, but also of powerlessness par excellence- from the viewpoint both of the masters of power and of those they crush. (Mbembe, 2001, p. 129)

Mbembe (2010) rightly points out that the autocratic can abolish or grant liberties in the postcolony. By so doing, a taboo is committed and according to Masaka and Chemhuru (2011, p. 134), "violation of taboos is perceived as direct provocation of spiritual forces which are the custodians of the moral code," which perhaps explains a perpetual condition of "kutanda botso" in Zimbabwe today. Winky D writes from a position of subalterity to give voice to the voiceless, a scenario that has refused to change in the post-Mugabe era in Zimbabwe as aptly argued by Moyo and Mavengano (2021). As already stated above, the socio-cultural and political context is pertinent in disambiguation in the process of meaning making. The musician's theological linguo and creative bricology also serve as an appeal to return to the lost moral codes which previously sustained a peaceful humanity.

Concluding Remarks: Adopting the Ethic of Love as a Guiding Political Thinking in Zimbabwe

As a way of concluding this study, the unresolved question remains nagging, what then can be suggested to alleviate the political polemics that define Zimbabwe today? It would be naïve to claim a finality of this topical issue, but all the same, making some recommendations is imperative to provoke further academic debate. The toxic political system is a product of multiple interconnected issues that include self-perpetuating logic, dictatorial rationality, among others. This means that finding a solution to the Zimbabwean political problem is not a matter of holding regular elections. The cumbersome mission to detoxify the long-contaminated socio-political system is multifaceted, thereby pointing at the need for ongoing academic conversations. Even among academics, there are a few greedy ones who derail from objective debates just to align themselves with power. However, bell hooks (1994) is of the opinion that the love ethic is at the core of all human relations. The new Zimbabwe is possible if the nation returns to a resilient African belief system anchored in caring for one another and solving disputes with love. For bell hooks, the ethic of love demands a shift from an ethic of domination and silencing. This implies that citizens should have voices to talk back to power and this could serve as a corrective mechanism whenever those in power attempt to deviate from the political ethos of the nation. Although hooks was talking about the love ethic in a different context, her views are relevant and insightful. hooks contends that without love, human efforts to liberate themselves and the world community from oppression and exploitation are doomed. This argument is supported by Sacks (2009) who points at the destructive power of hate which makes the world not a safe place. Zimbabweans need to arise beyond party politics and resist any manipulative intentions from conceited politicians especially during election times. There is an urgent need to rethink, thinking as a people and as a nation, to borrow Ndlovu-Gatsheni's terminology. Such self-introspection is imperative and could produce new sensibilities about Zimbabweanness that unifies all who cherish such an identity. Academics have an enormous task to re-educate the masses in order for them to regain their lost dignity and power for social and political change. The nation requires to create spaces of dialogue, inhibit the increase of unfair socio-political practices and foster reunion, mutual respect in an effort to foster national harmony.

References

Adichie, C. N. (2009, July). *The danger of a single story.* TED Lecture.
Agamben, G. (1998). *Homo sacer: Sovereign power and bare life* (D. Heller-Roaen, Trans.). Stanford University Press.
Allen, G. (2011). *Intertextuality.* Routledge.
Allen, L. (2004). Music and politics in Africa. *Social Dynamics, 30*(2), 1–19.
Althusser, L. (1971). *Lenin and philosophy and other essays.* Monthly Review Press.
Bakhtin, M. M. (1981). *The dialogic imagination.* University of Texas Press.
Bhebhe, N. (2023). *Winky D's new album saga: Hip Hop stars Holy Ten and Nadia Nakai regret.* https://www.myzimbabwe.co.zw/news/104365-winky-ds-new-album-saga-hip-hop-stars-holy-ten-and-nadia-nakai-regret.html
Chari, T. (2009). Continuity and change: Impact of global popular culture on urban grooves music in Zimbabwe. *Muziki: Journal of Music Research in Africa, 6*(2), 170–191.
Chigidi, W. L. (2009). Shona taboos: The language of manufacturing fears for sustainable development. *The Journal of Pan African Studies, 3*(1), 174–188.
Chikerema, A. F., & Chikunda, V. (2014). Political culture and democratic governance in Zimbabwe. *Journal of Power, Politics & Governance, 2*(1), 55–66.
Chitando, E., & Tarusarira, J. (2017). The deployment of a 'sacred song' in violence in Zimbabwe: The case of the song 'Zimbabwe Ndeye Ropa Ramadzibaba' (Zimbabwe was/is born of the blood of the fathers/ancestors) in Zimbabwean politics. *Journal for the Study of Religion, 30*(1), 5–25.
Chivasa, N., & Mukono, A. (2017). An analysis of the contributions of taboo system to peace among Shona communities in Zimbabwe. *International Journal of Research in Humanities and Social Studies, 4*(1), 24–32.
De Certeau, Mi. (1984). *The practice of everyday life.* University of California Press.
Dube, Z. (2016). Dancehall music and urban identities in Zimbabwe—A constructive postmodern perspective. *HTS Teologiese Studies/Theological Studies, 72*(4), 1–6.
Dziva, F. (2019). *Platinum Prince abducted, bashed over Mr President Ndoyacho Here song.* https://www.zimeye.net/2019/10/28/platinum-prince-abducted-bashed-over-mr-president-ndoyacho-here-song/
Eagleton, T. (2008). The rise and fall of theory. In D. Lodge & N. Wood (Eds.), *Modern criticism and theory* (3rd ed., pp. 824–834). Pearson.
Eureka! A word of discovery. https://learningenglish.voanews.com/a/eurika-word-discovery/3510636.html. TedED video was written by Armand D'Angour and animated by Zedem Media.
Ezenagu, N. (2014). Galvanising culture for Nigeria's development. *Agidigbo: ABUAD Journal of Humanities, 2*(2), 87–96.

Fanon, F. (1963/1961). *The wretched of the earth* (C. Farringdon, Trans.). Penguin.
Foucault, M. (1975/1995). *Discipline and punish: The birth of the prison*. Vintage Books: New York.
Gilroy, P. (1993). *The Black Atlantic: Modernity and double consciousness*. Harvard University Press.
Guzura, T., & Ndimande. J. (2015). Music, political space and power in Zimbabwe: A critique. *International Journal of Politics and Good Governance*, 6(4), 1–19.
hooks, b. (1994). *Teaching to transgress: Education as the practice of freedom*. London: Routledge
hooks, b. (2015). *Talking Back: Thinking Feminist, thinking black*, London: Routledge
Kadzura T. (2023). *Winky D latest 2023 Eureka Eureka album launch review: Musical coexistence as gateway to the nation's healing*. https://www.greedy south.co.zw/2023/01/winky-d-latest-2023-eureka-eureka-album.html
Kufakurinani, U., & Mwatwara, W. (2017). Zimdancehall and the peace crisis in Zimbabwe. *African Conflict and Peacebuilding Review*, 7(1), 33–50.
Manase, I. (2011). The aesthetics of Winky D's Zimbabwe urban grooves music and an overview of his social commentary on the post-2000 experiences in Harare and other urban centres. *Muziki*, 8(2), 81–95.
Masaka, D., & Chemhuru, M. (2011). Moral dimensions of some *Shona* taboos (*zviera*). *Journal of Sustainable Development in Africa*, 13(3), 132–148.
Mavengano, E. (2020). *A comparative stylistic analysis of selected Zimbabwean and South African fiction* (PhD thesis). North West University, Mafikeng. http://repository.nwu.ac.za
Mavengano, E., & Hove, M. L. (2019). Kaka country: An intertextual reading of national dysfunction in Bulawayo's *We Need New Names* and Jinga's *One Foreigner's Ordeal*. *Literator*, 40(1), a1595. https://doi.org/10.4102/lit.v40i1.1595
Mbembe, A. (1992). Provisional notes on the postcolony. *Africa*, 62(1), 3–37.
Mbembe, A. (2001). *On the postcolony*. University of California Press.
Mbembe, A. (2003). Necropolitics. *Public Culture*, 15(1), 11–40.
Mbembe, A. (2010). Fifty years of Africa's decolonisation [O]. https://www.chi murenga.co.za/archives/534. Accessed 20 March 2023.
Mhike, I. (2014, September 26). *Political violence in Zimbabwe's National Youth Service, 2001–2007*. Paper presented at the Nordic Africa Conference, Uppsala, Sweden.
Moyo, T., & Mavengano, E. (2021). A Déjàvu of Orwellian proportions: Re-reading animal farm in the context of Zimbabwean politics of change. In O. Nyambi, T. Mangena, & G. Ncube (Eds.), *Cultures of change in contemporary*

Zimbabwe: Socio-political transition from Mugabe to Mnangagwa (pp. 171–184). Routledge.

Muchemwa, K. Z. (2010). Galas, biras, state funerals and the necropolitan imagination in the re-construction of the Zimbabwean nation 1980–2008. *Social Dynamics: A Journal of African Studies, 36*(3), 504–514.

Muchemwa, K. Z. (2013). *Imagining the city in Zimbabwean literature 1949 to 2009* (PhD diss.). Stellenbosch University.

Ndlovu-Gatsheni, S. J. (2009). *Do Zimbabweans exist? Trajectories of nationalism, national identity formation and a crisis in postcolonial state.* Peter Lang.

Ndlovu-Gatsheni, S. J., & Ruhanya, P. (2020). *The history and political transition of Zimbabwe: From Mugabe to Mnangagwa.* Palgrave Macmillan.

Ndlovu-Gatsheni, S. J., & Willems, W. (2009). Making sense of cultural nationalism and the politics of commemoration under the *Third Chimurenga* in Zimbabwe. *Journal of Southern African Studies, 35*(4), 945–965.

Ngugi wa Thiong'o. (1994). *Decolonising the mind: The politics of language in African literature.* Heinemann.

Palmer, G. B. (1996). *Toward a theory of cultural linguistics.* University of Texas Press.

Pennycook, A., & Otsuji, E. (2015). *Metrolingualism. Language in the city.* Routledge.

Raftopoulos, B. (2009). The crisis in Zimbabwe 1998–2009. In B. Raftopoulos & A. Mlambo (Eds.), *Becoming Zimbabwe: A history from the pre-colonial period to 2008* (pp. 201–233). Weaver Press.

Sabao, C. (2018). Hegemonising Zimbabwe? The polity of *Mbare Chimurenga* lyrics in perpetuating Mugabe's and ZANU-PF's rule. *Muziki, 15*(1), 109–130.

Sacks, J. (2009). The dignity of difference: How to avoid a clash of civilizations. *Sacred Heart University Review, 25*(1), 20–46.

Sharifian, F. (2008). Cultural schemas in L1 and L2 compliment responses: A study of Persian-speaking learners of English. *Journal of Politeness Research, 4*(1), 55–80.

Sharifian, F. (2011). *Cultural conceptualisations and language: Theoretical framework and applications.* John Benjamins

Sharifian, F. (Ed.). (2017). *Advances in cultural linguistics.* Springer Nature.

Spivak, G. C. (1988). Can the subaltern speak? In C. Nelson & L. Grossberg (Eds.), *Marxism and the interpretation of culture* (pp. 271–313). Macmillan.

Tatira, L. (2014). Shona belief systems: Finding relevancy for a new generation. *The Journal of Pan African Studies, 6*(8), 106–117.

Tendi, B. (2010). *Making history in Mugabe's Zimbabwe: Politics, intellectuals and the media.* Peter Lang.

Tivenga, R. D. (2018). Contemporary Zimbabwean popular music in the context of adversities. *Tydskrif Vir Letterkunde, 55*(1), 134–148.

Vambe, M. (2004). Versions and sub-versions: Trends in *Chimurenga* musical discourses of post-independence Zimbabwe. *African Study Monographs,* 25(4), 167–193.

Veit-Wild, F. (1993a). *Teachers, preachers, non-believers: A social history of Zimbabwean literature.* Baobab Books.

Veit-Wild, F. (1993b). *Forms of syncretism in Southern Africa. Dambudzo Marechera and Lesego Rampolokeng: Dissonant voices writing back* (Unpublished paper). Annual Association of New English Literatures conference.

Wagner, V. (2002). History's mortal remains. In B. Neville & J. Villeneuvev (Eds.), *Waste-site stories: The recycling of memory* (pp. 165–176). SUNY Press.

CHAPTER 13

The Morbidity of Zimbabwe's Transformational Politics: Hope or Doom in the Post-coup Era?

Gift Gwindingwe

INTRODUCTION: ZIMBABWE'S POLITICAL TRANSFORMATIONAL PHASES

Zimbabwean politics has been characterised by different phases of hostilities between competing political parties (Raftopoulos, 2004). From 1980 to 1987, the country experienced conflict between Zimbabwe African Union (ZANU) and Zimbabwe African People's Union (ZAPU) which later united under a historic Unity Accord in 1987 to form ZANU-PF. The early 90 s witnessed political conflict between ZANU-PF and the Edgar Tekere-led Zimbabwe Unity Movement (ZUM). The period from 2000 to 2008 saw the worst politically motivated incidents of violence in

G. Gwindingwe (✉)
School of Heritage and Education, Masvingo, Zimbabwe
e-mail: ggwindingwe@gzu.ac.zw

Department of English and Media Studies, Great Zimbabwe University, Masvingo, Zimbabwe

© The Author(s), under exclusive license to Springer Nature Switzerland AG 2023
E. Mavengano and S. Chirongoma (eds.), *Electoral Politics in Zimbabwe, Vol II*, https://doi.org/10.1007/978-3-031-33796-3_13

Zimbabwe when 'Zanu PF... radically restructured the terrain of Zimbabwean politics towards a politics of frontal assault that had as its major targets the former colonial power, Britain, the local white population, the opposition Movement for Democratic Change (MDC), the civic movement' (Raftopoulos, 2004, ix), ostensibly because ZANU-PF's hold on to power had been visibly threatened by the Movement for Democratic Change (MDC).

This chapter focuses on the fifth segment of Zimbabwe's makeover politics. This phase is without the two political nemeses of Zimbabwean politics that had contested for over a decade: Robert Gabriel Mugabe and Morgan Richard Tsvangirai. Tsvangirai left the political stage due to death while Mugabe left it through a smart coup. Emmerson Dambudzo Mnangagwa led ZANU-PF, and Nelson Chamisa led MDC-Alliance. Of note in this phase is the change of tone, mood and atmosphere after the pronouncements by Emmerson Mnangagwa that Zimbabwe is in a new dispensation.

The questions that guide this chapter are: What new communication strategies and hope are Emmerson Mnangagwa and Nelson Chamisa bringing on the political field in the post-Mugabe/Tsvangirai era? Chitiyo (2019) pointed out that Emmerson Mnangagwa's government endeavoured to distinguish itself from Mugabe's leadership style, avoiding his drastic and 'ideologically driven language and policies'. This chapter examines the proclamations by Emmerson Mnangagwa on one side and those by Nelson Chamisa on the other side. Of particular focus in this chapter is an argument that both Mnangagwa and Chamisa have opted for populist politics that conceal certain morbidities that expose Zimbabwean politics as elitist but neither people centred nor nationalistic at the core. Noyes (2020, ii) argues that 'Mnangagwa promised to take the country mired in political and economic crisis for nearly two decades-in a new direction'. While the post-November 2017 political phase witnessed the most hilarious moments of Zimbabwean politics after 1980, the transformational phase is noted for its rudimentary elements of euphemistic oppression of the public to achieve elitist goals by both ZANU-PF and the MDC-A. Scholars such as Noyes (2020, p.viii) observed that 'there is a wide gap between the government's reform rhetoric and the reality on the ground'. An analysis of the propaganda techniques of glittering generalities, bandwagon and persuasion to hide the ills of Zimbabwe's transformational politics becomes the thesis statement of this chapter.

This chapter adopts a descriptive qualitative research approach that is rich in data. Purposive sampling was used to gather data from three rallies for each of the two political leaders. Textual analysis was also adopted to unpack the political statements and unravel their signifying values.

The chapter unpacks key concepts such as transformative politics and morbidity so as to operationalise them and put them into context. A section on theoretical framework is followed by the methodology that unpacks data gathering and data analysis. The findings and discussion follow. The chapter ends with a conclusion.

Unpacking Transformative Politics

This chapter places politics of change or change of politics at interparty level within the wider political continuum of transformative politics that is institutionally enshrined in 'universal liberal-democratic institutions' (Stokke & Törnquist, 2012, p. 8). In the Zimbabwean context, I focus on political transformation in the aftermath of Robert Mugabe and Morgan Tsvangirai. Soon after the post-Mugabe/Tsvangirai era, there was 'a need to develop democratic politics in order to alter the relations of power and to be able to build a substantive and substantial democracy that can generate and implement the laws and policies that people want' (Stokke & Törnquist, 2012, 8). I therefore choose to analyse the new models of popular engagement particularly through political communication and how they 'may open up renewed transformative strategies' (Stokke &Törnquist, 2012, p. 9). In the process, I unravel the deception underneath these popular engagement strategies.

In as much as transformative democratic politics is not synonymous with reform, it nevertheless has so much to do with 'reforms that are conducive to new reforms' (Stokke & Törnquist, 2012, 8). The fifth phase of Zimbabwe's political transformation has a reform agenda, and the phenomenon raised a lot of anticipation from various stakeholders.

The next section contextualises political morbidity.

Contextualising Political Morbidity

This subsection unpacks and contextualises the concept of morbidity. The term morbidity is largely a scientific one; in particular, it is applied in the field of medicine to imply certain illnesses. In this chapter, the term is applied metaphorically to suit the interdisciplinary context, particularly political communication. Morbidity is conceptualised in this chapter to insinuate political morbidity. The concept of political morbidity, simply put, connotes political ills. The Merriam Webster Dictionary defines morbidity as 'an attitude, quality, or state of mind marked by excessive gloo'.[1] Political communication, especially propaganda techniques such as glittering generality, aims to transpose electorates from this state of mind into political action. Rounaq Jahan (2008) cites Miria Matembe (1995) who posed a question in a Plenary Session on Governance, Citizenship and Political Participation, in Huairou, China, on September 3, 1995:

> With what qualities are women entering into the political arena and public life in a world where politics has been characterized by ills such as corruption, nepotism, dishonesty, sectarianism etc?

The ills referred to by Matembe are the political morbidities that are also referred to in this chapter. The chapter juxtaposes the communication strategies, specifically the propaganda techniques of glittering generalities, bandwagon and name-calling, with some of the morbidities that characterised Zimbabwean politics.

Theoretical Framework

This subsection focuses on the theory that informs this study. A theoretical grounding is very fundamental in guiding research. This chapter is premised on the Agenda setting theory with particular focus on the framing technique. A theory that dates back to Lipmann (1922) and McCombs and Shaw (1972), the Agenda setting, asserts that media are very central in producing and directing public opinion. This chapter discusses the Agenda setting theory in political communication in Zimbabwe. Central to the Agenda setting theory is mobilisation of people around certain sociopolitical goals and policies. McCombs and Shaw (1972) argue that the theory's focus is on election campaigns. Significantly, this chapter focuses on the race to set a political agenda between the two main political nemeses in Zimbabwe: ZANU-PF versus MDC-A and later ZANU-PF versus Citizens Coalition for Change (CCC).

---

[1] https://www.merriam-webster.com/dictionary/morbidity.

Both MDC-A and CCC are discussed under the leadership of Nelson Chamisa.[2]

Framing is the manner of representation or angling of news. This chapter employs the framing technique to discuss the 'principles of organisation that govern events' (Goffman, 1986, p. 10; Balmas & Sheafer, 2010), in this case, Zimbabwe's political events in the post-Mugabe era. In particular, the potential of the framing technique to anchor the discussion on persuasion and glittering generality as ideologically constituted means of concealing the morbidities of Zimbabwe's transformational politics by both Emmerson Mnangagwa and Nelson Chamisa is paramount. The endless debate on sanctions and corruption as having a causal effect on Zimbabwe's underperforming economy is best discussed under the framing theory that deals with problem definition, blame allocation and problem solution (Entman, 2006). The way problems are defined and blame is allocated is realised through the manner in which an issue is framed. The media influence the way the audience think about certain issues, and they do this through selection, emphasis, exclusion and elaboration (Entman, 2006). Arowolo (2017) posits that the media create frames by introducing news items with predefined and narrow contextualisation. This study fits well into Arowolo's (2017) assertion considering the narrow context in which both sanctions and corruption were put to the public by the two rivalry parties. Sanctions and corruption have been framed in such a way that they are mutually exclusive in order to make the frames more psychological than affective (Entman, 2006). Parveen (2017, 1) cites Fiske and Taylor (1991) who argue that:

> human beings are 'cognitive misers' by nature, which means that they tend to do as little thinking as possible. They prefer to have a quick way of processing information easily. This is done by 'frames' which help them understand the received messages.

Therefore, the framing technique of the Agenda setting theory facilitates the quick processing of information, thereby successfully telling the audience, not necessarily what to think, but what to think about.

---

[2] Soon after Tsvangirayi's death, Nelson Chamisa took over the leadership of MDC-A, only to leave it after being outwitted by Douglas Mwonzora to form the Citizens Coalition for Change (CCC) in 2022.

Methodology

In this section, I outline the research approach as well as the data gathering techniques that I employed. I also provide the sampling methods as well as the data analysis procedure. The research is chiefly qualitative as it aims for rich description of data to gauge the signifying value of the texts selected for discussion in this chapter. Through the use of textual analysis, the chapter aims to ascertain the extent to which propaganda by both the Zimbabwe African National Union-Patriotic Front (ZANU-PF) and the Movement for Democratic Change-Alliance (MDC-A) and later the Citizens Coalition for Change (CCC) has been used to conceal the morbidities of transformational politics during this political interregnum. Ifversen (2003, 61) pointed out that 'At a semantic level, a text can be said to constitute a certain unity of meaning, which contains sequences of sentences (other unities are morphemes, lexemes, syntagma and sentences)'. Besides, the effectiveness of such strategies is evaluated basing on the analysis of the content as captured on purposively selected rallies by both Emmerson Mnangagwa and Nelson Chamisa. I selected 2 rallies by Nelson Chamisa (29 January 2018 in Mutare, 12 February in Masvingo and 24 May 2021 at Chisamba Grounds) and 3 rallies by Emmerson Mnangagwa (1 November 2017 at ZANU-PF Headquarters; 26 August 2018, inauguration speech in Harare). I also used each political leader's campaign manifesto to pick certain content that I judged useful to discuss the ills of political transformation. I also referred to Al Jazeera online television station as well as YouTube videos. Discussion is done using textual analysis. Textual analysis is basically deducing meaning from media text submitted by the news consumers. Thus, one can get the meaning attributed to a media text only after analysing the engagements.

Findings

A textual analysis of the political statements by both Emmerson Mnangagwa and Nelson Chamisa in the period leading to the 2018 general elections and after revealing an over reliance on propaganda as a chief tool of political communication. Propaganda fits well in the discussion of the ills or morbidities of transformational politics in Zimbabwe in the post-Mugabe/Tsvangirai era because of its nature. Romarheim (2005, p. 5) posits that 'propaganda is derived from the Latin verb 'propagare', which means to spread and propagate'. Romarheim (ibid) then defines propaganda as 'the deliberate, systematic attempt to shape perceptions, manipulate cognitions, and direct behavior to achieve a response that furthers the desired intent of the propagandist'. Furthermore, Romarheim (2005, p. 5) states that 'words frequently used as synonyms for propaganda are lies, distortion, deceit, manipulation, mind control, psychological warfare, brainwashing and palaver' (p. 9). Deliberate propagation of distorted, deceitful, manipulative and brainwashing texts in order to shape perceptions and manipulate cognitions is in itself morbidity. Çelik's (2021) definition of political communication also explains the ills concealed by the political texts selected for the purposes of this study. Çelik (2021, 721) sees political communication as a 'way of understanding and explaining each other, and as two opposing ideas that see the main purpose as seizing power and benefiting from the blessings of power'. There is therefore a strong relationship between propaganda and Agenda setting, a theory that informs this chapter. Conveyance of distorted, deceitful and brainwashing texts is achieved through careful framing to achieve the intended agenda. The main purpose of propagandists is to seize power and to benefit from the blessings of such power (Çelik, 2021, 721). There is no space for the governed in this definition. As such, this chapter seeks to unpack the propaganda in texts such as the following:

1. The voice of the people is the voice of God (Emmerson Mnangagwa, 22 November 2017 at ZANU-PF headquarters, Harare).
2. Zimbabwe is open for business (Emmerson Mnangagwa, 26 August 2018 inauguration speech, Harare).
3. Nyika inovakwa nevene vayo (*A country is developed by its natives*) (Emmerson Mnangagwa's post-2018 election manifesto).
4. Video on $15 billion promised by Donald Trump (Nelson Chamisa, 29 January 2018 rally, Mutare).
5. Sanctions begging: Tikabvapo, tikainda kuGermany, tikabvapo....tichisunga, sunga one sunga dozen (*We moved from one Western country to the other, begging for sanctions*) (Nelson Chamisa, 12 February 2018 rally, Masvingo).
6. Connotations to election rigging: Hapana anogerwa asipo (no one can be hair dressed in absentia) (Nelson Chamisa rally, Chisamba grounds).

7. Generational consensus (Nelson Chamisa's MDC-A 2018 campaign manifesto) versus Operation Restore Legacy (Mnangagwa's Lacoste faction's justification for taking over power in ZANU-PF).
8. The sanctions versus corruption debate: participation as a site of ideological contestation between ZANU-PF and MDC-A/CCC.

Discussion

This section gives a discussion of the propaganda techniques used by both Emmerson Mnangagwa and Nelson Chamisa to conceal certain political morbidities in the post-coup era. It discusses glittering generality and the associated bandwagon by the electorate; the power-knowledge matrix in fighting wars of position and manoeuvre in the context of persuasion in political communication and lastly participation as a site of ideological contestation between ZANU-PF and MDC-A/CCC in the context of sanctions versus corruption debate.

Glittering Generality and the Post-Coup Bandwagon

The fifth phase of Zimbabwe's transformational politics, the new dispensation, is rife with the same disillusionment that characterised preceding phases. The period preceding this phase's harmonised election has been rife with propaganda. The term propaganda has been defined as 'spreading of rumours or information (false or correct), or an idea in order to influence the opinion of the society' and that it is 'misleading in nature and promotes a viewpoint or a political cause' (http://literarydevices.net/propaganda/). One of the techniques of propaganda is glittering generality, which implies use of 'vague, sweeping statements (often slogans or simple catchphrases) using language associated with values and beliefs deeply held by the audience without providing supporting information or reason' (Aaron Delwichin, https://www.ux1.eiu.edu/~bpoulter/2001/pdfs/propaganda.pdf). The glittering generality that is used to market a political brand is what probably Fanon (1963) would regard as pitfalls of national consciousness. Fanon (ibid) says that in young independent states, national consciousness was a failure; it did not achieve the desired results of economic and political independence. Rather, it was 'an empty shell, a crude and fragile travesty of what it might have been' (Fanon, 1963, p. 119). The legendary truths that are in the form of propaganda disguised as nationalist projects in the manifestos of the ruling governments (Fanon, 1963) resemble knowledge and power fused together. In the Zimbabwean post-coup era, the election manifestos/promises became coated lies that transpose citizens' mindsets into sheer and gullible believers. The dethroning of Robert Mugabe was met with relief and jubilation across the political divide. For the first time, all political parties joined hands to march against Robert Mugabe and his perceived cabal.

Soon after deposing Mugabe, Mnangagwa came with his political and economic promises. Chief among them were promises to curb corruption, job creation and re-engagement with the West. A close reading of these promises reveals nationalistic discourses that are all-embracing. The era after Mugabe became 'a new dispensation' or a 'second Republic'. These texts psychologically glittered. The overwhelming march against Robert Mugabe spoke to the glittering. A new dispensation implies a complete departure and negation of the past Mugabe ills. One such ill is corruption. However, events post-Mugabe showed the same corrupt tendencies ruling the roost in the new dispensation. A scandal that comes to mind is the Covidgate in which a former Minister of Health and Child Care, Obadiah Moyo, was alleged to have misappropriated US$20 million that was meant to combat the spread of COVID-19. Though the said minister was eventually fired, what remains questionable is the lack of checks and balances in the Second Republic in terms of awarding government tenders.

The glittering manifestos from the main opposition MDC-A were also quite enticing particularly to the masses of 'the working class of the towns, the masses of the unemployed, the small artisans and craftsmen' who 'line up behind this nationalist attitude' (Fanon, 1963, 125). A case in point is a rally addressed by Nelson Chamisa telling the crowd that he met Donald Trump who promised him fifteen billion United States of American dollars. At a rally on 29 January 2018 in Mutare, Nelson Chamisa said:

> Patakasangana naTrump, akatibvunza kuti vakomana muri kudei? Tikati tinoda fifteen billion.... (When we met (Donald) Trump, he asked us what we wanted. And we said that we need 15 billion United States dollars)

This was an indirect incitement of the public who were bitter over the alleged theft of the same amount by ZANU-PF leadership in the Marange Diamond mines under Robert Mugabe's government. This promised amount appeals more to the working class who suffered in poverty, the unemployed who yearn for employment and revival of the industries and the small artisans and craftsmen who want factories revived.

However, the ills of the text in the 29 January 2018 rally in Mutare were unmasked in a BBC Candid Talk interview between Stephen Sucker (a British journalist) and Nelson Chamisa (then leader of MDC-A) on 11 May 2018 where Chamisa denied such an utterance only to be exposed by being referred to the video about the rally by the interviewer/ journalist. Political communication, in particular propaganda communication, focuses on targeting. Friedrich Ebert Stiftung (2012) outlines three forms of audience targeting in political communication which are Demographic targeting, which focuses on age, gender and profession; Ideological targeting which finds major trends in political thought very crucial and Geographical targeting which looks at where the audience/ electorate live or work. The first two types of targeting are apt in this discussion. The urban young and professional (or learned) are the major political sphere of influence for Nelson Chamisa. However, the populist approach by Nelson Chamisa had its oversights as those exposed by Stephen Sucker on 11 May 2018. Propaganda is rooted in the magic bullet theory of the media which assumes that audience is tabula couch potatoes which wait to be filled with knowledge and information. Nelson Chamisa aimed to 'glitter' and endear himself to the electorate as a very potential leader, an effort embraced by many political leaders who know that 'media coverage of politics increasingly focuses on individual politicians rather than on political parties, even in parliamentary systems, in which the vote goes to parties and not to individual candidates' (Balmas & Sheafer, 2010, 1; Rahat & Sheafer, 2007). The submission by Sheafer (2008), Balmas and Sheafer (2010) and Sihite (2011) is that the political image of candidates is very central, and this is made possible through glittering generality.

The Fanonian nationalist catastrophe is relived in the post-coup period in Zimbabwe. Aphorisms like 'Operation restore legacy' (by Mnangagwa) and 'Generational Consensus' (by Chamisa) and their cyclonic effect on the minds of the citizens were a way of glittering and 'bandwagonning' everybody onto the political train. To restore legacy implied bringing back glorious days as those experienced soon after Zimbabwe's independence. This had a nostalgic effect on the electorate. To operate under a general consensus is to appeal to inclusivity that is implied under pluralist and representative democracy. But what eventually obtained is contained in Fanon's (1963: 131) lamentation when he says of the bankrupt leadership:

> They have come to power in the name of narrow nationalism…they will prove themselves incapable of triumphantly putting into practice a programme with even a minimum humanist content, in spite of the fine-sounding declarations which are devoid of meaning…

The aphorisms were used as weapons to fight wars of position and war of manoeuvre. War of position refers to cultural/ideological struggles within civil society while war of manoeuvre refers to use of forceful assaults against the masses (Brooker, 2003, p. 120). Mnangagwa's aphorism of 'Operation Restore Legacy' appeals to nationalistic values and beliefs and therefore more appealing to the old/aged electorate (class and age appeal) while Chamisa's dictum of generational consensus appeals to youths mostly (class and age appeal). These are the discourses that dissect the 'anatomical atlas' of the society (Foucault, 1974). This fine-sounding discourse and the various forms of knowledge imbedded in it become a ploughshare that dissects the anatomical atlas of the Zimbabwean society. Such mediated political statements bring together the youths, the adults and their respective classes depending on their geopolitical formation: The young and adults of the rural dissection are gorged more by Operation Restore Legacy mantra while the young and adults of the urban areas are motivated by the Generational Consensus dictum. At another level, the maxims employed by these leading politicians can be said to have been aimed at the broader political arena. Beardsworth et al., (2019, p. 3) argue that the dictum Operation Restore Legacy's aim was 'to legitimize a regime with dubious democratic credentials'. They further aver that it was aimed at 'persuading regional bodies and the international community to back—or at the very least acquiesce to—Mnangagwa's leadership' (Beardsworth et al., 2019, 3). Indeed, the African Union promised to work with Emmerson Mnangagwa's government and was eager to find out ways it can support it. The African Union's Commission Chairman Moussa Faki Mahamat revealed the continental body's decision to work with the Mnangagwa administration. At the funeral of

Morgan Tsvangirai, Nelson Chamisa's youths and security group popularly known as The Vanguard threatened to kill Thokozani Khupe, who was contesting a leadership wrangle with Nelson Chamisa. Later on in the race to lead MDC-A, Thokozani Khupe was stigmatised and labelled all sorts of names to paint her as unfitting to lead both MDC-A and the nation. On the other hand, Mnangagwa's Second Republic worked to symbolically annihilate the opposition MDC-A by denying the party visibility in state-controlled media such as the ZTV and major national newspapers such as *The Herald*, *The Chronicle*, *The Sunday Mail* and *The Sunday News*. All these were wars of position and wars of manoeuvre that negate the general consensus and the restoration of legacy, respectively.

Song has been used as an epistemological and phenomenological tool in the run-up to the 30 July 2018 watershed election by both the MDC-A and ZANU-PF. Political songs have a nationalistic and spiritual appeal and refreshment because like any form of music, a song is sentimental (Rimmon-Kenan, 2006). Music appeals because as a cultural product, it is a vector of knowledge and power (Gwindingwe, 2019, 104). Songs such as ED Pfee[3] by Chief Shumba and Kutonga Kwaro (Hero's leadership style) were designed to invoke a sense of an already won election before the actual voting. Kutonga Kwaro by Mukudzei Mukombe (aka Jah Prayzah) can signify the ruling tactics of a hero. Music has the capacity to produce knowledge and to enhance certain power positions in society (Randall, 2005). More so, music sentimentally appeals (Nausbam, 2010), thereby qualifying it as persuasive. The texts in music are naturally opinionated, but they are based on practical situations that are in constant change. The effect of this on power is axiomatic: opinionated and persuasive knowledge sentimentally moves the masses and leads to action or practice that brings forth change. That qualifies music as a tool for activism. The struggle over narratives or the competing truths can result in power shifts. In the next section, I discuss the power-knowledge matrix in fighting wars of position and war of manoeuvre in the context of persuasion in political communication.

---

[3] ED PFEE started as a slogan endorsing Emmerson Mnangagwa, and it was subsequently translated into a song by Chief Shumba.

The Power-Knowledge Matrix in Fighting Wars of Position and Manoeuvre: Persuasion in Political Communication

Zimbabwean politics in the fifth transformational phase was characterised more by political appropriation with the upshot of diluting the hopes and struggles of the less knowledgeable and the less powerful by taking advantage of their weak positions in society. Because they are less powerful, the masses sail in the belief that by belonging to this leader or that leader, one becomes privileged. The political grandstanding in both the MDC-A and ZANU-PF through the sugar-coated fine-sounding texts by MDC-A and billboard branding by ZANU-PF excoriated and concealed the political morbidities that stalled intra-party democracy. Even in the aftermath of vote casting, when the war of position failed (cultural/ideological struggles within civil society), the assumed defeat in the 31 July 2018 election, the level of contestation triggered anger in the opposition and ignited the war of manoeuvre (use of forceful assaults against the masses) (Brooke, 2003, p. 120). The early announcements of Chamisa's victory and speculated rigging by ZEC moved people who would otherwise have been patient and waited for ZEC announcements of the presidential election results. It is alleged that Tendai Biti announced a 'likelihood Chamisa victory', and as an opinion leader in the main opposition, he stirred anticipation and anxiety in the opposition masses.[4] The effect was street violence: a shift from the war of position to the war of manoeuvre. An announcement of a Chamisa victory and a possible rigging sparked anxiety and persuaded MDC-A supporters to take to the street to defend their vote. But later on, Nelson Chamisa labelled the demonstrating masses 'stupid' for not waiting for an official announcement of the result by ZEC.

The vulgar aphorisms such as ED Pfee by ZANU-PF and 'Kwekwe him', 'hapana anogerwa asipo' (No one can be hair dressed in absence) by the MDC-A leader, together with popular party songs blindfolded citizens into election euphoria. The meaning underneath these fine-sounding statements/slogans was that indeed the 'authoritative figures in our life have colossal power' to twist and turn the minds of the masses (Tiwari, 2018, p. 8). This has consequences that emanate from the knowledge and power vacuum created by propaganda.

---

[4] https://www.bbc.com/news/world-africa-45126593 BBC News on 9 August 2018.

Where Gramsci argues that the emancipation of oneself from (political/social) subjugation starts by freeing one's mind, Freire (1982) asserts that dialogue is an essential ingredient that is a 'co-operative activity' that leads to deepened understanding and enhanced social capital. The result is justice. A conflation of this pedagogy of hope by Freire is consequentially similar to the democratic pedagogy by Gramsci. According to Au (2012, p. 177), Frèire's (1982) pedagogy of hope in the oppressor-oppressed dichotomy in an unjust society explains the praxis that is at the centre of Freire's epistemology of the oppressed. Freire's (1982) liberatory pedagogy evokes the concept of critical consciousness which involves 'people in search of self-affirmation' (Au, 2012, 801). This is equated to Gramsci's moment re-articulation and disarticulation because Freire (1982) avers that humans are beings of praxis, that is, people of action and reflection. The war of manoeuvre and war of position as 'actions' to liberation is, in Freire's (1982) philosophical terms, the attempt by humans to liberate themselves. Through consciousness, humans (as subjects) act to transform or change themselves, that is, to change their reality. The reality of the proletariat is lack of power and knowledge to some extent.

There are Fanonian's 'fine-sounding declarations which are devoid of meaning' which are used to persuade the masses. The ZANU-PF team went to the electorate with the rhetoric of 'The Voice of the people is the voice of God' and 'Servant leadership' among other fine-sounding rhetorics. The MDC-A team took to the people such rhetoric like 'God is in it'. These were ostensibly meant to persuade the mindsets of the electorate to move along with the leadership. If the voice of the people is the voice of God, then the people's choice on Mnangagwa is divine and correct. In other words, you choose/vote Mnangagwa, you make a wise decision because he is presumably accountable to the people! In the same manner, MDC-A's rhetoric is meant to hoodwink the electorate into believing that the journey and destination to freedom is reachable because 'God is in it'.

Notable from these fine-sounding texts is that there was massive persuasion by both ZANU-PF and MDC-A to woo supporters towards the 2018 plebiscite. The fundamental question that recurs in the researcher's mind is whether these rhetorics were superficial or not. If the observer missions indeed observed and concluded relative peace, were the observations down to the political core of the field of contestation, that is, did this include intra-party observations? The next section looks at participation as a site of ideological contestation between ZANU-PF and MDC-A/CCC.

PARTICIPATION AS A SITE OF IDEOLOGICAL CONTESTATION BETWEEN ZANU-PF AND MDC-A/CCC: SANCTIONS VERSUS CORRUPTION DEBATE

This section discusses the centrality of participation as a site of ideological contestation between ZANU-PF and MDC-A/CCC. The discourse on sanctions imposed on Zimbabwe by the United States of America in 2001 forms the core of the discussion. The debate revolves around whether the sanctions are consequential to Zimbabwe's poor economy, or it is corruption that has drained the economy.

This chapter also discusses the raging debate on sanctions imposed by the United States of America on Zimbabwe under the Zimbabwe Democracy and Economic Recovery Act (ZIDERA) in 2001. Because of the scope of this research, I will not get into the major details of ZIDERA but will refer to some as the need arises. It also looks at how the two political nemeses, ZANU-PF and CCC, frame the debate on sanctions versus corruption as the root causes of the economic meltdown in Zimbabwe. Are sanctions against Zimbabwe impactful or inconsequential to the economy? Is corruption the sole cause of poor performance of Zimbabwe's economy? These questions lead to the critical issue of political polarisation in Zimbabwe. Participation in this debate has exposed the ideological contestation between power and citizen in Zimbabwe on the one hand, and this chapter also discusses this relationship between power and citizen from the Foucauldian perspective on power and knowledge.

ZANU-PF vehemently blames sanctions as very impactful on the deteriorating economic performance in Zimbabwe. Matyszak (2019, 1) argues that:

> The Government has framed these measures as an international trade embargo against Zimbabwe and, because they do not have the imprimatur of the United Nations Security Council, maintains that they are illegal.

There are numerous social media debates, including on Twitter, where the CCC and Western embassies make reference to the 1990s when the Zimbabwean economy began to nosedive as an era when there were no sanctions imposed on Zimbabwe, but corruption was rampant.

Kudzai Chikowore, a Human Rights Activist, is quoted in *The Tribune* (6 December 2020) saying that corruption has been grown, cultivated and nurtured in Zimbabwe, and the effects have been very dire and have 'pushed the country into severe economic conditions'.

At the centre of this debate on sanctions versus corruption are the political elites and spin doctors who then relay their views to the general public in order to influence public opinion and perception. The fundamental influence of the Agenda setting theory and its associated techniques of framing and salience transfer comes into play. The framing by ZANU-PF aims to hoodwink its supporters into believing in sanctions as the major factor in the declining economy, hence the newly framed motto: Nyika inovakwa nevene vayo (A country is developed by its natives). This positions sanctions a chief 'proprietor' of Zimbabwe's suffering and juxtaposed to that is a resilient leadership puling its citizens to bust the sanctions through cooperation and support to the ruling government.

The CCC, on the other hand, lambasts the ZANU-PF government for running down the economy due to corruption. An image is therefore built of a gigantic beast called corruption, and sanctions are dwarfed by the word 'targeted'. However, contrary to these claims, Nelson Chamisa refers to the need for renewed sanctions on Zimbabwe. His rally on 12 February 2018 in Masvingo illuminated the need for renewed sanctions when he talked about moving from one European country to the other, begging for sanctions renewal: '*Ndikabvapo, ndikainda kuDenmark; Ndikabvapo, ndikainda kuGermany...Ndichisunga, sunga one sunga dozen...*' (I travelled from Denmark, then to Germany... tightening the (sanction renewal) screws). The call for renewal of sanctions against Zimbabwe is a direct indication of their impact on Zimbabwe.

My conclusion on the sanctions versus corruption debate is hinged on the Foucauldian perspective on power and knowledge. Knowledge is always inextricably entangled in relations of power (Hall, 1997:75; Foucault, 1980). In his extensive discussion on power and knowledge, Foucault rejects the class reductionist approach or focus of the Marxists and argues that all political and social forms of thought are caught up in the interplay of knowledge and power (Hall, 1997). Hall (1997:76) says that Foucault (1977), who is fond of the term 'power/knowledge', has the following to say about this relationship:

Knowledge linked to power, not only assumes the authority of 'the truth' but has the power to make itself true. All knowledge, once applied in the real world, has effects, and in that sense at least, 'becomes true.' Knowledge, once used to regulate the conduct of others, entails constraint, regulation and the disciplining of practice. Thus, there is no power relation without the correlative constitution of a field of knowledge, nor any knowledge that does not presuppose and constitute at the same time, power relations.

Both ZANU-PF and MDC-A/CCC conceal certain realities and expose others. The CCC does not clarify the two-edged sword in sanctions where there are ZIDERA (2001/2019) and the National Emergencies Act (50 U.S.C. 1601, 1622(d)) that entails presidential powers mandating the President of the United States of America to 'impose sanctions on individuals and entities anywhere in the world using powers under the International Emergency Economic Powers Act' (Matyszak, 2019, p. 5). The two forms of sanctions seem unclear to the general citizens. ZANU-PF is loud on the detrimental effects of sanctions but is inactive in curbing corruption in the public service. The actions by the CCC frame corruption vividly, thereby transferring attention to it as a sole cause of Zimbabwe's economic woes when ZIDERA has a permanent injury on the same economy if sanctions are not lifted. ZANU-PF directs all media attention on sanctions as the root causes of the economic poor performance of the country, thereby looming large the picture of sanctions in the electorate's mind and downplaying corruption as a minor cause. It is that knowledge gap that is occupied by propaganda.

Conclusion

I argued that propaganda as a political communication tool has devastating effects on the gullible audience or voters. It is also this chapter's submission that framing and salience transfer are unsaid conveyors of propaganda. Well-framed deceptive media texts are in themselves propaganda. Selection and exclusion necessitate salient transfer in communication. Also, the Foucauldian knowledge/power matrix points to the fact that the powerful and knowledgeable occupy the centre, and the less knowledgeable and the less powerful are at the periphery in knowledge production. Information radiates from the centre going outwards. What is propagated by political elites comes from them, at the centre. Therefore, the discourse that circulates from the centre is the discourse of the powerful and the knowledgeable.[5] The centre analyses the periphery to know their specifics and adjust their action so as to achieve the preferred goals. In conclusion, I invite the reader to continue reflecting on the following overarching question: With this recurrent political field, does political communication in Zimbabwe spell hope or gloom?

References

Aleksić, D. & Stamenković, I. (2021). *Propaganda techniques in fake news published by Serbian Mainstream Media*, Conference paper on "30 years of higher education in journalism and communication in Eastern Europe after 1989: From conquering the freedom of expression to embracing digital communication", Media Studies and Applied Ethics pp. 33–48.
Arowolo, O. (2007). *Media violence*. Lagos State University.
Arowolo, S. O. (2017). *Understanding framing theory*, Researchgate. https://doi.org/10.13140/RG.2.2.25800.52482
Au, W. (2012). *Epistemology of the oppressed: The dialectics of Paulo Freire's theory of knowledge*. http://www.jceps.com/wp-content/uploads/PDFs/05-2-06.pdf Accessed on 11 March 2018.
Aziz, A. (2013). *Siyasal İletişim (4. Baskı)*. Nobel Yayınları.
Balmas, M., & Sheafer, T. (2010). Candidate image in election campaigns: Attribute agenda setting, affective priming, and voting intentions. *International Journal of Public Opinion Research*, 1–27. https://doi.org/10.1093/ijpor/edq009
Beardsworth, N., Cheeseman, N., & Tinhu, S. (2019). Briefing Zimbabwe: The coup that never was, and the election that could have been. *African Affairs*, 1–17. https://doi.org/10.1093/afraf/adz009.
Bond, P., & Manyanya, M. (2003). *Zimbabwe's plunge: Exhausted nationalism, neoliberalism and the struggle for social justice*. Merlin Press
Brooker, P. (2003). (2nd Ed) *A glossary of cultural theory*. Arnold.
Çelik, R. (2021). Political communication; A conceptual evaluation, *International Journal of Disciplines Economics & Administrative Scienves Studies*, (e-ISSN: 2587-2168), 7(33), 713–722.
Chikowore, K. (2020). In *The Tribune*, 6 December 2020.
Chitiyo, K. (2019) *Zimbabwe after Mugabe*, Chatham House.
Chitranshi, B. (2015). *Transforming the political—politicizing transformation: Beyond developmentalism*. Ambedkar University Delhi.

---

[5] McQuail, D. (2010) on the authoritarian normative media theory of the media.

Crenshaw, K. W. (1991). Mapping the margins: Intersectionality, identity politics, and violence against women of color. *Stanford Law Review*, *43*(6), 1241–1299.
Entman, R. M. (2006). Punctuating the homogeneity of institutionalized news: Abusing prisoners at Abu Ghraib versus Kiling Civillians at Fallujah. *Political Communication*, *28*(2), 215–224. https://doi.org/10.1080/10584600600629844
Fanon, F. (1963). *The wretched of the earth*. Penguin Books.
Fiske, S. T., & Taylor, S. E. (1991). *Social cognition (2nd ed.)*. McGraw-Hill.
Foucault, M. (1974). Prisons et asiles dans le mécanisme du pouvoir' in *Dits et Ecrits*, *t. II*. Gallimard.
Foucault, M. (1977). *Discipline and punish: The birth of the prison*, trans. Vintage Books.
Foucault, M. (1980). *Power/Knowledge*. Harvester.
Freire, P. (1982). *Education as the practice of freedom*, In Education for critical consciousness, pp. 1–84. Continuum Publishing Co.
Goffman, E. (1986). *Stigma: Notes on the management of spoiled identity*. Simon and Schuster Inc.
Gwindingwe, G. (2019). (PhD Thesis). *Reflection and representation: Modes of communicating Zimbabwean historical narratives through popular music*. University of Fort Hare.
Hall, S. (1997). *The work of representation* in S. Hall (Ed.), Representation: Cultural representations and signifying practices. Sage Publications.
Ifversen, J. (2003). Text, discourse, concept: Approaches to textual analysis. *KONTUR Nr*, *7*, 60–69.
Jahan, R. (2008). *The practice of transformative politics*, Centre for Asia-Pacific Women in Politcs: University of Colombia.
Jowett, G. S., & O'Donnell, V. (1999). *Propaganda and persuasion* (3rd ed.). Sage.
Lippmann, W. (1922). *Public opinion*. Harcourt.
Manheim, J. B. (1994). *Strategic public diplomacy and American foreign policy: The evolution of influence*. Oxford University Press, 1994.
Matembe, M. (1995, September 3). Member of parliament, constituent assembly, Uganda, plenary session on *governance, citizenship and political participation*, NGO Forum.
Matyszak, D. (2019). *Sanctions: The EU, US and Post-Mugabe Zimbabwe*, Firinne Trust.
McCombs, M. E., & Shaw, D. L. (1972). The agenda-setting function of mass media. *Public Opinion Quarterly*, *36*(2), 176.
Noyes, A. (2020). *A New Zimbabwe?* Rand Corporation.
Nussbaum, C. (2010). *Sentiment and sentimentality* in Music in Pennanen, R. K. (Ed.), Music and Emotions. Helsinki Collegium for Advanced Studies.

Parveen, H. (2017). *Framing theory, agenda setting theory*, Alirgah Moslem University.
Raftopoulos, B. (2004) *Unreconciled differences: The limits of reconciliation politics in Zimbabwe.* In Brian Raftopoulos and Tyrone Savage (Eds.), Zimbabwe: Injustice and political reconciliation, South Africa: Institute for Justice and Reconciliation, pp. vii–xxii.
Rahat, G., & Sheafer, T. (2007). The personalization(s) of politics: Israel, 1949–2003. *Political Communication, 24*, 65–80.
Randall, A. J. (Ed.). (2005). *Music, power and politics.* Routledge.
Rimmon-Kenan, S. (2006). *Concepts of narrative* in Hyvarinen, M., Korhonen, A. and Mykkenen, J. (Eds.), The travelling concepts of narrative. Helsinki Collegium of Advanced Studies, (10–19).
Romarheim, A. G. (2005). *Definitions of strategic political communication*, Norwegian Institute of International Affairs.
Sheafer, T. (2008). Charismatic communication skill, media legitimacy and electoral success. *Journal of Political Marketing, 7*, 1–24.
Sihite, R. (2011). *Political communication strategy of the opposition political party: A case study of PDI-P Website.* In Heri Budianto (Ed.), "MEDIA DAN KOMUNIKASI POLITIK". Pusat Studi Komunikasi dan Bisnis Universitas Mercu Buana, ISBN: 978-602-19217--2-3.
Stiftung, F. E. (2012). *Running for office: A guide to effective political communication in cameroon, Yaoundé*: Située Face Ambassade de Russie. ISBN 978 9956-0-9220-8.
Stokke, K., & Törnquist, O. (2012) *Transformative democratic politics: A historical and comparative perspective.* 9780230370036_02_cha01.
Stromback, J., & Kiousis, S. (2014). *Strategic political communication in election campaigns*, pp. 109–128.
Tiwari, S. (2018). *Foucault's power, knowledge and discourse in the teaching of musical composition.* New York University.
https://www.merriam-webster.com/dictionary/morbidity

CHAPTER 14

The Rhetoric of Onoma: The Intersection of Memory and Power Dynamics in Naming and Name-Calling in Zimbabwe's Electoral Politics

Esther Mavengano and Thamsanqa Moyo

INTRODUCTION

The death of Morgan Tsvangirai, a founding member of the opposition party, Movement for Democratic Change (MDC) which was later renamed MDC-Tsvangirai in Zimbabwe, put the highly regarded as a

---

E. Mavengano · T. Moyo (✉)
Department of English and Media Studies, Faculty of Arts,
Great Zimbabwe University, Masvingo, Zimbabwe
e-mail: thamsmoyo@gmail.com

E. Mavengano
Research Institute for Theology and Religion, College of Human Sciences,
UNISA, Pretoria, South Africa

Alexander von Humboldt Postdoctoral Research Fellow at TU, Institute of English and American Studies, Faculty of Linguistics, Literature and Cultural Studies, Department of English, Technische Universitat Dresden, Dresden, Germany

© The Author(s), under exclusive license to Springer Nature
Switzerland AG 2023
E. Mavengano and S. Chirongoma (eds.), *Electoral Politics in Zimbabwe, Vol II*, https://doi.org/10.1007/978-3-031-33796-3_14

resilient political opponent into chaos. Mwonzora and Hodzi (2021, p. 1) observe that:

> [B]oth MDC and ZANU-PF were personified in Tsvangirai and Mugabe respectively, the two leaders used their incumbency to maintain widespread grassroots support—making any challenge to their leadership at party congresses untenable. Mugabe's dominance only ended in November 2017 with his ouster from power in a putsch that involved the military elite in what came to be referred to as the 'military assisted transition'. Tsvangirai's grip on the MDC was cut short by his death in February 2018.

One major challenge that is visible in Zimbabwean political terrain today is a deep-seated culture of denigrating the political Other. This attitude is not only the ruling party's defining character but is also evident within the opposition camps. Key political figures in Zimbabwe do not tolerate different views coming from either within or outside their parties. These leaders want to enjoy being surrounded by praise-singers. This culture has produced cultic political outfits where those who are around party leaders become zombified and muted loyalists in the presence of a godified and hero-worshipped leader. Such a political culture has made it difficult for the parties to meaningfully discuss a succession plan because raising the subject is perceived as undermining the seating leadership. Moyo (2020, p. 79) rightly remarks that 'the reasons for the splits in MDC revolved around ideological contradictions, structural incoherence, deficiency in internal democracy, and succession or leadership renewal questions'. It is, however, not the focus of this study to pursue this debate.

Going back to the politics of onoma, Lynch (2016) expounds that names, and the ability to name, are inherently political due to the power relations involved and the discourses and actions they facilitate and hinder. Name-givers determine the anthroponyms (or name-calling) that fulfil their communicative needs and perceptions (Mensah & Rowan, 2020). Likewise, Nyambi et al. (2016) posit that names provide nuanced semantic layers in human communication. Yet, they have been often understudied as imperative sociopolitical-cultural sites on which some of the most significant events and processes of the post-colony can be read. De Klerk (1996, p. 18) also commenting on the prominence of names in the South African context, opines that "names: are vital in social construction since the process of naming is a linguistic act which is linked with anticipations, values, qualms and events in people's lives."

Of interest is Pitcher's (2016) view that names provide information on momentous historical events indicative of private or communal carnivals, tensions or crises. In this regard, names function as necessary retention clues to propagate the continuity of such undertakings.

Background to the Study

Up until 2018, Morgan Tsvangirai, the founding leader of the Movement for Democratic Change (MDC) since its establishment in 1999, and Robert Mugabe, Zimbabwe's long-serving president and leader of the Zimbabwe African National Patriotic Front (ZANU-PF), dominated Zimbabwe's multiparty 'democracy' (Mwonzora & Hodzi, 2021, p. 1). Recently, an ensuing power battle accentuated the pervasiveness and dialectics of onoma in Zimbabwe's present-day politics. The battle of onoma saw the two political offshoots, one led by Douglas Mwonzora and the other one by Nelson Chamisa, from the opposition party, the Movement of Democratic Change (MDC), approaching the courts to resolve the issue. Derogatory names were constructed which amplified the conflict leading to the split and the ultimate formation of a new political party named Citizens Coalition for Change (CCC) (Mwonzora & Hodzi, 2021). These politicians use party names and naming to mobilise memory as a political instrument in recent power dynamics and electoral discourses in Zimbabwe. Both opposition camps within the MDC wanted to align and identify themselves with the late founding father Morgan Richard Tsvangirai and build on his political legacy. While this battle defines the present-day opposition politics of these two splinter groups, the ruling party, the Zimbabwe African National Union Patriotic Party (ZANU-PF), has its own share of problems after the demise of Robert Mugabe since it was already struggling with factionalism (Hove, 2021; Ndlovu-Gatsheni & Ruhanya, 2020).

The primary purpose of this study is to locate the debate in this tension-filled terrain and further argues that the dialectics of onoma entrenched in current Zimbabwe are not only emanating from a quest for political identification, but also serve as political subterfuges to accentuate self-image and disparage electoral opponents. Furthermore, the study examines striking semantic connotations as embedded discourse of such naming and name-calling as counter discourses or political strategies to denigrate other contenders especially as the country is heading for the 2023 elections. By doing this, the study foregrounds the relevance of linguistic and political inquiry into names and naming as part of Zimbabwe's political culture. Most notably, the onoma disputes usually intersect with emerging power cleavages, clashes over electability and a longing to monopolise recent historical narratives. Pragmatics and socio-onomastics provide essential analytical lens utilised to interrogate political signification and perlocutionary insinuations embedded in semantics of names and naming practices. Thus, the chapter is located in the context of troubled transitional politics in Zimbabwe. It also foregrounds the view that the corridors of power in Zimbabwe are occupied by egoistical leaders who serve their self-interest at the expense of the masses who continue to suffer due to sociopolitical stasis (Moyo & Mavengano, 2021). This further complicates Zimbabwe's contemporary power dynamics and aggravates political conflict. It is from this discursive angle that this study considers names and (mis)naming as compelling lexical items which shape the public's political views (Holland, 1990). A pragmatic view treats language as a semiotic system whose meanings could be understood through a critical reflection on specific sociocultural, historical and political contexts (Halliday, 1978). This idea is salient as the discussion in this study considers the sociopolitical context of namegivers, the named and naming practice. The study seeks to address the following guiding research questions:

Why do names and naming matter in Zimbabwe's emerging opposition power dynamics?

What are the embedded discourses in names, name-calling, and naming of political personalities in Zimbabwe?

How do insights from pragmatics and socio-onomastics offer refreshing political sensibilities about the significance of onoma in Zimbabwe's present-day electoral discourses?

Pragmatics and Socio-Onomastics Conceptual Frameworks

The study's theoretical gaze is on a multifaceted academic sphere that privileges the intersection of political semiotics, pragmatics and sociolinguistics. The intersection of related fields is necessary as it is aimed to develop thought-provoking readings pertaining the dialectics of onoma in Zimbabwe's transitional politics. It is odd that anthroponyms and naming practices have not yet received much scholarly responsiveness, particularly in the context of electoral process despite the visible and enduring politics of onoma in power contest. In another context, Likaka (2009) explicates that names establish the essence of the individual, embodying their experiences, memories, thoughts and actions. He further asserts that names are sites of human perception which are also deployed as sites for encrypting myths, metaphors and for discerning the world. Following Mensah and Rowan's (2020) argument, this study asserts that anthroponyms provide conspicuous sites for the nexus between language and power struggle in Zimbabwe. Raper (1987, p. 17) draws our attention to the relevance of onomastic inquiry when he postulates that "names are an integral part of a language, and a primary function of a language is to communicate." It would then, appear to be irrational to accept that "names have no meaning at all." Raper (1987, p.78) also explains that onomastics has as its object the study of proper names. A proper name, like any other linguistic sign, entails of a sound sequence, which may be signified graphically, and has a 'sense' or 'meaning'. It also has the purpose of referring to, or designating, an extra-linguistic entity (Okello, 2020). For Suzman (1994, p. 253), names are not arbitrary labels, but they have sociocultural meanings and possess referential functions. Similarly, Mbali (2004, p. 25) notes that onomastics as a study, goes beyond not only the interrogation of the linguistic features of names, but also concerned with the sociocultural and psychological (political and socio-historical) factors that influence the choice of a name given to an entity by the namer. This situates the onomastic field within a multifaceted web of potentially meaningful relations with other disciplines (Butler, 2013). In the context of Zimbabwean politics, names and naming are interlaced with discourses of power, tropes of memory and motifs that speak about the present situation. Thus, the notions of history and memory overlap in compelling ways in this study. Pragmatics is a sub-discipline of linguistics which overlaps with sociolinguistics and semantics (Halliday, 1978). It is concerned with meaning in the context of use, therefore is located in poststructuralist paradigm (Bakhtin, 1981; Kristeva, 1980). In this study, pragmatics and socio-onomastics complement each other in the discussion of the politics of memory and naming in Zimbabwe's electoral dialectics. The study proffers the ideas that the control of memory is a form of power, and naming practice is also semantics of power. Both pragmatics and socio-onomastics are socially oriented theories, which bring into consideration the extra-linguistic factors that generate intricate layers of meanings in human communication.

Naming/Disnaming/Misnaming as a Political Trope in Zimbabwe

The subjects of names and naming practices have attracted interdisciplinary academic inquiry over the years. The topicality of onomastic research is derived from its interconnectedness to the human beings' socio-psychological disposition and their daily interaction with universal semantics (Meiring, 1993). In line with this view, Anderson (2007) and van Langendonck (2007) are among scholars who have elucidated that anthroponyms have both denotational and connotational semantic functions, and their significance in discourse has been particularly intrigued linguists and language philosophers. Udu (2019, p. 100) also endorses the importance of names and naming in the Africans' existence by asserting that names are reflective of the cosmology or worldview of the people. For Windt-Val (2012), names and naming constitute essential parts of nation-building, and there is a link between a person's given name and their sense of self. In the same vein, Tiav (2012, p. 165) affirms that:

> the practice of naming has greater social (and political) significations than merely giving an individual a nomenclature. First, through names, individuals relate and interact with the world around them. Second, a name provides elemental evidence of a person 's being or humanness—some rudimentary information on the background of the bearer. Third, a name could be a philosophical statement and a means of acting on the world.

These views about names and naming practices are also shared by Zimbabweans today. With reference to the Zimbabwean political landscape, the politics of names and naming has for long been part of the arsenal of legitimating and delegitimising discourses in political and electoral contestations. It is what Chari (2017) calls framing practices in politics. Pongweni (1983) observes that African names and naming were employed as part of subversive political discourse during the war. Names such as *Gariraneo Mabhunu* 'ambush the Boers,' *Farai Tichatonga* 'be happy, we shall rule,' *Rovai Mabhunu* 'destroy the Boers', *Teurai Ropa* 'spill blood', *Yeukai Chimurenga* 'remember the revolution', *Mabhunu Muchaparara* 'Boers, you will perish', *Kupisa* 'how hot my bullet is', *Amerika Mudzvanyiriri* 'America Oppressor and *Zvido Zvevanhu*' 'the people's wishes' played imperative civic mobilisation against the colonial regime. Although this strategy has been used since 1980, it is beyond the purview of this chapter to delve into backwards in time, rather the chapter's discussion will focus on the period of 2000 and beyond. Mushati (2013, p. 69), making reference to the Zimbabwean context, observes that:

> Onomastics is foregrounded to demonstrate the impact of ondonyms on the construction of post-colonial discourses about the nation, sociopolitical organization, negotiation of power relations, national identity, linguistic and cultural heritages. The act of naming is a signifier of authority and power over the discursive space and is therefore influenced by vested interests.

The chapter draws also upon Derrida's (1967) argument about "the violence inherent in the act of naming." This violence is particularly discernible in various acts of misnaming, disnaming and labelling in the Zimbabwean body politic. We conceive misnaming as calling someone out of their name, as to insult (Medina-Lopez, 2020) and disnaming, though it has similar connotations, as symbolic mutilation of a person's name (Francoise, 2013). The politics of naming is a political resource used by the leaders and supporters alike to influence the way voters view a given political contender. It is a form of "rhetorical violence" (Medina-Lopez, 2020) relied upon when individuals decide to hit below the belt for political capital. We argue that the strategy of political naming is meant to influence perceptions, attitudes and actions that follow that named entity. It ascribes certain identities of a political nature and is "perspective representation of political actors themselves and evolving of their relationship to each other" (Kowert & Lego, 1996, p. 435). Mpande (2006) avers that names are the most meaningful lexical items in the vocabulary of any language and a vital part of language inventory. In other words, names have the effect of constructing social reality and attempts to create particular regimes of truth. In the same vein, Gee (2014, p. 9) asserts that "looking closely at the structure of language as it is being used can help us uncover different ways of saying things, doing things and being things in the world." This implies that language that is including its onomastic character performs certain functions in human communication. For instance, names and name-calling could serve as a linguistic manifestation of factional politics, hate speech and counter-discourse among others. According to Derrida (1988), this is the power of proper names. The more visible the political figure and the greater the perceived threat he/she poses, then the greater the circulation of the ascribed identity through misnaming. In a political environment characterised by intolerance, majoritarianism and emotions than reasoned engagements in politics, the politics of naming has contributed to the flagrant toxicity and political polarisation. The next section examines the technologies of disnaming selected political personages extant in Zimbabwean politics post-2000.

MISNAMING AND DISNAMING AS CONTEST FOR POLITICAL SPACE AND (IL) LEGITIMACY

The hallmark of Zimbabwean political contestation is that where rational delegitimation and describing the other fail, people resort to arguing against the person to besmirch their reputation and injure their standing in society. This involves a deliberate process of 'hunting' for specific entry points to scatter and immobilise the political other. Names and (re)naming become the classification strategies to delineate the "appropriate and (the) inappropriate" candidates (Gross, 2004, p. 286). This comes about because "naming is first of all dividing, demarcating, and drawing lines of pertinence between the similar and the different" (ibid). It is a complex process of psychologisation that has the effect of writing out certain subjectivities from the realm of political acceptability. The associations inherent in such naming practices prod and cajole the electorate to act in accordance with the identities that the names dredge up. This view is in line with Ashley's (2003, p. 10) observation that "names are, like all art, distortions of reality, when they are experienced within texts (or discourses), they arguably serve as a linguistic representation of a desired referential intention." In other words, the potent connotative capacity that names possess gives them a noteworthy semantic command within a given context of use. Thokozani Khupe is a Zimbabwean politician who was instrumental in the formation of the Movement for Democratic Change in 1999, having worked with its founding leader, Morgan Tsvangirai, during their days as trade unionists. She was elected deputy to Tsvangirai and went on to become Deputy Prime Minister between the years from 2009–2013 in the Government of National Unity (GNU). Conflict arose when Tsvangirai appointed two other vice presidents into the party, Nelson Chamisa and Elias Mudzuri. After Tsvangirai's death, Khuphe was mandated by the constitution to superintend the affairs of the party pending the election of a substantive leader at congress. But Chamisa slyly assumed the leadership of the party by brushing aside the only elected candidate, Khupe. She was to later break away to lead what she termed the original MDC-T while Chamisa remained with the MDC-Alliance after a court ruling in her favour. This political fallout had adverse onomastic implications for her identity as a politician, woman and a person from a minority cultural group in Zimbabwe.

Subsequent to the war of attrition between the two MDC formations, Khuphe was vilified as a "sellout" (Marowa, 2009) with the attendant threat of violence and potential death that the word carried. She was cast as an overly ambitious woman, a prostitute and a dissident. The party that felt aggrieved by the wresting of the MDC-T logo, symbols and slogans deployed naming as a strategy to mark her out as unelectable and doomed from the very word go. Overnight, Thokozani Khupe was burdened with the clumsy name Thokozanu. A character-destroying attempt at rhyme and onomatopoeia transplanted her identity as an MDC member to being an inveterate ZANU-PF accomplice in the destruction of the hitherto buoyant opposition party. In examining the effect of the name on her, we draw upon Gross' (2004, p. 287) theorisation that "names...correspond to the realities this denotes, and, realities so that they coincide with their conventional designations." Thokozanu is a designation that disqualifies her from representing the interests of the MDC which is normally constructed as the antithesis of ZANU-PF. The associative force of the name invites scorn and hatred; it dramatises motives that are decidedly anti-people. In this way, according to Mawere (2019, 29), "one way in which to deal with Thokozani was to rename her Thokozanu, implying that she had sold out to ZANU-PF and so she needed to be purged from the MDC leadership." This was a strategy of writing her out of the discourses of liberation from the totalitarianism of the ruling party; it is a means of ordering social and political reality so as to appeal to most people's sense of the anachronistic.

It was not only Thokozani's first name that was subjected to misnaming/disnaming but her surname as well. From Khuphe, it was easy for her detractors to coin the insulting name Khupenga/Kupenga so that, according to Mawere (2019), the Kalanga surname is converted to Shona for wide circulation of the negative identity. Implicit in the violence on the surname was that she had gone bonkers; that she was unhinged. It is, however, not clear why fighting for one's constitutional rights and wanting to be president could be equated to madness, but popular views disqualified her because she was a woman in a male-dominated electoral playing field.

The patriarchal and militarist nature of Zimbabwean politics does not, for now, imagine a woman as a potential president of the country. This must be understood against the plots and manoeuvres that attended Joice Mujuru and Grace Mugabe's assumed presidential aspirations. Mujuru was hounded out of the party with the complicity, ironically, of a fellow woman for threatening the position of Robert Mugabe. In the case of Grace, it had to take the intervention of the army to snooker her apparent presidential ambitions. This shows the misogynistic nature of the Zimbabwean political terrain. For Khuphe, the odds against her did not end there; she also belonged to a minority cultural group in a country where leaders are expected to come from the dominant Shona group. In this line of reasoning, she was mad enough not to interrogate her minority status against her ambitions to lead a Shona-dominated MDC outfit. More than that, she was constructed as a sellout and a whore where "other narratives positioned her as one of Mnangagwa's several lovers" (Mawere, 2019, p. 28). This was circulated in order to concretise her deviance because, according to Gaidzanwa (2004), only married women are respectable enough to vie for leadership positions; otherwise, the unmarried ones use their bodies to try and climb the ladder of power, and their ascension to power becomes the naturalisation of a cultural aberration. Thus, in the fight for leadership of the MDC against Chamisa, Khuphe was viewed as the insane woman "resembling an estranged other intending to steal her son's (Chamisa's) inheritance and disturb the natural family order" (Mawere, 2019, p. 51). All this had the cumulative effect of exteriorizing, silencing and banishing her from the opposition family. In certain political contexts, and as part of the storytelling that materialises certain identity ascriptions, she was pathologised as Thokozamu—a frontal attack and reference to her being a victim of breast cancer that left her other breast devastated. Thokozamu means Thoko of the one breast fame—a reflection of the ways in which political contestation in the country sinks so low as to elicit sympathy for the named person. But the strategy is deliberately meant to handicap the individual and sow seeds of suspicion so as to exclude.

In Zimbabwe's politically charged terrain, the names that are given to people attempt to "structure and nuance the way we imagine and understand the world" (Lynch, 2016, 208). This is particularly so in a masculinist society that views women's spaces to be in the domestic sphere and under the gaze of men. The deployment of the trope of prostitute/*hure* on Khuphe should not be seen as an aberration but part of a sustained strategy to marginalise women who seek political positions in the country. Gaidzanwa (2004) sees this as a male strategy to normalise patriarchal views of leadership. Such phallocentric practices deny women opportunities to actively contribute to the character of national politics in Zimbabwe. This machismo culture further unmasks the mechanisms of domination which are put to use by a long-established hegemonic masculinity. It orchestrates a view that women should not be taken seriously in politics. As a trope of exclusion, *hure* was deployed on Grace Mugabe and Joice Mujuru in order to render them unattractive for the positions for which they sought personal fulfilment. It cannot be overstated that Zimbabwe needs to deconstruct such hegemonic masculinity practices in order to develop a new gender complementarity political philosophy (Mavengano & Marevesa, 2022).

Douglas Mwonzora took over the reins of party leadership (MDC-T and later MDC-Alliance) from Thokozani Khupe in 2020. Before that, he was a senior member of the party even prior to the death of the party's founder, Tsvangirai. After his ascendance to the leadership post, he became notorious for recalling many members of parliament who showed affiliation to the other MDC formation led by Chamisa. Mwonzora tried to create a leadership identity by adopting a less radical and adversarial stance towards national politics and ZANU-PF. He argued that such radicalism tends to polarise more than unify the nation. That he was the leader of the other MDC formation and the fact that he was less confrontational put him on a collision course with the Chamisa formation. The apparent compromise with the establishment earned him the less-than-savoury name Mwozorewa. Thus, in examining the politics of the ascribed name and the identity it conjures up, we invoke Dzimiri et al., (2014, p. 227) argument that naming is implicated in "struggles for power, relevance and memory." The name given to Mwonzora carries the negative weight of history; it carries the burden of selling out, compromise, collaboration and shooting the self in the foot. Medina-Lopez (2020, p. 73) posits the view that:

> We are our names, and our names carry specific rhetorical weight and value. Names signify something about our bodies, lives, and experiences they are attached to. Names give place, purpose, and identity.

The identity given to Mwonzora becomes associated with Bishop Abel Muzorewa of the infamous Internal Settlement of 1978–79. The Internal Settlement was a product of the not-so-open negotiations between Ian Smith, leader of the racist Rhodesian regime on the one hand, and Muzorewa, Ndabaningi Sithole and Chief Jeremiah Chirau, seen as Smith's puppets, on the other. These negotiations were an act of delegitimating the liberation struggle and its potential for a broad-based participation of Blacks in the political destiny of their country for selfish gains. These negotiations resulted in Muzorewa becoming Prime Minister of Zimbabwe-Rhodesia. It was a façade in that it sought to perpetuate white domination and control of politics in the country. Accordingly, it was unpopular with nationalist parties who commanded a lot of grassroots support than Muzorewa could ever do. The settlement was emblematic of Muzorewa's delusions of grandeur. He failed to realise how much of a political dwarf he was in the scheme of things, and, by virtue of being Prime Minister, he began to view himself as very powerful. Suffice to say the bubble burst sooner than he realised.

It should be noted that naming at times brings out the history of the nation, especially negative history. Naming has the effect of making individuals connect the past with the present. As a strategy, such naming practices create identifications and dis-identifications to orchestrate a sense of disgust and anger at a given contemporary contender who seems not to have learnt important lessons from the past. Mwonzora's association with Muzorewa disqualifies him as a political alternative to ZANU-PF. In fact, he is figured as sleeping with the enemy, as a pawn in the hands of the ruling party and wittingly or unwittingly, helping the party to maintain its stranglehold on power. Taking advantage of the general disregard people have for ZANU-PF, the name implies that Mwonzora's political oblivion is guaranteed and that it is only a matter of time just as was the case with Muzorewa. It also carries the implication that Mwonzora's political myopia is as legendary as that of Muzorewa who tended to punch above his weight when he began to see himself as more important than the nationalists. The name constructs Mwonzora as egotistic, as hell-bent on smothering the flames of people's liberation from the claws of the ruling party. The technique of historical knee-jerking consigns Mwonzora to a Zimbabwean askari whose irrelevance is politically assured.

Chamisa, leader of the Citizens Coalition for Change, is negatively named Khamisa, a Ndebele word for widely opening the mouth. In the ruling party circles, he is figured as someone with the propensity to approach politics with his mouth open and his mind shut. He is, therefore, constructed as a mere storyteller who regales his supporters with tall tales "full of fury but signifying nothing," re-enacting Shakespearean much ado about nothing. In such constructions, he is reduced to student politicking, as given to mere trouble-rousing without any coherent political strategy. So, his visions of spaghetti trains, bullet trains, etc., are seen as the hallucinations of an optimistic idealist. The crowds that he pulls at his rallies are seen as manifestations of people who would seize any opportunity that provides entertainment. In this way, Chamisa is viewed as presidential contender to be tolerated in the name of democracy but whose political acumen is at best dubious and at worst infantile. Trudgill (1974) notes that 'names are a good example of the social function that is often fulfilled by language, and are also a very important means of establishing and maintaining relationships' (p. 13). This language-culture nexus also plays out in the naming system with heightened significance through the depiction of the crises which are often transferred into caricature and memes invoking colonial narratives of African tribalism.

Conclusion

From the above discussion, it is apparent that names and naming are semantically populated and troubled by power dynamics at both party and interparty levels. The terrain of (dis)naming in Zimbabwe's political discourses is characterised by mud-slinging, denigration and defacing of the political Other. The power dimensions of onomastic semiosis in the context of contemporary Zimbabwean electoral politics convey the use of often odd and disparaging names meant to serve as public confrontation. This hampers the efforts to develop the new political dispensation. This problem is further exacerbated by the fact that naming practices assume performance of power by the namer, which is then resisted by the named, thereby promoting an ongoing political tension. In other words, name-calling becomes a site of construction of harmful exclusions and Otherisation which further amplify divisions rather than addressing the problems that have incapacitated the nation for nearly three decades. As a way of concluding, this study has contributed to the understanding of political pragmatism and complications entrenched in names and naming practices in the Zimbabwean political discourse. It has also exposed the political ineptness and immaturity which gave birth to factionalism and ultimate split within the previously famous MDC-Tsvangirai party. This symbolic development refracts profound political fissures, and it has a serious impact on the landscape and substance of national politics as the country is heading for the second elections in the absence of Mugabe and Tsvangirai. Reflecting upon these unpleasant scenarios, the question that remains unresolved is, will Zimbabwe rise again to observe the tenets of democratic politics in the current transition era after the demise of both Mugabe and Tsvangirai? Quite unnerving for the ordinary citizens is the central question: is Zimbabwe heading towards economic and sociopolitical recovery or another dead end is already looming? Following on these questions, this study recommends a change in political thinking and practices which would foster serene political dispositions aimed at nation-building and prosperity.

References

Ashley, L. R. N. (2003). *Names in literature*. Author house (formerly 1st Books).
Anderson, J. M. (2007). *The grammar of names*. Oxford University Press.
Bakhtin, M. M. (1981). *The dialogic imagination*. University of Texas Press.
Butler, O. J. (2013). *Name, place, and emotional space: Themed semantics in literary onomastic research*. PhD thesis. Glasgow University.
Chari, T. (1988). Electoral violence and its instrumental logic: *Mapping Press Discourse on Electoral Violence During Parliamentary and Presidential Elections in Zimbabwe, 16*(1), 14-40.
Derrida, J. (1988). *Otobiographies. The teaching of Nietzsche and the politics of the proper name*. Translated by Avital Ronell. *The ear of the other. Otobiography, transference, translation*. Texts and discussions with Jacques Derrida. English edition edited by Christie McDonald.
Derrida, J. (1967). *Gramatology*. John Hopkins University.
Dzimiri, P., Dzimiri, C. T., Mazorodze, W., & Runhare, T. (2014). Naming, identity, politics and violence in Zimbabwe. *Studies in Tribes and Tribals, 12*(2), 227–238.
Francoise, K. (2013). Misnaming and mis-labelling in the namesake by Jhumpa Lahiri, *Appelation(s), 36*(1), 93–101
Gaidzanwa, R. (2004). *Gender, women and electoral politics in Zimbabwe*. EISA Research Report 8.
Gross, S. (2004). The politics of names. *French National Centre for Scientific Research, XVIII*, 2, 275–302.
Halliday, M. A. K. (1978). *Language as social semiotic: The social interpretation of language and meaning*. Arnold.
Holland, T. J., Jr. (1990). The many faces of nicknames. *Names, 38*(4), 255–272.

Hove, M. L. (2021). Spectacles of transition: Texts and counter-texts in the historiography of Zimbabwe in transition, In *Cultures of change in contemporary Zimbabwe: Socio-political transition from Mugabe to Mnangagwa*, (Eds.), Nyambi, O. Mangena, T. and Ncube, G. (pp. 156–170). Routledge Publishers.

Kristeva, J. (1980). *Desire in language: A semiotic approach to literature and art.* Columbia University Press.

Kowert, P. & Legro, J. (1996). Norms, identity and their limits: A theoretical reprise. In P. Kartzenstein (Ed.), *The culture of national security.* Columbia.

Likaka, O. (2009). *Naming colonialism, history and collective memory in the Congo, 1870–1960.* University of Wisconsin Press.

Lynch, G. (2016). What's in a name? The politics of naming ethnic groups in Kenya's Cherangany Hills, *Journal of Eastern African Studies*, 10(1), 208–227.

Mavengano, E. & Marevesa, T. (2022). Re-conceptualising Womanhood and Development in Post-colonial Zimbabwe: A Social Conflict Perspective. In: Chitando, E., Kamaara, E. (Eds.), *Values, identity, and sustainable development in Africa. Sustainable development goals series.* Palgrave Macmillan, Cham. https://doi.org/10.1007/978-3-031-12938-4_15

Marowa, I. (2009). Construction of sellout identity during Zimbabwe's war of liberation: A case of Dandawa Community of Hurungwe District, 1975–1980. *An Afro-Asian Dialogue*, 10(1), 121–131.

Mawere T. (2019). Gender and sexual imaginations. The 2018 Zimbabwean E(r)ections and the Aftermath. *Centre for Sexualisation, AIDS and Gender.* University of Pretoria

Mbali, A. M. (2004). *Naming, identity and the African renaissance in a South African context*, PhD Thesis. University of Natal.

Medina-Lopez, K. (2020). Pardon my acento: Racioalphabetic ideologies and rhetorical recovery through alternative writing systems. *Latinx Writing and Rhetoric Studies*, 1(1), 57–79.

Meiring, B. A. (1993). The syntax and semantics of geographical names, pp. 269–289 in P.S. Hattingh, N. Kadmon, P.E. Raper and I. Booysen (Eds.), *Training course in toponym for Southern Africa*. University of Pretoria.

Mensah, E., & Rowan, K. (2020). African anthroponyms: Sociolinguistic currents and anthropological reflections. *Sociolinguistics Studies*, 13(2–4), 157–170.

Moyo, T., & Mavengano, E. (2021). A Déjàvu of Orwellian proportions: Re-reading animal farm in the context of Zimbabwean politics of change. In O. Nyambi, T. Mangena, & G. Ncube (Eds.), *Cultures of change in contemporary Zimbabwe: Socio-political transition from Mugabe to Mnangagwa* (pp. 171–184). Routledge Publishers.

Moyo, C. (2020). Party foot soldiers, quasi militia, vigilantes and the sceptre of violence in Zimbabwe's opposition politics. *Modern Africa: Politics, History and Society, 8*(1), 65–103.

Mushati, A. (2013). Street naming as author (iz) ing the collective memory of the nation: Masvingo's Mucheke suburb in Zimbabwe, *International Journal of Asian Social Science, 3*(1), 69–91.

Mwonzora, G., & Hodzi, O. (2021). Movement for democratic change and the rise of Nelson Chamisa. *Journal of Asian and African Studies, 56*(2), 1–16.

Ndlovu-Gatsheni, S. J., & Ruhanya, P. (2020). *The history and political transition of Zimbabwe: From Mugabe to Mnangagwa*. African Histories and Modernities Series (AHAM). Palgrave: Macmillan. Press

Nyambi, O., Mangena, T., & Pfukwa, C. (Eds.) (2016). *The postcolonial condition of names and naming practices in Southern Africa*. Cambridge Scholars Publishing.

Okello, B. (2020). What's in a name? *Reinventing Luo naming system in Kenya's ethnopolitical landscape, African identities*. https://doi.org/10.1080/147 25843.2020.1791687

Pongweni, A. J. C. (1983). *What's in a name?* Mambo Press.

Raper, P. E. (1987). Aspects of onomastic theory. *Nomina Africana, 1*(2), 27–45.

Tiav, T. A. (2012). Nigerian names as enactments of the human essence: An analysis of Tiv personal names. *Makurdi Journal of Language and Literature, 2*(1), 164–173.

Udu, T. T. (2019). Names as repositories of worldview: Empirical evidence from the morphological and semantic analysis of Tiv personal names. *International Journal of Language and Linguistics, 6*(4), 100–108.

van Langendonck, W. (2007). *Theory and typology of proper names*. Mouton de Gruyter.

Windt-Val, B. (2012). Personal names and identity in literary contexts. In B. Helleland, C.-E. Ore & S. Wikstrøm (Eds.), *Names and Identities, Oslo Studies in Language, 4*(2), 273–284.

CHAPTER 15

The Effectiveness of Social Media in Mitigating Unfair Mainstream Media Electoral Coverage in Zimbabwe

Lucia Chingwena and Isaac Mhute

Mass media play a pivotal role in transmitting political information and through them, a framework for understanding the past, present and future events is shared with the electorate. There is an extensive debate about the impact and effectiveness of mass media in politics because, whereas some theorists believe that they facilitate democracy by allowing expression of various views, others (Olaniran, 2020; Reisach, 2021; Rogers, 2020) consider them anti-democratic due to their power to manipulate people's perception on politics. Holt et al., (2019, p. 861) define mass media as "legacy news media organisation ... characterised by certain, often hierarchical, organisational structures and traditional publishing routines". Mass

L. Chingwena
Zimbabwe Broadcasting Cooperation, Harare, Zimbabwe

I. Mhute (✉)
Department of Language, Literature and Culture Studies, Midlands State University, Zvishavane, Zimbabwe
e-mail: isaacmhute@gmail.com

© The Author(s), under exclusive license to Springer Nature Switzerland AG 2023
E. Mavengano and S. Chirongoma (eds.), *Electoral Politics in Zimbabwe, Vol II*, https://doi.org/10.1007/978-3-031-33796-3_15

media was established prior to the advent of the digital age (Wimmer & Dominick, 2013, p. 2). Holt et al., (2019, p. 861) opine that mass media "fulfil a societal function by enabling public discourse through the provision of topics of general interest that are oriented on facts, selected by professional actors and published following professional rules". This allows considerable censorship of the news that gets published often in favour of ruling parties in undemocratic societies.

In response to the foregoing, the past decade has transformed political discourses immensely as political actors have increasingly adopted social media platforms such as Twitter, WhatsApp and Facebook for connecting with their stakeholders (Maarek, 2014). The Internet is now playing a significant role in providing information on political events, engaging its users and encouraging them to get involved in offline political activities. Social media offer favourable circumstances for public discourses due to their relatively open access and overall structure that supports networking and sharing of information. Social media play a critical role in reconnecting and reviving political parties' ties with their civic roots by providing the basis for a more democratic mode of organisation. Other scholars like Lipow and Seyd (1996) as well as Wring and Horrocks (2000) add that social media further existing trends toward the micro-management of voters and centralised control by techno-literate elites. Thus, social media communication brings political parties closer to their potential voters and provides a platform for politicians to communicate faster and reach citizens in a more targeted manner without the intermediate role of mass media practitioners. Social media have reshaped methods and structures of contemporary political communication by influencing how politicians and citizens interact with each other. However, the effectiveness of this approach in increasing political engagement and electoral participation is yet to be established in different environments which is the focus of the study.

Mainstream Media Coverage of Zimbabwean Political Parties

Mass media plays a pivotal role in the transmission of political information and various researchers suggest that the use of mainstream media is positively associated with democratic outcomes (Boulianne, 2011). However, due to selfishness, in developing countries, the main role of the mainstream media has become forcing the public into accepting the ruling parties which usually control the mainstream media whilst at the same time framing the opposition party as evil. The Zimbabwean mass media typically castigates opposition parties as traitors advancing regime change agenda in order to reverse gains of the liberation struggle. This is the reason Mukasa (2003) note that due to threats from the governments, media owners, be it public or private, are usually forced by governments in developing countries through their newspapers or broadcast stations to promote ruling party's selfish interests by advancing their political agendas.

Zimbabwe provides an interesting case study of election media coverage as broadcasting has remained a state monopoly in the country. The government has total control over the two big media companies in the country which are the Zimbabwe Broadcasting Corporation (ZBC) and Zimpapers. The ZBC is a parastatal owned by the state through the Ministry of Information and Publicity in accordance with the ZBC Commercialization Act (2001). The corporation owns most radio stations which are Radio Zimbabwe, National FM, Classic 263 and Power FM and one television channel ZBC TV. Zimpapers, on the other hand, is a state-controlled Zimbabwe mass media company which expanded its operations to include radio, commercial printing and television. Zimpapers is the proprietor of the daily newspapers which are The Herald, The Chronicle and H Metro and it owns two Sunday papers which are The Sunday Mail and The Sunday News. The company has provincial newspapers and it also publishes two local language papers, Kwayedza and Umthunywa. It runs the national commercial radio station, Star FM, and three national commercial radio stations, Capitalk, Diamond FM and Nyaminyami FM, as well. While licenses for Capitalk and Nyaminyami are held by Kingstons Holdings Pvt Ltd, these stations are run by the Zimpapers Group. The Zimpapers also has a television station called the Zimbabwe Television Station (ZTN).

In a democratic set up, no one group or set of interests is systematically preferred over another and that the information available to citizens is accurate and impartial. As such, the ZBC, as a public broadcaster is expected to give equal coverage to all political parties. Scholars like Moyo and Darnolf (1997) argue that the ZBC has a tendency of making it impossible for opposition parties to have access to coverage. The ruling party (ZANU-PF) in the 1990 elections not only violated the requirements of equal access, but also ethical standards of advertising by running intimidating radio and television adverts that likened voting for the opposition to choosing death. One of the adverts featured a coffin being lowered into a grave, accompanied by a stern warning: "Aids kills. So does ZUM. Vote Zanu PF" (ibid.). The following tweets capture the situation further:

> @upenyu18 replying to @NyereSamaringa and @ZBCNewsonline No sympathy card, Howard. Plain irony. ZBC only reports on CCC when it trashes or demonized it, or quote leaders out of context, but it religiously covers Zanu-pf functions, even the commissioning of Bush pumps and bins. CCC gets coverage on SABC, which has a wider reach, they 😒The opposition was generally denied access to the electorate in the state-owned media.

> @CodyKambon Replying to @ZBCNewsonline How about they lobby over ZBC's biased coverage of CCC ? To be honest, ZBC, your entire reporting ethos needs a major overhaul. Zimbabweans are truly tired of the rubbish you put out hence all the satellite dishes. If it wasn't for mandatory license fees you would have been gone.

Before the 1995 election campaign, the ZBC appointed an Election Coverage Committee (ECC) which decided that parties running in at least fifteen constituencies would receive at least thirty minutes of free airtime on TV1, while parties with fewer candidates would receive only five minutes. However, ZBC reserved the right to edit the party's tape before airing it (Darnolf, 1997, p. 59). The contest over access to broadcasting came to a head in 1999, when the ZBC refused to broadcast paid for advertisements from the National Constitutional Assembly (NCA). The NCA took the ZBC to court on the basis that: ZBC is a public broadcaster, and the sole broadcasting house in the country funded mainly by the state, as well as by fees paid by the public. As a public broadcaster, it has a duty to reflect a broad spectrum of views across the nation, and not just those of the government and ZANU-PF (Zimbabwe Independent, 26 February 1999).

According to the Media Monitoring Project Zimbabwe (2000), in the 2000 Parliamentary election campaign, the ZBC is said to have devoted about 91% of its coverage to the ruling ZANU-PF, and the remaining 9% to all the opposition parties. A similar pattern of unequal access was also maintained in the run-up to the Presidential election of 2002. Justice

Joseph Mafusire, a Zimbabwean High Court judge, in a judgement dated 19 June 2019, ruled that the Zimbabwe Broadcasting Corporation (ZBC) and Zimpapers acted unconstitutionally during Zimbabwe's 2018 elections as they failed to provide a fair opportunity for the presentations of divergent views and dissenting opinions. The Media Monitors of Zimbabwe Report (2020) states that the ZBC has always been used by the government and ruling party ZANU-PF as its mouthpiece, with no editorial independence since the colonial period. The ZBC has often been run like a private institution and it is well documented that the President appoints the Minister of Information and Broadcasting Services entrusted with the power to hire or fire key personnel to ensure the coverage of government-related stories of interest. As such, the ZBC and Zimpapers did not afford the MDC with necessary coverage when they rebranded their political party to CCC. The ZBC only mentioned in passing in the middle of the Main Bulletin on the 25th of January 2022 that Advocate Chamisa had launched a new political party. Zimpapers also did the same as the story found space in the middle of The Herald newspaper dated 26 January 2022, indicating that the story was of no considerable importance to them. The unfair coverage of CCC was lamented in various tweets like;

> @Nhlanhl79435621 Mar 5 Replying to @ZBCNewsonline Why is **ZBCnews** not reporting on the Rallies held by **CCC**? We're all Zimbabweans despite our political affiliation. We expect **ZBCnews** to be very much apolitical unless if yu're an extension of ZANU PF party.

> @BishopAMagaya Interesting to observe that contrary to the usual dramatic coverage of MDC A and MDC T fights by the ZBC, they went mum on the announcement of the new party name CCC by Chamisa.

That is why Okwudishu (1988) posits that if government controls the media, it controls all its media coverage and content and manipulate the same media to achieve its desired agenda and because of this, the opposition parties never find a place in the mainstream media where they get equal and unbiased coverage. It has contributed to the continued dominance of the elites and exploitation of the oppressed majority and opposition parties. As such, the ZBC and Zimpapers have remained an instrument of ruling party propaganda as they are dependent on government subsidies for their survival. To demonstrate the seriousness of the matter, in the Newsday of 18 March 2022, the ZANU-PF official, Mike

Fig. 15.1 News article where a ZANU PF official was telling CCC to campaign on social media

Bimha, was quoted saying that the CCC should leave the ZBC alone and make use of social media for their campaigns. This is captured in Fig. 15.1.

New Media and Political Coverage

The new media have radically altered the way government institutions operate, the way political leaders communicate, the way elections are contested as well as citizen engagement. Social media have transformed the political media system, redefined the journalists' role as well as the way elections are contested, and how citizens engage in politics. Gibson and McAllister (2012) evaluated online social ties and political engagement, examined how online platforms increase political interaction and they established that online social contact fosters offline participation. Similarly, political participation and engagement via different online and offline channels allow political participants to get involved in politics and express their opinions openly.

Internet and all other e-activities improve the knowledge of online users about politics and spurs political engagement and participation. E-campaigning directly connects and engages Internet users before and after elections. Rainie et al. (2012) investigated social media and political engagement and found that 39% of adults in the United States used social media and one out of every eight adults used social media for civic and political purposes. Social media has, thus, become a pervasive force in politics, altering the communication dynamics between political leaders, journalists, and the public. Social media opened up wider avenues for instantaneous political discourse and debate. It generated new trends for political participation and changed the patterns of political communication. Siluveru (2015) endeavoured to dig out the facts about social and digital media in political communication and concluded that social media is being used for the purpose of social relations and updating the users about developments. Biswas et al. (2014) examined the influence of social media in India, on voting behaviour, and their results show that social media unites people within political parties.

There is evidence to suggest that social media allow political leaders to end the usual run around the public mainstream media as it is often aligned to the ruling party. Social media have become ubiquitous communication channels for candidates during election campaigns with platforms like Facebook, WhatsApp and Twitter enabling candidates to directly reach out to voters, mobilise supporters, and influence the public agenda. These fundamental changes in political communication present election candidates with a widened range of strategic choices. Social media have the potential of relaying information directly to individuals without the intervention of editorial or institutional gatekeepers. Democracy is enhanced in the process as members of the public are also capable of recording and posting videos that could go viral and influence the course of events. Politicians in different parts of the world are increasingly turning to social media to outwit the mainstream press' control over the news agenda. Social media have become a key communication tool in campaigns and other political activities before, during, and after the 2016 Ghana presidential and parliamentary elections.

In Zimbabwe, Sengere (2018) notes that the Voice of Zimbabwe in 2018 conducted a poll and it established a phenomenal rise in the use of social media as news platforms, with 52.3% of Zimbabweans getting their news from WhatsApp, Twitter and Facebook. The same study established that 32.5% of Zimbabweans think that social media is a reliable source of news (Sengere, 2018). Consequently, the Zimbabwean mainstream media seems to have been outpaced by social media. Opposition parties have always had difficulties in mobilising their political actions, communicating with mass audiences and their possible supporters through the mainstream media, hence, the MDC Alliance made use of social media when they rebranded to CCC. It solely used this medium to cover critical developments that took place ever since the party was formed, from the infighting that resulted in several splits, the latest of which is the one that resulted in the formation of the CCC. In a tweet urging supporters to fully utilise social media, Nelson Chamisa tweeted:

> @nelsonchamisa May 31 Citizens you are lit, # faka pressure on all social media. Your voices must be heard, make use of it citizens. Blessed day.

Theoretical Framework

The study adopted the honeycomb framework. Kietzmann, Hermkens, McCarthy and Silvestre developed a honeycomb framework in 2011 that identifies seven functional building blocks of social media which are identity, conversations, sharing, presence, relationships, reputation and groups. According to them, each block provides a platform to unpack and examine a specific facet of social media user experience and its consequences for organisations (Kietzmann et al., 2011).

Research Methodology

This study used the qualitative research approach and obtained data through virtual ethnography, which is an online research approach for exploring the social interactions that take place in virtual environments like internet sites. Virtual ethnography includes a broad range of methodological approaches aimed at answering the complexities of the object of research and the different ways in which the object has been constructed.

Findings

Accessibility of Political News on Social Media

The CCC used social media as its media channel to announce their new party, which was announced on January 24, 2022 and was broadcasted live on the CCC Facebook page. Its politicians and analysts in support of the CCC use social media to access people, make announcements and to interact with the followers and get feedback. Hopewell Chin'ono's tweet on the 26th of January 2022 states that his discussion with the CCC's vice president Tendai Biti had 48 100 audiences tuned in and it had been replayed for 26 900 times by different people as shown below:

> @daddyhope Jan 26 So far 48,100 people have tuned into my @Twitte rSpaces conversation with Citizens Coalition for Change VP, Tendai Biti @BitiTendai It has been replayed 26,900 times since it ended hours ago. Context; @HeraldZimbabwe sells less than 5000 copies a day. **CCC must use social media.**

The party also hosted virtual candidate launch on the 16th of March to showcase their candidates who were running in the March 26 byelections and the message was retweeted by 187 people and liked by 364 whilst the live launch was watched by 7 800 people. The CCC also kept its followers and prospective voters updated through their frequent posts on the official party's handle as well as through the retweets by the party's leadership and followers. All the party's launch rallies were broadcasted live on their Facebook page and photos were also shared on their Twitter page. The CCC Star rally which was held on the 20th of February 2022 in Highfields was first advertised on Twitter on the 15th of February 2022 and it was retweeted 533 times and liked by 1 120 people. Live updates were shared by ZimLive with 18 890 people watching and also different people who had attended the star rally shared their photos on the CCC page. CCC official page had one hundred and thirty-seven tweets which only focused on the different bi-elections campaign launch which were done in different provinces.

The party's official Facebook page has 203 000 followers, and it has above 150 live streaming videos uploaded from the day they announced the party rebrand on January 26 up to May 2022 and these live videos included but not limited to the election rally launches, press conferences, Independence Day message and workers' day message from Chamisa and a live streaming of when Chamisa was voting in the March 26 byelections. Many people mainly learnt of the CCC's political launch, rallies, vision, mission, and goals through social media. Many CCC followers encouraged the rebranded party to make use of social media to market the new party as shown by the following tweet:

@daddyhope. This evening at 8PM, I will be hosted by @ChangeRadioZW and @CCC_Diaspora to discuss the power of Social Media, and why the opposition must use it, and also why the citizen must understand the strength of the RETWEET and SHARE buttons going into 2023.

The CCC mainly used Twitter and Facebook as their social media tools in creating political awareness and these platforms have the greatest number of users as compared to other social media platforms. Supporters from different provinces, regions and continents created CCC groups to cater for their audiences and, on Facebook, CCC has more than 50 pages with a minimum of 10 000 followers in each group. Most supporters from the social media groups encouraged the party to make use of these two social media sites to communicate with their potential voters. Below are some tweets encouraging the CCC leadership to make use of Twitter and Facebook to raise awareness:

@The_zim_patriot May 2 It should be a mandate for every **CCC** leader to take part on Twitter and Facebook. They should be informed of how to bypass the ruling party propaganda. A quality leader should use these **social media** sites to update the people on his doings and encourage the citizens.

Citizen Coalition for Change @Son_of_Dzamabwe Jan 31 Citizens, we need to build momentum and awareness of our campaign and party. We only have **SOCIAL MEDIA**. Please use the power of RETWEET on all #CCC information PLEASE. @daddyhope, @advocatemahere, @ProfJN Moyo, @JobSikhala1, @DarkForceGirl01.

This study noted that most people followed the party's events either directly on Twitter and Facebook or from the links they learned from these networks. These worldwide social media tools are in the centre of the network cluster of the CCC's campaign awareness since they have a higher amount of connectivity to other Webpages related with the political party as this tweet indicates:

@victor_takaruva. Replying to @daddyhope, @TwitterSpaces, and 2 others, How do we get the link to listen 12:26 PM Jan 26, 2022 Twitter for Android.

These social media sites were also used by other political blogs and websites to promote their links and to reach more people. Besides sharing photos, videos, live broadcast links, these websites are used as discussion platforms. The blogs, folksonomies and activist websites are also remarkable social media tools that are used by political activists to discuss and argue on the ongoing political events. Using their viral nature, the blogs and activist websites reach much more people than their own followers.

Appropriateness of Social Media Use

People consider it appropriate for their current situation as evident in the following tweet:

> **Citizen Coalition for Change** @Son_of_Dzamabwe Jan 25 We don't have TV stations like Zanu Pf, we don't have Radio stations like Zanu Pf, we don't have Papers like Zanu Pf. ALL WE HAVE IS **SOCIAL MEDIA**.

They lauded the engagement aspect involved as evident in the tweets:

> @ProJamesTeam1 Replying to @EfieZethu and @LynneStactia The beauty about new communication platforms like Twitter& Facebook is engagement, Unlike the one traffic Jonso enjoyed at ZBC/TV then as Min of Information for Zanu PF. He imposed his ideas on disarmed people. Today the CCC structure he crying loud for are engaging him right here 8:35 AM Jun 18, 2022 Twitter for Android.

> @Ishmaelmandinye Jun 30 Replying to @daddyhope This is what Munangagwa is ignorant about. Propaganda on tv is a thing of the past now. People spend much of their time on social media than on television. Not even a single day **CCC** never appeared **onzbc** since its formation but managed to hammer Zanu-pf in the by elections.

> @MusekiwaThemba Jan 26 Replying to @daddyhope, @engineer_eden, and 3 others Very true. Zanu monopoly on state media is being broken by social media. Kuno kwaMasembura, the trend is changing from state media (mostly Zbc) to sosho media. It's now common to hear someone saying, ndakazvinzwapa Whatsapp [I learnt about it on the Whatsapp platform].

> @tapiwapi Replying to @daddyhope, @TwitterSpaces, and 2 others, Lol. @HeraldZimbabwe, and @ZBCNews\online r outdated. U don't have to wait 4 the restricted media 2 get news about censored people or groups.

> U get it direct. It's 2021 media has moved on. But they're stuck believing they can mute opposition through their narrow channels.12:50 PM Jan 26, 202 Twitter for Android.
>
> @FreshmanJoni Replying to @daddyhope @TwitterSpaces and 2 others Since Zbc is Captured! ! Social media will be Number 1. For CCC to communicate with its Supporters and The Whole World 12:35 PM Jan 26, 2022 Twitter for Android.

One participant stated that it facilitates unprecedented engagement:

> Sunrise tweets: @zuvarabuda01 Replying to @nelsonchamisa Finally, was waiting for a word from you president. Handeimberi! One president anotaura nevanhu vake pasosho media.[Lets continue moving forward! One of the few presidents who communicates with his supporters via the social media platform].

Another participant pointed out that "twitter messages are a good example of engaging the political consumer on burning political issues and Chamisa is doing well in engaging with the citizens without looking down on anyone" which was also noted from the Newshawks tweet:

> @NewsHawksLive Starting tomorrow, Zimbabwe's main opposition Citizens Coalition for Change leader Nelson Chamisa will be engaging on live social media conversations - in this case Facebook Live - to increase personal interaction with voters, address their concerns and tap into their ideas.

It was noted that the participants agreed on the importance of engagement as they believe that it is the key to a political brand's success. They also stated that without the political consumer engagement, the CCC will just be flooding the cyber space with noise.

Social Media Effectiveness in Political Brand Storytelling

The study noted that political brand storytelling needed to resonate with the political consumers as one participant pointed out:

> The stories told need to resonate with the audience and remain true to the brand.... CCC no matter the story they are sharing, must always find

a way to resonate with their supporters.... Every time there is a story to be told, we need to make sure that the story is accessible and that it resonates with the people.

When probed about the approaches to political branding, the participants felt that it was vital to consider the emotional connection people make with the brand. In Rhetoric, Aristotle spoke about the three emotional appeals where the speaker is able to persuade his audience through logos, ethos, and pathos. The notion of emotional appeal that political parties can create is important as captured in the tweets:

> @arnoldJmpofu, @nelsonchamisa is a bigger brand in Zimbabwe. As I was analysing Masvingo 2018 results, I realized he is loved even kumamisha [in the rural areas]. I can assure you CCC under Chamisa is in good hands, we must work hard in many rural areas to increase the support base 10:32 AM Mar 29, 2022 Twitter for Android.

> @Bright_CFIS Replying to @PedzisaiRuhanya and @nelsonchamisa This is absurd. Was about to tweet that Nelson Chamisa as a brand, is more popular than all the bugatti and rolls royce vehicle models in Zimbabwe. No amount of political schemes can ever replace our association to CCC. #Nero_chibaba_zve!

The yellow color was also properly sold as the symbol through the social media platform starting with Chamisa himself stating on his tweeter handle that yellow was a color of change:

> @nelsonchamisa Feb 6 **YELLOW** IS THE **COLOUR** OF CHANGE! IT'S A REVOLUTION. A CITIZEN'S REVOLUTION. FOR THE CITIZENS. BY THE CITIZENS. FROM THE CITIZENS. **YELLOW** is #CCC Blessed Sunday!!

One responded saying that the yellow color which the CCC chose as the party color is too bright and can be easily noticed by the colour-blind person. A lot of pictures and short phrases were used for brand storytelling to promote the CCC 's brand. Supporters shared photos of yellow bananas, yellow sunflowers, and yellow sun with various captions that supported the new party as vibrant (See index 1 for various yellow photos). Chamisa as the leader also sent a yellow bouquet on Twitter wishing his supporters a "yellow weekend". Images of yellow hearts and yellow box were shared on the main CCC handle as a sign of support for the new brand. Below are a few excerpts that were retrieved on the CCC and Chamisa Twitter handle on what the colour yellow symbolises:

> @CCCZimbabwe: "Yellow is a color that symbolizes hope, energy & a fresh start. The CCC citizen movement has thrown ZPF into panic mode so they are desperately trying to dampen the spirits of the people who are ready to win the nation for change. They won't succeed. CCC is here to stay...".
>
> @Washington0010 Jan 28 #YellowFriday#CCC#RegisterToVoteZW **Coloryellow** is bright and refreshing.
>
> @Starrinvictus Jan 28 There is a big difference between the fading **yellow color** on the Zanu Pf flag and the vibrant, lively **yellow** on the **CCC**. While the former symbolizes decay and death, the latter symbolizes life and a new hope.
>
> @Shelaz007 Jan 24 **Yellow** is the **color** for prosperity, **yellow** is the **color** for victory. Let's paint the whole place **yellow**. Retweet and like. Behold the NEW. #CCC.

An interviewee also said:

> Yellow is fresh, yellow is reviving and tiri wero naNero. [we are well, with Nero- the codename for Nelson Chamisa].

Other prominent members applauded the colour, for instance, Temba Mliswa said:

> Welcome to the Yellow Army @nelsonchamisa and @CCCZimbabwe. God had already shown us that yellow is the color. What others do which is good, it's great that you follow. The Yellow Army is an undefeated army. You have wisdom.

Former deputy secretary general of the MDC Alliance Jameson Timba also backed the yellow colour saying:

> We are bold and we are yellow. Choose the New. #RegisterToVoteZW #NgaapindeHakeMukomana. [let the young men inhabit/takeover the presidential office].

15 THE EFFECTIVENESS OF SOCIAL MEDIA IN MITIGATING ...

Similarly, human rights activist Evan Mawarire echoed:

ZVADIRWA YELLOW! 💚 [everything has turned Yellow!] Congratulations to my comrade in arms @nelsonchamisa and the entire team @CCC Zimbabwe on the launch of a brand-new season and strategy for bringing change to Zimbabwe. #CCC.

The CCC effectively used the visual narrative on social media, showing the emotional engagement with the political consumers of various ages. For example, various photos were uploaded with Chamisa mingling with supporters of varying ages and with evidence of the party's appeal to the elderly in different areas (rural and urban) quite evident. Some of the pictures posted on the CCC pages included here were not coincidental but they are pregnant with meaning. For instance, they received many likes, comments and retweets on both the CCC Twitter page and Chamisa's page as they were telling a story behind a story on the CCC branding as evident in Figs. 15.2, 15.3 and 15.4.

Fig. 15.2 Old grannies at mutare rally

Fig. 15.3 Old woman dancing to CCC songs

Fig. 15.4 Chamisa chatting to an elderly man

It was discovered that the brand stories were presented in different ways and themes with some showing Chamisa as a humble leader, loving and lovable character and listening leader. Data collected for this study showed that the dress code for Chamisa as posted on social media platforms mirrored both his connection with his predecessor the late Tsvangirai as noted by one respondent who said:

Nero identifies with all classes of people, through his character and that is what we love most about him. He took the good lessons from Save.

The brand-based perceptions by audiences are created on what they associate the brand with and in that vein, the CCC rebranding came at a time when the party and the leaders were desperate to present an image that would associate them with the electorate. In a leaked US cable, the founding president of the MDC, Morgan Tsvangirai, was described as an 'indispensable leader', therefore, in order to invoke the memory of Tsvangirai during the election campaign, Chamisa to some extent, mimicked Tsvangirai's dress code, though with a slight variation. Tsvangirai had created the image of a humble leader by wearing popular safari bush jackets during campaigns, and Chamisa could have adopted the same dress code for similar reasons. Chamisa's actions presented him as a leader anointed by Tsvangirai whose footsteps he was following. It also supported his claim that he was the anointed one rather than the other contesting rivals like Dr Thokozani Khupe. This image which was being portrayed by Chamisa would in a way give the voters the impression that Chamisa, though young and different, was as powerful as Tsvangirai. Second, the dress code depicted a humble, ordinary leader who was not corrupted by political power represented by the expensive suits paraded by most of the local politicians. By appearing as a down-to-earth man in the social media platforms, Chamisa was reaching out to and identifying with the ordinary voters, most of whom live below the poverty datum line (Fig. 15.5).

From the data collected for this study, it was clear that social media became a platform to share political communication about Chamisa's spiritual values. Images that represented his spiritual values were shared on his page as well as CCC's page and data collected showed that these politicians are aware that the majority of Zimbabweans take issues of spirituality seriously when choosing political leaders. This could also have been inspired by the suffering and killings that have become typical of the nation especially during elections which made people think that only a God-fearing person could rescue the situation. Chamisa shared pictures with verses and some when he was in the forest with his bible and videos of his visits to some of his supporters praying for them and one respondent said:

Fig. 15.5 Chamisa mingling with the public at the Workers' Day commemorations

I love Chamisa because he is a man of God and many people love him and his party because he is grounded in the word of God.

Another image presented a prayer for thanksgiving after they won the March byelections. The meaning embedded in these social media images, videos and verses was that Chamisa was the ideal, anointed, God-fearing man who could take Zimbabwe forward. The sense of religious conviction and a love of God coming from the candidates was also important for his followers as Zimbabwe is mainly a Christian nation.

Chamisa's use of social media to present the CCC to tell the party's story from the day they introduced it to the world appealed to the public properly too. One respondent stated that Chamisa's natural use of social media helped the rebranding process tremendously, as he managed to maintain and build the CCC brand image as approachable and relatable. Chamisa was viewed as a leader who was consistent in his social media behavior throughout the rebranding process and always available to take part in conversations and answered questions from his followers, regardless of their status and where they come from. This contrasted immensely with the usual inaccessible leaders known for their many guards meant to keep them away from the voting public.

Effectiveness of Social Media in Disseminating Political Information

Comparing the findings from the chosen social media platforms, expert interviews and the qualitative content analysis, all the datasets indicated that to a greater extent, social media was an effective media channel in disseminating political information to the target audiences. The research findings showed that social media has given birth to so many movements which recorded a huge success in Zimbabwe, for example the #Tajamuka, #This Flag and #Bring back Moby (after the alleged murder of a CCC member). Social media has changed people's perceptions and convictions on such political issues as it seeks to enlighten some, while it creates fanatics in some people. It was discovered that, through social media, movements were promoted, and the government felt the heat responding at times by shutting down the internet in the country to avoid the sharing of updates and news on the scheduled protests. Further confirmation of success comes from the considerable victory of the CCC in the March 2022 byelections, it has been seen winning even in ZANU-PF strongholds like Gokwe. Thus, despite these social media drawbacks, its instant and cost-efficient nature enables citizens journalism which is a great help to social movements since mainstream media stays behind. Citizens journalism during the CCC rallies proved that social media is a very effective tool for spreading the information all over the world and creating political awareness and solidarity with people who live far away. We can note as well the arrests and considerable detentions of the CCC activists like Job Sikhala and Makomborero Haruzivishe. Others include Pastor Evan Mawarire in July 2016 for producing and sharing protest videos on social media and Jacob Ngarivhume in July 2020 who was coordinating a scheduled demonstration on social media against the government, and both got arrested on accusations of inciting public violence.

In a Twitter message, the CCC complained of poor network coverage as they were trying to beam their Star rally in Highfields. Many supporters in Zimbabwe also confirmed the poor connectivity as they also failed to connect to the Facebook live stream and as an active participant for this study's sake, I also witnessed the same challenge of poor connectivity until the rally ended on Facebook. The government knew the power that was embedded in social media, hence, the deliberate move to cut the internet connection in order to deprive people of the live broadcast by ZimLive and also the sharing of photos and small video clips as people followed the proceedings.

It was, however, noted that the effectiveness of social media depends on a lot of factors like educational background, preferences, age, gender, and location of the people. The youths in the rural areas can have a different view from those in the urban areas. In as much as it is easy to view the number of followers, love, like and retweets in a group alone are not enough to ascertain if the members are not ghost accounts and are interested in the messages sent. The number of followers cannot translate into votes and that becomes difficult to tell if social media channels are effective in transmitting political messages.

It was also discovered that political groups had regular people who follow and comment on issues as compared to the entertainment pages that belong to some socialites like Madam boss or Mai Titi, for example, where people spend the whole day commenting on celebrity fights. From the interview conducted for this study, it became apparent that most youths do not engage themselves in political dialogue as they believe it is for the older generation yet on the CCC and other political activists' pages, they are encouraging the youths to register to vote as noted from responses from the interviews:

> I don't follow politics because I am still young and my interest is in music and football.

> I am not interested in politics since it's a serious and boring discussion I cannot be entertained by those "f..." debates of who is better between Chamisa and ED.

This failure to appeal to these scores of the young generation on such critical topics, which is the focus of the CCC, then reduces the credibility of social media messages. The research also established that there are people who do not believe in anything that comes from social media unless it is authenticated by the ZBC. They can actively participate on social media but at the end of the day, they will turn to the ZBC to verify if it is true. One of the study participants noted that this is the reason why in some heated debates on the authenticity of messages circulating in WhatsApp groups, they often get resolved when one says, "it's true, it was aired on television". This demonstrates that, to some extent, mainstream media remain a threat to social media success in appealing to society on critical issues.

Challenges Faced in Social Media Use

Though some followers were comfortable and perceiving these social media sites as effective in disseminating information and creating awareness amongst the potential voters, others argued that the CCC must not mainly focus on these sites as they only accommodate the elite and those in diaspora. A college student said that Facebook helps him to follow political events though associated with some challenge:

> I have a Facebook account where I am a group member for a CCC group but sometimes it is difficult to follow messages since they will be covered in porn videos and messages from traditional healers adverts.

Some Twitter followers complained about the expensive data and poor network connections which often hinder accessing the CCC messages on time and urged the party to make use of WhatsApp by sending short videos and audios. One of the study participants made the following comment:

> ...I do not have an account for both Facebook and Twitter and I don't know how it is used. I have WhatsApp which I rely on for all the updates....

Below are some tweets showing that some people are of the view that some of the social media sites are not of great importance in creating awareness, especially to the people who are in Zimbabwe and are able to vote:

> @mashabhinisabhu Mar 31 replying to @hwendec: SG truly speaking **CCC** is mainly **on social media** but the majority of rural folks don't use Twitter, plz action on the ground.

> @ogknot Jan 26 Replying to @daddyhope, @TwitterSpaces, and 2 others True social media needs to be fully utilized, especially WhatsApp. We need short and precise messages that we can listen to in our villages. The problem with twitter is that it's not the majority of our electorate. A significant number there is the diaspora which cannot vote.

@gthandazam Replying to @daddyhope, @TwitterSpaces and 2 others Download it to WhatsApp if possible and will flood the market 12:19 PM Jan 26, 2022 Twitter for Android.

@realnigelndlovu Replying to @daddyhope, @TwitterSpaces,and 2 others, Do not forget that very few Zimbabweans are on Twitter, data is now very expensive and Twitter does not win elections mdara [old man or my man]. These leaders must go to the people. 2:55 PM Jan 26, 2022 Twitter for Android.

@its_peejay_ Replying to @daddyhope, @BMrehwa, and 3 others. He should take the campaign to ZUPCO busses, flea market, rural areas. Twitter does not reach out to that audience. It is restricted to those who afford data the diaspora, on campus students, the elite and social media addicts. What's the Location of where ura [you are] tweeting? The most popular social media in Zim? My gut feeling is whats app - if I am right CCC will need to use short videos, which can be shared cheaper. Twitter is used mostly by diaspora @ProfJNMoyo.

It was discovered that despite the CCC being launched live on various social media platforms, some people in the remote rural areas were not aware and some got to know about it later through word of mouth from other people. This was captured by a tweet:

@IshmaelMaz·Jan 27 Replying to @daddyhope, @TwitterSpaces, and 2 others Granted, BUT social media reach in rural #Zimbabwe is not as effective as in towns & cities which are already @CCCZimbabwe strongholds. We need a blend of social media & traditional media. ZANU PF must free state-controlled media @ZBC+Newsonline, @HeraldZim babwe, @SundayMailZim.

Conclusion

The chapter has demonstrated that, whilst in Zimbabwe mainstream media is arguably fully captured by the ruling party, social media is proving to be a perfect alternative for the coverage of electoral politics. The way Chamisa and the CCC brand have become household names even for the elderly (who have traditionally refused to hear of anything other than the ruling party) courtesy of social media confirm how much the approach is capable. The impact social media has caused for the opposition party has also been indicated, for instance, by the alleged efforts often made to interfere with internet connections within the country as a way of disturbing accessibility of the various CCC events. However, there are challenges associated with the platform even in other African countries like Uganda such as data charges, government interference through tempering with internet connectivity and accessibility of the material being posted to rural voters, though one could argue that even televisions, radios and newspapers have always experienced challenges too when it comes to reaching these rural citizens.

REFERENCES

Biswas, A., Ingle, N., & Roy, M. (2014). Influence of social media on voting behavior. *Journal of Power, Politics & Governance, 2*(2), 127–155.
Boulianne, S. (2011). Stimulating or reinforcing political interest: Using panel data to examine reciprocal effects between news media and political interest. *Political Communication, 28*(2), 147–162.
Darnolf, S. (1997). Critics or megaphones? News coverage during the parliamentary campaigns in Botswana 1994 and Zimbabwe 1995. *Democratization, 4*(2), 167–191.
Gibson, R. K., & McAllister, I. (2012). Online social ties and political engagement. *Journal of Information Technology & Politics, 10*(1), 21–34.
Holt, K., Ustad Figenschou, T., & Frischlich, L. (2019). Key dimensions of alternative news media. *Digital Journalism, 7*(7), 860–869.
Kietzmann, J. H., Kristopher H., Ian P., McCarthy & Bruno S. S. (2011). Social media? Get serious! Understanding the functional building blocks of social. *Business Horizons, 54*(3), 241–251.
Lipow, A., & Seyd, P. (1996). The politics of anti-partyism. *Parliamentary Affairs, 49*(2), 273–285.
Maarek, P. J. (2014). Politics 2.0: New forms of digital political marketing and political communication. *Trípodos, 34*, 13–22.
Media Monitoring Project Zimbabwe. (2000). https://worldcat.org/identities/lccn-no2002045738 Accessed on 22 October 2022.
Moyo, J. N. (1992). State politics and social domination in Zimbabwe. *The Journal of Modern African Studies, 30*(2), 305–330.
Mukasa, S. (2003). Press and politics in Zimbabwe. *African Studies Quarterly, 7*(2), 171–183.
Newsday. (2022, march 18). https://www.newsday.co.zw/category/10/news
Olaniran, B., & Williams, I. (2020). Social media effects: Hijacking democracy and civility in civic engagement. *Platforms, Protests, and the Challenge of Networked Democracy, 2020*, 77–94. Palgrave Macmillan, Cham.

Okwudishu, C. (1988). Patterns of ownership and accessibility to information and media facilities in democratizing the media in Nigeria. *Africa Media Review, 3*(1), 121–133.

Rainie, L., Smith, A., Schlozman, K. L., Brady, H., & Verba, S. (2012). Social media and political engagement. *Pew Internet & American Life Project, 19*(1), 2–13.

Reisach, U. (2021). The responsibility of social media in times societal and political manipulation. *European Journal of Operational Research, 291*(3).

Rogers, R. (2020). Deplatforming: Following extreme internet celebrities to Telegram and alternative social media. *European Journal of Communication, 35*(3), 213–229.

Sengere, L. (2018). 52.3% Of Zimbabweans say social media is their source of News. *TechZim.* https://www.techzim.co.zw/2018/02/52-3-percent-zimbabweans-say-social-media-source-of-news on 14/03/19.

Siluveru, M. (2015). Social and digital media in political communication. *International Journal of Scientific Research, 4*(6), 768–770.

The Media Monitors of Zimbabwe report. (2020). https://www.mediamonitors.org.zw/wp-content.

Wimmer, R. D., & Dominick, J. R. (2013). *Mass media research.* Cengage learning.

Wring, D., & Horrocks, I. (2000). *New media and politics.* Routledge.

ZBC Commercialization Act. (2001). https://www.veritaszim.net/node/249 Accessed on 22 October 2022.

Zimbabwe Independent, 26 February 1999.

PART III

Traditional Leaders and Religious Discourses in Zimbabwe's Electoral Politics

CHAPTER 16

Traditional Leaders as Vote Brokers and 'Kingmakers' in Zimbabwe's Elections

Gift Mwonzora

INTRODUCTION

The chapter seeks to examine the role of traditional leaders in undermining electoral integrity in Zimbabwe through acts of clientelism including coercion and vote buying on behalf of the incumbent. The chapter shows that traditional leaders play a significant role as kingmakers who deliver rural votes on behalf of the ruling Zimbabwe African National Union–Patriotic Front (ZANU-PF) party. It would seem appropriate to focus our analytic gaze on Zimbabwe which makes an interesting case considering the long-acknowledged role of traditional leaders in undermining democratic politics through partisan involvement in electioneering processes. It does seem, however, that Zimbabwe is not totally divorced from other African countries. Indeed, in Africa and the rest of the world, politicians have at varying times utilised different strategies and tactics of electoral mobilisation (Bayer, 2018; Brierley & Nathan, 2021; Frye et al.,

G. Mwonzora (✉)
Institute for Institutional Change and Social Justice, University of Free State (UFS), Bloemfontein, South Africa
e-mail: giftmwonzora@gmail.com

© The Author(s), under exclusive license to Springer Nature Switzerland AG 2023
E. Mavengano and S. Chirongoma (eds.), *Electoral Politics in Zimbabwe, Vol II*, https://doi.org/10.1007/978-3-031-33796-3_16

289

2019; Koter, 2013). This often involves the deployment of acts of clientelism (Baldwin, 2013; Dawson et al., 2023; Frye et al., 2019; Medina & Stokes, 2007; Stokes, 2005).

In Zimbabwe, this trend became more pronounced in the post-2000 era. In polities in Africa and elsewhere, where clientelist acts are rife, the power of intermediaries has gained prominence. As scholars opine 'instead of reaching out to the public on the basis of impersonal ties, politicians can create constituencies through personal connections between voters and their leaders' (Koter, 2013, p. 193). These intermediaries (middlemen) often involve powerful local politicians, traditional elites, leaders and activists—understood as the brokers. Mares and Young (2016, p. 268) conceive brokers as 'the actors who mediate in the relationship between candidates and voters'.

That traditional leaders have played a significant role as vote brokers in voter and electoral mobilisation in Africa has long been obvious (Bayer, 2018). In such contexts, scholars view clientelist acts, relationships and behaviour as underpinned by 'quid pro quo' whereby the trading of electoral support by the agent is premised on an agreed conduct by the principal (Hickens, 2011; Mares & Young, 2016, p. 270). It should be noted that so far, Zimbabwean-based research has concentrated on the (ab)use of traditional leaders by the incumbent. One downside of this strand of literature is that it fails to systematically analyse the utility and significance of traditional leaders as vote brokers who stand to benefit from incumbent victory.

Before proceeding further, a clear note on case selection is in order. The Zimbabwean context provides an ideal case for an exploration of the involvement of traditional leaders in the electioneering and voting processes against the dictates of democratic politics. This is reflected in how these actors coerce and offer promises to voters. Zimbabwe is also unique because the country has experienced what scholars term 'turnout buying' (Larreguy et al., 2016; Nichter, 2008). This then provides a good entry point for examining the role and influence of traditional leaders as vote brokers in the country's elections. The inquiry is relevant as it contributes to a nuanced theoretical discussion on electoral integrity in Africa, where elections are often flawed with the help of state and non-state actors.

The chapter helps in advancing our empirical understanding of the role of vote brokers, clientelism and how this impacts the realisation of electoral democracy and more specifically democratic accountability (Stokes,

2005). Such an analysis informs policy literature and discussions regarding election administration in Zimbabwe and in Africa and on social and distributive justice. The latter relates to the public policy articulations and concerns over the distribution of social welfare programmes. The study could not have been timelier. This is considering the enduring trend where traditional leaders continue to influence the voting patterns and dynamics in Zimbabwe's 2023 elections and even beyond. The chapter relies on qualitative research methodologies, including a critical review of grey material (literature), journal articles, content analysis of newspaper and online articles, critical discourse analysis of written and spoken text including political pronouncements at campaign rallies, party conferences, press statements, rally speech, video evidence and author's observations. The next section turns to the conceptual discussion underpinning the study.

Conceptualising Clientelism and Voter Brokering

This chapter focusing on the Zimbabwean case study, utilises the theoretical lens of clientelism, specifically situating the discussion within the patron-client relationship (Nichter & Peress, 2017). The discussion focuses on how traditional leaders, particularly local chiefs, headmen and village heads, in collusion with party activists, councillors and party candidates, continue to undermine electoral democracy through clientelist acts (Ndoma, 2021; Zimbabwe Human Rights NGO Forum, 2018, p. 27). As will be argued throughout the chapter, these acts often involve positive inducements (Frye et al., 2019; Nichter, 2008). These 'positive inducements include vote buying involving offers of rewards such as money, goods or favours' (Mares & Young, 2016, p. 270). Clientelistic acts also extend to negative inducements (Mares & Young, 2016) aimed at swaying voters to vote in a particular way. This often involves, for example, the use of coercion (Mares & Young, 2018). As further argued, 'negative inducements include the threat of economic or physical sanctions for an individual's voting behaviour' (Mares & Young, 2016, p. 270). As Lemarchand and Legg posit:

Political clientelism, in short, may be viewed as a more or less personalised, affective, and reciprocal relationship between actors, or sets of actors, commanding unequal resources and involving mutually beneficial transactions that have political ramifications beyond the immediate sphere of dyadic relationships. (Lemarchand & Legg, 1972, pp. 151–152).

Taping from the clientelism literature, the chapter also utilises the vote broker model (Auerbach & Thachil, 2018; Baldwin, 2013; Brierley & Nathan, 2021; Frye et al., 2019; Hicken & Nathan, 2020) to examine how traditional leaders act as intermediaries who influence voting behaviour and dynamics. Thus, engendering electoral manipulation in Zimbabwe and even beyond. Scholars define brokers as 'the actors who mediate in the relationship between candidates and voters' (Mares & Young, 2016, p. 267).

As scholars argue, 'patrons have an incentive to broker relationships between voters and politicians not because they are benevolent but because they gain materially from doing so' (Baldwin, 2013, p. 795). No one puts it across laconically than Baldwin writing in the Zambian case study who described patrons as:

> Unelected leaders at the zenith of the socioeconomic hierarchy in their communities. This puts them in a unique position to lobby on behalf of their communities, to obtain information on problems, to organise local resources, and to ensure community participation in programs. The embeddedness of patrons within their communities gives them the capacity to broker relationships between voters and politicians, and the incentive to do so. (Baldwin, 2013, p. 795).

The question then is why vote brokering occurs with regularity and in particular contexts and not in others. I, however, offer a caveat in the sense that while pursuing this line of thought one must be attentive to the country's socio-economic, political and cultural context. After presenting the introduction and conceptual framing, the chapter maps the background/historical context before engaging with the literature discussion. This is followed by an empirical analysis before concluding the discussion and making recommendations for future research.

Historical Context

At independence, Zimbabwe was on course to become a beacon of democracy especially after the black African government led by Robert Mugabe popularised reconciliation in acts and in deeds with the former white settler regime. The country held its first competitive election in 1980, where Robert Mugabe triumphed.

In years to follow, the country was to hold periodic elections in 1985, 1990, 1995, 1996, 2000, 2005, 2008 (March and June -Run-off), 2013, 2018 and the next election slated for 2023. Despite the varying contentious issues affecting electoral integrity in all these elections, it was apparent that the incumbent had the upper hand. Thanks to the manipulation and (ab)use of instruments of the state, including the security element (soldiers, secret service and police) (Masunungure, 2009), traditional leaders as well as the use of the judiciary to delay—if not rubber stamp electoral disputes (Mwonzora & Xaba, 2020).

Though traditional leaders were pushed to the periphery and neglected since independence, this only changed in 1998 when they were accorded more rights and privileges under the Traditional Leaders Act. Again, the ZANU-PF party utilised traditional leaders to shore up support in the 2000 era, when the prospect of losing power to the newly formed Movement for Democratic Change (MDC) loomed large. Since then, traditional leaders were roped in as 'party functionaries' or 'commissars' who would canvass for votes on behalf of ZANU-PF (Zimbabwe Human Rights NGO Forum, 2018, pp. 27–34). This occurred with open disdain or defiance of the Traditional Leaders Act of 1998 (Government of Zimbabwe, 1998) and the country's constitution, which proscribe the partisan dabbling of traditional leaders in party politics (Ndoma, 2021). The traditional leadership structure in Zimbabwe, as is the case elsewhere in Africa—for instance, in Malawi and Zambia, recognises and holds in high esteem traditional leaders as custodians of culture, heritage, customs, traditional values and traditions (Baldwin, 2013; Chigwata, 2016; Ndoma, 2021). On this basis, they are supposed to divorce themselves from active party politics, including electioneering on behalf of any party. While, this is expected of Zimbabwe's traditional leaders, they have veered from their expected roles as evident in their direct involvement in elections as vote brokers (Ndoma, 2021). In this regard, it should come as no surprise that:

The role of traditional leaders in Zimbabwe depicts a picture of a traditional authority whose existence is held in tension between the citizen expectations for it to be a neutral vanguard of the traditions custom and community development on one hand and ruling elites demands for it to be loyal and serve the interest of the incumbent party (ZESN, 2018, p. 1).

The above depiction raises several questions regarding traditional leaders' conduct, powers, limitations and overstretching. In what follows, I engage with the literature debates on clientelism, vote broking and the role of traditional leaders in election and voter mobilisation.

CLIENTELISM, VOTE BROKERING AND TRADITIONAL LEADERS

The clientelism literature has underscored the interdependence of politicians and traditional leaders (Koter, 2013), and such an analysis has helped shed light on why traditional leaders often involve themselves in voting and electoral processes (Baldwin, 2013). Existing studies often observe that politicians need traditional leaders as intermediaries who will drum up support for their parties, and traditional leaders also need politicians for legitimation (Matiashe, 2022; Ndoma, 2021). Though traditional leaders' authority and powers are derived from traditional leadership structures (e.g. lineage), they also seek and require legitimation that comes with the formally recognised rights by their respective governments (Baldwin, 2014; De Kadt & Larreguy, 2018). In other words, they also need to safeguard their positions from the government, especially in the wake of dethronement as in the case of Zimbabwe (Matiashe, 2022).

However, significant gaps abound in this corpus of scholarship as evident in the sparse literature focusing on broker compensation (Brierley & Nathan, 2022). This is save for African literature (De Kadt & Larreguy, 2018; Nathan, 2019) detailing how traditional leaders are compensated for their clientelist acts by the incumbent. Existing scholarly accounts further underscore the mutual dependence of political actors and traditional leaders (Krämer, 2016, p. 122) with others characterising the relationship as exemplifying a *quid pro quo* alliance (De Kadt & Larreguy, 2018). This win–win relationship may even extend further to cater for the 'legal safeguards of traditional leaders often including legislation that improve their material welfare and financial wellbeing' (Bayer, 2018, pp. 10–11). This is aptly demonstrated in the South African context during the past decades, where traditional leaders sought legal tenure, which was tenuous by trading votes in what they term 'political quid pro quo' (De Kadt & Larreguyz, 2014, p. 2).

In their quest to bring a richer perspective to the vote broker literature, scholars have examined the efficacy of brokers in how they (struggle to) monitor voter behaviour (Kitschelt & Wilkinson, 2007; Nichter, 2008; Zarazaga, 2014). The monitoring dilemma has been raised in several research studies in varying jurisdictions, including in Argentina (Stokes, 2005), Venezuela, Russia (Frye et al., 2019), Ghana (Nathan, 2019) and Zambia (Baldwin, 2016). Other scholarly accounts, however, argue that monitoring vote choice remains challenging though possible (Koter, 2013, p. 194; Kramon, 2017; Nichter, 2018). Questions still linger within empirical studies on how we account for voters' decision-making and whether voters maintain and respect the orders and instructions of brokers (Koter, 2013; Nichter, 2008). Nuancing this debate, scholars raise critical questions on how and in what ways politicians and brokers can monitor and access voter behaviour in the context of secret balloting (Nichter, 2008; Stokes, 2005). However, others quickly observe that voters will still vote as directed as they are beholden to brokers due to the power of clientelist exchanges.

Varied strands of research exist detailing the role of traditional leaders in undermining election integrity in Zimbabwe (Masunungure, 2009; Mwonzora & Mandikwaza, 2020) but with little focus being paid to the dynamics of vote broking, especially by traditional leaders (Matiashe, 2022; Zimbabwe Human Rights NGO Forum, 2018). This for example involves the nature of promises made (pre- and post-electoral benefits). Scholars also observe that politicians working with intermediaries also underscore 'post-electoral re-distribution to sway voters' (Koter, 2013, p. 198). The Zimbabwean election administration scholarship specifically dwells on the complexities facing traditional leaders in vote broking utilising the competing principles dilemma. This entails complexities of balancing allegiance and authority to government/state *vis-à-vis* the need to maintain the allegiance to the people (ZESN, 2018).

Although the role of traditional leadership in electoral mobilisation in Africa and Zimbabwe has received increased scholarly attention, significant gaps still exist (Kurebwa, 2020; The Zimbabwe Human Rights NGO Forum/The Zimbabwe Peace Project, 2021). While the role of traditional leaders have long been acknowledged, much emphasis is on the capture of chiefs and their subsequent role in electoral contests (Baldwin,

2016; Bayer, 2018; CIASA, 2021; Kurebwa, 2020). Such analyses largely overlook, underplay and circumvent the role, contribution and influence of other local-level traditional leaders (for instance, headmen and village heads) and elected officials like councillors in vote broking as is the case in Zimbabwe (Ndoma, 2021; ZESN, 2018). Though chiefs often issue top-level directives, they rarely get involved in localised electoral mobilisation. This is not to suggest that they do not matter. Their influence is still felt within communities owing to their respected roles, authority and power within their jurisdictions. This often translates into voters following what has been termed elsewhere as 'chiefly endorsements' (Brierley & Ofosu, 2021). It is valuable to review different legislative frameworks guiding the conduct and role of traditional leaders in Zimbabwe as will be shown in the ensuing discussion.

Legislation on Traditional Leaders in Zimbabwe

In Zimbabwe, the institution of traditional leaders is respected and recognised under Section 16(3) of the Zimbabwean Constitution (Government of Zimbabwe, 2013). Further, the conduct and rights of traditional leaders is regulated by the Traditional Leaders Act of 1998 under Section 49(1) and 49(2) (Government of Zimbabwe, 1998). However, what is of concern is that despite the existence of such legislative measures and statutes, Zimbabwe's traditional leaders still renege on their duties and dabble in partisan politics and, in doing so, contribute to the erosion of democracy. This is evident in the involvement of village heads, chiefs and headmen in various acts of electoral manipulation through, for example, coercing community members to vote in a particular manner (Ndoma, 2021).

In most—if not all—cases, they act as vote brokers on behalf of the incumbent. Such conduct goes against the dictates of the Constitution, specifically Section 281(2) [a] and [c], which stipulates that traditional leaders must not only act neutrally but seen to be maintaining neutrality in partisan issues (Government of Zimbabwe, 2013; Zimbabwe Human Rights NGO Forum, 2018). However, this has not been the case as in every election traditional leaders act as voter brokers who coerce and intimidate villagers into voting for the incumbent or else they will be denied material benefits or chased away from the community. In 2018, the European Union Election Observation Mission [EU EOM]

Observers report 'confirmed that traditional leaders were involved in the campaign, including intimidating and influencing voters' (2018, p. 55). In the wake of the enduring involvement of traditional leaders in politics in Zimbabwe, the Observer Mission then made recommendations to the effect that: 'Effective mechanisms should be introduced for monitoring and sanctioning of partisan behaviour by traditional leaders and civil servants, to help ensure the impartiality of state structures in the election' (ibid; 2018, p. 55). The fact that, for example, the High Court ruled that the President of the National Council of Chiefs, Fortune Charumbira, acted *ultra vires* the Constitution (Section 281), 2[a] by instructing traditional leaders to support ZANU-PF seems to not have stopped some Zimbabwean traditional leaders from acting in a partisan manner. This wanton disregard for the rule of law (court rulings) underscores the strength of the party-state embeddedness and how this continue to undercut electoral democracy. What has been peculiar in Zimbabwe though is the progressive efforts at restraining traditional leaders who act in a partisan manner (Kurebwa, 2020; Zimbabwe Human Rights NGO Forum, 2018, pp. 28–29). The question, though, remains whether such acts of restraint often including litigation are effective in reining their conduct, especially in a country famed for the disregard of the rule of law, particularly court judgements that are disfavourable to the incumbent or those sympathetic/aligned to the ruling elite (Zimbabwe Lawyers for Human Rights, 2018). The case mentioned below is instructive:

> In a matter filed by the Election Resource Centre v. Chief Charumbira, National Council of Chiefs, Minister of Local Government, Public Works and National Housing, Case No. HC 1718/2018, the court ruled that disciplinary proceedings against a traditional leader supporting ZANU PF in public statements should be initiated by the Minister of Local Governance, while the National Council of Chiefs should establish the Integrity and Ethics Committee of Chiefs, provided under the Constitution to monitor such conduct. (European Union Election Observation Mission [EU EOM], 2018, p. 41).

That the courts adjudicated on the matter and made a pronouncement is commendable. However, the jury is still out on whether such a ruling sets a precedent in advancing electoral democracy by proscribing the partisan conduct of traditional leaders (vote brokers) who work to pursue the interests of a single party. This is particularly relevant if examined in the context of ongoing defiance of court rulings and the wanton disregard of the rule of law by chiefs who perceive themselves as 'untouchable' and acting in behaviour of those above the law. A percipient example is when Chief Charumbira was ordered by the court to retract a public statement in support of the ZANU-PF party, a retraction that never came (CIASA, 2021). This far, I have mapped the legislative terrain guiding the conduct of traditional leaders, I now turn to a discussion on the efficacy of traditional leaders as election brokers.

TRADITIONAL LEADERS AS KINGMAKERS IN ZIMBABWEAN ELECTIONS

Traditional leaders in Zimbabwe's rural communities have become notorious for strategically handing in material benefits a few days before elections. Village heads usually hand out food stuffs and farming inputs donated by the government to households/party supporters in their jurisdiction. This amounts to vote buying, which is an act of clientelism (Zimbabwe Human Rights NGO Forum/Zimbabwe Peace Project, 2021). The monopolisation of food aid (maize) (Human Rights Watch, 2003), farming inputs including seed and fertiliser as well as the partisan distribution of food handouts have been used by both local ZANU-PF activists, local leaders and headmen and chiefs to curry favour with voters (Mwonzora & Mandikwaza, 2019; Zimbabwe Human Rights NGO Forum/Zimbabwe Peace Project, 2021). In doing so, these traditional leaders utilise positive and negative inducements (Mares & Young, 2016), as explained earlier. Nowhere is this more evident than in the revelation below:

> Conduct of traditional leaders in Zimbabwe is such that they influence both electoral outcomes and processes by not only sealing off space for opposition political players, but also subverting the will of the people under their jurisdiction through intimidation, making public pronouncements to the effect that they support ZANU-PF and partisan distribution of food aid and farming inputs. The reality on the ground is that traditional leaders are fully engaged with electoral and political processes in their communities(CIASA, 2021).

While this trend persists, the net effect is that it remains a source of concern as it engenders what Stokes (2005) terms perverse accountability, as will be explained later. Not only that, the dishing of handouts—or withholding of such has affected the quality of leaders that emerge from electoral contests. There are good reasons to suggest that these clientelist acts undermine electoral democracy.

Although there are parallels in how brokers utilise clientelist acts, the trend is not limited to Africa (Baldwin, 2013; Koter, 2013) or Zimbabwe. Examples abound in some countries in Latin America and elsewhere. Stokes gives an excellent example of how and why one voter in Ukraine once revealed that he voted for Viktor Yanukovych instead of his preferred opposition candidate Viktor Yuschenko because of the promise of getting a wheelchair by the local nurse if he switched his vote (Stokes, 2005, p. 316). This shows the effectiveness of vote brokers in local elections, which is the case in some Zimbabwean rural constituencies where food handouts and farming inputs are promised by traditional leaders, specifically headmen and village heads as more pronounced from the 2000s era to the contemporary. Even though in the above case, it was a non-food item that swayed the voter's mind, this is telling of how voters not only in Ukraine but elsewhere can be manipulated through the promise of material rewards to trade their votes. From this perspective, we are bound to concur with scholars who observe that 'if a voter's benefactor profits from the election of a particular candidate or party, such a voter can expect to experience diffuse benefits' (Koter, 2013, p. 193).

While there are reasons to argue that the fear factor (harvest of fear) plays a role in determining voter choice and behaviour in Zimbabwe's rural communities (Zamchiya, 2013), one cannot rule out the moral obligation that accompanies one to fulfil his/her promises to the vote broker. Taking from the Ukraine case, such acts diminish accountability as voters fail to checkmate politicians and punish them for misbehaving, make them account for their failure to deliver, and their lack of responsiveness (Stokes, 2005, p. 316). Such behaviour further 'reduces the pressure on governments to perform well and to provide public goods, keeps voters from using elections to express their policy preferences, and undermines voter autonomy' amounting to perverse accountability (Stokes, 2005, p. 316).

In the Zimbabwean context, this act of vote broking is particularly acute in rural areas where the incumbent face stiff competition from the opposition or in battleground constituencies where there is a likelihood of incumbent defeat. The stakes are so high in such contexts that the incumbent relies on traditional leaders, including headmen and chiefs who collaborate with local party activists, leaders and members. They then act as power brokers who decide how the community members are supposed to vote. This resonates with several case studies in the Global South. As some scholars opine:

> In highly competitive areas, electoral inducements—such as money or food parcels—offered by parties to voters may serve to mobilise supporters who are disinclined to turn out or it may help sway the vote choice of weakly opposed voters who are marginally inclined to support the competing party (Dawson et al., 2023, p. 2).

In the Zimbabwean context, village heads and headmen continue to play a significant role in identifying and co-ordinating development and public social welfare programmes, including the compilation of beneficiaries' lists (see, Zimbabwe Human Rights NGO Forum/The Zimbabwe Peace Project, 2021). This privileged position is thus used either as a 'stick' to punish or a 'carrot' (Frye et al., 2019) to entice voters who harbour and entertain the thoughts of voting against the ZANU-PF party. The evidence to support this claim is apparent in the 2018 election. In the build-up to the polls, 'traditional leaders were involved in the campaign and influencing voters by threatening to cut food aid and agricultural inputs if they did not vote for ZANU-PF' (European Union Election Observation Mission [EU EOM], 2018, p. 21). The above acts should also not cause us to forget the unique embeddedness of traditional leaders within the ZANU-PF party state. As noted by one election watchdog:

> The fault lines in the traditional leadership's interference in elections and electoral process despite the Constitution and subsidiary laws prohibiting are to be found in the history's long relationship between traditional leadership and the political elite both during colonial and in deposited colonial era' (ZESN, 2018, p. 1).

To fully account for the above outlined nexus, we must understand the love-hate relationship between citizens and their local traditional leadership. In Koter's (2013, p. 193) observation, this happens mainly because:

The relationship between local leaders and their followers is complex in that it can be based both on reciprocity and on some degree of exploitation. Voters can trust and rely on their leaders but also feel trapped in their subordinate position (Koter, 2013, p. 193).

The same is true of the Zimbabwean rural voters who feel obliged to vote for the incumbent at the behest of local party leaders, activists and traditional leaders. In many rural areas including in Manicaland (Buhera South) and Mashonaland East (Mudzi), Muzarabani (Mashonaland Central) among other places during the 2018 elections traditional leaders and ZANU-PF members implemented '*sabhuku nevanhu vake*' (a village head and his subjects)—loosely translated 'rally behind your headmen' in voting for the incumbent (Zimbabwe Human Rights NGO Forum, 2018, p. 31). This practice relates to how voters/community members are shepherded to vote as a bloc. The aim is to intimidate and monitor voting behaviour, especially those viewed as 'deviant' and sympathetic to the opposition.

Writing on the conduct of clientelist parties with specific reference to Argentina, one scholar made the following revelation:

> Political machines (or clientelist parties) mobilise electoral support by trading particularistic benefits to voters in exchange for their votes. But, if the secret ballot hides voters' actions from the machine, voters are able to renege, accepting benefits and then voting as they choose (Stokes, 2005, p. 315).

It is observed from the above that the utilisation of a secret ballot complicates the voter-broker relationship mainly in what others term commitment and reciprocity dilemma (Finan & Schechter, 2012; Hicken & Nathan, 2020; Nichter, 2008). Recently, scholars have begun asking: 'how can clientelism be a viable electoral strategy if voters can renege on their commitments to politicians?' (Hicken & Nathan, 2020, p. 277). However, in seeking to provide answers to such questions, they also have solutions in mind. As Hicken and Nathan further elucidate, the panacea to (re)solving the commitment dilemma with voters rests with instituting monitoring and enforcement mechanisms (Hicken & Nathan, 2020, p. 277). For some observers, this seems easier stated than done considering the ubiquity of secret voting in many—if not all—jurisdictions.

This then raises an enforcement nightmare regarding how parties monitor and verify how one votes. For example, how do traditional leaders in Zimbabwe including chiefs, village heads and headmen monitor how voters vote in particular elections and do the electorate vote according to the orders issued by these powerful local elites?

In Zimbabwe, it remains difficult to monitor how voters vote despite those headmen, village heads and chiefs who entice and threaten voters to vote for ZANU-PF candidates. This is because vote monitoring is more challenging due to the constituency and polling station-based voting model. While the temptation would be to view incumbent victory as a reflection of broker effectiveness, this is also difficult to verify. For example, in contexts of an opposition victory, how can brokers explain voting behaviour? In the Zimbabwean case, brokers can only speculate, witch hunt and single out opposition sympathisers for reprisals without knowing how voters voted. It is only then that they can now sanction or promise rewards.

As scholars enunciate, there is a solution to vote transaction: 'giving handouts not to die-hard supporters whose loyalty and support is guaranteed but 'to people whose future support is in doubt' (Stokes, 2005, p. 316). Even in such constituencies, there is no guarantee that positive and negative inducements will produce the desired results (Mares & Young, 2016). This is even though traditional, leaders rely on their 'social clout to induce compliance' (Koter, 2013, p. 195).

It should, however, not be disputed that in Zimbabwe, vote brokers, mostly village heads and headmen have also actively engaged in coercion. A local human rights organisation noted in the context of the 2018 elections how 'food aid and agricultural inputs were also used as tools of coercion by mostly traditional leaders' (Zimbabwe Human Rights NGO Forum, 2018, p. 6). Media reports revealed some traditional leaders (village heads) who were seen recording names of voters in books at polling stations. There is also evidence that leading to the polls, some traditional leaders coerced villagers to submit serial numbers of their biometric voters' roll slips (Zimbabwe Human Rights NGO Forum, 2018, p. 6).

While we can persuasively advance the claim that traditional leaders remain influential power brokers who decide election outcomes in some African polities, others opine that they make or break politicians. As Richard Sklar writes in a different context, which still resonates with the Zimbabwean case study, 'the traditional kings are not power brokers behind the throne, they are the thrones behind the power of the sovereign state which they help to legitimate' (Sklar, 2005, p. 8).

Worryingly, in 2018 the Chiefs Council declared its support and allegiance to the ZANU-PF party. The fact that the Chiefs Council was to declare its allegiance to one political party is an affront to the dictates of the Constitution and the Traditional Leaders Act. In a matter brought to the bench by Mr Elton Mangoma of the (now defunct)—Renewal Democrats of Zimbabwe—Justice Mawadze of the High Court ruled that traditional leaders cease to involve themselves or interfere with partisan processes (Zimbabwe Lawyers for Human Rights, 2018). That the traditional leaders have continued on this path is unsurprising. This is considering that Zimbabwean traditional leaders particularly chiefs have been pampered with material gifts and benefits including cars (Zimbabwe Human Rights NGO Forum, 2018, p. 29), electricity provision to their households, farming inputs and monetary compensation among others by the ZANU-PF government (Chigwata, 2016; Matiashe, 2022). This is viewed as amounting to buying their loyalty especially during election periods.

As recent as 2020, traditional leaders continued to get involved in partisan registration of food aid beneficiaries in rural areas, such as Tsholotsho, favouring ZANU-PF supporters and members at the expense of all vulnerable beneficiaries (Heal Zimbabwe Trust, 2020). Such vote brokering behaviour is bound to persist, considering that Zimbabwe's traditional leaders benefit from political patronage and remuneration from the incumbent government (Chigwata, 2016). Hence, they 'become willing collaborators' during and off election season(s) (ZESN, 2018). This is against the wishes of communities as established in a 2021 Afrobarometer survey (see, Ndoma, 2021). Without change of conduct, clientelist acts led by traditional leaders will continue to sway voters thus affecting their free will to choose leaders of their choice in the 2023 elections. It is foreseeable that such a practice will continue to undercut participatory and electoral democracy in Zimbabwe even beyond the 2023 polls.

Conclusion

This chapter has made a case on why we should study and understand the role of Zimbabwean traditional leaders in influencing democracy through clientelist acts (as vote brokers). The study has highlighted that the relationship between traditional leaders and the incumbent ZANU-PF involves a quid pro quo arrangement. The discussion underscored the continuities in the use of coercion, material rewards (promises and fulfilments) and other clientelist exchanges in swaying voters. In this and in many ways, voters are left with no option than to trade their votes for the promised guarantees. The study underscored that even in a context where legislation prescribing and proscribing the conduct and behaviour of traditional leaders exist, they remain willing and 'useful' actors who can deliver votes on behalf of the incumbent (ZANU-PF) party. The study concludes that absent change of behaviour and conduct, Zimbabwean traditional leaders (chiefs, headmen and village heads) will remain an albatross on the neck of citizens who yearn to meaningfully realise electoral and liberal democracy by participating in free, fair and credible electoral processes freed from coercion and manipulation. Future empirical work should be directed in understanding how polarisation, partisanship, political economy, fear and violence continue to influence voter decision-making and vote choice in Zimbabwe's rural areas where traditional leaders still enjoy unbridled power and influence.

References

Auerbach, A. M., & Thachil, T. (2018). How clients select brokers: Competition and choice in India's slums. *American Political Science Review, 112*(4), 775–791.

Baldwin, K. (2013). Why vote with the chief? Political connections and public goods provision in Zambia. *American Journal of Political Science, 57*(4), 794–809.

Baldwin, K. (2014). When Politicians cede control of resources: Land, chiefs, and coalition-building in Africa. *Comparative Politics, 46*(3), 253–271.

Baldwin, K. (2016). *The paradox of traditional chiefs in democratic Africa*. Cambridge University Press.

Bayer, A. (2018). *Ensuring each other's post?: Exploring personal ties between politicians and traditional leaders* (Doctoral dissertation).

Brierley, S., & Kramon, E. (2018). *Party campaign strategies: Rallies, canvassing and handouts in a new democracy*. Working paper.

Brierley, S., & Ofosu, G. (2021). Do chiefs' endorsements affect voter behaviour?.

Brierley, S., & Nathan, N. L. (2021). The connections of party brokers: Which brokers do parties select? *The Journal of Politics, 83*(3), 884–901.

Brierley, S., & Nathan, N. L. (2022). Motivating the machine: Which brokers do parties pay? *The Journal of Politics, 84*(3), 1539–1555.

Chigwata, T. (2016). The role of traditional leaders in Zimbabwe: Are they still relevant? *Law, Democracy & Development, 20*(1), 69–90.

Citizens in Action Southern Africa [CIASA]. (2021). *The role of traditional leaders in elections*, 29 November 2021 available at: https://kubatana.net/2021/11/29/the-role-of-traditional-leaders-in-elections/

Dawson, S., Charron, N., & Justesen, M. K. (2023). Electoral competition, political parties and clientelism: Evidence from local elections in South Africa. *Democratization*, 1–22.

De Kadt, D., & Larreguyz, H. A. (2014). Agents of the regime? Electoral clientelism and traditional leaders in South Africa. Unpublished manuscript, Massachusetts Institute of Technology Political Science Department Research Paper No. 2014-24.

De Kadt, D., & Larreguy, H. (2015). Agents of the regime? Traditional leaders and electoral clientelism in South Africa. Working Paper, Department of Political. Science. Massachusets Institute of Technology.

De Kadt, D., & Larreguy, H. (2018). Agents of the regime? Traditional leaders and electoral politics in South Africa. *The Journal of Politics, 80*(2), 382–399.

European Union Election Observation Mission [EU EOM]. (2018). *Final report: Republic of Zimbabwe harmonised elections (European Union, October 2018)* available at: https://www.ecoi.net/en/file/local/1449201/1226_1541592190_eu-eom-zimbabwe-2018-final-report.pdf

Ferree, K. E., & Long, J. D. (2016). Gifts, threats, and perceptions of ballot secrecy in African elections. *African Affairs, 115*(461), 621–645.

Finan, F., & Schechter, L. (2012). Vote-buying and reciprocity. *Econometrica, 80*(2), 863–881.

Frye, T., Reuter, O. J., & Szakonyi, D. (2019). Vote brokers, clientelist appeals, and voter turnout: Evidence from Russia and Venezuela. *World Politics, 71*(4), 710–746.

Government of Zimbabwe. (1998). *Traditional Leaders Act, Chapter 29:17.* Government Gazette, Printflow.

Government of Zimbabwe. (2013). *Constitution of Zimbabwe Amendment (No. 20).* Government Printers, Harare: Government of Zimbabwe.

Heal Zimbabwe Trust. (2020). *Abuse of traditional leaders in Tsholotsho during food aid registration a cause for concern*, 10 November 2020 available at: https://kubatana.net/2020/11/10/abuse-of-traditional-leaders-in-tsholotsho-during-food-aid-registration-a-cause-for-concern/

Hicken, A. (2011). Clientelism. *Annual Review of Political Science, 14*, 289–310.

Hicken, A., & Nathan, N. L. (2020). Clientelism's red herrings: Dead ends and new directions in the study of nonprogrammatic politics. *Annual Review of Political Science, 23*, 277–294.

Human Rights Watch. (2003). *Not eligible the politicization of food in Zimbabwe*, 24 October 2003, available at: https://www.hrw.org/report/2003/10/24/not-eligible/politicization-food-zimbabwe

Krämer, M. (2016). Neither despotic nor civil: The Legitimacy of chieftaincy in its relationship with the ANC and the State in Kwazulu-Natal (South Africa). *The Journal of Modern African Studies*, 54(1), 117–143.

Kramon, E. (2017). *Money for votes: The causes and consequences of electoral clientelism in Africa*. Cambridge University Press.

Kitschelt, H., & Wilkinson, S. I. (Eds.). (2007). *Patrons, clients and policies: Patterns of democratic accountability and political competition*. Cambridge University Press.

Koter, D. (2013). King makers: Local leaders and ethnic politics in Africa. *World Politics*, 65(2), 187–232.

Kurebwa, J. (2020). The capture of traditional leaders by political parties in Zimbabwe for political expediency. In S. Chhabra (Ed.), *Civic engagement in social and political constructs* (pp. 196–219). IGI Global.

Larreguy, H., Marshall, J., & Querubin, P. (2016). Parties, brokers, and voter mobilization: How turnout buying depends upon the party's capacity to monitor brokers. *American Political Science Review*, 110(1), 160–179.

Lemarchand, R., & Legg, K. (1972). Political clientelism and development: A preliminary analysis. *Comparative Politics*, 4(2), 149–178.

Medina, L. F., &Stokes, S. (2007). Monopoly and monitoring: An approach to political clientelism. *Patrons, clients, and policies* (pp. 68–83).

Mares, I., & Young, L. (2016). Buying, expropriating, and stealing votes. *Annual Review of Political Science*, 19, 267–288. Masunungure, E. (2009). 'A Militarised Election: The 27 June Presidential Run-off', in Masunungure, E. (ed.) *Defying the Winds of Change: Zimbabwe's 2008 Elections*. Harare: Weaver Press.

Masunungure, E. (2009). A militarised election: The 27 June presidential run-off. In E. Masunungure (Ed.), *Defying the winds of change: Zimbabwe's 2008 elections*. Weaver Press.

Matiashe, F. S. (2022). Zimbabwe: How ZANU-PF uses traditional chiefs to buy votes in rural areas, 3 January 2022 available at: https://www.theafricareport.com/162456/zimbabwe-how-zanu-pf-uses-traditional-chiefs-to-buy-votes-in-rural-areas/

Mwonzora, G., & Mandikwaza, E. (2019). The menu of electoral manipulation in Zimbabwe: Food handouts, violence, memory, and fear–Case of Mwenezi East and Bikita West 2017 by-elections. *Journal of Asian and African Studies*, 54(8), 1128–1144.

Mwonzora, G., & Xaba, M. B. (2020). From the booth to the dock: 2018 elections in Zimbabwe and the elusive search for electoral integrity. *Commonwealth & Comparative Politics*, 58(4), 433–451.

Nathan, N. L. (2019). Does participation reinforce patronage? Policy preferences, turnout and class in urban Ghana. *British Journal of Political Science, 49*(1), 229–255.

Ndoma, S. (2021). Zimbabweans see traditional leaders as influential but want them to stay out of politics. *Afrobarometer Dispatch No. 469*, 3 August 2021, Afrobarometer available at: https://www.afrobarometer.org/wp-content/uploads/2022/02/ad469-zimbabweans_see_traditional_leaders_as_influential_but_want_them_out_of_politics-afrobarometer-3aug21.pdf

Nichter, S. (2008). Vote buying or turnout buying? Machine politics and the secret ballot. *American Political Science Review, 102*(1), 19–31.

Nichter, S. (2018). *Votes for survival: Relational clientelism in Latin America.* Cambridge University Press.

Nichter, S., & Peress, M. (2017). Request fulfilling: When citizens demand clientelist benefits. *Comparative Political Studies, 50*(8), 1086–1117.

Sklar, R. (2005). The premise of mixed government in African political studies. In O. Vaughan (Ed.), *Tradition and politics: Indigenous political structures and politics in Africa* (pp. 3–25). Africa World Press.

Stokes, S. C. (2005). Perverse accountability: A formal model of machine politics with evidence from Argentina. *American Political Science Review, 99*(3), 315–325.

The Zimbabwe Human Rights NGO Forum /The Zimbabwe Peace Project. (2021). *The politics of food: A contextual analysis of the distribution of food aid in Zimbabwe*, March 2021 available: https://data.zimpeaceproject.com/api/files/1615803851127r38eqzh83co.pdf

Zamchiya, P. (2013). The MDC-T's (un) seeing eye in Zimbabwe's 2013 harmonised elections: A technical knockout. *Journal of Southern African Studies, 39*(4), 955–962.

Zarazaga, R. (2014). Brokers beyond clientelism: A new perspective through the Argentine case. *Latin American Politics and Society, 56*(3), 23–45.

Zimbabwe Human Rights NGO Forum. (2018). Human rights violations in the context of the 2018 Harmonised elections, Elections Report, available at: https://ntjwg.uwazi.io/api/files/1572944113287d5g3mfabq2w.pdf

Zimbabwe Lawyers for Human Rights. (2018). High Court bans all traditional leaders from politics, 17 May 2018 available at: https://kubatana.net/2018/05/17/high-court-bans-traditional-leaders-politics/

CHAPTER 17

The Institution of Traditional Leadership and Partisan Politics in Zimbabwe

Jeffrey Kurebwa

INTRODUCTION

The role of traditional leaders in governance processes has always followed the dictates of the ruling regimes since colonial Zimbabwe. Traditional leaders are always willing enablers to the government in all aspects, by design, default, and coercion. While the Constitution of Zimbabwe (2013) made a distinct departure in making clear provisions as to their role, the practice has continued to be opposite and defiant (Baldwin, 2020). The roles of traditional leaders in rural communities continue to be important as it has been argued that they reduce transaction costs on behalf of the government, facilitate faster and grounded decision-making and access to justice while maintaining their cultural functions and superintending over land access and use. Their role in electoral processes in Zimbabwe has always attracted the interest of stakeholders such as Civil Society Organisations (CSOs), citizens, and political parties. It can be

J. Kurebwa (✉)
Department of Peace and Governance, Bindura University of Science Education, Bindura, Zimbabwe
e-mail: jkurebwa@buse.ac.zw

argued, from the onset, that electoral malpractice and fraud have long shifted from the ballot box and polling day to the political environment where traditional leaders have taken a partisan role. It is in this arena that traditional leaders seem to superintend with unfettered power (Mamdani, 2018). Their partisan participation in politics has been criticised for having an effect in diverting the will of the people and free choice through intimidation.

The ZANU-PF government has always been accused of often using financial and non-financial rewards to gain traditional leaders' active support and verbal public endorsements during election campaigns. The partisan participation of traditional leaders in politics can either be coercive or cooperative. This has important implications for electoral accountability and democratic responsiveness (Baldwin, 2013; Gottlieb, 2017). Several complaints have been raised by opposition political parties regarding the partisan role of traditional leaders in electoral processes. Traditional leaders have also been co-opted into campaign teams of the ruling ZANU-PF (Neiwaai, 2003). In the process, chiefs have lost their historical role as custodians of tradition and culture and become political agents and puppets of the post-colonial state, often participating in the oppression of their own subjects (Ncube, 2011).

Defining Traditional Leadership

Various definitions have been given as to what constitutes traditional leadership. Some of these definitions are discussed below.

Traditional leaders are defined as unelected elites who derive their leadership position from the historical socio-cultural customs of their communities (Baldwin, 2020; Mamdani, 2018).

Other scholars such as Holzinger, Kerny, and Kromrey (2017) define traditional political leadership as an institution whose legitimacy is based in part on its association with customary modes of governing a community. These institutions are political in the sense that they make decisions regulating and providing for the collective, and they are traditional in the sense that they are popularly believed to be connected to custom. These definitions emphasise that these institutions are associated with custom in the popular imagination, not that they are accurate reflections of historic governance practices (Baldwin & Hozinger, 2019).

Weber (1922/1958) defines traditional authority as that which gains legitimacy through the sanctity of tradition. This is distinct from a rational-legal authority, which is manifested mostly in the bureaucratic state and maintains power through the support of the normative rules (i.e. laws) and those who issue them. The existence of traditional authority in most developing countries has been controversial. Weber (1922/1958) argued that societies will transition from traditional to rational-legal authority in a linear fashion, without the two ever necessarily co-existing. The Traditional Leadership and Governance Framework Act (2003) of South Africa defines traditional leadership as "the customary institutions or structures, or customary systems or procedures of governance, recognised, utilised or practiced by traditional communities". Traditional leadership is an institution governing a particular tribe according to customary law and has developed over many hundreds of years in Africa (Khanyisa, 2010; Khunou, 2009).

Structure of Traditional Leadership in Zimbabwe

Traditional structures vest extensive powers in appointed individuals who comprise a prescribed hierarchy—Chief, Headmen, and Village Heads. These individuals are appointed based on custom which is governed by hereditary, rather than elective democratic principles (Matyszak, 2011). For rural communities, the most immediate form of local governance is that of traditional and customary institutions, which have been given the authority of statute (Constitution of Zimbabwe, 2013; Traditional Leaders Act, 2000) which run parallel to and, in some instances, in conjunction with the Provincial Development Committees (PDCs) and Rural District Councils (RDCs).

The institution of traditional leadership in Zimbabwe has been at the centre of rural local governance before and after independence. Between 1930 and 1980, traditional leaders became the anchor of rural local government, progressively being assigned tax collection, judicial and land allocation functions, and other associated powers. Traditional leaders have enjoyed 'fluctuating fortunes' (Makumbe, 2010). Over the years, traditional leaders have been alternatively empowered and disempowered in various roles as extensions of colonial rule, conservation allies, and sources of political mileage (Holleman, 1968; Mutizwa-Mangiza, 1985; Scoones & Matose, 1993). Traditional leaders exist at the village level (village heads), which is the basic organising unit of rural life in Zimbabwe outside commercial farming areas. The number of headmen in a ward and the chiefs in a district or province largely depends on traditions in different parts of the country as well as the influence of formal administrative boundaries (Chatiza, 2008).

LEGISLATIVE FRAMEWORK FOR TRADITIONAL LEADERSHIP IN ZIMBABWE

This section will focus on the Constitution of Zimbabwe (2013) and the Traditional Leaders Act (2000) as key instruments that recognise the institution of traditional leadership in Zimbabwe. These two instruments will be discussed below.

The Constitution of Zimbabwe (2013)

The Constitution of Zimbabwe (2013) recognises and formalises the authority and legitimacy of the institution of traditional leadership. It provides the powers and responsibilities that are vested in traditional leaders.

Section 282(1) of the Constitution Zimbabwe further states that:

1. Traditional leaders have the following functions within their areas of jurisdiction-

    a. to promote and uphold cultural values of their communities and, in particular, to promote sound family values;
    b. to take measures to preserve the culture, traditions, history and heritage of their communities, including sacred shrines;
    c. to facilitate development;
    d. in accordance with an Act of Parliament, to administer Communal Land and to protect the environment;
    e. to resolve disputes amongst people in their communities in accordance with customary law; and
    f. to exercise any other functions conferred or imposed on them by Act of Parliament.

The challenge however, has been that traditional leaders do not perceive their role to be derived from the Constitution of Zimbabwe. They have argued that it is derived from historical traditional authority governed by rules embedded in cultural practices. However, these cultural practices have been politically corrupted by the colonial and post-colonial regimes.

Traditional Leaders Act (2000)

The appointment of traditional leaders into office is dealt with in Section 45(2) of the Traditional Leaders Act (2000). It states that:

> No chief, headmen or village head shall canvass, serve as an election agent, or nominate any candidate for election as a state President, Member of Parliament or Councillor in any local authority whilst still holding office as Chief, headman or village head.

Traditional leaders, however, may exercise their right to vote in any national or local government election or referendum. A traditional leader may be suspended by the Minister of Local Government if charged with any offence involving dishonesty or after an investigation by Ministerial appointees into *misconduct in relation to the customs and traditions observed in his area* ordered by the Minister. If a traditional leader is found guilty of any of the offences or misconduct, the Minister may recommend to the President that the traditional leader be removed from office in terms of Section 7(5) (a) of the Traditional Leaders Act.

THEORETICAL FRAMEWORK

The study of traditional leaders has been heavily driven by theoretical expectations derived from the prominent frameworks used to study traditional political institutions. For the most part, these theoretical frameworks have been pessimistic about the compatibility of traditional institutions and modern democratic states. For example, the modernisation theory contrasts traditional political institutions with an ideal type of rationalised bureaucratic authority (Huntington, 1968). A major strand of democratic theory emphasises the role of elections in creating accountability, implying that unelected traditional institutions are likely to provide poor leadership. Theories of clientelism suggest that traditional leaders can make politicians less accountable to citizens by serving as vote brokers who drum up electoral support via coercion and contingent exchanges (Lemarchand & Legg, 1972).

As a result, some scholars have argued that traditional leadership restricts the individual rights of citizens and inhibits the development of democratic states (Hariri, 2012; Ntsebeza, 2005). Other scholars have, however, challenged these claims with empirical evidence suggesting the compatibility of traditional institutions and democracy (Logan, 2013).

Some literature has also made the counter-argument that traditional leaders can serve citizens' interests by helping to broker government resources and/or coordinating collective action (Baldwin, 2016; Honig, 2019). Since colonialism, the powers of traditional leaders have been subjected to the consent of formal governments. At both a national and local level, politicians have shown greater discretion regarding how much autonomy to give traditional leaders, especially in areas related to land allocation and revenue collection (Boone, 2003). The fact that government officials allow traditional leaders to retain some power, despite being able to take away this power, requires explanation. Why would government officials allow traditional leaders who are potential political rivals to maintain their powerful status? During the colonial era, the answer was the chiefs provided control over citizens as the British used indirect rule in Ghana (Baldwin, 2016). This study argues that such an explanation is not satisfying in the current political climate of free and fair elections where candidates want to actively cultivate voters. It further argues that due to their strong cultural power, traditional leaders serve as more effective vote mobilisers than anyone in helping politicians get elected. Politicians, therefore, allow chiefs to continue to have an administrative presence in their communities. Removing such powers would mean a reduction in the status of traditional leaders and a loss for the politicians of the most effective mobilisers available to them. The establishment of competitive elections means that traditional leaders have become clientelistic agents of ruling political parties. Rather than just serving as village 'big men' that keep local order and peace, traditional leaders can provide a path towards formal governmental control for politicians (Baldwin, 2016). Due to the weaknesses of political parties and other forms of organisation, local politicians have relied more on traditional leaders to mobilise for votes. On the contrary, Ntsebeza (2001) has argued that traditional leaders have played, and continue to play, an important role in the governance and development of communities, particularly, in rural areas. Ntsebeza (2001) further argues that most rural communities have not known any other form of governance, or authority, except traditional leaders. Opponents of traditional leaders have argued that traditional leadership is a regressive step that undermines progress towards democratic consolidation.

According to Dipholo et al. (2011), the governance of rural communities in Africa has been associated with traditional leadership. These authors argue that traditional leadership has been instrumental in protecting and preserving customs and cultures. In addition, traditional leadership also plays a significant role in protecting African tradition from Western influence. However, on the one hand, some authors, such as Reddy and Mkala (2008, p. 3), are of the opinion that traditional leadership has to change or move with the times, lest they become irrelevant.

Political endorsements can provide important information to voters in complex electoral contests with limited information (Lau & Redlawsk, 2001; Lupia, 1992). Voters use endorsements from political parties (Hobolt, 2007), individuals (Dominguez, 1994), and other groups (Arceneaux & Kolodny, 2009; Stone et al., 1992) as signals to determine which candidate or policy proposals will serve their interests (Lupia, 1992). Scholars of political behaviour have suggested that voters are influenced by the positive endorsements of groups or individuals they believe share their interests and who are less likely to mislead them (for example, someone with a reputation for honesty or credibility) (Lupia, 1992). Credible groups or individuals are those who consistently provide accurate and valuable information or perform useful services to the voter (Sobel, 1985).

Political endorsements can be defined as public praise of and direct appeal to subjects to vote for a party's candidate by a traditional leader. In this study, the expression of explicit electoral support is an essential component of chiefly political endorsements (Arceneaux & Kolodny, 2009). Such endorsements may occur at a traditional leader's place of residence, traditional ceremonial grounds, or a political party campaign rally. Politicians can make routine visits to traditional leaders in their constituencies during election campaigns to "ask for permission" to mobilise support among their subjects (Lau & Redlawsk, 2001). Such visits by politicians are necessary and a sign of respect before organising rallies and house-to-house campaigns in a traditional leader's jurisdiction (Dominguez, 1994). These events may serve as an occasion for a traditional leader to endorse a candidate. However, in some cases, such visits do not constitute an endorsement. Previous studies in Zimbabwe have shown that some traditional leaders have given an audience to all political parties (Kurebwa, 2020). In the Zimbabwean case, for example, traditional leaders have openly expressed their support for ZANU-PF candidates. Traditional leaders have been accused of being partisan and appreciating the contribution of ZANU-PF in the provision of local public infrastructure and social programmes and in some cases appealed for more. Traditional leaders have also called for their subjects to vote for the ZANU-PF government.

Research Methodology

This study relied on the qualitative research approach. This was aimed at assessing and analysing the roles of various participants in traditional leadership and partisan politics in Zimbabwe. Data was collected using key informant interviews and documentary searches. Key participants chosen for the study included two traditional leaders, one member from each of the two major political parties namely, ZANU-PF and Citizens Coalition of Change (CCC), two members from the Civil Society Organisations (CSOs), and one District Development Coordinator (DDC). The data collection methods allowed the researcher to obtain first-hand information because these methods involved the collection of a variety of empirical material, such as case studies, introspection, personal experiences, interviews, observations, and historical, interactional, and visual texts.

Study Findings and Discussion

The findings of the study indicated that traditional leaders in Zimbabwe have an influence both on electoral outcomes and processes. This has been done through sealing off space for opposition political players, subverting the will of the people under their jurisdiction through intimidation, making public pronouncements to the effect that they support ZANU-PF, and partisan distribution of food aid and farming inputs.

While addressing traditional leaders and ZANU-PF supporters at Nemamwa Growth Point in Masvingo Province, ZANU-PF Second Secretary, Kembo Mohadi mentioned that:

> We want our leaders in the party to work in unison with our traditional leaders because traditional leaders play a very important role in spearheading development in rural communities where the majority of the people live. (The Herald 9 June 2022)

Mohadi further promised to give traditional leaders, including all village heads, US$50 monthly and a bicycle. He repeated the same statement while addressing traditional leaders and ZANU-PF supporters in Beitbridge, Zaka, and Chiredzi districts. This move was seen by political opponents and CSOs as a vote-buying gimmick meant to force community leaders to mobilise for the ZANU-PF party. The use of traditional leaders by the ruling party is one of the issues usually raised by opposition parties like the Citizen Coalition for Change (CCC) as a rigging tactic used by ZANU-PF to threaten rural people (Bulawayo News 24, 25 June 2022).

In response to Mohadi's utterances, a CCC member indicated that:

> All what Mohadi was doing in Masvingo is nonsense, considering that he cannot come and make a declaration that all village heads are now chairpersons of ZANU-PF cells in their villages. A traditional leader is for all people; including those in opposition hence they should not be involved in politics. (Bulawayo News 24, 25 June 2022)

During the interview, a member of the CCC castigated traditional leaders for being partisan by stating that:

> We have seen a situation where traditional leaders have punished those who belong to our party through denying them food aid and agricultural inputs. We have also been denied access to campaign in some rural areas especially in Masvingo and Mashonaland Central provinces.

The fact that traditional leaders are openly partisan, working towards furthering the interests of ZANU-PF goes against the principles set out in Chapter 15 of the Constitution of Zimbabwe (2013). The gatekeeping role of traditional leaders was evident when Village Head Nhamoinesu Nemanwa of Chivanhu Village in Masvingo Province mobilised ZANU-PF supporters to participate in pre-emptive attacks against members of the MDC-Alliance on Monday, 11 October 2021. To enable traditional leaders to perform this gatekeeping role with relative ease, the ZANU-PF government has made the institution of traditional leadership very strong, with traditional leaders receiving hefty perks such as top-of-the-range vehicles, hefty salaries, electrification of their homes, rehabilitation of roads that lead to their homes, among other provisions.

In December 2021, Chief Murinye of Masvingo was castigated by Vice President Constantino Chiwenga after telling mourners that he was tired of thieves who were surrounding President Emmerson Mnangagwa. Chief Murinye stated:

> We are fed up, we do not want this anymore, and thieves in Zimbabwe should stop. Mnangagwa is my nephew, but if he does not listen to

my advice, he will not make it in the 2023 elections. (Myzimbabwe, 16 December 2021)

The above statement infuriated Chiwenga who later told in a Chief's council meeting in Harare that Chief Murinye should be investigated for his utterances. Chiwenga stated that:

> What has been done by Chief Murinye is going to be investigated by the Minister of Local Government, the President of the Chiefs Council, his deputy, and his committee and if found guilty then appropriate disciplinary action will be taken. This is the Republic of Zimbabwe, this is not done. Such foolishness is not done. I hope you understand me. Chiefs are appointed and they are removed too. From here, 2021, you must dig holes in the tar and spit in them, declaring that such words are not uttered. (The Zimbabwe Mail, 16 December 2021)

During the ZANU-PF annual conference in Bindura, Mashonaland Central Province, Chief Fortune Charumbira, the President of the Zimbabwe Council of Chiefs vowed that traditional leaders were never going to leave ZANU-PF. He stated that:

> On behalf of all chiefs in the country, I want to tell you that we are together. It's true we are together. We are behind you. I want to repeat this because there are people who ask why we come here. Firstly, if you know where ZANU-PF came from, then you will not ask why Chief Charumbira is here. But if you don't know the origins of ZANUPF then you will continue asking why we are here. (Zim Live, 30 October 2021)

He went on to state that:

> We are the owners of ZANUPF. The reason why ZANU-PF exists is all about traditional leadership. So, you cannot separate the struggles about land on this continent from the traditional leadership. We will never leave ZANU-PF. (Zim Live, 30 October 2021)

In 2018, Justice Clement Phiri of the High Court of Zimbabwe ordered Chief Charumbira to publicly retract comments he made in 2017. However, Chief Charumbira has refused to comply. Justice Phiri ruled that:

The remarks made by Chief Charumbira on October 28, 2017, on the occasion of the annual conference of the Council of Chiefs and on January 13, 2018, to the effect that traditional leaders have been supporting and must continue to support ZANU-PF and its presidential candidate at the forthcoming 2018 elections be and is hereby declared to be in contravention of the Constitution of Zimbabwe. Chief Charumbira be and is hereby, ordered to retract in writing the statements that he made to the effect that traditional leaders should support and vote ZANU-PF by issuing a countermanding statement and shall publish the countermanding statement in a newspaper with a national circulation and endeavour to make a statement available to private and public media houses and the national broadcaster within seven days of being served this order. (Bulawayo 24, 10 May 2018)

Section 281(2) of the Constitution of Zimbabwe states that:

2. Traditional leaders must not-

   a. Be members of any political party or in any way participate in partisan politics;
   b. Act in a partisan manner;
   c. Further the interests of any political party or cause; or
   d. Violate the fundamental rights and freedoms of any person.

The Constitution of Zimbabwe (2013) is very clear in terms of what traditional leaders ought to do and ought not to do in respect of politics and elections. However, traditional leaders often wantonly disregard the law, often with impunity. This impunity was evident when the Election Resource Centre sued Chief Charumbira over unconstitutional utterances pledging support to the ruling ZANU-PF. The court found the Chief President to be out of order and ordered him to withdraw the statement, an order he did not abide by. Instead, Chief Charumbira has gone on to make more statements to the same effect with no consequence. Speaking during the annual Chiefs Conference in Bulawayo on the 28th of October 2017, Chief Charumbira was quoted encouraging traditional leaders to campaign for the ruling ZANU-PF party in the upcoming 2018 harmonised elections. Chief Charumbira personally declared his allegiance to ZANU-PF highlighting that the institution of traditional leaders will support and vote for the ruling ZANU-PF in the 2018 elections.

A participant from the CSO castigated Chief Charumbira's partisan support for ZANU-PF by stating that:

The utterances by Chief Charumbira are reckless, unfortunate and a direct contradiction of Section 281 of the constitution which states that traditional leaders should not act in a partisan manner or participate in partisan politics. We strongly condemn in the strongest terms the remarks attributed to Chief Charumbira who openly declared his allegiance to ZANU-PF in clear contradiction of the Constitution.

Another CSO participant stated that:

The statement by Chief Charumbira is in total breach of the role that traditional leaders are expected to play. We expect traditional leaders to be apolitical, embracing all their subjects regardless of their political persuasion and allowing their subjects to exercise their freedom of choice and association.

A District Development Coordinator indicated that:

Traditional leaders are expected to abide by the provision of the Constitution. The Constitution of Zimbabwe is very clear in terms of their duties and responsibilities and that they ought not to participate in partisan politics. As public servants it's very difficult to tell them not to meddle into partisan politics as we will also be labelled opposition supporters.

The role of traditional leadership in the politics of Zimbabwe has always been controversial. Traditional leaders have been playing partisan roles in the elections mainly to prop up the ZANU-PF party, for instance, by directly campaigning for the party. For example, Chiefs Sogwala, Gobo, Ruya, and Ntabeni of Midlands Province were accused of banning the holding of opposition party rallies or wearing party regalia in their areas. In Mashonaland East, some chiefs and village heads were accused of urging people to vote for the ZANU-PF party so that they would not be evicted from their respective villages. Such reports were also made in Manicaland Province where Chief Chifodya of Nyanga district allegedly campaigned for the ZANU-PF party while in Zaka district, Village Head Nedowa allegedly campaigned on behalf of the ZANU-PF parliamentary candidate during the 2008 harmonised elections and even forced people to buy party cards (Ruhanya, 2012). The Village Head was also reportedly the vice-chairperson of the ZANU-PF district branch in the area. These developments were particularly disturbing given that traditional leaders are supposed to be neutral. Some traditional leaders, however, reportedly remained neutral, urging people to vote for candidates of their choice (ZESN, 2008).

Since the formation of the MDC in 1999, many traditional leaders have been manipulated to entrench and protect the power of ZANU-PF (Ruhanya, 2012). The ZANU-PF-led government realised the general acceptance of traditional leaders and harnessed this institution for its personal benefit (Makumbe, 2010). In carrying out their duties, the traditional leaders must not be influenced by any considerations of race, tribe, place of origin, creed, gender, or political affiliation (Zimbabwe Institute, 2005).

The provision to political neutrality was reinforced in the Global Political Agreement (GPA) (2008) signed by Zimbabwe's three main political parties (ZANU-PF, Movement for Democratic Change-Tsvangirai, and Movement for Democratic Change-Mutambara on 15 September 2008). Article 14.1 of the Agreement provided that:

> Recognising and acknowledging that traditional leaders are community leaders with equal responsibilities and obligations to all members of their communities regardless of age, gender, ethnicity, race, religion, and political affiliation, the Parties hereby agree to:
>
> a. Commit themselves to ensuring the political neutrality of traditional leaders; and
> b. Call upon traditional leaders not to engage in partisan political activities at national level as well as in their communities.

These provisions were brushed aside by ZANU-PF as the country prepared for the 2013 harmonised elections (Matyszak, 2011). In October 2010, several meetings of traditional leaders were held to ensure and utilise their allegiance to the ZANU-PF party. A meeting of 30 Chiefs and army officers is reported to have taken place at military barracks in Harare to discuss election strategies that would ensure the ZANU-PF's party's retention of power (The Zimbabwean 10 November 2010).

The annual national conference of Chiefs held in Kariba in October 2010 endorsed President Robert Mugabe (now late) as their favourite Presidential candidate. In an address by former Vice President Joice Mujuru at the same conference, Chiefs were specifically informed that they were entitled to engage in politics "as pioneers of the struggle for freedom" (The Herald 01 October 2010). She further emphasised the status of traditional leaders by stating:

> Chiefs are not ordinary people. You are the tower lights of our culture and the icons of our identity. (The Herald 01 October 2010)

A member of ZANU-PF during the interview supported the partisan nature of traditional leaders by stating that:

> There is no way you can separate traditional leaders from ZANU-PF. Traditional leaders have always supported the party from the time of the liberation struggle. Check the role that Chief Rekai Tangwena played in assisting former President Robert Gabriel Mugabe in crossing into Mozambique during the liberation struggle. There is an umbilical code between ZANU-PF and traditional leaders.

The then Zimbabwe National Army Brigadier-General (now late) Douglas Nyikayaramba formerly of 3 Brigade in Manicaland Province in 2010 summoned 200 traditional leaders from the province to a 'workshop' at the army barracks during which they were told to prevent members of the main opposition party, MDC-T, from campaigning and receiving agricultural inputs from the government (The Zimbabwe Independent 12 November 2013). The former Brigadier-General is further reported to have stated that:

> I want to make it clear to all Chiefs gathered here today that if President Mugabe loses in the next year's (2011) elections [later held in 2013], you will have a case to answer. Gone are the Rhodesian days when Chiefs were apolitical. (The Zimbabwe Independent 12 November 2013)

Traditional leaders as argued in this study are the guardians of the customs and traditions. Their powers in this regard have been abused to evict opposition supporters from villages in several instances, suggesting that ZANU-PF's policy of co-opting traditional leaders has been at least partially successful (Zimbabwe Institute, 2005). This policy has been pursued by leaving ultimate authority over traditional leaders and structures with the central government through the restoration of powers to the Chiefs (which can be used against political opponents). For example, Chiefs at one point received non-taxable allowances 15 times higher than those of Ward Councillors in addition to benefits such as housing, rural electrification programme, and subsidised vehicles (Zimbabwe Institute, 2005). These benefits underlie the importance of traditional leaders as sources of political mileage (Wines, 2001). In return for the benefits, traditional leaders are supposed to remain loyal to the ruling party ZANU-PF and the government. Traditional leaders have rendered their unconditional support to ZANU-PF for fear of losing the above benefits. Makahamadze, Grand, and Tavuyanago (2009) indicated that Chief Gama of Buhera district had remarked 'ZANU PF chefs are eating and we chiefs are eating. So let them rule forever'.

Chief Chitsa of Gutu district likened the late President Mugabe to God. Such thinking reflects the mentality of most traditional leaders in Zimbabwe who owe their allegiance and livelihood to the ZANU-PF party. Most traditional leaders do not raise any concerns with regard to the violation of the human rights of their subjects by politicians during election periods (Makahamadze et al., 2009).

The CCC party argues that traditional leaders should not act like ZANU-PF political commissars and described their problem as "not only reprehensible but also patently illegal and unconstitutional". In Manicaland Province, traditional leaders were reportedly intimidating opposition supporters, and traditional leaders accused of not supporting ZANU-PF was being ousted ahead of the 2018 harmonised elections. In response, the MDC-T Spokesperson maintained that:

> Traditional leaders are supposed to be apolitical. This is very clear and unambiguous provision in terms of Section 281(2) of the Constitution of Zimbabwe. We have maintained that traditional leadership should not be politicians. The problem is that the ZANU–PF regime routinely forces traditional leaders to act as their political commissars in the areas under their jurisdiction. (Kubatana 31 October 2017)

This followed allegations that Chiefs Nerutanga and Marange of Buhera and Marange districts respectively were intimidating traditional leaders they deemed loyal to the MDC-T and other opposition parties. Chief Marange was alleged to have told a gathering of local villagers that 'We will not allow MDC-T and Zimbabwe People First (ZIMPF) to hold their meetings in my area. This area is secured' (Kurebwa, 2018).

The MDC-T in its paper entitled 'Policy Position towards the Traditional leadership' indicated that:

As the country moves into the future, the MDC recognises not only the traditional role of the Chiefs and Headmen as custodians of our cultures and language and history but also as representatives of the people under their administration and their importance in maintaining our unique character as Africans. All of this is under threat, first by the abuse of the leadership by political parties in pursuit of their own agendas and by the process of modernisation and development. If these threats are not resolved and dealt with they will threaten the very foundations of our society. (The Zimbabwean, 24 August 2015)

Jackson and Marqutte (2005) argued that traditional leaders had become 'glorified civil servants'. The effect has been to elevate the status of Chiefs above that of elected councillors and this has exacerbated existing tensions between elected officials and traditional leaders. This policy continues to the present and the traditional leaders' demand for acknowledgement of their elevated status has been accorded recognition by the Ministry of Local Government, Public Works, and National Development. In 2010, an official in the Ministry of Local Government defended the distribution of vehicles to Chiefs. He argued that:

> Chiefs made the demands for twin cabs, saying it is the only way of restoring their status and that they cannot be seen driving single cabs when Members of Parliament (MPs) are driving twin cabs. (The Standard, 10 October 2010)

The Ministry official was supported by a Chief from Matabeleland South Province who indicated that:

> It was long overdue. We are more important than MPs and we cannot be seen to be lesser to them. (The Standard, 10 October 2010)

Politicians of all persuasions realised the substantial influence traditional leaders wield in rural Zimbabwe, most notably through mediums such as tribe, clan, totem, custom, and tradition. Both before and after independence, politicians have sought the assistance of traditional leaders in order to influence the electoral and governance processes as indicated in the above cases. Traditional leaders are also best positioned to communicate programmes and ensure community participation in such programmes (Chatiza, 2008). The colonial governments, for example, made effective use of traditional leaders to mobilise the African people to participate in selected government programmes largely aimed at ensuring the people's compliance with colonial rules (Makumbe, 2010). Political parties in government have tended to have an edge in rallying traditional leaders to their cause, be it during elections or in the delivery of government programmes. Traditional leaders are an effective communication tool given their hierarchical nature (chiefs, headmen, village heads). They are present in all parts of rural Zimbabwe, except for commercial farming areas and mining regions (Matyszak, 2011). Their support is therefore invaluable. Though the law prevents them from participating in politics or, more specifically seeking elective office, they remain a major player in governance, especially at the local level.

The institution of traditional leadership in Zimbabwe has gone through colonial and post-colonial acceptance, usage, and political corruption (Mamdani, 1996; Mbembe, 2001). It has also shown considerable resilience and clout by influencing sub-national development processes and increasingly national political structures. There are inherent contradictions in terms of the functions of the institution that Zimbabwe's ruling elite (ZANU-PF) has exploited, capitalised on and its continued legitimacy in the eyes of the majority of Zimbabweans (Matyszak, 2011). The fact that it is provided for in the Constitution of Zimbabwe has been an additional source of strength if not endurance (Chatiza, 2008). As an institution, traditional leaders have been willing and coerced state partners into controlling, ordering, and developing spaces.

While many chiefs continue to support ZANU-PF, a growing number have stood their ground and refused to participate in the repression of their people. In Matabeleland, a growing number of chiefs have been at loggerheads with Mnangagwa's government. The clashes have mainly been about the restoration of the Ndebele kingdom in that province. In July 2018, three prominent chiefs from Matabeleland North Province won a court order against the Minister of Home Affairs, Obert Mpofu who they allege was interfering with their work. In Midlands Province, a number of traditional leaders addressed their subjects on the need to maintain tranquillity during the electoral season. In Manicaland Province, chiefs have castigated politicians from most political parties for fanning divisions among their subjects based on political affiliation. Other traditional leaders have even defended their subjects by simply ruling that they would not tolerate political violence in their chiefdoms (Newsday, 30 June 2018).

Traditional leaders who supported the opposition MDC-T party had their privileges withdrawn. For example, Chiefs Ziki and Sengwe of Chiredzi districts in Masvingo Province had their monthly allowances withdrawn for backing the MDC-T party in the run-up to the 2008 harmonised elections (BBC News, 2008; Ncube, 2011). Such developments underline the serious adulteration that the institution of chieftainship has undergone in the post-colonial period and the extent to which it has been patronised by the ZANU-PF party.

Conclusions and Recommendations

The role of traditional leaders in electoral processes requires a concerted effort in both understanding and regulation. While the Constitution of Zimbabwe is clear on its functions and principles of engagement, the Traditional Leaders Act which is the enabling legislation is yet to be aligned thereby making implementation ad hoc, haphazard, and manipulated. Traditional leaders can indeed assist in building a democracy, but they have been a hindrance owing to unclear legislation, manipulation by the ZANU-PF government, and unclear proposals as to how they can facilitate democratic electoral processes going forward. Traditional leaders should respect the constitution and reassure citizens that they are non-partisan and should perform their duties and responsibilities in a non-partisan manner that allows all citizens regardless of political affiliation equal access to resources and guaranteed non-discrimination.

References

Arceneaux, K., & Robin, K. (2009). Educating the least informed: Group endorsements in a grassroots campaign. *American Journal of Political Science, 53*(4), 755–770.

Baldwin, K. (2020). Chiefs, democracy, and development in contemporary Africa. *Current History, 119*(817), 163–168.

Baldwin, K., & Holzinger, K. (2019). Traditional political institutions and democracy: Reassessing their compatibility and accountability. *Comparative Political Studies, 15*(12), 1747–1774.

Baldwin, K. (2016). *The paradox of traditional leaders in democratic Africa.* Cambridge University Press.

Baldwin, K. (2013). Why vote with the chief? Political connections and public goods provision in Zambia. *American Journal of Political Science, 57*(4), 794–809.

BBC News. (2008). *Africa betrayed.* www.bbcnews.com
Boone, P. (2003). Chiefdom: A universal political formation? focal-European. *Journal of Anthropology, 43,* 76–98.
Bulawayo News 24. (2022, June 25). ZANU-PF Subverts Traditional Leaders. www.bulawayonews24.com
Bulawayo News 24. (2018, May 10). High Court Judge Embarrases ZANU-PF Chief. www.bulawayonews24.com
Chatiza, K. (2008). *Opportunities and challenges in institutionalizing participatory development: The case of rural Zimbabwe.* Unpublished Doctoral Thesis, Swansea University.
Conroy-Krutz, J. (2018). Individual autonomy and local-level solidarity in Africa. *Political Behaviour, 40*(3), 593–627.
Dipholo, K. B., Mafema, E., & Tshishonga, N. (2011). Traditional leadership in Botswana: Opportunities and challenges of democratic decentralization in sustaining local government in Botswana and South Africa. *The Journal of Public Administration, 46*(4), 1431–1444.
Dominguez, C. B. K. (1994). Does the party matter? Endorsements in congressional primaries. *Political Science Quarterly, 64*(3), 491–505.
Gottlieb, J. (2017). Explaining variation in broker strategies: A lab-in-the-field experiment in Senegal. *Comparative Political Studies, 50*(11), 1556–1592.
Government of Zimbabwe. (1998). *Traditional Leaders Act* [Chapter 29: 17]. Harare, Government Printer.
Government of Zimbabwe. (2013). *Constitution of Zimbabwe Amendment* (No. 20) Act 2013. Harare, Government Printer.
Hariri, J. G. (2012). The autocratic legacy of early statehood. *American Political Science Review, 106*(5), 471–494.
Hobolt, S., & Binzer, J. (2007). Taking cues on Europe? Voter competence and party endorsements in referendums on European integration. *European Journal of Political Research, 46*(2), 151–182.
Holleman, J. F. (1968). *Chief, council and commissioner.* Koninkelijke Van Gorcum
Holzinger, K., Kern, F. G., & Kromrey, D. (2017). Traditional institutions in sub-Saharan Africa: Endangering or promoting stable domestic peace? *Forschung DSF.* Retrieved from https://bundesstiftung-friedensforschung. de/wp
Honig, L. (2019). *The struggle for land in Africa: The state, customary authorities and citizens.* Boston College.
Huntington, S. (1968). *Political order in changing societies.* Yale University Press.
Jackson, P., & Macquittee, M. (2005). *Citizen and subject: Contemporary Africa and the legacy of late colonialism.* Princeton University Press.

Khanyisa, G. (2010). *The role of traditional leadership in governance and rural development: A case study of the Mgwalana traditional authority.* Unpublished dissertation. Port Elizabeth: Nelson Mandela Metropolitan University.

Khunou, S. F. (2009). Traditional leadership and independent Bantustans of South Africa: Some milestones of transformative constitutionalism beyond Apartheid. *Potchefstroom Electronic Law Journal, 12*(4), 81–125.

Koter, D. (2013). King makers: Local leaders and ethnic politics in Africa. *World Politics, 65*(2), 187–232.

Kurebwa, J. (2020). The institution of traditional leadership and local governance in Zimbabwe. In Information Resource Management Association (Eds.), *African studies: Breakthroughs in research and practice* (pp. 715–732). IGI: GLOBAL Publishers.

Kurebwa, J. (2018). The institution of traditional leadership and local governance in Zimbabwe. *International Journal of Civic Engagement and Social Change, 5*(1), 1–22.

Lau, R. R., & David, P. R. (2001). Advantages and disadvantages of cognitive heuristics in political decision making. *American Journal of Political Science, 10*(5), 951–971.

Lemarchand, R., & Keith, L. (2017). *Political clientelism and development: A preliminary analysis.* Routledge.

Lemerchand, R. (1972). Political clientelism and ethnicity in Tropical Africa: Competing solidarities in nation-building. *American Political Science Review, 66*(17), 68–90.

Logan, C. (2013). The roots of resilience: Exploring popular support for African traditional authorities. *African Affairs, 112*(8), 353–376.

Lupia, A. (1992). Busy voters, agenda control and the power of information. *American Political Science Review, 86*, 390–403.

Makumbe, J. (2010). Local authorities and traditional leadership. In J. De Visser., N. Steytler., & N. Machingauta (Eds.), *Local government in Zimbabwe: A policy dialogue.* Community Law Centre, University of the Western Cape.

Makahamadze, T., Grand, N., & Tavuyanago, B. (2009). The role of traditional leaders in fostering democracy, justice and human rights in Zimbabwe. *The African Anthropologist, 16*(1&2), 33–47.

Mamdani, M. (1996). *Citizen and subject: Contemporary Africa and the legacy of late colonialism.* Princeton University Press.

Mamdani, M. (2018). *Citizen and subject: Contemporary Africa and the legacy of late colonialism.* Princeton University Press.

Matyszak, D. (2011). *Formal structures of power in rural Zimbabwe.* https://www.researchandadvocacyunit.org

Mbembe, A. (2001). *On the post colony.* University of California Press.

Mutizwa-Mangiza, N. D. (1985). *Community development in pre-independent Zimbabwe: A study of policy with special reference to rural land*. University of Zimbabwe.

My Zimbabwe. (2021, December 16). Brave Chief Murinye Blasts Mnangagwa and Top ZANU-PF Bigwigs, warns their Actions Could Lead to Coup. www.myzimbabwe.co.zw

Ncube, G. T. (2011). Crisis of communal leadership: Post-colonial government reform and administrative conflict with traditional authorities in the communal areas of Zimbabwe, 1980-2008. *African Journal of History and Culture*, 3(6), 89–95.

Neiwaai, E. (2003). The new relevance of traditional authorities in Africa. *Journal of Legal Pluralism and Unofficial Law*, 37(38), 27–29.

Ntsebeza, L. (2001). Traditional authorities and rural development. In J. Coetzee, J. Graaff., J. Hendricks., & F. Wood. (2002). *Development: Theory, policy and practice*. Oxford University Press.

Ntsebeza, L. (2005). *Democracy compromised: Chiefs and the politics of the land in South Africa*. Brill.

Reddy, P. S., & Mkala, T. (2008). *Traditional leadership and local governance in a democratic South Africa: "Qua Vadis."* Democracy Development Programme and the University of KwaZulu-Natal.

Ruhanya, P. (2012). Democratic forces must corner ZANU-PF. https://www.theindependent.co.zw

Scoones, I., & Matose, F (1993). Local woodland management: Constraints and opportunities for sustainable resource use. In P. N Bradley & K. McNamara (Eds.), *Living with trees: Policies for woodland management in Zimbabwe* (pp. 157–198). World Bank.

Sobel, J. (1985). A theory of credibility. *The Review of Economic Studies*, 52(4), 557–573.

Stone, W. J., Ronald, B. R., & Abramowitz, A. I. (1992). Candidate support in presidential nomination campaigns: The case of Iowa in 1984. *The Journal of Politics*, 54(4), 1074–1097.

The Herald. (2020). *ZANU-PF Values Traditional Leaders*. www.theherald.co.zw

The Zimbabwe Mail. (2021, December 16). Chiwenga breathes fire over Chief's Funeral Address. wwwthezimbabwemail.com

Weber, M. (1922/1958). The three types of legitimate rule. Translated by Hans Gerth. *Publications in Society and Institutions*, 4(1), 1–11.

Wines, A. (2001). *On the postcolony*. University of California Press.

Zimbabwe Institute. (2005). Thirteen principles to guide the decentralisation process in Zimbabwe. *Local Government Policy Review*. Zimbabwe Institute.

Zim Live. (2021, October 30). Chiefs will never leave ZANU-PF- Chief Charumbira in shock new ourburst. www.zimlive.com

CHAPTER 18

The Role of Traditional Leaders and Culture in Zimbabwean Elections

Takavafira Masarira Zhou

INTRODUCTION

The chapter analyses the role played by traditional leaders (village heads, headmen, and chiefs) in Zimbabwean elections. It is our argument that ZANU-PF has since 1980 endeavoured to manipulate the traditional institution to serve the agenda of maintaining power. The role of the institution of indigenous authority in governance processes in Zimbabwe has constantly followed the injunctions of the ruling regimes since the colonial period. Traditional leaders have been enthusiastic enablers to the government in many aspects, by plan, default, and compulsion. Their role in electoral processes in Zimbabwe has increasingly attracted the attention of stakeholders including civil society, citizens, political parties, and scholars. Arguably, electoral malpractice and fraud have long shifted from the ballot box and polling day to the political environment before, during, and after elections. It is in this arena that traditional leaders seem to control with unencumbered power. Traditional leaders have the imposing

T. M. Zhou (✉)
Progressive Teachers' Union of Zimbabwe, Harare, Zimbabwe
e-mail: takavafira1967@yahoo.co.uk

© The Author(s), under exclusive license to Springer Nature Switzerland AG 2023
E. Mavengano and S. Chirongoma (eds.), *Electoral Politics in Zimbabwe, Vol II*, https://doi.org/10.1007/978-3-031-33796-3_18

331

power to manipulate, appropriate, expropriate, and divert the will of the people and free choice through intimidation and discrimination, thereby stifling the conduct of free, fair, and credible elections.

PATRON-CLIENT THEORY

The patron-client system can be defined as a mutual arrangement between a person that has authority, social status, wealth, or some other resource (patron) and another who benefits from their support or influence (client). In the substantial literature on the patron-client theory (Arriola, 2009; Campbell, 1964; Clapham, 1982; Eisenstadt & Roniger, 1984; Foster, 1963; Galt, 1973; Stein, 1984; Wolf, 1966), one point of consensus is the functional or beneficial character of the relationship for the client. Patron-client systems are organized by people of, and in power, who build and keep the loyalty of people of more humble positions. Both patrons and clients regard the link between them as a personal attachment like the bond of affection holding members of a family or kin group together. However, unlike families, where the linkage is regarded as permanent and often is taken for granted, a patron-client relationship must be renewed constantly and renegotiated continuously. Throughout history, clients have provided the work, popular acclaim, votes, political allegiance, and support that patrons need to maintain power and position. Clients have in return gained protection, access to resources or information, group identity, personal emoluments, and opportunities for improvement. In this chapter, we also draw attention to certain dysfunctional characteristics of patronage which have not previously been highlighted by scholars. Only Galt (1973) and Stein (1984) posit that the spurious success of patronage requires the continuing presence of the very stress with which it helps its clients to cope. While the patronage-client relationship might be functional in the short run and at a superficial level of analysis, it is dysfunctional in the long run and at a deeper level of analysis. The chapter, therefore, examines the functional and dysfunctional trajectories in the patron-client relation between the ruling party and traditional leaders, respectively.

Historical Background

The advent of colonialism in Africa inaugurated changes to the system of indigenous governance and abused traditional leaders against their own people. Ranger (1967) and Beach (1986) argue that traditional leaders commanded the respect of the highest order among their people as they were key to the governing structures. Historically, traditional leadership can be divided into three periods: pre-colonial, colonial, and post-colonial. The pre-colonial period was an epoch when Africa was authentic to itself, it had not yet encountered many other worldviews. This era was governed by chieftaincy (Beach, 1994; Ranger, 1970), with deep-seated interests in socio-political and economic matters affecting the general populace, besides being the custodian of customs and culture. Freedoms of expression and after-expression were guaranteed and respected in Africa's own allegedly ancient and distant indigenous system. It is noteworthy that ordinary villagers were able to participate in the decision-making process by voicing their opinions freely at council meetings and village assemblies (Ayittey, 1999). Above all, a consensus was reached after debating various views. Customary African leaders did not arrest, confine, and kill those who differed with them. There was always an unwritten law that guaranteed freedom of expression to reach a consensus.

During the colonial period, traditional leaders were coerced into becoming the extension of colonial administration. As a strategy, colonial powers removed and even killed traditional leaders who opposed white supremacy. Following the 1896–1897 rising, objecting Shona traditional leaders were arrested and replaced with western educated appointees who were compliant, while Ndebele traditional leaders became salaried officials (Ranger, 1967, 1970). The colonial system used or even exploited the traditional system of governance as chiefs were forced to supply forced labour to colonialists and maintain colonial law and order (Phimister, 1988; Van Onselen, 1976; Zachrisson, 1978). This, increasingly, became the preferred trend under the brutal colonial rule with many people turning against traditional leaders. Mkhwanazi (2012) asserts that as people became suspicious of traditional leaders, the trust they previously had in them was compromised and some completely lost confidence in them. Consequently, the institution of traditional leadership lost both its legitimacy and influence since it was being used as a strategy by means of which the divide-and-rule principle could be carried out.

The Rhodesia Front further sealed the demise of traditional leadership during the colonial period. The formation of the African Council of Chiefs in 1960 established a patron-client relationship where chiefs constantly met and made resolutions in support of the colonial government in return for personal emoluments from the colonial government (Ndawana & Hove, 2018). As a preparation for the Unilateral Declaration of Independence (UDI), the then-new Prime Minister of Southern Rhodesia, Ian Douglas Smith, who replaced Winston Field gathered the chiefs at Domboshava in November 1964 (Southern Rhodesia, 1964) and tricked them into voting unanimously for UDI. At that infamous chiefs' Indaba, most of the chiefs had no idea whatsoever of what they had been invited for by the government. They were just advised to raise their hands each time they saw their few 'enlightened' colleagues raising their hands in this sham and fraudulent voting process for UDI. They were hoodwinked into thinking that the settler government wanted to restore their authority which the young and educated were trying to usurp from them. After the declaration of UDI on 11 November 1965, the chiefs were thanked by a tour of India and Europe aboard an airplane and generously supplied with jelly, ice cream, liquor, and jam during the tour (Ibid). By this stratagem, Smith deceitfully convinced the world that he had the support of Africans over UDI as chiefs were regarded as representatives of Africans. By this feat, chiefs antagonized nationalists and earned the label of traitors for collaborating with the brutal Rhodesian Front.

There were, however, exceptions to this traditional institution of collaboration, patronage, and clientelism, epitomized by chief Rekai Tangwena in Gairezi area of Manicaland. Tangwena offered herculean resistance against colonial appropriation and expropriation of African land. He fiercely resisted his people's eviction from their ancestral lands by the racist white minority settler government and refused to make way for the white settlers (Chigwanda, 2019). Despite being arrested more than a dozen times, he continued to resist and rebuild even after his people's homesteads had been destroyed by settler forces. He even preferred to stay in the bush than accept to be resettled. He earned great respect from his people and even assisted many liberation fighters crossing into Mozambique and back into Zimbabwe. He is also well known for assisting Edgar Tekere and Robert Mugabe cross into Mozambique in 1975 to join the African National Liberation Army (ZANLA) guerrillas who were waging a fierce bush war against Smith's Rhodesian government (Tekere,

2007). Not surprisingly when he died in 1984, he was accorded national hero status and is buried at the National Heroes Acre in Harare.

Admittedly, early African political leaders linked to liberation movements were instrumental in the demise of—or at least attempts to do away with—the institution of traditional leadership. According to Mkhwanazi (2012, p. 19), "Nkrumah's government contributed significantly to the further diminution of the status and significance of chieftaincy in Africa ... [as he] ... created a problematic polarity between chieftaincy and the modern political state." The ZANU-PF government that took over the country in 1980 deliberately discredited the institution of chieftainship. Lazarus Nzarayebani, the then Member of Parliament for Mutare South cited by Ranger (2001, p. 47) remarked: "At Independence in 1980, we did revolutionarily so well. Ours was change; change in the administration of our public affairs and public lives…Some institutions where necessary must simply be allowed to wither away. One of these institutions might be chieftainship." The government undermined the institution of traditional leadership whose role in the liberation was ambivalent. As much as some critics argue that Nzarayebani's statement cannot be taken as representing the position of the government as he was somewhat regarded as a rebel in ZANU-PF, it is important to focus on government actions in the 1980s that resonate with his utterances. The reform measures introduced in the 1980s sought to undermine the authority of traditional institutions in judicial and land matters in the communal areas; firstly because of their perceived pre-independence role as functionaries of colonial oppression; secondly because some elements within the new Government viewed traditional institutions as antithetical to their modernization project to transform rural society; and thirdly because other elements in the new Government perceived traditional institutions as centres of alternative authority to that of the formal state. The government enacted several policies and laws that reduced the powers of traditional leaders. In 1981, the Customary and Primary Courts Act was enacted. This Act replaced the courts of chiefs and headmen with elected officers. Zhou and Makahamadze (2012) argue that the 1982 Communal Lands Act gave District Councils authority over land allocation, eliminating the Colonial Tribal Land Authorities in the process. In 1984, Ward District Committees and Village Development Committees were elected. These were intended to be the major conduits of government-initiated development projects in the rural areas (Tavuyanago et al., 2011). The election of these officers, however, became the major source of conflict at the village level as they were interpreted as usurping the powers of traditional leaders (Zhou & Makahamadze).

The government assumed the role of appointing and anointing chiefs to ensure that the right candidates for chieftaincy posts were chosen. It tasked the Ministry of Local Government and Community Development with that duty. To qualify for the post of a chief, one had to satisfy two requirements: allegiance to the ruling party and a clean criminal record (Ibid). People opposed to ZANU-PF did not qualify for the post. At times the government installed incompetent candidates if they supported the party ardently. Ironically, ZANU-PF opposed the appointment of chiefs by the colonial regime during the liberation struggle citing the abuse associated with the practice. They argued that the involvement of the government in appointing chiefs was a way of silencing chiefs of the gross injustices perpetrated by the settler regime (Tavuyanago et al., 2011).

Mugabe's Patron-Client Relationship with Traditional Leadership

Much as Moorcraft (2011) stresses the use of military power by Mugabe to entrench his reign, one must also consider patronage as a powerful tool Mugabe used to get support from traditional leaders. After eighteen years of independence, the ZANU-PF government made a sudden shift regarding the way they related to the institution of traditional authority (*Traditional Leaders Act*, 1998). The then Minister of Local Government, John Landa Nkomo, announced in 1999 plans to create new Ward and Village Assemblies that would be led by chiefs and headmen. Following this announcement, the allowances of the chiefs were increased from Z$2 083 to Z$10 000 per month. The headmen's allowances increased from Z$680 to Z$5000 per month. These hefty increments were followed by President Mugabe's public apology for neglecting the chiefs since independence (Ranger, 2001). Thereafter, the powers of the chiefs (including those of allocating land and trying certain cases) were returned. Chiefs were given powers to spearhead development programmes in their areas including distributing land to their subjects. They were also tasked with the role of promoting cultural values and norms in their communities (*Traditional Leaders Act*, 1998; Government of Zimbabwe (1999)).

The great question of the day is: What informed this sudden twist? The sudden turn was informed by the politics of expediency, notably the emergence of the Movement for Democratic Change (MDC) in 1999 and the support that it commanded from the urban dwellers. The ruling party realized that the only way to curb the advancement of opposition and ensure election victory in the rural areas was to win the allegiance of the traditional rulers. Like Kwame Nkrumah (Yaw, 2006), Mugabe successfully endeavoured to manipulate the institution to serve his agenda of maintaining power. In a bid to woo the traditional leaders, he raised their social status by giving them lucrative incentives that surpassed those of the most senior civil servants. Zhou and Makahamadze (2012) argue that the chiefs were given cars, tractors, and farm equipment, while the salaries of all traditional leaders were also reviewed upwards from time to time. The chiefs also benefited from the housing schemes initiated by the government. The government saw to it that the homes of the chiefs were electrified and that water pipes were put in place. The chiefs were also given the mandate to distribute government food handouts in times of drought. In addition, they benefited from the Land Reform Programme with some of them becoming holders of multiple farms although they did not have enough farming skills (Ibid). Overwhelmed by the benefits that emanated from Mugabe's patronage, chief Chiwara (Cuthbert Kasikai) from Gutu in Masvingo Province likened President Mugabe to the son of God when he remarked, "*Uyu mwana wamwari chaiye!*" (This one is the son of God himself) (Zengeya, 2022). Such an utterance was an acknowledgement that Mugabe was a saviour who provided for his people. In a way, Mugabe was likened to the biblical Jesus whom Christians believed was the redeemer of the world.

It is interesting to note that Mugabe was not the only leader who courted the affection of chiefs to gain support in Southern Africa. President Festus Mogae who took over from Sir Ketumile Masire appointed Ian Khama as the Vice President who was the chief (*kgosi*) of the Bamangwato people. The subsequent landslide victory of the party was attributed to the chief's influence over his people. His appointment to the post of Vice President could be viewed as a sign of gratitude by President Mogae (Nyamnjoh, 2003). South Africa witnessed a hike in the stipend of traditional leaders when the African National Congress (ANC) won overwhelming support in KwaZulu Natal (Beall et al., 2005). It is believed that chiefs in KwaZulu Natal contributed to ANC victory by encouraging their people to vote for the party. However, chiefs in these countries, unlike those in Zimbabwe are not coerced to campaign for political parties. They enjoy some degree of autonomy as they are not totally controlled by the ruling party. In return for Mugabe's generosity, some chiefs rendered unconditional support to the ruling party and expelled from their constituencies those villagers who did not support ZANU-PF. The then President of the Chief's Council, Jonathan Mangwende, was responsible for evicting several peasants in the period 2000–2002 on allegations that they were MDC members (Zhou & Makahamadze, 2012). He also made various pronouncements in support of the ruling party. On one occasion, he remarked that the return of the bottom half of the Zimbabwean bird after many years in Germany was a symbol of ancestral support for Mugabe's regime (Ibid). According to the Zimbabwe Human Rights (ZHR) NGO Forum (August 2001), in 2000 chief Chiweshe, a staunch supporter of Mugabe disrupted a funeral service for an MDC supporter who had been killed because of political violence. He vowed that as the chief he would not allow the burial of an MDC activist in his territory and informed relatives of the slain victim to take the body to London for burial. In a similar incident in the same year (2000), the family members of another slain MDC activist in Muzarabani had to pay a bull as a fine and they were made to vow that they would never support the opposition before they could bury their relative in that area (Ibid).

The incumbent President of the Chief's Council, Fortune Charumbira, expressed the chiefs' support for Mugabe's presidential candidature for 2008 polls (Zhou & Makahamadze, 2012). He whipped chiefs, headmen, village heads, and villagers into submission to ensure that Mugabe retained his position as president. In the run-up to the elections, headmen and village heads were given instructions to lead their people to ZANU-PF rallies and to the voting stations where the villagers were forced to cast their ballot papers under the watchful eyes of war veterans and youth militias. In 2008, many chiefs declared their constituencies, no-go areas for the opposition MDC formations. Some traditional leaders in rural areas went to the extent of evicting opposition members from their areas. Some denied opposition members food handouts that were provided by the Non-Governmental Organizations. To get the handouts, villagers were supposed to be holders of ZANU-PF party cards. The chiefs, who in most cases supervised the distribution of this food, announced that the drought relief was meant for those who supported the government and ZANU-PF was the government (Ibid). Furthermore, they allowed armed youth militia to establish military bases in their areas. The Legal Monitor of the 29th of June 2009 also reported that chiefs in Bikita and Nyanga Districts encouraged ZANU-PF supporters to loot chickens, goats, beasts, and other valuables belonging to MDC supporters during the run-up to the June 2008 elections. The animals were slaughtered at the military bases where opposition members were tutored about the liberation struggle and sometimes tortured and forced to repent. Thus, many chiefs during this period functioned as Mugabe's auxiliaries and lackeys, as well as 'vote banks' for ZANU-PF politicians.

In March 2012, chiefs openly declared their support for Mugabe (in the then 2013 forthcoming elections) at a four-day chiefs' conference in Bulawayo. However, they infuriated even ZANU-PF Vice President, John Nkomo, when they in turn, as clients, demanded farms, an increase in their allowances, a share of the Community Development Fund paid to Members of Parliament, guns, free duty on vehicles, bodyguards during elections, and diplomatic passports (*Daily News*, 10 March 2012). At a meeting at chief Masunda's homestead in Zvishavane in September 2012, the then Local Government, Rural and Urban Development Minister, Ignatius Chombo, revealed government plans to buy new luxury vehicles for all the country's then 282 chiefs. "It has also been realised that it is not fair to select cars for chiefs. They should choose. If they want an Isuzu, Prado, Pathfinder or even a Mercedes Benz, let them have the cars," remarked Chombo (*The Zimbabwean*, 15 August 2012). He accused the then Finance Minister, Tendai Biti of failing to consider the 'plight' of chiefs, claiming that Biti was working to strip traditional leaders of their dignity. The move was a political manoeuvre by ZANU-PF to guarantee the chiefs' loyalty and that of their subjects ahead of 2013 elections. As already reflected above, most chiefs have been used to force their subjects to support ZANU-PF, particularly in the rural areas. They have also been the key perpetrators of partisan distribution of food aid, farming inputs, and other schemes supposed to benefit all without regard for political affiliation.

It is noteworthy that the Constitution of Zimbabwe Amendment (No. 20) Act 2013 (Government of Zimbabwe, 2013) recognizes and formalizes the authority and legitimacy of the traditional institutions. The Constitution explicitly lists a variety of powers and responsibilities of traditional leaders. Traditional leaders play very critical roles in the process of good governance. They play an advisory role to government and participation in the administration of rural areas. In their developmental role, they complement the government's efforts in mobilizing rural communities in implementing developmental projects, sensitizing them on health issues such as HIV/AIDS, promoting education, encouraging economic enterprises, inspiring respect for the law and urging participation in the electoral process and conflict resolution (Sections 280, 282). In principle, the constitution is clear on how traditional leaders can be utilized in urging citizen participation in electoral processes. Section 281(2) states that traditional leaders must not:

(a) be members of any political party or in any way participate in partisan politics;
(b) act in a partisan manner
(c) further the interests of any political party or cause; or
(d) violate the fundamental rights and freedoms of any person.

Yet sound as this may appear, in practice traditional leaders are part of ZANU-PF's political arsenal against opposition parties in Zimbabwe and therefore stifling democracy, political pluralism, and egalitarianism.

Mnangagwa and Continued Traditional Institutional Patronage and Clientelism

President Mnangagwa's new dispensation or the Second Republic was established through the November 2017 military coup and legitimized through the July 2018 elections. Since November 2017, Zimbabwe has become a country run by parasitic and predatory militarized political elites aided by a bureaucratic bourgeoisie who raid and empty state coffers while speaking the neo-liberal economic language. Mnangagwa has continued with Mugabe's pursuit of politics of expediency by winning the allegiance of traditional leaders to curb the advancement of opposition and ensure election victory in the rural areas (Zhou, 2019b). Like Mugabe, Mnangagwa has successfully endeavoured to manipulate the traditional institutions to serve his agenda of maintaining power. Towards the 2018 elections, there was a deliberate attempt to raise traditional leaders' social status by giving them lucrative incentives such as increased salaries, double-cab cars, housing schemes, tractors, and farm equipment, among many other things. According to the Zimbabwe Human Rights Commission (ZHRC, 2018), chiefs were also given the mandate to distribute Presidential inputs (ZHRC, 2018). Traditional leaders have become salaried officials or ZANU-PF functionaries amenable to partisan politics rather than promoting their traditional role of upholding the cultural values of communities and preserving the traditions, history, and heritage of their communities (Section 282 of Constitution 2013).

In direct contravention of Section 281 (2) of the Constitution which states that traditional leaders must not 'be members of any political party or in any way participate in partisan politics,' just before the 2018 elections, the President of the Chief's Council, Fortune Charumbira, expressed that traditional leaders would support the ZANU-PF presidential candidate in the 2018 harmonized elections (ZHRC). The European Union Election Observation Mission (2018, p. 21) reported several "traditional leaders involved in the campaign and influencing voters by threatening to cut food aid and agricultural inputs if they did not vote for ZANU-PF." Arguably, traditional leaders have routinely and wantonly disregarded the law with impunity. Although the Election Resource Centre sued chief Charumbira over unconstitutional utterances pledging support to the ruling ZANU-PF, and the High Court found the Chief President to be out of order and ordered him to retract in writing the statements that he made (Election Judgement, 2018), he did not abide by this order. Instead, he has gone on to make more statements to the same effect with no consequence. Conversely, by aligning himself with ZANU-PF, chief Charumbira, like chief Jeremia Chirau during Ian Smith's time in the 1970s, has entered active partisan politics. This is unfortunate for a traditional leader whose mandate is to judiciously serve his subjects irrespective of their political persuasion. It is also noteworthy that in May 2018, Justice Garainesu Mawadze of Masvingo High Court issued a judgement banning all traditional leaders from partisan politics or making political statements and declaring allegiance to any political party. Yet sound as these judgements may appear, they have been ignored with impunity by many traditional leaders in Zimbabwe largely because of ZANU-PF's patron-client relationship with traditional leaders for its political expediency.

The conduct of traditional leaders in Zimbabwe is such that they influence both electoral outcomes and processes by not only sealing off space for opposition political players, but also subverting the will of the people under their jurisdiction through intimidation, making public pronouncements to the effect that they support ZANU-PF and partisan distribution of food aid and farming inputs. The gatekeeping role of traditional leaders was evident when village head, Nhamoinesu Nemanwa, of Chivanhu village in Masvingo mobilized citizens under the ZANU-PF banner to participate in pre-emptive attacks against members of the MDC Alliance on 11 October 2021 (Mathanda, 2021). In June 2022, a village head in Mudzi District by the name of John Mukota Rongai informed all people under his jurisdiction not to attend Citizens Coalition for Change (CCC) meetings, and that anyone who defies his ban would be fined a goat (Chengeta, 2022). This situation is prevalent in all rural areas of Zimbabwe. In June 2022, village heads in Chitumbama area under chief Matope in Mt Darwin South ordered CCC members and women to attend ZANU-PF cell meetings and to vote for ZANU-PF in the 2023 elections (Maphosa, 2022). In July 2022, a village head in Hurungwe East constituency who is also a secretary for ZANU-PF Masikati District in Tengwe area summoned more than 50 CCC members at his homestead to interrogate why they were no longer attending ZANU-PF meetings (Mandava, 2022). Addressing farmers at a Cotton Company of Zimbabwe (COTTCO) in Hurungwe in July 2022, chief Njelele, Moses Misheck Njelele, expressed that he had banned opposition parties in Gokwe and did not want to hear about opposition supporters in an area under his jurisdiction. In the words of chief Njelele, *"Kuna President, madzishe aripo, uye pane madzishe ndipo pane ZANU-PF* (where the president is, chiefs are there, and where the chiefs are, is where ZANU-PF is)" (Muonwa, 2022). Arguably, the reality on the ground is that traditional leaders are fully engaged with electoral and political processes in their communities.

The role of the traditional institution goes far beyond what is provided for in the Constitution of Zimbabwe. They are clearly an appendage of the ruling ZANU-PF without shame nor apology. Even President Mnangagwa confirmed this when he remarked:

> *Saka nde ndichikumbira kuti kubva the 12 wards dziri kwaChirumanzu, hanzi sabhuku kumberi, chairman wedistrict mushure nevanhu, councilor aripo, kwava kuno vhota. Hatidi, tetichiziva kuti polling station imwe neimwe ina maresults ayo. Toziva kuti ko polling station ino, vabvepi, vapinda nepapi. Chisingazvikanwi kufamba kwacho, rufu. Rufu haguna zhira, asi anovhota ane zhira* (Of the 12 wards in Chirumanzu, the village head must be in front, the district chair behind him leading the people, the councillor must be present and then we go and vote. We are aware that every polling station has its own results. We would want to know where

opposition would come from and how they will penetrate any polling station. What cannot be predicted is death, you can't determine how it comes, but a voter has a pathway) (Mnangagwa, May 2022).

Surveys conducted by CCC Interim provincial committees in Midlands (2022) and Masvingo (2022) show that 83% and 94% of traditional leaders, respectively, are politically aligned to the ruling ZANU-PF and have used their positions to punish those who belong to opposition political parties. This is in total violation of the national constitution and High Court judgements, as reflected above. To enable traditional leaders to perform the gatekeeping role with relative ease, the ZANU-PF government has made the institution of traditional leadership very strong, with traditional leaders receiving hefty perks such as top-of-the-range vehicles, hefty salaries, electrification of their homes, upliftment of the roads that lead to their homes, among other emoluments. As reflected above, they also participate in the partisan distribution of farming inputs and food aid. After suffering a humiliating defeat at the hands of CCC in March 2022 by-elections, ZANU-PF has moved a gear up in its use of patronage and clientelism. In total pursuit of political expediency ahead of the 2023 watershed elections, ZANU-PF has offered a new package for traditional leaders comprising: payment of US$50 and ZWL$30,000 to village heads, and more for headmen and chiefs; bicycles for village heads and headmen, and servicing of chiefs' cars by government and receipt of brand new ones after every five years; medical aid, monthly fuel coupons, and airtime for ease communication; funeral assistance, free ZUPCO[1] travel and a suit every year; and devolution led by the village heads, headmen, and chiefs (Chiseva, 2022; *The Herald*, 12 May 2022). It is within this framework that the current leading participation in voter registration by traditional leaders, their threats to banish CCC supporters from many rural constituencies under their jurisdiction, as well as threats to villagers that those who support CCC will risk not having other villagers attend and assist during funerals of their family members, must be fully comprehended.

---

[1] This is a bus company owned by the state and it plies both urban and rural routes.

Exceptions to Patronage and Clientelism

Some traditional leaders have not supported ZANU-PF despite threats from war veterans, youth militias, and even government officials, while some have condemned high-profile corruption that has become routine rather than episodic. Some traditional leaders discouraged operations of youth militias in their constituencies and they showed sympathy for the opposition since Mugabe's reign. By so doing, they risked losing their positions as chiefs and even their lives. For instance, chief Makuvise of Buhera was stripped of his traditional regalia, humiliated before his subjects, and murdered in broad daylight in 2002 for supporting the MDC. His son reported that the chieftaincy has since been given to a member of the next family who support the ruling party (Makuvise, 2012). Chief Nhlanhlayamangwe Ndiweni of Ntabazinduna was a progressive traditional leader who was non-partisan and concerned about the welfare of his people. He stood out as one of the few traditional leaders in Zimbabwe who spoke out against the government's failure to resolve the country's political and economic crises, and human rights abuses (Takawira, 2019). For his genuine efforts at representing the general populace under his jurisdiction, and resistance to government patronage and clientelism, he was labelled a 'security threat' and physically attacked by rogue ZANU-PF youth militias. He was finally deposed by the government in December 2019.

Equally critical is chief Murinye who in December 2021 stunned government officials attending a funeral in Masvingo rural when he warned President Mnangagwa to stop the looting in the country or risk losing 2023 elections. He even dared to encourage the Zimbabwe defence forces commander, Valerio Sibanda, to stage another coup, in similar fashion to the 2017 'military assisted coup.' "We are fed up with these criminals that surround the President. This is nonsense and it must stop; this country does not belong to anyone. You can kill me if you want, but stop this," chief Murinye remarked (*Masvingo Mirror*, 15 December 2021). He also stated that he would rather be a poor chief than have "filthy wealth in the midst of poverty." For this voice of reason, chief Murinye and other traditional chiefs were rebuked by the Vice President, Constantino Chiwenga. In a related incident, the 95-year-old traditional leader, chief Sigola was candid to the Deputy Minister of Local Government and other government officials who visited him at his homestead in Esiphezini, Umzingani District in Matabeleland South that he was living in a dilapidated farmhouse that had no electricity, no running water, and with no trafficable road leading to his homestead. He made it clear that if he dies, he does not want anyone to start fixing the road, restoring electricity so that they attend his funeral. He made it categorically clear that if that cannot be done while he was alive, it better not be done at all (*The Herald*, 12 May 2022). In another related incident, in July 2022, village head, Njelele bemoaned the low prices of cotton offered to villagers in Gokwe and indicated that some such villagers have not been paid since 2020, while others were offered mazoe (drink), cooking oil, and other groceries (Muonwa, 2022). He wondered what type of a country Zimbabwe has become to allow this to prevail. Chief Siabuwa in Binga North, is also very progressive and tries to strike a balance by allowing both ZANU-PF officials like Kembo Mohadi, and CCC Member of Parliament, Prince Dubeko Sibanda, to address village heads under his jurisdiction. Due to his non-partisan posture, he has been accused of '*bhora musango*' (kicking the ball into the bush, a euphemism for supporting the opposition) antics, with ZANU-PF supporters recommending disciplinary measures against him in July 2022 (Sibanda, 2022). It is evident that due to challenges under the current predatory government, some traditional leaders have decided to voice the concerns of the villagers under their jurisdiction, thereby riddling ZANU-PF patronage and clientelism. Some such traditional leaders have remained progressive under excessive difficulties. They judiciously execute their responsibilities as custodians of traditions, culture, and customs and treat their subjects impartially, irrespective of their political affinity. However, their voices in the Chiefs' Council meetings where decisions are taken through majority votes have been suffocated.

The position of some chiefs during this period has been ambivalent. The case of chief Mutambara epitomizes this scenario. Towards the 2005 elections, two men claiming to represent chief Mutambara told the MDC supporters at a rally in Mutare at Chisamba grounds that the chief had disowned Arthur Mutambara, for joining an MDC faction led by Welsman Ncube. It was claimed that the chief could not attend because of advanced age. According to the envoys, the chief and the Mutambara clan recognized Morgan Tsvangirai as the legitimate leader of MDC nationwide (Tavuyanago et al., 2011). However, following an investigation by members of the Central Intelligence Organization, Chief Mutambara denied ever sending the two men. He declared, "I am a very strong ZANU-PF cadre and I am very proud of that. I want everybody to know that I am the chief and the only one who can speak about issues pertaining to the Mutambara clan" (*The Standard*, 4 June 2006). This declaration is in line with what one participant cited in Alexander (2006, p. 172) stated: "He [Chief Mutambara] was an active and loyal supporter of the freedom fighters during the war of liberation which led to his detention... He supports the present government to the hilt. He commands great political respect among the people and chiefs in this district." Thus, while some chiefs have tried to retain their degree of autonomy to a small extent, most chiefs have largely become ZANU-PF puppets, clients, and lackeys that can be counted on for rural votes during elections.

Conclusion

By and large, as much as traditional leaders can assist in building a democracy, they have been a hindrance owing to manipulation by the government and the ruling party. Having realized that force and repression alone cannot sustain a government and political party, ZANU-PF leaders have adopted a convenient core of regime consolidation and extended their tenure in office through patronage and clientelism. This involves co-opting and coercing traditional leaders to stop their subjects from supporting parties of their choice and banning the political activities of other parties. Traditional leaders are, therefore, undermining democracy and perpetuating political harassment and discrimination. Indeed, the role of the traditional authorities in the electoral process and in the distribution of food aid, among other functions and processes, has been brought into question as their bias towards the ZANU-PF party has distorted and reduced their function to being affiliates and at times touts of the ruling party. Traditional leaders have repeatedly been engaged to distribute agriculture inputs, land, food aid, farming inputs, and welfare funds to ZANU-PF party faithful. Reports are rampant during election time of traditional authorities discriminating against those labelled as members of opposition parties and in extreme cases, some politically motivated violence has been meted out with the knowledge or even sanction of some traditional leaders. Considering the foregoing, it is imperative to:

1. Align the Traditional Leaders Act (1998) and all other ancillary statutory instruments to the Constitution of Zimbabwe so that traditional leaders can stay out of politics and let people decide for themselves how to vote.

2. Continue to monitor and document activities of traditional leaders for evidence-based advocacy, litigation, and future reference in reform advocacy.
3. Put more effort in capacity training of traditional leaders to understand their roles, provisions of the Constitution, and the aligned enabling legislation.
4. Facilitate evidence-based litigation to push traditional leaders, the ruling party, and government to implement provisions of the constitution.
5. Strengthen citizen awareness of the provisions of the constitution on traditional leaders, their political limitations, and what citizens can do in the event of infringements.

References

Alexander, J. (2006). *The unsettled land: State-making and the politics of land in Zimbabwe, 1893–2003*. James Carrey.
Arriola, L. R. (2009). Patronage and political stability in Africa. *Comparative Political Studies, 42*(10), 1339–1362.
Ayittey, G. N. B. (1999). *Africa in chaos*. St Martin's Griffin.
Beach, D. N. (1986). *War and politics in Zimbabwe, 1840–1900*. Mambo Press.
Beach, D. N. (1994). *A Zimbabwean past*. Mambo Press.
Beall, J., Mkhize, S., & Vawda, S. (2005). Emergent democracy and 'resurgent' tradition: Chieftaincy and transition in KwaZulu-Natal. *Journal of Southern African Studies, 31*(4), 755–771.
Campbell, J. (1964). *Honour, family and patronage*. Clarendon Press.
CCC Masvingo Interim Provincial Committee (2022). Scanning of traditional leaders in Masvingo Province Report.
CCC Midlands Interim Provincial Committee (2022). Scanning of traditional leaders in Midlands Province Report.
Chengeta, T. (2022, July 20). Interview, Marondera.
Chigwanda, L. (2019). Chief Tangwena's legacy. blog.zimtribe.com. Accessed 20 July 2022.
Chiseva, B. (2022, June 21). Panicky: ZANU-PF dangling US$50, badges to traditional leaders. *Tellzim*.
Clapham, C. (Ed.). (1982). *Private patronage and public power: Political clientelism in the modern state*. Printer.
Daily News. 10 March 2012.

Eisenstadt, S. N., & Roginer, L. (1984). *Patrons, Clients and friends: Interpersonal relations and the structure of trust in society (themes in social sciences)*. Cambridge University Press.

Election Judgement. (2018). Election Resource Centre v. Charumbira. Available at: Election Resource Centre v. Charumbira • Page 1 • Election Judgments – IFES. Accessed 2 August 2022.

European Union Election Observation Mission. (2018). *Final Report Republic of Zimbabwe Harmonised Elections 2018*.

Foster, G. (1963). The dyadic contract in Tzintzuntan: Patron-client relations. *American Anthropologist*, 65(6), 1280–1294.

Galt, A. (1973). Carnival on the island of Pentelleria: Ritualised community solidarity in an atomic society. *Ethnology*, 12(3), 325–339.

Government of Zimbabwe. (1998). *Traditional Leaders Act [Chapter 29:17], 1998*.

Government of Zimbabwe. (1999). *Statutory Instrument 430A: Traditional Leaders*. Harare: Gvt Printers.

Government of Zimbabwe. (2013). *Constitution of Zimbabwe Amendment (No.20) Act 2013*.

Makuvise, B. (2012, February 20) Interview, Mutare.

Mandava, B. (2022, August 1). Telephone Interview.

Maphosa, J. (2022, June 29). Interview, Bindura.

Masvingo Mirror (2021, December 15). Video.

Mathanda, E. (2021, October 25). Rein in traditional leaders: ERC. *News Day*.

Mkhwanazi, E. (2012). Nkrumah and the chiefs: Contending epistemologies of democracy. *Journal of African Philosophy*, 4, 18–28.

Mnangagwa, E. (2022, May). Audio recorded at a meeting addressed by the President.

Moorcraft, P. (2011). *Mugabe's war machine, saving or savaging Zimbabwe*. Pen & Sword Military.

Muonwa, J. (2022, August 1). Chief saya 'insane' opposition parties banned in Gokwe. Available at: www.newzimbabwe.com/chief-says-insane-opposition-parties-banned-in-gokwe. Accessed 2 August 2022.

Ndawana, E., & Hove, M. (2018). Traditional leaders and Zimbabwe's liberation struggle in Buhera District, 1976–1980. *Journal of African Military History*, 2, 119–160.

Nyamnjoh, F. B. (2003). Chieftaincy and the negotiation of might in Botswana's democracy. *Journal of Contemporary African Affairs*, 21(2), 233–250.

Phimister, I. R. (1988). *An economic and social history of Zimbabwe, 1890–1948: Capital accumulation and class struggle*. Longman.

Ranger, T. O. (1967). *Revolt in Southern Rhodesia, 1896–1897: A study in African resistance*. Heinemann.

Ranger, T. O. (1970). *The African voice in Southern Rhodesia, 1898–1930.* Heinemann.
Ranger, T. O. (2001). Democracy and traditional political structures in Zimbabwe 1890–1999. In N. Bhebe & T. O. Ranger (Eds.), *The historical dimensions of democracy and human rights in Zimbabwe, volume one: Pre-colonial and colonial legacies* (pp. 31–52). University of Zimbabwe Publications.
Sibanda, P. D. (2022, July 28). Telephone Interview.
Soouthern Rhodesia. (1964). The Domboshava 'indaba': The demand for independence in Rhodesia: Consultation with African tribesmen through their chiefs.
Stein, H. F. (1984). A note on patron-client theory. *Ethos, 12*(1), 30–36.
Takawira, L. (2019). Government deposes chief Ndiweni. Available at: https://bustop.tv/government-deposes-chief-ndiweni/
Tavuyanago, B., Grand, N., & Makahamadze, T. (2011). Traditional leadership and democracy in Zimbabwe: Past and present. *Journal of History and Development, 2*(1), 56–75.
Tekere, E. (2007). *Edgar '2Boy' Zivanai Tekere: A life of struggle.* Sapes Trust.
The Herald. (2022, May 12).
The Zimbabwean, (2012, August 15).
Van Onselen, C. (1976). *Chibaro: African mine labour in Southern Rhodesia, 1900–1933.* Pluto Press.
Wolf, E. (1966). Kinship, friendship, and patron-client relations. In M. Banton (Ed.), *The social anthropology of complex societies.* Routledge.
Yaw, A. (2006). Chieftaincy and royalty in Ghana: Are we throwing away the Baby with the Bath water? Available at: http://www.ghanaweb.com/GhanaHomePage/features/artikel.php?ID=112177. Accessed 20 October 2009.
Zachrisson, P. (1978). *An African area in change: Belingwe, 1894–1946.* University of Guthernburg.
Zengeya, H. (2022, July 20). Interview, Gutu Growth Point.
Zhou, T. M. (2017). Poverty, Natural Resources "Curse" and Underdevelopment in Africa. In M. Mawere (Ed.), *Underdevelopment, development and the future of Africa* (pp. 279–346).
Zhou, T. M. (2019a). The historiography and politicisation of drought in Colonial Africa. In A. Nhemachena & M. Mawere (Eds.), *Necroclimatism in a spectral world (dis)order?: Rain petitioning, climate and weather engineering in 21st century Africa* (pp. 69–107).
Zhou, T. M. (2019b). Governance, democratisation and development in post-Mugabe Zimbabwe. In F. Duri, N. Marongwe, & M. Mawere (Eds.), *Mugabeism after Mugabe? Rethinking legacies and the new dispensation in Zimbabwe's Second Republic* (pp. 75–144). Africa Talent Publishers.

Zhou, T. M., & Makahamadze, T. (2012). *Asset or liability? The leadership of Mugabe in Independent Zimbabwe*. Lambert Academic Publishing.
Zimbabwe Human Rights Commission. (2018). *Harmonised Election Report.*

CHAPTER 19

A Critique of the Responsibility of Traditional Leaders in the Electoral Process: A Zimbabwean Experience

Sibiziwe Shumba

INTRODUCTION

In contemporary Zimbabwe, traditional leaders have been playing varied crucial political roles. This chapter examines the traditional authority whose existence is held in conflict with the citizens' expectations in order for it to be a neutral vanguard of the traditions, customs and community development, on the other hand, satisfying the ruling elite's demands for it to be loyal and serve the interests of the incumbent party (Zimbabwe Election Support Network, 2019). Therefore, the main purpose of this chapter focused on critiquing the role of traditional leaders in elections and the electoral processes, with particular emphasis on contemporary Zimbabwe. The nature of the responsibility of traditional leaders in the

S. Shumba (✉)
University of South Africa, Pretoria, South Africa
e-mail: Shumba-shumbasibiziwe@gmail.com

Department of Humanities, Business Development and Arts Education, Midlands State University, Gweru, Zimbabwe

© The Author(s), under exclusive license to Springer Nature Switzerland AG 2023
E. Mavengano and S. Chirongoma (eds.), *Electoral Politics in Zimbabwe, Vol II*, https://doi.org/10.1007/978-3-031-33796-3_19

351

elections and the electoral process was examined. The other issue was to bring to the fore challenges faced by the traditional leaders in the execution of their duties during the elections and electoral processes and establish the strategies to overcome the challenges faced by traditional leaders.

Background to the Study

Mgojo (1977) asserts that Plato in his Cratylus once said, "To teach a thing rightly it is necessary to define its name". As such, it is necessary in this instance to define the term traditional leaders and then explore the background of traditional leaders in relation to elections and electoral processes in contemporary Zimbabwe. Traditional leaders are defined as local elites who derive legitimacy from custom, tradition and spirituality (Honig, 2019). On the other hand, Baldwin (2016, p. 21) defines traditional leaders as "rulers who have power by virtue of their association with the customary mode of governing a place-based community". It is important to note that while their claims to authority are local, traditional leaders or chiefs are also integrated into the modern state in a variety of ways.

The New Constitution of Zimbabwe Amendment (No. 20) Act 2013 posits that a traditional leader is responsible for the execution of the cultural, customary and traditional functions of a chief, or village head as the case may be for their community. In addition to this, Chigwata (2016) asserts that traditional leaders deliver various government responsibilities in some parts of Zimbabwe where the state has no or limited presence. Their legitimacy, control and influence in rural areas remain widespread and demonstrate remarkable resilience, despite facing various threats. Therefore, traditional leaders play many roles in Zimbabwean communities, culture and families.

According to Citizens in Action Southern Africa, CIASA (2021) the role of traditional leaders in the government processes has always followed the dictates of the ruling party since colonial Zimbabwe. In this case, the traditional leaders have always been willing enablers of the government by design, default and coercion. The New Constitution of Zimbabwe Amendment (No.20) Act 2013 recognises among other things, the role of the institution of traditional leadership which operates alongside modern state structures (Chigwata, 2016). While strengthening the role and status of the institution, this new constitution strictly controls the conduct of the traditional leaders. Although the Constitution of Zimbabwe (2013) made a distinct departure in making clear provisions as to the role of traditional leaders, the practice has continued to be opposite and defiant.

The Ought to and Ought not to of Traditional Leaders

Citizens in Action Southern Africa CIASA (2021) argue that the 2013 Constitution recognises and formalises the authority and legitimacy of the traditional institutions. According to Chigwata (2016) and Ndoma (2021), the Constitution explicitly lists numerous powers and responsibilities of traditional leaders. The New Constitution of Zimbabwe 2013 posits that traditional leaders have various functions within their jurisdictions. First, traditional leaders are required to encourage and maintain the cultural values of their communities, and to uphold sound family values. It is a prerequisite that traditional leaders preserve the culture, traditions, history and legacy of their communities, including sacred shrines. More so, traditional leaders ought to promote development in the communities where they lead. In accordance with an Act of Parliament, they administer communal land and protect the environment. Kerbela cited in Chigwata (2016) posits that traditional leaders are utilised in urging citizen participation in electoral processes. Above all, the traditional leaders are supposed to resolve disputes among people in their communities in agreement with customary law and even to exercise any other functions conferred or imposed on them by the Act of Parliament. Hence, traditional leaders play very critical roles in the process of good governance.

The foregoing idea was also echoed by Kurebwa (2020) who noted that traditional leaders play important developmental, administrative and political roles in the rural areas, despite modern state structures. They are respected leaders in the communities who regulate rural life, control access to land and settle various disputes within their areas of jurisdiction.

The 2013 Constitution of Zimbabwe stipulates the tenets that have to be observed by traditional leaders. Firstly, traditional leaders must act in accordance with this constitution and the laws of Zimbabwe. They are also supposed to observe the customs pertaining to traditional leadership and exercise their functions for the purposes for which the institution of traditional leadership is recognised by the Constitution. Traditional leaders are supposed to treat all persons within their areas equally and fairly.

On the other hand, the same 2013 Constitution of Zimbabwe clearly specifies what ought not to be done by the traditional leaders. Firstly, they must not be a member of any political party or in any way partake in partisan politics. Traditional leaders should not act in any partisan manner, or further the interests of any political party or cause. They should not violate the fundamental rights and freedoms of any person. Ndoma (2021) reiterates the above idea by pointing out that the Constitution of Zimbabwe bars traditional leaders from being members of any political party, participating in partisan politics, and furthering the interests of any political party or cause. Despite this constitutional provision, some traditional leaders in Zimbabwe have been accused of dabbling in politics, typically in support of the Zimbabwe African National Union-Patriotic Front (ZANU-PF) party.

Kurebwa (2020) echoes the same view by pointing out that traditional leaders have played a pivotal role in ensuring that the ZANU-PF government remains in power since 1980. In principle, traditional leaders should not be drawn into party politics and their role should remain one of neutral leadership style. If a traditional leader assumes a political-party role, one should appoint a substitute to handle their traditional role to avoid conflict of interest.

From the above information, it is evident that the Constitution of Zimbabwe is clear in terms of what traditional leaders ought to do and not to do in terms of politics and elections. Despite all the clear stipulations, the traditional leaders often wantonly disregard the law, with impunity. For instance, according to Kurebwa (2020), this impunity was shown when the Election Resource Centre sued Chief Charumbira over unconstitutional utterances pledging support to the ruling ZANU-PF party. The court ruled that the president was of order and ordered him to withdraw the statement, an order by which he did not abide. As if that was not enough, he went on to make more statements to the same effect.

Chigwata (2016) affirms that the New Constitution of Zimbabwe that was adopted by the Zimbabweans among other things recognises the role of the institution of traditional leadership which operates alongside modern state structures. While strengthening the role and status of the institution, this New Constitution strictly regulates the conduct of traditional leaders. Despite this upliftment and strict regulation, the role and relevance of the institution of traditional leadership is under significant scrutiny. Traditional leaders often clash with State structures, particularly rural local governments, which are largely attributed to competition for power, resources and legitimacy.

The Role of Traditional Leaders in Zimbabwe

The Citizens in Action Southern Africa CIASA (2021) posits that the conduct of traditional leaders in Zimbabwe is such that they influence both electoral outcomes and processes by not only sealing off space for opposition political players but also destabilising the will of the people under their jurisdiction through intimidation, making public pronouncement to the effect that they support ZANU-PF and partisan distribution of food aid and farming inputs. The Citizens in Action Southern Africa CIASA (2021) went on to say that the reality on the ground is that traditional leaders are fully engaged with electoral and political processes in their communities. Furthermore, the Citizens in Action Southern Africa CIASA (2021) notes that the role of traditional leaders even goes beyond what is provided in the Constitution of Zimbabwe. The leaders are clearly an appendage of the ruling ZANU-PF without shame or apology.

Chigwata (2016) notes that a study undertaken by Rukuni in Bikita District established that 94% of traditional leaders in the district are politically aligned with the ruling ZANU-PF and have used their positions to punish those who belong to opposition political parties. Chigwata (2016) further notes that the fact that traditional leaders are openly partisan, working towards furthering the interests of a political party goes against the principles set out in Chapter 15 of the Constitution of Zimbabwe. Thus, by implication, the above scholar suggests that the gatekeeping role of traditional leaders was evident when Sabhuku Nhamoinesu Nemamwa of Chivanhu village in Masvingo mobilised citizens under the ZANU-PF banner to participate in pre-emptive attacks against members of the MDC Alliance on Monday, October 11, 2021.

Zimbabwean traditional leadership is deeply entrenched in politics. The ruling party openly rallies behind traditional leaders by treating them better than its own civil service. For instance, they are often given exorbitant monetary allowances and even vehicles so that they can push their agenda in their constituencies. It, therefore, makes it easy for Charumbira to openly declare his allegiance to ZANU-PF thereby defying the constitutional statutes. According to news from https://www.zimeye.net/2018/12/31 as well as https://www.kubatana.net/2018/01/17, Chief

Fortune Charumbira openly declares his political allegiance to ZANU PF. As the President of the Chiefs' Council, he has on several occasions openly whipped his constituency to support ZANU-PF. According to Dube (2019), those who have gone against this position have been victims of scorn and punishment. A recent example is that of Chief Ndiweni who lost his chieftaincy in Ntabazinduna in Matabeleland North and has since relocated to the United Kingdom on a political asylum of some sort. The reality of the roles of the traditional leaders is therefore clearly and directly guided by the ruling party which believes that opposition parties are led by people representing Western countries in their quest to reverse the gains of independence.

The Role of Civil Actors

The Civil Society known as the Citizens in Action Southern Africa CIASA (2021) points out that the Civil Society of Zimbabwe has played an important role in exposing the unconstitutional practices of the traditional leaders in electoral processes. This largely included capacity building of traditional leaders to understand their roles, documentation and litigation on behalf of citizens.

In the preceding section, the background that should provide the base and direction of this chapter has been delineated. Having explored the background to the study, the next section focuses on the theoretical framework.

Theoretical Framework

The theoretical framework is an important component of the research study. It serves as the guide on which to build and support the study. It also provides the structure to define how one will philosophically, epistemologically, methodologically and analytically approach the dissertation as a whole (Grant & Osalo, 2014). The social reconstruction theory illuminates this chapter. According to Letsiou (2014), the process of social reconstruction seeks to make culture relevant to the current problems. The principles of this theory emphasises on the view that there is a time when we can maintain the status quo in the society and yet there is a time when change is highly called for. The main purpose of this chapter focused on critiquing the role of traditional leaders in elections and the electoral processes, with particular emphasis on contemporary

Zimbabwe. The main argument raised in the discussion was that the role of traditional leaders in the running of the elections and the electoral processes cannot remain constant if they are to serve the current modern-day Zimbabweans. If the social, political and economic situations have changed, definitely, the way people operate should also change. The coming of the Constitution in Zimbabwe should reconstruct and redefine traditional leaders' roles in elections and electoral processes, since people are now being guided by Constitutionalism and Human Rights issues. In modern Zimbabwe, the traditional leaders are no longer the supreme guiding law of the land, but the Constitution defines and redefines what should be done in the running of elections and electoral processes in modern Zimbabwe. The Constitution is now the Supreme law of the land. Having outlined the theoretical framework, the next section focuses on the research methodology.

Research Methodology

In this chapter, a qualitative research approach was used. Qualitative research is based on an interpretive paradigm. This kind of research approach was used because it has several benefits in this study. First, Cohen and Manion (1994) posit that interpretive approaches to research have the purpose of understanding the world of human experience. This suggests that reality is socially constructed as propounded by Mertens (2000). Creswell (2010) asserts that the interpretive researcher relies on the participants' views of the situation under study and takes cognisance of the impact of their own experiences on the research. Creswell (2010) goes on to say that the interpretive researcher mostly relies on qualitative data collection methods and analysis, or a combination of qualitative and quantitative methods. In this chapter, qualitative methods were used to adequately describe or interpret a situation in relation to a critique of the responsibilities of traditional leaders in the electoral processes of Zimbabwe.

For the research design, a case study research design was adopted. The case study design was applied for its numerous benefits as posited by (Lohman & Boyd, 2021; Moorhead & Griffin, 1995). According to these scholars, the case study design has the advantage of permitting the researcher to explore situations in detail. In this case, it was used to get an in-depth analysis of a single setting of the populace within Zimbabwe. In addition to this, Gaulle (2018) postulated that a case study is inexpensive.

The costs associated with this method involve accessing data which can often be done for free. In this case, it is important to note that even when there are in-person interviews, the costs of reviewing the data are minimal. This design had the advantage of permitting the researcher to probe one situation in detail, yielding a plethora of descriptive and explanatory data (Gaulle, 2018; Lohman & Boyd, 2021). The case study design also facilitated the unearthing of unanticipated relationships as well as exploring deeper causes of the phenomena (Lohman & Boyd, 2021). Therefore, the use of a case study design was quite commendable in this research study.

However, it is worth noting that a case study had some limitations, for instance, data produced through a case study could not be readily generalised to other situations because the data generated is closely tied to the situation studied (Lohman & Boyd, 2021; Zainal, 2007). In this case, it was difficult to generalise the findings from one case study to another. Consequently, the data may again be biased towards the researcher's closeness to the situation (Gaille, 2018; Lohman & Boyd, 2021). Above all, a case study research design tends to be very time-consuming (Gaille, 2018). Therefore, when applying a case study research design, such constraints were taken into consideration. So the use of a case study had its own weaknesses to be taken note of.

Purposive sampling was used to select participants for the study. Using this type of sampling provided the researcher with the justification to make a generalisation from the sample that was being studied (Sharma, 2017; Editor in Chief, 2018). Purposive sampling was commendable because it helped by saving time and money while collecting the data (Editor in Chief, 2018; Alchemer, 2021). It offered a process that was adaptive as circumstances changed, even if it occurred in an unanticipated manner. For the above scholars, this technique enabled the researcher to target niche demographics to obtain specific data points. Furthermore, the sampling technique made it possible for the researcher to select everyone in the population for the study. Hence, the method was useful in making sure that people who did not fit the conditions of the study be excluded. A sample of forty-five participants from rural areas was chosen comprising five chiefs, twenty village heads and twenty villagers from a rural setting.

However, it is important to note that purposive sampling had disadvantages. For instance, Alchemer (2021), retrieved December 30, 2022, from https://www.alchemer.com/purpos... notes that it is a technique which is prone to researcher bias due to the fact that researchers are making subjective or generalised assumptions when choosing participants for their study. To overcome this disadvantage, a diverse and qualified team was chosen to plan, write and conduct the study. To overcome sub-group exclusion, the researcher ensured that everybody in the chosen audience was accounted for. Hence, in this research study, it was ensured that much bias was eliminated.

For research instruments, focus group discussions were conducted with thirty-five participants made up of fifteen village heads and twenty villagers. The use of focus group discussions enabled the collection of general and complex information on the role of traditional leaders in the electoral process in modern Zimbabwe within a short space of time (Miller, 2020; Writing, 2019). It yielded rich information as the villagers and village heads were able to respond to each other's comments and raised unexpected answers. Focus group discussion was a cost-effective way to get information and even provided time-saving opportunities (Miller, 2020). Together with that, using such an instrument did not require participants to be literate. Above all, the use of focus group discussions in the research study provided an enjoyable experience for the participants to dialogue with each other. This instrument allowed for more brainstorming opportunities with individual participants to create new ideas and approaches yielding a rich amount of data (Miller, 2020) on the role of traditional leaders in elections and electoral processes.

However, using focus group discussions had a disadvantage for some participants who were a bit reluctant to express their true feelings in the group because of fear of victimisation (Writing, 2019). In this case, some of the participants could not express their honest and personal opinions on the role of traditional leaders in elections and electoral processes in Zimbabwe. Hence, focus group discussions were not as efficient in covering maximum depth on a particular issue.

In-depth interviews were used to solicit data from five chiefs and five village heads from Zimbabwe who were information-rich. This tool assisted in uncovering rich descriptive data on the personal experiences of the participants and they remained focused on the topic under discussion (Rutczynska-Jamroz, 2022). Using the in-depth interviews enabled a deeper understanding of participants and observing the said as well as the unsaid (Abawi, 2017). The interviews had the advantages of keeping the costs down, having the flexibility of questioning as well as wide geographic access (Rutczynska-Jamroz, 2022). In addition to this, in-depth interviews enabled the researcher to have more control over the order and flow of the questions (Abawi, 2017). Above all, since it was more personal, it even allowed the researcher to have a high response rate (Abawi, 2017). The interview results were tape-recorded and later transcribed after the interviews using a "speech to text" application. In-depth interviews created a free atmosphere which permitted the participants to reveal their innermost feelings and experience as regards the responsibility of traditional leaders in the election and electoral processes in Zimbabwe.

However, using in-depth interviews had the challenge that they were time-intensive since they required a large amount of preparation beforehand (Rutczynska-Jamroz, 2022). They were also quite time-consuming since they were transcribed, organised, analysed and reported (Abawi, 2017). The in-depth interviews had a challenge in that this type of interview must be conducted by an appropriate employee who is fully prepared and engaged so as to avoid data loss. Hence, in-depth interviews were the most demanding in terms of time and financial resources (Rutczynska-Jamroz, 2022). Having outlined the research methodology, the next section presents a discussion of the findings.

Discussion of Findings

This section critiques the responsibilities of traditional leaders in the electoral processes in Zimbabwe being illumined by the Social Reconstruction Theory. This theory reiterates the view that if the social, political and economic situations have changed, definitely, the way people operate should also change. The New Constitution of Zimbabwe Amendment (No.20) Act 2013, notes that traditional leaders have certain responsibilities that they should play in the election and electoral processes. The discussion has shown that in the execution of their duties, they often face various challenges. However, there are several strategies that can be used to overcome those challenges.

Roles Played by Traditional Leaders in the Elections and Electoral Processes

From the interviews and focus group discussions, and responses, it was noted that the traditional leaders in Zimbabwe conscientise and mobilise people to participate in elections and electoral processes. For instance, Interviewee A (Chief), interviewed on 1 July 2022 noted that:

> The traditional leaders in Zimbabwe conscientize and mobilise people to participate in elections and electoral processes by encouraging them to register and vote. They even advocate for peace and harmony during elections and after elections.

The above assertion was reiterated by Interviewee E (Chief), interviewed on 3 July 2022. Hence, from the above view, it is noted that traditional leaders ensure that people register and vote in great numbers. The participants in the focus group discussions pointed out that traditional leaders encourage peace and harmony during and after elections and electoral processes.

It was also revealed that the traditional leaders mobilised support for the ruling ZANU-PF party. Such a stance shows that these leaders are biased towards supporting the ruling party. For instance, Interviewee B (Chief), interviewed on the 4th of July 2022 posited that:

> The traditional leaders work with the party leadership from the cells of the party to branches up to the wards. Traditional leaders are party cadres and they are actively involved in party politics. This is even shown by their actions and speeches in line with party politics.

More so, the focus group discussion responses also pointed out that the traditional leaders together with party village chairpersons, district chairpersons and coordinating committees prepare registers of party members right from the cells and the members are assisted in getting identity documents. Thus, one can say the traditional leaders prepared a fertile ground for the election and electoral processes since they actively participate in them.

The above idea is supported by the Zimbabwe Election Support Network ZESN (2019) which stipulates that traditional leaders in Zimbabwe have been blamed for manipulating communities under their rule to vote for the ruling party. These allegations were authenticated by an appeal presented by the highest traditional leaders' structure, the Chiefs' Council pronouncement of support to the ruling ZANU-PF and its presidential candidate ahead of the 2018 harmonised elections (Mail & Guardian, 2018). This bias compromises free and fair elections.

Fayayo (2018) supports the foregoing idea by postulating that ZANU-PF uses a strategy of assimilating traditional leaders into indiscernible party structures. This was achieved through making kraal heads and other traditional leaders ZANU-PF cell chairpersons but not permitting them to have positions beyond, for example the district or provincial level. Thus, it has been noted that traditional leaders in Zimbabwe are part of the ZANU-PF mobilisation stratagem at the very basic level, clandestinely encouraging the villagers to vote for the ruling party in great numbers at levels where distant observers would not observe.

In Matobo, Matabeleland South region, some chiefs purportedly deprived those who were not ZANU-PF members access to food aid, while others reported opposition party supporters to the ZANU-PF structures or the police for victimisation (Fayayo, 2018). Consequently, opposition parties could not field candidates in some wards in Matabeleland as their members/supporters were threatened and some had to flee for their lives to neighbouring urban areas like Bulawayo, Plumtree and Gwanda. All this implies that opposition parties were really in great trouble since traditional leaders were vigorously mobilising people for the ruling ZANU-PF.

From interview responses, it was revealed that the Chief's Council is partisan. For instance, according to Interviewee J (Village Head) interviewed on 22 July 2022,

> President of the Chief's Council Mr Fortune Charumbira is a ruling party cadre just like all the other chiefs. We also noted that during some of the past elections, traditional leaders literally drove their subject people to polling stations where they were made to vote for the ruling party.

Interviewee C (Chief) interviewed on 7 July 2022 postulated that, "In the 2018 elections, members of some communities in the rural areas had to fake illiteracy due to fear of being victimised". The issue of being forced to fake illiteracy was also mentioned by Interviewee H (Village head), interviewed on 18 July 2022. This was also supported by the responses from focus group discussions where it was noted that during the 2018 elections in areas like Mashonaland West and Mashonaland Central, some voters pretended to be illiterate or to be blind so that they could be helped when voting at polling stations since they were afraid of being victimised. This is an indication that traditional leaders had roles of ensuring that the electorate voted for the ruling party. Therefore, making traditional leaders non-partisan will remain a pipe dream if the generation which brought about the country's independence is still in existence.

Challenges Faced by Traditional Leaders in the Execution of Their Duties in the Elections and Electoral Processes

From the responses, it was revealed that the non-partisan traditional leaders encountered some challenges in the execution of duties during the election and the electoral processes. Interviewee D (Chief), interviewed on the 16th of July 2022 posited:

> The non-partisan traditional leaders' main challenges were that they would see the need for electoral reforms but they did not have effective ways of bringing about such reforms. Such reforms can be brought about by the Chief's Council because debating about electoral reforms is its mandate.

This view was also supported by the responses from the focus group discussions held in Matabeleland South. It was pointed out that non-partisan leaders had difficulties in that although they may have ideas of bringing electoral reforms, their hands were tied. Hence, the non-partisan traditional leaders are at times in a difficult position as far as the execution of their duties is concerned. Their challenging situation is worsened by their lack of resources because of their non-partisanship.

Coupled with this, the responses revealed that the country's constitution stipulates that traditional leaders are supposed to be non-partisan and apolitical. It was also shown that some of the non-partisan traditional leaders do not come to the open due to fear of victimisation. The enlightened or educated ones who try to call for reforms end up losing their positions. A case in point is the dethroned Chief Ndiweni, who is currently in the United Kingdom. This Chief is petitioning the SADC, the EU and the United Nations to compel the government of Zimbabwe to make room for the diaspora vote. His main argument is that most of the people in the diaspora contribute to the economy through remittances back home and therefore they must be afforded an opportunity to choose representatives in government. Hence, one can say he is like a "lone prophet" crying in the wilderness, with slim chances for anything to come out of it.

What has been raised in the above paragraph is in line with what was raised by the Zimbabwe Electoral Support Network (2019) which argued that, just like during the colonial era, Zimbabwe's opposition parties have been punished, therefore compelling traditional leaders to toe the line. As a result, there is a perception that the entire traditional institution is pro-ZANU-PF which is the ruling party. Therefore, some non-partisan traditional leaders during the elections and electoral processes may not give a nonconforming voice due to the fear of victimisation.

On the other hand, the interview and focus group discussion responses show that the partisan traditional leaders are part and parcel of the ruling party, and they are helping to uphold the existing policies of the established order. They do not see any challenges in the electoral processes because they result in the victory of the ruling party. They do not see the need for change. The partisan traditional leaders are in support of the status quo. For them, the ruling party must rule forever. Based on the abovementioned points, it is apparent that the challenge of some traditional leaders is the lack of democratic space during the elections and electoral processes. The ideology and the propaganda of the ruling party are what is followed by the partisan traditional leaders.

The focus group discussions and interview responses also revealed that some traditional leaders in Zimbabwe find it difficult to remain apolitical as far as the elections and electoral processes are concerned since they enjoy a lot of benefits. This view was echoed by Interviewee F (Village Head), interviewed on 10 July 2022 who posited that:

> The traditional Chiefs have top-of-the-range vehicles, receive monthly fuel allocation and a monthly salary as well as other several packs including mechanised farm equipment and farm implements which makes it difficult for them to be apolitical.

This view was also supported by Interviewee I (Village Head), interviewed on 20 July 2022 and Interviewee J (Village Head), interviewed on 23 July 2022, who pointed out that some traditional leaders have failed to be apolitical due to the financial and material benefits that they get as a result of unwavering support to the ruling party. Hence, at times a traditional leader during elections and electoral processes may operate as a court prophet who dares not "bite the hand that feedeth thee". Resultantly, most of the traditional leaders are partisans due to the payment of some benefits such as cars, farms, money, etc., from the government via the ruling party.

The above view is in line with what has been raised by the Zimbabwe Election Support Network (ZESN, 2019). According to the ZESN, the constitutional and institutional frameworks in Zimbabwe make adequate provisions that clearly prohibit traditional leaders from partaking in elections and electoral processes to advance the interest of any political party or candidate. What is challenging is the implementation because the political elite who are supposed to guarantee enforcement are beneficiaries of the status quo. On the other hand, traditional leaders are willing collaborators because they benefit from political patronage. Therefore, the traditional leaders have challenges of not advancing the interest of any other political party since they will be benefitting from the existing status quo.

In addition to this, the responses also portrayed that the traditional leadership in elections and electoral processes is affected by political polarisation which has its roots and tentacles in binary statecraft. For instance, according to Interviewee G (Village Head) interviewed on the 14th of July 2022:

> In Zimbabwe, we see the conflagration of state and party politics, which to a great extent is the cause of particular politicisation of the institution of traditional leadership. Therefore, traditional leadership in the elections and electoral processes are affected by political polarisation.

Hence, from the above response, one can say that in Zimbabwe, the traditional leadership in elections and electoral processes is greatly influenced by political polarisation which has its roots and tentacles in binary statecraft.

Strategies for Overcoming Challenges Faced by Traditional Leaders in the Elections and Electoral Processes

From the interview and focus group discussion responses, it was noted that the thinking or mind-set of most traditional leaders in Zimbabwe can only be changed by the same leaders of the ruling party. However, this might be something which is impossible because that will be like removing itself from power. Hence, the following groups of people may bring about electoral reforms. Firstly, the House of Parliament, that is the legislative assembly and senate. The House of Parliament is comprised of Members of Parliament of both the ruling party and the opposition, so through a debate on electoral reforms, a level electoral field can be achieved.

In addition to this, the responses showed that the laws of the country must be aligned with the 2013 Zimbabwean Constitution. Pressure groups can also help to bring about electoral reforms. Together with that, the SADC, the EU and the United Nations can as well help in bringing out electoral reforms in Zimbabwe. It was also revealed by the study participants that while to politicalise is more utopian, it is the levels of *Zanufication* that leave a lot to be desired. The ideal would be that traditional leaders leave it to the decision of individuals to exercise their right to choose political leadership of choice rather than to conscript all to vote for a particular party.

Along with this, there should be a monitoring instrument for traditional leaders. In this case, the civil society must continue to monitor and document the activities of traditional leaders for evidence-based advocacy, litigation and future reference in reform advocacy (The Citizens in Action Southern Africa CIASA, 2021).

In line with what was put forward by the Zimbabwe Electoral Support Network (2019), the Zimbabwean traditional leaders must promote social cohesion and refrain from getting involved in elections and politics. Moreover, traditional leaders must not accept any dictates that demand them to unduly influence citizens under their jurisdiction to exercise their Constitutional right to elect leaders of their choice.

Together with this, Sect. 49 of the Traditional Leaders Act 1998 should be accordingly amended to inhibit possible political abuse. The Electoral Act 2018 must be amended to ensure explicit provisions for the role of traditional leaders and the Code of Conduct in the Act has to be revised to have specific clauses on prohibited conduct. The Parliament of Zimbabwe must ensure that all citizens enjoy ultimate freedom and human rights, including freedom of association, assembly and expression in line with SADC Principles Guiding Democratic Elections.

There should be capacity building and sensitisation of traditional leaders to understand their roles. More effort should be put into capacity training of traditional leaders to understand their roles and the provisions of the Constitution. In addition to that, there should be more education on litigation processes. Above all, the traditional leaders of Zimbabwe should borrow a leaf from traditional leaders in South Africa in that during elections, their job is to reinforce the electoral process as a national programme that it is not an end in itself but a means to a developmental end. In this case, the traditional leaders should make their areas of jurisdiction accessible to all aspirant parties and candidates.

Conclusion

All in all, in line with the social reconstruction theory, the role of traditional leaders in the running of the elections and the electoral processes cannot remain constant if they are to serve the current modern-day Zimbabweans. If the social, political and economic situations have changed, definitely the way people operate should also change. The coming of the Constitution in Zimbabwe should reconstruct and redefine traditional leaders' roles in elections and electoral processes since people are now being guided by Constitutionalism and Human Rights issues. The role of the traditional leaders goes far beyond what is provided in the Constitution of Zimbabwe. More so, the traditional leaders assist the government either by design, default or coercion. They are fully engaged with the electoral and political processes in their communities. In the execution of those duties, they even face certain challenges. The non-partisan traditional leaders' main challenges were that they would see the need for electoral reforms but they did not have effective ways of bringing about such reforms. The non-partisan traditional leaders do not come in the open due to fear of victimisation. There are certain strategies that can be used to overcome those challenges. There should be capacity building and sensitisation of traditional leaders to understand their roles. Section 49 of the Traditional Leaders Act 1998 should be accordingly amended to inhibit possible political abuse.

References

Abawi, K. (2017). Data collection methods (Questionnaire and Interview) Training in Sexual and Reproductive Health Research. Geneva Workshop 2017.

Adom, D., Hussein, E. K., & Adu- Agyem, J. (2018). Theoretical and conceptual framework: Mandatory ingredients of quality research. *International Journal of Science Research.*, 7(1), 438–441.

Alchemer (2021). Purposive sampling. Retrieved December 30, 2022, from https://www.alchemer.com/purpos

Baldwin, K. (2016). *The Paradox of Traditional chiefs in Democratic Africa.* University Press.

Chief Charumbira Declares Open Allegiance to ZANU PF-*ZimEye*. Retrieved December 2022, from https://www.zimeye.net/2018/12/31

Chigwata, T. (2016). The role of traditional leaders in Zimbabwe: Are they still relevant? *Law, Democracy and Development.* Law, devor. Dev. Cape Town.

Citizens in Action Southern Africa CIASA: The Role of Traditional Leaders in Elections. November 29, 2021.

Cohen, L., & Manion, L. (1994). *Research methods in education* (4th ed.). Routledge.

Constitution of Zimbabwe Amendment, (No.20) ACT 2013.

Creswell, J. W. (2010). *Qualitative research design: Choosing among five approaches.* Sage.

Dube, G. (2019). *Some traditional leaders dump powerful Zimbabwe Chief Ndiweni.* Retrieved December, 30, 2022, from https://www.voazimbabwe.com/a/zimbabwe-chiefs-removal-ndiweni-from-office/5168932.html

Editor- in- Chief (2019). *18 Advantages and disadvantages of purposive sampling in connectus.* Retrieved December 30, 2022, from https://www.connectusfund.og.on

Fayayo, R. (2018). *Zimbabwe's 2018 elections: The changing footprints of traditional leaders.*

Gaille, B. (2018). *Case study method: Advantages and disadvantages.* Retrieved December 30, 2022, from https://www.brandongaille.com/12-case

Grant, C. & Osanloo, A. (2014). Understanding, selecting and integrating a theoretical framework in dissertation research: Creating the blue print for your "House". *Administrative Issues Journal: Connecting Education, Practice and Research.* https://doi.org/10.5929/2014.4.2.9

Honig, L. (2019). *Traditional Leaders and Development in Africa.* https://doi.org/10.1093/acreforce/9780190228637.013.821.

In-depth Interviews: Data Collection Advantages and Disadvantages. Retrieved December, 30, from https://www.cfrinc.net/cfrblog/indepth-interviewing

Interviewee C(Chief), interviewed on 7 July 2022.

Interviewee D (Chief), Interviewed on 16 July 2022.

Interviewee G (Village Head), interviewed on 14 July 2022.
Interviewee A (Chief), interviewed on 1 July 2022.
Interviewee I (Village Head), interviewed on 20 July 2022.
Interviewee H (Village Head), interviewed on 18 July 2022.
Interviewee E(Chief), interviewed on 3 July 2022.
Interviewee F (Village Head), interviewed on 10 July 2022.
Interviewee J (Village Head), interviewed on 23 July 2022.
Interviewee B (Chief), interviewed on 4 July 2022.
In-depth interviews-advantages and disadvantages in spark the strategic insight agency. Retrieved December 30, 2022, from https://www.sparkmr.com/blog
Kurebwa, J. (2020). The Capture of Traditional Leaders by Political Parties in Zimbabwe for Political Experience. https://www.igi-global.com/chapter/the-capture-of-traditional-leaders-by-political-in-zimbabwe-forpoliticalexpediency/247632
Letsiou, M. (2014). *ART intervention and social reconstruction in education: Secondary education*, ART education researched, Athens School of Fine Art, Greece.
Lohman, L. & Boyd, N. (2021). *Case study design: Examples, steps, advantages and disadvantages*. Retrieved December 30 2022, from https://www.study.com/learn/lesson
Mertens, D. M. (2010). *Research and evaluation in education and psychology: Integrating diversity with quantitative, qualitative and mixed methods* (2nd ed.). Sage.
Mgojo, E. K. M. (1977). Prolegomenon to the study of Black Theology. *Journal for Theology for Southern Africa, 21*, 25.
Miller, B. (2020). *17 Advantages and disadvantages of a focus group*. Retrieved December 30, 2022, from https://www.greengarageblog.org/17advantages-and-disadvantages-of-a-focus-goup
Moorhead, G., & Griffin, R. (1995). *Organizational behavior: Managing people and organizations*. Houghton Mifflin Company.
Ndoma, S. (2021). Zimbabweans see traditional leaders as influential but want them to stay out of politics. *Afro barometer*. Dispatch no. 469.
Rutczynska-Jamroz, E. (2022). *Advantages of in-depth user interviews*. Retrieved December 30, 2022, from https://www.start-up.house/en/blog/articles/in-depth-user-interviews
Sharma, G. (2017). Pros and Cons of different sampling techniques. *International Journal of Applied Research, 2017*, 749–752.
Traditional Leaders Must Remain Impartial and Non-Partisan. *Kubatana.Net*. Retrieved December 30, 2022 from https://www.kubatana.net/2018/01/17
Writing, A. (2019). Advantages and disadvantages of A Focus Group in *Chron Newsletters*.

Zainal, Z. (2007). Case study as a research method. *Jurnal BIL*, June 2007.
Zimbabwe Election Support Network. (2019). Position Paper: Role of Traditional Leaders in Elections and Electoral Processes in Zimbabwe in *Kubatana*.

CHAPTER 20

Abusing the Traditional Sceptre: Chiefs and Electoral Collusion in Zimbabwe

Edmore Dube

This chapter interrogates the electoral choices of indigenous leadership from the onset of colonial times. Core to the chapter is deciphering how the chiefs and their leadership structures have used their indigenous sceptres over the past century, and how that can help us postulate their stand in the crunch 2023 harmonised elections. In an attempt to answer whether the chiefs could be on a reformative path attempting to live by the democratic consensus entrenched in their indigenous insignia of office or the current constitution, the research finds them more at home with representative democracy (rule in which the choice made by the leader summarises the wishes of the led). The representative democracy in which the indigenous leaders' choices become the sum and summit of individual choices has its source in colonialism. To survive colonial pressure leaders chose collusion against community democratic consensus. Their personal political choices were cascaded as the summary of the

E. Dube (✉)
Department of Philosophy and Religious Studies,
Great Zimbabwe University, Masvingo, Zimbabwe
e-mail: edube@gzu.ac.zw

© The Author(s), under exclusive license to Springer Nature Switzerland AG 2023
E. Mavengano and S. Chirongoma (eds.), *Electoral Politics in Zimbabwe, Vol II*, https://doi.org/10.1007/978-3-031-33796-3_20

choices of their constituencies, even when those choices were against common good. The chapter finds them moving in the same direction, albeit with insignificant individual variations. This contribution emphasises the limitations of representative voting (chiefs voting on behalf of their constituencies), which gradually develops into 'acclamative' voting (accepting the chief's choices through simultaneous verbal noise). The constituencies of indigenous leaders acclaim the choices of their leaders, well-knowing that variations lead to negative sanctions.

This chapter is a result of desktop research, which limits its sources to the information already in the public domain (Goundar, 2012). Desktop research is one of the well-known qualitative methodologies. It is a low-cost method in which one collects information from repositories while sitting at a desk. It is not a result of empirical research which dwells much on fieldwork (Walliman, 2011). The methodology is often called "documentary research" because it does not encourage the researcher to get back to the field to gather information already documented, though often for quite different purposes (Sileyew, 2019). It rather constructs an interpretive argument from available literature to postulate new outcomes—and in the present case, the position of chiefs in the 2023 harmonised elections. Available literature paints a gloomy picture in relation to what the chiefs may do. It would appear electoral collusion remains central to block-voting, in which territorial areas are expected to vote by cue after their indigenous leaders. The postcolonial theory is utilised in understanding the erroneous behaviour of chiefs and their administrative structures, at tangent with their mandates. Their mandates require democratic consensus as opposed to pseudo-consensus which must always be in tandem with the whims of the ruling elite (Gwaravanda, 2018).

The chapter opens with a brief section on the background to the current electoral collusion, followed by a look at the postcolonial theory as an interpretive methodology. An attempt is then made to clarify how independent Zimbabwe tried to deal with the problems of the errant colonial representative voting. Emphasis is placed on the period from 2000, when impediments to democracy lay in the numerous incentives of complicity afforded indigenous leaders, corrupting them beyond expectation. The section on government perks whetting the appetite of leaders for the purpose of electoral collusion is followed by an examination of hopes for reformation and positive contribution. The chapter concludes on a pessimistic note with regard a return by chiefs to the pristine values of democratic consensus, allowing individuals voices to be heard in the run-up to the 2023 harmonised elections.

Indigenous Leadership and the Background to Current Electoral Collusion

This section looks at how indigenous leadership migrated from using their powers for the benefit of their communities to that of the state. By moving at tangent with the requirements of their mandates, their actions resulted in lost opportunities by their communities and stalled independence. Pre-colonial chiefs were custodians of peace, democracy and group rights, through wide consultations and council consensus (Gwaravanda, 2018). Human life was sacrosanct, as guaranteed by the spiritual world, which made sceptred leadership sanctuaries for the troubled. At the onset of colonialism, indigenous leadership was intact, with territorial interests safeguarded and reinforced by spirit mediums to ensure internal democracy (Daneel, 1971; Schofelees, 1979). That chiefs and their subordinate structures loved their territories was clear in the pro-independence rebellions of the 1890s, whose crippling effects saw political powers of indigenous leadership (chiefs, headmen, village heads) being curtailed by the colonial regime up to the 1920s (O'Meara, 2019). Gradual pacification saw chiefs, headmen and village heads ceding their allegiance to the colonial enterprise even against their own people (and sometimes against their own will too). They had been entrusted with religious, political, economic and administrative duties prior to the coming of whites, and continued to hold onto these in a very limited way with the onset of colonialism. Most of their powers had been subsumed by the colonial administrators (Kurebwa, 2020). Once they became appendages to 'native' commissioners in charge of local government affairs, the Rhodesian government pejoratively regarded them as "the legitimate voice for African aspirations" (O'Meara, 2019, p. 72). Their utterances were becoming more and more personal, and therefore divorced from the legitimate aspirations of fellow Africans, for which the incumbents held the ruling sceptres.

The institution of indigenous leadership was reasonably restored in the 1960s when the cost of bureaucracy had become too expensive in the face of nationalist malcontents (Alexander, 2018, p. 10). Chiefs were given a 'role' in the Senate, which though insignificant was considered the only legitimate political voice for the indigenous people. In this way, the Rhodesian Front of Ian Smith, the last colonial ruler, used indigenous structures as cushions against nationalist (opposition) politics. The chiefs and their subordinates owed their legitimacy to the colonial enterprise, which appointed and salaried them, and "alienated large numbers of their indigenous supporters" (O'Meara, 2019, p. 72), creating problems for them. They were isolated by their communities for electing to legitimise an oppressive colonial regime. They tried their best to please both the appointing authority and their indigenous constituencies, sometimes falling short of either. They were allowed limited powers to allocate land and settle numerous indigenous disputes.

As elsewhere in Africa, chiefs tended to defend patronage benefits even against liberation struggles, which irked liberation parties and liberation icons (Nkomo, 2020, p. 156). They used their authority to allocate land as a prime source of production to whip people into line, on behalf of the government of the day. The government restored their powers over land allocation through the enforcement of the Tribal Trust Land Act of 1967, which reaped dividends as indigenous authorities did their best to forestall resistance to the central government. Karekwaivenane (2017, p. 47) adds that "African Law and Tribal Courts Act 1969, gave chiefs powers to grant justice commensurate to the norms of society… [but] The major aim was not custom but making chiefs enforce the unpopular government policies". The chiefs committed electoral fraud by enforcing unpopular government policies against the nationalist demands of one-man-one-vote. By doing so, indigenous leaders had entered an unholy alliance with the colonial regime in which chiefs became the sum and summit of African voices (summarising their ballot positions). The chiefs became willing gatekeepers of a system that could easily be put to rest through the individualistic system of "one man-one vote" (The Voice of the Tribes, 1968). The chiefs became divisive at a time when bureaucracy had become too expensive and the final push, with the indigenous leadership leading the way, was a real possibility. At that golden moment, the chiefs and their administrative structures were fished out of the African nationalist opposition, incentivised and used as fake voices for all Africans. Their electoral collusion sent wrong signals to the world, delaying liberation assistance from external donors. The chief was afforded more allowances commensurate to the amount of taxes he collected from his constituency, which further alienated him from his impoverished people. It is noteworthy that the problem is not limited to chiefs of the colonial period, because "with the introduction of salaries and new administrative policies, the office of chieftaincy was compromised in both the colonial and post-colonial periods" (Makahamadze et al., 2009, p. 33). It is important to postulate theoretically why the problem of abuse of the indigenous ruler's sceptre outlived the colonial times. The next section, therefore, looks at the postcolonial theory and its explanations of continuity of electoral collusion.

THE POSTCOLONIAL THEORY AS INTERPRETIVE METHODOLOGY

The argument that follows gives greater fault for electoral collusion by the indigenous leadership to colonialism. For centuries, chiefs and their subordinate leadership used open consensus democracy (down-up mode) to elect people's choices from *dare/idale* discussions (Gwaravanda, 2018). With the coming of colonialism, open democracy was largely subverted by administrative impositions in the top-down fashion, with indigenous leadership at the centre of advancing colonial interests. The postcolonial theory as an interpretive methodology helps us to understand the permanence of colonial residue in our minds, visible in the way we react to issues many years after independence. Arora (2007, p. 29) argues that the "ghost of colonialism is so powerful that the literary necromancers are mystified and do not know how to eliminate its evocative memories that are so stamped on the memories of people". This stress underscores that once colonised, nations struggle to be their old selves without success even after attaining political independence. In this way, we understand why indigenous leadership failed to restore the worthy of their traditional sceptres despite regaining their territorial powers in independent Zimbabwe.

The sceptre of leadership belonged to the departed forbearers who continued to be its owners through territorial mediums. They had become territorial spirits able to specify their choices sometimes in the face of missionary challenges (Matsuhira, 2013). The choice of an indigenous leader was first and foremost the duty of a territorial medium because the mantle of leadership belonged to the departed fathers. The one most adjudged to stand up to the common good as expected by the "living dead" was selected and anointed as leader (Schoffellus, 1979). He was specifically oriented to understand that he held the ruling sceptre only vicariously, on behalf of its rightful owners now in the divine realm. With the sceptre, he stood for the common good reflective in the *dare/*

dale consensus verdict. In that the chief or his representative ruled by consensus. He elected to advance the group opinion, which colonialism seriously varied. It did that, first, by sideling the territorial mediums and directly appointing the incumbent. Then, by redefining the common good as that which engendered the whims of the state (Dube, 2018). By wielding the powers to appoint, incentivise or remove the incumbent, the colonial government effectively managed to redefine the loyalties of a chief. That was done despite him continuing to claim the indigenous sceptre as befitting a true representative of the people. Holding onto the sceptre in circumstances not advancing its benevolent use of justifying the good was the advent of abuse. The colonial state largely survived by corrupting existing territorial leadership, than creating purely new genealogies of leadership. The postcolonial theory helps us to understand why this misdemeanour by the colonial state has continued to stand despite political independence. The next section discusses attempts by the independence government to rectify colonial electoral fraud by the indigenous leadership.

Failure to Annihilate Electoral Collusion in New Zimbabwe

This section accesses the methods used by the newly independent Zimbabwe to correct the flawed colonial contribution by chiefs. It concludes that the constricting methods were only possible in the first five years of independence when the ruling Zimbabwe African National Union-Patriotic Front (ZANU PF) was still popular. As opined by the postcolonial theory, ZANU PF soon began to court the collusion of traditional leaders to prop up its waning popularity.

In Zimbabwe as elsewhere, complicity with the colonial enterprise disadvantaged chiefs, headmen and village heads, forcing them to enter yet other anti-democracy pacts with the ruling regimes. Bishi (2015, p. 40) notes that "post-colonial governments in Africa were faced with the task of whether to incorporate indigenous leaders or not, since many chiefs were part of the colonial administration". President Kwame Nkrumah diced with the abolition of the institution altogether as Ghana attained its independence ahead of the rest of 'Black Africa' in 1957. In Uganda, the institution of indigenous leadership was reinstated in 1986, after being dumped twenty years earlier, in 1966 (Foundation for Human

Rights Initiative, 2004, p. 5). In Tanzania, such abolition was accompanied by the nationalisation of the land, to nib the power of chiefs in the bud (Green, 2011). Indigenous leaders were labelled sellouts by the pro-independence parties (Nkomo, 2020). As a result, Zimbabwe's independence government adopted a hostile stance against indigenous leadership in the areas of politics and administration. The official excuses related to the anachronistic nature of indigenous leadership as opposed to the modernist-socialist agenda being fronted by the victorious revolutionists (Bhebe & Ranger, 2001). In reality, ZANU PF was still lulling from overwhelming support to the extent that it needed no political allies in the form of indigenous leaders (Ncube, 2020, p. 200). When the opposite became conspicuous, government empowered chiefs through the Traditional Leaders Act (No. 25 of 1998), which only became enforceable after the government lost a referendum to the opposition forces in February 2000 (Ncube, 2020, p. 213). To be 'empowered', indigenous leaders were forced to openly fraternise with the ruling ZANU PF, even against the constitution and their sceptres.

At independence, the chiefs' judicial powers were subsumed by government-appointed quasi-courts. Chiefs and headmen used to fighting their own battles during colonialism bulldozed their selection/election into the local courts by manipulating indigenous support structures and chauvinist support for ZANU PF. They fiercely campaigned against their relegation. They held steadfastly to the grassroots support with the result that the ruling party was not able to wrestle such support. More so, the so-called modern approach to local courts was equally peopled with the same indigenous leadership which ZANU PF intended to punish for colluding with the colonial legal and electoral processes, including places in the Rhodesia Senate. Having failed to turn around the political and administration of justice without local indigenous leadership, the nascent government had to change tact. Ordinary villagers continued to accord excessive respect to the indigenous leadership despite its past dealings with the colonial government, "for historical, cultural and existential reasons" (Nkomo, 2020, p. 154). By 1985, the government rhetoric had shifted to the return of the chiefs' powers, thawing away open hostility towards chiefs holding political sway in the majority of rural constituencies.

The government was never worried about the restoration of the powers of the indigenous leaders per se, but the voter mobilisation consequent to that move. Such self-interested attempts were matched by indigenous leadership equally unconcerned with democratic roles intrinsic to their sceptres. They were playing it for benefits, which they did not want to fall into the hands of those outside current royal genealogies. That placed them in the willing hands of politicians rather worried about the "chiefs' legitimating and mobilising capabilities in the context of waning political fortunes" (Nkomo, 2020, p. 152). The return of their powers was therefore premised on their service to the politicians, which needed to be complete and unadulterated. In that regard, the generality of the indigenous leadership did not disappoint: they "played a pivotal role in ensuring that the ZANU-PF government remains in power since 1980" (Kurebwa, 2020, p. 715)—way before any talk of the restoration of their powers. That thawed and consolidated their relations with the ruling elite, which accepted nothing short of victory. That was sardonically against the legal statutes that any chief wishing to negate the principle of neutrality by joining active politics should appoint a surrogate chief to help solve the problem of conflict of interest.

ZANU PF was not alone in courting the undivided support of indigenous leadership to remain in power. The mobilisation capabilities of chiefs were never in doubt across Africa (Ainslie & Kepe, 2015). Thus, while the independence government of Zimbabwe continued to sideline chiefs, Chief Mangwende cautioned the ruling party saying that the party would certainly come to terms with their invaluable importance despite currently living in poverty (Hansad, 1987, para. 564). When the ZANU PF government finally repented of their earlier position, the new political mantra presented chiefs as "the eyes and the ears of the government" (Herald, 1987, September 16). The chiefs chose power by colluding with the rulers who granted them lucrative incentives to turn the tables against their 'legitimate' competitors. Their roles pertained protecting the grassroots from opposition political parties and helping in the implementation of government plans (Nkomo, 2020, p. 156). They were clear to ZANU PF that "you will not win without us" (Hansad, 1998, para. 68), and of course, the relevant reply would be 'you cannot exist without us'. The ruling party decided to gradually increase the chiefs' powers, but only to the extent that they would be willing to mobilise for ZANU PF and no other political party (Chigwata, 2016). Nkomo (2021, p. 47) reiterates that "as in the colonial era, the relationship continued to be defined by the political interests and strategies of the governing regime". In that regard, indigenous leadership was revived and strengthened as a prop to up ZANU PF power and may not survive outside that pact at the moment. The need to prop up ZANU PF became more evident with the loss of the referendum in 2000. The importance of leadership collusion became more invaluable, and therefore, a separate section has been created for the period beyond 2000.

Chiefs and the Electoral Fraud Beyond 2000

This section discusses how electoral collusion was more amenable to the colonial period when indigenous leadership was used as a threat to the security of those of contrary views to state policy. Chiefs continued to be a source of fear among the rural folk from colonial times, a thing which worsened in the years following the fast-track land reform initiated in 2000 (Nkomo, 2020). What is worse is that "they have overseen violence, denied people legitimate access to resources and services, and banished villagers linked to opposition politics, among other things, on behalf of beleaguered governments" (Nkomo, 2020, p. 157). The idea has been to shut out revolutionary ideas originating in urban setups from flowing into rural communities. The trauma that went with banishments of those daring to bring such ideas into rural setups, and other sanctions associated with abuse of the indigenous sceptre is beyond imagination. Maslow's hierarchy of needs has security needs as basic and transformative. One reacts positively to the one threatening insecurity and suspension of basic needs. The carrot and stick approach superintended by the indigenous leadership has been the best cog in the rigging mechanism in favour of the ruling elite. In other words, rigging has been a process covering the whole period from one election to the other, leaving Zimbabwe in a perpetual election mood. The approach ensures that there is no lapse in 'the party' building and defence; ensuring that there is no penetration by opposition parties.

It is clear that "the state's realignment of its relations with chiefs had a political context" (Nkomo, 2020, p. 170). The chiefs had to return a giving hand by acting as the vanguard against opposition intrusion into rural setups. First, the chiefs and their subordinate administrative structures had to shun opposition politics before directing their subjects to do the same, though the incentives from government only covered the leadership from chief to village head, in diminishing order. In that regard, the rural leadership approach ran counter to the inclusive benefits approach interred in the 'holding in trust' traditions of the forefathers, the owners of the indigenous sceptre. The expectation was that one who wielded the indigenous sceptre also held wealth in trust for all in the territories covered by his authority. Unfortunately, that has not happened since the colonial era. As it stands,

> it is the political alignment of indigenous leaders with the ruling party, however, which raises significant conflicts of interest. Most indigenous leaders openly align themselves with the ruling ZANU-PF in contradiction of the Constitution which requires their non-involvement in politically related activities. (Chigwata, 2016, p. 90)

Even the reputed anti-corruption and veteran liberation icon, Edgar Tekere, failed to woo chiefs to his Zimbabwe Unity Movement (ZUM) despite the nobility of his cause and the extensive tour of Mhondoro and Manicaland communal lands (Nkomo, 2020). The failure was due to the symbiotic relationship between chiefs and government based on exclusive patronage omitting the general citizens from benefits. When chiefs encouraged farm invasions, it was more to do with individual benefits than the generality of their constituents. It is clear that those who control land also control those who benefit from it (Cabaye, 1999, p. 11). In that regard chiefs were prepared to have land as a source of more power.

The chiefs utilised their vicarious control of resources to dictate who should rule and who should not. They made philosophical arguments based on such proverbs of continuity as: *Hakuna zuva rinobuda rimwe risati radoka* (there is no sun that rises before the other one has set); *Machongwe maviri haariri pamutanda mumwe* (two cocks never crow from the same wood pedestal); and *Hakuna musha unoita machongwe maviri* (there is no home with two cocks) (Takudzwa, 2023, p. 1). As cultural pundits, they made extensive use of the proverbial lore, more suitable for indigenous leadership. In the ideal indigenous context, hereditary leadership works with councils that actually run the show with the leader only pronouncing the verdict already reached by consensus. The indigenous leader is not there to try cases per se, but to pronounce the verdict of the council on particular cases. In that case, the same decision can still be arrived at and validated even in the case of an incapacitated leader, and therefore, there is no need for appointing 'another cock' before his death. In the past, the council had to remain impartial because it still had to contend with the spirit mediums, whose focus was on justice and the sanctity of life (Dube, 2018). For that reason, it was not possible to have a new leader while the other one was still alive. Death signified by the setting sun ushered in new leadership in normal cases. One had to leave through death or misdemeanour for which the voice of the ancestors was prominent. In the case of death, the sun will have 'set', and the reigning cock would have left space for the new one. The proverbs became more rampant in the last days of the nonagenarian, Robert Mugabe, Zimbabwe's long-time ruler. The idea was that there was no vacancy in the presidency and the opposition was to call off their campaign in the rural areas. In fact, they were unwelcome in their capacity as the 'intransigent new cock' sardonically crowing in competition to the 'old cock'. The same is true with the octogenarian incumbent, President Emmerson Mnangagwa, for whom the Citizens Coalition for Change (CCC) should give space by not seeking to 'crow' from the same pedestal (competing for leadership). This indigenous stance will continue to determine the indigenous leaders' standard in any election unless they are sanctioned by a competent court under an impartial administration.

The adage goes, "Without the approval of the elder council, a traditional leader was powerless as he neither could pass any legislation nor make political decisions" (Dusing, 2001, p. 77). The chiefs, headmen and village heads have equated such a leader whose decision was clearly corporate to the current elected head of state who has legislative and executive authority—able to ignore parliament and the judiciary with impunity. The anachronistic interpretations of the presidency as equivalent to the role of indigenous leadership have led chiefs and their subordinate structures to campaign for political leaders whom they see as their larger image. The conditions of the indigenous leadership are not replicated in the Zimbabwean presidency, though indigenous leadership marry such presidency to indigenous proverbs. In the former, real authority was vested in the council, while in the latter it is vested in the president. While the council could chastise the chief, the cabinet can only do the same to the president in theory. Sadly, the current chief, like the president, can override the council, scuttling grassroots democracy in matters pertaining to national politics. The overarching hand of the president, featuring like a colossus, dwarfing every other centre of authority has attracted all those interested in more vicarious power. Of course, nobody is forced to be an indigenous leader, but to be one, the incumbent must meet a certain disposition in favour of the ruling party. That means an openly pro-opposition member may not ascend the throne. It also takes a lot of meritable courage to resist the conditional perks that go with the posts. Some of these are discussed below.

Conditional Perks Impelling Indigenous Leadership to Dice with Democracy

This section analyses some of the conditional perks afforded indigenous leadership, in order to buy its loyalty. In general, chiefs, headmen and village heads have found the perks too lucrative to resist. Both colonial and post-independence governments availed an array of perks for those vetted to be compliant with the system. To be an indigenous leader across the divide, one had to be vetted to the satisfaction of the appointing authority—the current government through some statutory instrument. Those openly opposed to the ruling party were not tolerated. For example,

> Chief Makuvise of Buhera was stripped of his indigenous regalia, humiliated before his subjects and murdered in broad daylight for supporting the MDC. One of his sons reported that the chieftaincy has since been given to a member of the next family who supported the ruling party. (Makahamadze et al., 2009, p. 43)

The first advantage was for the indigenous leader to be seeded above the rest, which for the colonial government meant that an indigenous leader was the sole consultant on African affairs. Consulting the indigenous leader was 'consulting all'. As a result, some indigenous leaders openly loathed and castigated the one-man-one-vote being advanced by the revolutionary parties (The Voice of the Tribes, 1968). That, notwithstanding such democratic stalwarts as Rekai Tangwena, Chief Mangwende and Chief Chiweshe, stood with their people even at the peril of death (Martin and Johnson, 1981; Moore, 2005). These and others in the minority fought for one-man-one-vote, while the rest stood for consultative democracy, with themselves as the sole consultants enjoying mediatory roles as agents of the establishments. Jocelyn Alexander (2018, p. 1) distinguishes the two groups more succinctly thus:

> Some chiefs became outspoken opponents of the Rhodesian state, making common cause with nationalism. A small number made their way to the guerrilla camps in Zambia and Mozambique. Others went on state-sponsored tours of empire, robed in invented costumes and embodying newly created institutions and constituencies.

Those who distanced themselves from individual representation through the ballot, failed to go back to the pre-colonial period where consultative democracy could apply through the *dare/idale* (Dube, 2018). Instead, the *dare/idale* system ceased to be relevant as the chief became the personification of "All of You" (Achebe, 1958). Plausibly, despite their own ego, the chiefs had hard choices to make during the Second Chimurenga (liberation war) because of the contending colonial and liberation forces (Ndawana & Hove, 2018, p. 119). The colonial regime was bent on improving personal perks for chiefs and headmen to prevent them from partaking in the liberation struggle, while the liberation forces were bent on including all Africans in the liberation agenda.

The second perk by both governments was putting in place a separate electoral college for sending chiefs to the senate. This set them apart from the rest of the society. Although representatives of the chiefs in the senate were not always docile, playing to the whims of the regime, they did not reject their representative status as speaking for the people. Quite often, however, they remained self-interested; firmly believing that they could achieve much more than the rest of the population combined. This is why Senator Chief Mangwende criticised ZANU PF for its reliance on the masses rather than chiefs. He reacted to the ruling party's approach with a threat, noting that "sooner or later, you will hunt for us in our little huts" (Hansad, 1987, para. 564). Chief Naboth Makoni added in the following year: "you will not win without us" (Hansad, 1998, para. 68). The chiefs used these policy-making forums for honorific purposes, to lobby for more power over their indigenous constituencies. Their resilient autocratic stimuli remained intact since colonial times. Fortune Charumbira, the president of the Chiefs' Council, was even more arrogant; stating that "We [chiefs] own ZANU PF" (Centre for Innovation and Technology [CITE], 2021). ZANU PF being their project, chiefs were therefore called upon to openly fraternise with it, well-knowing that it is against the country's constitution (Constitution of Zimbabwe 2013, Sect. 281 [2]). Charumbira has had to be reprimanded by the courts, with no visible sanction from ZANU PF leadership and government.

Then the provision of infrastructure and amenities for compliant chiefs was added to the perks. Chiefs in deep rural areas, where modern accommodation and amenities were scarce had modern houses constructed for them by the government through the Ministry of Rural Housing (Makahamadze et al., 2009, p. 41). Electricity and water reticulation were connected to the houses, drastically shifting the social status of many rural chiefs. They were made 'lords' of their societies. They took charge of the distribution of government aid to communities, spreading the news of such aid as originating from the party. In doing that, they were defending their perks which gave them a higher standing in society. In addition, transport for chiefs was availed ahead of the crunch 2008 election, in which many claimed a Morgan Tsvangirai victory over the ZANU PF candidate, Robert Mugabe. The chiefs were given double cab vehicles and government-paid chauffeurs where the incumbents could not drive. Fuel was at government's expense. The relevant roads to chiefs' homesteads were upgraded. Indigenous leadership also "benefited from the Land Reform Programme and the Farm Mechanisation Programme. Some of them now own vast tracks of land which they cannot even use effectively. Through the latter programme, they received tractors, seeds, ploughs, carts and fertilizers" (Makahamadze et al., 2009, p. 41). All these helped to tether them to ZANU PF whims in any election in the foreseeable future.

The volatile late 1990s saw a drastic increase in the perks for indigenous leaders. In 1999, remunerations for indigenous leaders were drastically increased, accompanied by the unusual apology from President Mugabe over the sidelining of chiefs since independence in 1980 (Ranger, 2001). The chiefs' monthly allowances were increased from Z$2,083 to Z$10,000 [USD335.43 to USD1610.31], and that of headmen from Z$680 to Z$5,000 [USD109.50 to USD805.15] (LikeForex.com, 2023; Ranger, 2001). The jump was so enticing, forcing the indigenous leadership to tackle Tsvangirai and the Movement for Democratic Change (MDC) by the 'horns'. Chiefs and headmen had to defend their allowances by standing stiffly in the way of democracy, by being openly partisans. They threatened those who thought otherwise, with death or expulsion. The threats had nothing to do with the defence of the masses, but strictly for personal gain, attributed to patronage by senior politicians wanting to hold onto power by any means possible.

The final perk, associated with such patronage, relates to immunity from arrests for threatening or visiting subjects with violence, including refusal of burials for opposition members. Some bereaved relatives were fined by the indigenous leaders before they could bury their dead in their normal areas of domicile (Makahamadze et al., 2009, p. 42). Such violence against the dead is worthy of prosecution, but the culprits go unpunished because they are on the 'correct side' of the law—in support of the ruling elite. To receive food and inputs, ZANU PF membership cards were required. Some chiefs in Muzarabani, Buhera, Nyanga and Bikita were implicated in the murders of MDC members, which became dynamites hanging from their necks should they desist from openly advancing ZANU PF causes. Because of the lucrative perks, indigenous leaders went into over-drive, sanctioning the confiscation of livestock from MDC members to be eaten at ZANU PF repentance camps in 2008 (Ibid, p. 42). This drove those of chicken hearts and those of limited means to confess before rejoining ZANU PF, to save wealth and to receive food handouts and farm inputs. Lessons from the past were painful; "Chiefs Ziki and Sengwe of Chiredzi districts in Masvingo province had their monthly allowances withdrawn for backing the MDC-T party in the run-up to 2008 harmonised elections" (Kurebwa, 2018, p. 11). Punishments matted on those correctly utilising their sceptres throw doubt on indigenous leadership standing for the common good in the 2023 harmonised elections as discussed below.

Prospects for a Neutral Indigenous Leadership in the 2023 Elections

There are no signs that political patronage and the love for personal gain by indigenous leaders are on the wane. There is, therefore, no reason to dream of a positive pro-democracy involvement of chiefs, headmen and village heads in the 2023 harmonised elections. Most rural areas are still regarded as no-go areas for the opposition CCC. That has been the same with the MDC since 2000. Constitutional restrictions have never been invoked for those indigenous leaders who openly support ZANU PF, and there is no sign in the recent years that they will be brought to order (Ndoma, 2021). Court verdicts in relation to the conduct of indigenous leaders campaigning for the ruling party during elections have not been openly seen to be complied with (CITE, 2021). A 2018 High Court verdict banned all indigenous leaders from engaging in active politics in support of any political party, but chiefs were still present at the ZANU PF congress four years later. The Afrobarometer estimates their influence on the rural vote at about fifty per cent and that "almost three-quarters (72%) want indigenous leaders to stay out of politics and let people decide for themselves how to vote" (Ndoma, 2021, p. 2). The wish to have them out of politics, however, remains a pipe dream as no one in the echelons of power appears prepared to vary their 'life-and-death' marriage with the ruling party.

It is quite evident that the institution of indigenous leadership was revived largely "to implement technocratic edicts [and] or enforce partisan loyalties" (Alexander, 2018, p. 2). Outside these mandates, the institution has no political will. Its cultural value/role is more cosmetic, meant as a smokescreen to portray politicians as lovers and protectors of indigenous cultural norms and institutions. The fronting of tradition by politicians tallies very well with indigenous leaders' "interests in wealth and office" (Alexander, 2018, p. 2). Both politicians and indigenous leaders have interests to serve apart from what appears on the surface. In other words, chiefs, headmen and village heads are equally not focused on pristine indigenous democracies, which affect their colleagues in politics adversely, risking their own lucrative posts. Moreover, some of those chiefs who think that their indigenous powers are linked to territory believe that the departure of ZANU PF in a democratic election may mean the return of the land restituted through the Fast Track Land Reform. They hold on to the ruling party as a way of salvaging their own power.

The second scenario is that ZANU PF wins despite their support. In such a case, they risk their roles being reverted to the 1980s, when elected village development committees, ward development committees and court presiding officers assumed their various roles in development, administration and judiciary (Alexander, 2018). Their ego was more visible in cases where they were excluded through elections to these new bodies altogether, leading to total emasculation. They ranted and raved that the elections were not free and fair, but once in, they fought to have the same powers through the restoration of indigenous leadership in which there were fewer contestants—only of royal families. They argued that traditionally elected courts were stealing their birthright as the sole local rulers (Ncube, 2020). In many cases, situations became unbearable until spaces were created for them on the elected benches. To date, they are still worried about these powers to the extent that they are prepared to bury their pre-colonial partner—the spirit medium—for the sake of personal power. In that case, they still cannot be trusted with a positive role in the 2023 crunch election.

More so, indigenous leaders are certainly being watched to ensure that they live to their expectations of "political mobilization, surveillance and punishment" of non-compliant members of their communities (Alexander, 2018, p. 16). This is why Chief Fortune Charumbira, the president of the chiefs' council, continues to stress that all chiefs must openly support ZANU PF even in contravention of the supreme law of the land—the Constitution of Zimbabwe. Recently, elderly citizens from Murehwa rural were thoroughly beaten by the alleged ZANU PF militia (Bwanya, 2023), and no word of solidarity with the victims has come from the chiefs. Instead, the fact that "they are respected leaders in their communities" presents them with room for self-actualisation unperturbed (Kurebwa, 2018, p. 1). They manipulate respect as an honorific reason to be listened to in all matters. They assume the indigenous godfatherly figure whose consensus word was law; except that the pristine father figure was consultative and well-meaning. The current one is selfish and materialistic. Such tendencies prey on the fact that indigenous rule is the most acceptable form of governance among the rural folk (Kurebwa, 2018, p. 2). In the absence of a sanction, the indigenous leadership shall continue to abuse Sect. 45 (2) of the Traditional Leaders Act, which states that:

> No chief, headmen or village head shall canvass, serve as an election agent, or nominate any candidate for election as a state President, Member of Parliament or Councillor in any local authority whilst still holding office as Chief, headman or village head.

The Nyikayaramba syndrome is still prevalent. The Zimbabwe National Army Brigadier-General (now [late] Major-General) Douglas Nyikayaramba formerly of 3 Brigade in Manicaland Province summoned 200 indigenous leaders from the province to a 'workshop' at the army barracks during which they were told to prevent members of the main opposition party, MDC-T, from campaigning and receiving agricultural inputs from the government (Kurebwa, 2018, p. 11).

Currently, indigenous leaders and civil servants are being mobilised from across Zimbabwe to attend the Herbert Chitepo School of ideology at an army barrack at Dadaya, west of Zvishavane town. State security continues the Nyikayaramba oversight over indigenous leadership, and it may be risky to act otherwise. This is especially because the government has faith in the effectiveness of the hierarchical nature of indigenous authority. It is the hierarchical role of indigenous leaders which raises constitutional questions without answers (Chigwata, 2016, p. 69). Politicians maximise the use of these willing and/or squashed rulers who control nearly seventy per cent of Zimbabwe's (rural) population, with some living in areas scarcely in effective government control. The strategic alliance between indigenous authorities and ZANU PF has resulted in chiefs in parliament always voting with ZANU PF, besides "rallying rural constituencies as vote banks for the ruling party in the elections" (Ncube, 2020, p. 215). This chiefly representation with Western secular underpinnings has departed from the African perspectives and there is no indication the chiefs are prepared to get to the original African institution with mediums and African spirituality (Chakunda & Chikerema, 2014, p. 74). To worsen the situation, an executive president appoints a chief; the minister appoints the headmen; and the permanent secretary appoints village heads nominated by the chief. All this is done according to the Traditional Leaders Act, 2007, which allows for their removal if that satisfies the political appointing authority. As it is, the worst crime is supporting anyone else other than the appointing authority (Kurebwa, 2018, p. 11). In all this, there is no hope for a neutral indigenous leadership in the 2023 harmonised elections. As a precursor to the 2023 harmonised elections, violence was reported in several rural by-election constituencies in 2022, followed by muted indigenous leadership (Garusa, 2022). This is a pointer to the fact that they will remain blind to violence orchestrated by ZANU PF on its legitimate competitors.

Conclusion

The foregoing has demonstrated that indigenous leadership headed by chiefs metamorphosed with the change of the appointing authority. It shed its links with African spirituality and procedure by creating new synergies with secular authorities. Though they still assume hereditary posts of chief, headman and village head, they do not act on indigenous consensus to save lives in a democracy. The introduction of the payroll and other perks has turned chiefs and their subordinate structures into anti-democracy stumbling blocks with mercenary characteristics. During the colonial period, they supported programmes that defeated the nationalist ethos of one-man-one-vote. The majority of the chiefs were visibly willing to move around, masquerading as spokespersons of their communities, pretending that all was well. They voted for representative democracy in which the chief spoke for all, alienating the whole society by misrepresenting it. After independence in 1980, they became so partisan to the extent of killing, maiming, expelling and fining opposition members on behalf of ZANU PF. They sealed off the rural areas from opposition parties as a way of attaining and defending lucrative perks from the government. They have been vocally on record that every chief must campaign and vote for ZANU PF. Chiefs in the senate have always voted with ZANU PF, and there is no sign that this is on the wane. Complaints about being excluded from receiving food aid as punishment for belonging to opposition parties are already rampant in the run-up to the harmonised 2023 elections. The minority canvassing for change has often been publicly humiliated, with perks being withdrawn at the least. Overall, the current mode of chieftainship is a ZANU PF project that may be withdrawn at the president's pleasure. In reality, the vetting that goes into appointment does not leave room for neutrality, leaving no hope for a neutral indigenous leadership in the 2023 harmonised elections. It may be worthwhile, however, to interrogate the voices of the elderly now visible in the opposition CCC, to see whether this signifies a wind of change in the senior citizenry.

References

Achebe, C. (1958). *Things fall apart*. Heinemann.

Ainslie, A., & Kepe, T. (2015). Understanding the resurgence of traditional authorities in post-apartheid South Africa. *Journal of Southern African Studies*, 42(1), 1–14.

Alexander, J. (2018). *The politics of states and chiefs in Zimbabwe*. University of Oxford Press.

Arora, S. C. (2007). Responsible and responsive bureaucracy. *Indian Journal of public Administration*, 53(2), 1-15.

Bhebe, N. & Ranger, T. (2001). Introduction. In N. Bhebe & T. Ranger (Eds.), *The historical dimensions of democracy and human rights in Zimbabwe, Volume One: Pre-colonial and colonial legacies* (pp. i–xxix). The University of Zimbabwe Publications.

Bishi, G. (2015). *The colonial archive and contemporary chieftainship claims: The case of Zimbabwe, 1935 To 2014*. The University of the Free State.

Bwanya, M. (2023, January 7). Harrowing video captures Zanu PF thugs flogging elderly CCC supporters. *ZimLive*. https://www.zimlive.com/graphic-footage-captures-zanu-pf-militia-flogging-elderly-ccc-supporters/

Cabaye, E. (1999). Land use in eastern Cameroon. Yaounde: Institute of Natural Resource Policy.

Chakunda, V., & Chikerema, A. F. (2014). Indigenisation of democracy: Harnessing traditional leadership in promoting democratic values in Zimbabwe. *Journal of Power Politics and Governance*, 2(1), 67–78.

Chigwata, T. C. (2016). The role of traditional leaders in Zimbabwe: Are they still relevant? *Law, Democracy and Development*, 20(1), 69. https://doi.org/10.4314/ldd.v20i1.4

CITE. (2021, Novermber1). High Court must punish Charumbira for continued ZANU PF Support: Ndiweni. *Centre For Innovation and Technology.* https://cite.org.zw/high-court-must-punish-charumbira-for-continued-zanu-pf-support-ndiweni/

Daneel, M. L. (1971). Old and new in southern shona independent Churches 1.

David, M. & Johnson, P. (1981). *The struggle for Zimbabwe: The chimurenga war.* Faber and Faber.

Dube, E. (2018). The search for justice and peace: Reflections on the *jambanja* discourse as an articulation of justice foreshadowing peace. In E. Masitera & F. Sibanda (Eds.), *Power in Contemporary Zimbabwe* (pp. 15–30). Routledge.

Dusing, S. (2001). *Traditional leadership and democratisation in Southern Africa: A comparative study of Botswana, Namibia and South Africa.* Transaction Publishers.

Foundation for Human Rights Initiative. (2004).Uganda: A situation of systematic violations of civil and political rights. *Alternative report to the government of Uganda's first periodic report before the United Nations human rights committee.* Retrieved from http://www.refworld.org/pdfid/46f1469c0.pdf

Garusa. T. (2022, August 26). Gokwe violence: Police urged to investigate and hold to account suspected ZANU PF thugs who assaulted journalists. *New Zimbabwe.* Retrieved from https://www.newzimbabwe.com/gokwe-violence-police-urged-to-investigate-and-hold-to-account-suspected-zanu-pf-thugs-who-assaulted-journalists/

Goundar, S. (2012). *Research methodology and research method: Methods commonly used by researchers.* Victoria University of Wellington.

Green, E. (2011). The political economy of nation formation in modern Tanzania: Explaining stability in the face of diversity. *Commonwealth and Comparative Politics, 49*(2), 223–244. https://doi.org/10.1080/14662043.2011.564474

Gwaravanda, E. T. (2018). Epistemic injustice and Shona indigenous conceptions of political power. In E. Masitera & F. Sibanda (Eds.), *Power in Contemporary Zimbabwe* (pp. 56–70). Routledge.

Hansad, (1987, September 9). Chief Jonathan Mangwende. *Parliamentary debates*, para. 564.

Hansad. (1998, July 30). Chief Naboth Makoni. *Parliamentary debates*, para. 68.

The Herald (1987, September 16). Chiefs—Enos Nkala.

Karekwaivenane, G. H. (2017). Customising justice and constructing subjects: State, 'customary law' and chiefs' courts, 1950–1980. *The struggle over state power in Zimbabwe: Law and politics since 1950* (pp. 47 – 80). Cambridge University Press. https://doi.org/10.1017/9781316996898.003

Kurebwa, J. (2020). The institution of traditional leadership and local governance in Zimbabwe. *African studies: Breakthroughs in research and practice.* IGI

Global, 715–732. https://doi.org/10.4018/978-1-7998-3019-1.ch038Abstract

Kurebwa, J. (2018). The institution of traditional leadership and local governance in Zimbabwe. *International Journal of Civic Engagement and Social Change*, 5(1), 1–18. https://doi.org/10.4018/IJCESC.2018010101

LikeForex.com. (2023). 1999 Zimbabwe Dollar to US Dollar, 1999 ZWL to USD Currency Converter. https://www.likeforex.com/currency-converter/zimbabwe-dollar-zwl_usd-us-dollar.htm/1999

Makahamadze, T., Grand, N., & Tavuyanago, B. (2009). The role of traditional leaders in fostering democracy, justice and human rights in Zimbabwe. *African Anthropologist*, 16(1), 33–47.

Martin, D., & Johnson, P. (1981). *The Struggle for Zimbabwe: The Chimurenga War*. Faber & Faber.

Matsuhira, Y. (2013). Rain making ceremony in the Nyandoro region, Zimbabwe. *African Religious Dynamics*, 1, 165–182.

Moore, D. S. (2005). *Suffering for territory: Race, place, and power in Zimbabwe*. Weaver Press.

Ncube, G. (2020). *A comparative study of the politics of chieftaincy and local government in colonial and postcolonial Zimbabwe, 1950–2010*. The University of South Africa.

Ndawana, E., & Hove, M. (2018). Traditional leaders and Zimbabwe's liberation struggle in Buhera District, 1976–1980. *Journal of African Military History*, 2, 119–160.

Ndoma, S. (2021, August 3). Zimbabweans see traditional leaders as influential but want them to stay out of politics. Afrobarometer Dispatch No. 469. Retrieved from https://www.afrobarometer.org/wp-content/uploads/2022/02/ad469-zimbabweans

Nkomo, L. (2020). Winds of small change: Chiefs, chiefly powers, evolving politics and the state in Zimbabwe, 1985–1999. *Southern Journal for Contemporary History*, 45(2), 152–180. https://doi.org/10.18820/24150509/SJCH45.v2.7

Nkomo, L. (2021). The small matter of sellouts: Chiefs, history, politics, and the state at Zimbabwe's independence, 1980–1985. *African Historical Review*, 52(1), 47–71. https://doi.org/10.1080/17532523.2022.2047283

O'Meara, P. (2019). The past in the present: Chiefs in Rhodesia. *Rhodesia*. Cornell University Press. Retrieved from https://www.degruyter.com/document/doi/https://doi.org/10.7591/9781501744723-008/pdf

Ranger, O. T. (2001). Democracy and traditional political structures in Zimbabwe 1890–1999. In N. Bhebe & T. Ranger (Eds.), *The historical dimensions of democracy and human rights in Zimbabwe: Pre-colonial and colonial legacies*, 1 (pp. 31–52). The University of Zimbabwe Publications.

Schoffeleers, J. M. (Ed.), (1979). *Guardians of the land*. Mambo Press.

Sileyew, K. J. (2019). Research design and methodology. *ItechOpen*. https://doi.org/10.5772/intechopen.85731

Takudzwa T. (2023). Shona Proverbs Association. British Council IELTS. https://studylib.net/doc/25679407/shona-proverbs-ass

The Voice of the Tribes. (1968). *Rhodesia's Chiefs*. https://www.rhodesia.me.uk/voice-of-the-tribes/

van Nieuwaal, A. (1996). States and chiefs: Are chiefs mere puppets? *Journal of Legal Pluralism, 28*(37), 39–78.

Walliman, N. (2011). *Research methods: The basics*. Routledge.

CHAPTER 21

Traditional Leaders, Electoral Politics and Impregnability of the Rural Constituency in Zimbabwe

Pedzisai Ruhanya and Bekezela Gumbo

INTRODUCTION

This chapter examines the role of traditional leaders in the electoral impregnability of the rural constituency in Zimbabwe. The main research question is: Why has it been so difficult to achieve political transition in Zimbabwe using competitive elections as a medium of transition? This study conceptualises electoral impregnability to mean the difficulty encountered by a contesting opponent to unseat the incumbent in an election in a given constituency. Thus, electoral impregnability of the rural constituency as used in this study refers to electoral impregnability of those constituencies that are outside urban areas of Zimbabwe. Electoral impregnability exists where above 50% of the total valid votes cast were needed by the opposition to surpass votes given to the incumbent in a previous general election.

P. Ruhanya (✉) · B. Gumbo
Harare, Zimbabwe
e-mail: pruhanya@gmail.com

© The Author(s), under exclusive license to Springer Nature Switzerland AG 2023
E. Mavengano and S. Chirongoma (eds.), *Electoral Politics in Zimbabwe, Vol II*, https://doi.org/10.1007/978-3-031-33796-3_21

The chapter is organised into three thematic sections. The first section examines the theoretical and empirical background literature undergirding this study. This first section begins with a summary review of basic principles that enable political transition via elections. It then analyses agency theoretical and empirical literature to explain the background institutional designs that have influenced the conduct of traditional leaders in electoral politics vis-a-vis the identified basic principles that enable political transition through elections. The second section investigates the state of electoral impregnability in the rural constituency in Zimbabwe. This section reviews electoral outcomes of the past legislative elections since 2000 and brings out key observations that single out the traditional leaders and their relationships with the ruling elite as a sufficient condition determining electoral impregnability of the rural constituency. The third section interrogates how the capture of traditional leaders and attendant impregnability of the rural constituency has been institutionally designed.

Background Literature: Agency Theory and Transitology Literature

This chapter categorises background literature explaining the role of traditional leaders in electoral politics and attendant electoral impregnability of the rural constituency in Zimbabwe into two main topics. First is the agency theory of political transition whereas the second presents the three transitology schools of thought explaining political transition in Zimbabwe.

The Agency Theory of Political Transition

This study uses agency theory of transition to examine the role of traditional leaders in electoral and transition politics in Zimbabwe. The underlying argument in the agency theory within transitology studies is that political change is determined by political elites' deliberate acts of commission or omission who are willing to compromise to achieve an end (Grugel, 2002). Agency perspectives posit that transition does not depend on structural context but relies on the ruling elite and business actors who create it—their commitment and willingness to initiate, institutionalise and accomplish the transition (Grugel, 2002). Rustow, one of the leading proponents of the agency theory posited that transition to democracy, is a dynamic process created by conscious actors through a "prolonged and inclusive political struggle" involving committed majorities of citizens (Rustow, 1970, pp. 350–352). O'Donnell et al. (1986) emphasised the study of pacts, interactions, bargains, authoritarian leaders and democracy promoters. These negotiations and pacts are what Rustow (1970) conceived as the preparation and decision stage by elites which are important foundations of transition. The role of traditional leaders in Zimbabwe's electoral politics and their relationships with the ruling elite cannot be ignored in transitology.

Political transition that uses elections as its medium relies on the elites' creation and institutionalisation of at least three basic democratic principles. First is free flow of contesting political narratives through which the voter gets informed to make his/her decision in the ballot box (Dahl, 1971; O'Donnell et al., 1986; Schumpeter, 1950). This includes fair state media coverage of contending candidates, accessible private media, civil society organisation and political parties freely conduct civic education and voter education work. Second principle is free association and assembly by competing parties (Dahl, 1971; O'Donnell et al., 1986; Schumpeter, 1950). This includes the presence of institutions that enable voter mobilisation activities and equal access to the constituency for political mobilisation. Third is the presence of a fair legal and institutional environment involved in voting, vote counting and announcement of results (Cox, 2007; Diamond, 2002; Howard & Roessler, 2006; Merkel, 2004; Ottaway, 2003). This last principle deals more with the independence of electoral management bodies. These three create the minimum requirements for political transition to be possible through elections at constituency level. A limitation in these conditions makes the constituency electorally impregnable. The role of traditional leaders in electoral politics in Zimbabwe is examined in relation to the extent of these three basic principles of democratic elections as an analytical framework.

Three Transitology Schools of Thought

There are three identifiable transitology schools of thought in the background literature that use the agency theory to explain the main factors hindering Zimbabwe's political transition using elections as a medium. First are studies that point to the competitive authoritarian regime that capture the legislature, judiciary, the media and the electoral arena and use these institutions to manipulate electoral outcomes and ensure the opposition always loses (Bogaards & Elischer, 2016; Carothers, 2018; Cox, 2007; Diamond, 2002; Howard & Roessler, 2006; Levystky & Way, 2002, 2010; Mainwaring, 2012; Schedler, 2002, 2006; Yardımcı-Geyikçi, 2020). This group of studies locate Zimbabwe in the competitive authoritarian regimes category where elections without democracy are held to maintain the ruling party in power and make opposition defeat certain before elections are counted. Competition is, thus, real but blatantly unfair (Levitsky & Way, 2010; Mainwaring, 2012; Matti, 2010). Evidence from Zimbabwe's electoral history presented in Appendix 1.1 confirms these observations. However, this school of thought does not explain the defiant electoral victory of the opposition in urban constituencies and dismal performance in rural constituencies of Zimbabwe and the role of the relationships between the ruling elite, the military and the captured institutions.

The second school of thought comprises studies that point to the conflation of the ruling party, the state and the military which has resulted in the militarisation of elections, electoral violence and attendant election manipulation to keep the ruling party in power (Mandaza, 2016; Masunungure, 2011; Masunungure & Bratton, 2008; Moyo, 2014; Ndlovu-Gatsheni, 2006; Rupiya, 2005; Tendi, 2013). These studies emphasised the subservice of the military and all other institutions to the ruling party in electoral politics. This has been challenged by empirical evidence where the military removed the ruling elite from power through the November 2017 coup détat and replaced them with its members and allies. This development revealed the subservience of the ruling party and all other state institutions to the military elite who play a decisive role in political transitions in Zimbabwe (Gumbo & Ruhanya, 2022). This leads to the third group of studies that point to the securocratic state problem, a political system wherein the military elite capture the ruling party, populate it with their members and allies and then deploy it to infiltrate state institutions that administer electoral politics.

The third group of transitology studies in Zimbabwe, building on the former two groups of studies, pointed to the decisive role of the military that has infiltrated and captured key state institutions responsible for ensuring political transition through democratic elections and used then to ensure ZANU PF wins (Gumbo & Ruhanya, 2022; Maringira, 2017, 2021; Ndawana, 2020; Ruhanya, 2020; Zimbabwe Democracy Institute [ZDI], 2017). In a securocratic state, all features of a competitive authoritarian regime identified by the first group of studies exist within a framework of a government whereby the military elite plays a decisive role in transition and electoral politics (Gumbo & Ruhanya, 2022). The military elites infiltrate and capture the ruling party in addition to the judiciary, legislature, electoral process and media and deploy these institutions to effect its direct and indirect direction of the political economy of the nation-state (Gumbo & Ruhanya, 2022; Ruhanya, 2020; ZDI, 2017). This study associates with this conceptual perspective in terms of identifying the role of traditional leaders in the rural constituency impregnability problem and attendant electoral politics.

In sync with the securocratic state school of thought, this chapter observes that, for three times in history, the military elites have played a decisive role in determining political transition in Zimbabwe. The first being the 1975 Mgagao Declaration where Zimbabwe African National Liberation Army (ZANLA) a military wing of ZANU party assisted the late President Mugabe to depose then leader of ZANU Ndabaningi Sithole (Chung, 2006; Riley, 1982; ZDI, 2017). This was the most important period in history because the military elite from this point onward begun to determine who leads Zimbabwe and how the leader ensures inclusion of the military in state institutions. The second interference was the 1983–1987 Gukurahundi massacre of opposition Zimbabwe African Peoples Union (ZAPU) supporters to support a one-party state ideology of their chosen ZANU leader Mugabe (Catholic Commission for Justice and Peace [CCJP] 7Legal Resources Foundation [LRF], 1999; Stauffer, 2009). This epoch saw the metamorphosis of a what was conceptually defined as a de facto one-party state that legally allowed multipartyism but in practice, did not tolerate opposition and used coercion as a mobilisation strategy during elections to maintain a one-party dominant political; system (Mandaza & Sachikonye, 1991; Sachikonye, 1990). Opposition parties such as ZAPU in 1980–1987 and the Zimbabwe Unity Movement (ZUM) in 1990 were allowed to contest but subjected to electoral violence and unfair electoral processes that made the victory of the ruling party very certain (Laakso, 2003; Sachikonye, 1990).

The third instance was the June 2008 presidential rerun election where the military elites deployed the army in all provinces of Zimbabwe to unleash violence against opposition supporters in a bid to ensure re-election of ZANU PF candidate Robert Mugabe who had lost the first round of elections to the opposition leader Morgan Tsvangirai (Masunungure, 2011). This epoch saw Zimbabwe's transition to democracy via elections being barred. The last intervention to save ZANU PF from self-destruction was seen in November 2017 when the military elite deployed the army to wage a military coup d'état against the then President Robert Mugabe and the faction of ZANU PF linked to his wife and replaced them with President Mnangagwa as a faction of ZANU PF linked to him (Gumbo & Ruhanya, 2022). This was a critical juncture for political transition that was captured and determined by the military elite and a securocratic state was reinstalled. Read together, the two groups of studies highlight two common issues that the electoral environment has for years failed to pass the test of minimum standards for democratic elections. They also concur that the ruling elites in Zimbabwe have created and institutionalised conditions that inhibit the possibility of political transition via elections.

On the contrary, parliamentary elections have proven to be less susceptible to the conditioning capacity of the competitive authoritarian regime and its menu of electoral manipulation. Two key observations corroborate this claim. Firstly, the opposition has managed to win most of the legislative and local authority elections in urban areas and some rural areas since year 2000. Secondly, where the opposition has lost legislative and local authority elections, there have been very few cases of disputed results since 2000. This raises two key implications on findings of previous studies reviewed above. First being that the capture of democratic and electoral institutions to ensure victory of the ruling elite applies to presidential elections but not legislative and local authority elections in Zimbabwe. Second being that the ruling elite prioritises capture of the presidential election since it serves as the means to the highest office and control of state machinery and leaves the legislative election open to electoral uncertainty.

Another observation is that the ruling party continues to lose votes in the urban constituency and maintains a stronghold in the rural constituency. In addition to the factors identified in existing studies reviewed above, an additional factor, unique to the rural constituency buttressing ruling elites' victory, is perceivable—the traditional leaders. Although background literature correctly identified key constituents of the problem, they did not bring the pieces together into a schematic framework that can explain the ruling elite's electoral performance variations between urban and rural constituencies. The rural vote has been very instrumental in defining the winner and attendant election-based transition trajectory in Zimbabwe. Therefore, this chapter creates a nuanced conceptualisation of the problem bedevilling elections as a medium of political transition in Zimbabwe. It combines constituents of the problem identified in background literature to produce a new explanatory thesis that Zimbabwe's political transition has been hindered by electoral impregnability of the rural constituency where traditional leaders exercise their influence.

ELECTORAL IMPREGNABILITY PROBLEM IN THE RURAL CONSTITUENCY

A common observation from a comparative analysis of legislative elections in the 2000–2005 electoral cycle, 2005–2008 electoral cycle, 2008–2013 electoral cycle and 2013–2018 electoral cycle has been that the ruling ZANU PF party has always won the rural constituency unlike urban constituencies that have been won by the opposition. This ZANU PF consistent victory in the rural constituency has defied the corrosive impacts of economic decline and elite dis-cohesion believed by previous studies to lead to the defeat of the ruling elite. Previous studies have shown that ruling elites usually lose elections: (i) when they go to elections with internal factional conflicts (Geddes, 2005; O'Donnell et al., 1986; Schedler, 2010) or (ii) when they go to elections with a bad record of economic decline (Duch & Stevenson, 2008; Hellwig, 2010; Lewis-Beck & Stegmaier, 2000, 2007). Although these studies concede that there are some determinants of electoral outcomes, the state of the economy and elite dis-cohesion have proven to be among the most important determinants. Figure 21.1 gives an analytical presentation of the defiant impregnability of the rural constituency since 2000 in Zimbabwe. To determine electoral impregnability percentage of the rural constituency per province, this study calculated the opposition's margin of loss vis-à-vis ZANU PF at a given constituency calculated as a percentage of total valid votes cast at that constituency plus 1%, then the average percentage of all sampled rural constituencies in each province was used to get the provincial percentage. This gives the estimated percentage vote needed by the opposition to defeat ZANU PF in the rural constituency in each province.

As shown above, two times in electoral history of Zimbabwe since 2000, ZANU PF entered the electoral race deeply divided (66%). First was the 2008 election wherein ZANU PF was divided between elites associated with the late retired General Mujuru and the late President

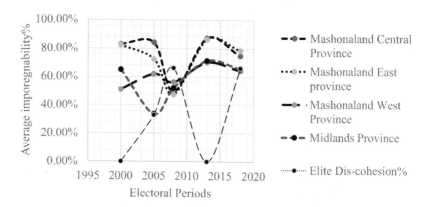

Fig. 21.1 Elite dis-cohesion vs. electoral impregnability (*Source* Author's analysis of ZEC election statistics in Appendices 1.2 and 1.3)

Robert Mugabe. Supporters of the former made what was known as a "bhora musango" campaign which means "kicking the ball into the bush, a euphemism for swaying the vote to the opposition" which resulted in many citizens in sampled areas voting against ZANU PF to the benefit of the opposition. The second instance was 2018 where ZANU PF entered the electoral race divided between the supporters of the late President Mugabe and supporters of current President Mnangagwa. Although findings show some dwindling in impregnability of the rural constituency that coincides with elite dis-cohesion, the extent of impregnability remained so high (above 50% average) across these electoral periods.

On the other hand, Nadeau et al. (2013) after conducting 40 surveys from Denmark, France, Germany, Greece, Ireland, Italy, the Netherlands, Portugal, Spain and the UK found that: "the economy is not a mirage. Voters see it, and see it rather clearly [...] Economic perceptions, properly understood, have a greater impact than previously imagined" (p. 565). This conclusion not only applies to overseas electoral politics, but it has been established through comparative studies of 653 elections from 1960 to 2010 across Africa (Hausken & Ncube, 2014). Percentage changes in average electoral impregnability per province based on sampled constituencies vis-a-vis percentage changes in average economic indicators per electoral season presented in Table 21.1 give a very defiant and/or resilient picture of ZANU PF elites in the rural constituency.

Table 21.1 Percentage changes in economic growth Vs rural impregnability

	2000–2005 (%)	2005–2008 (%)	2008–2013 (%)	2013–2018 (%)
Mashonaland Central Province	1	−41.31	76.67	−14.33
Mashonaland East province	−11.94	−34.44	82.07	−9.04
Mashonaland West Province	21.41	−9.22	25	−8.29
Midlands Province	−48.00	54.00	37.19	−8.00
Average GDP per capita growth (annual %)	−7.70	−9	11.60	0.57
Average Human Development Index growth (annual %)	−0.20	0.41	4.50	1.20

Source Author's average and percentage change analyses based on results for sampled constituencies

As shown above, the deepest economic decline in history experienced in the 2005–2008 electoral cycle failed to erode electoral impregnability of the rural constituency as it remained above 50%. Since the year 2000, the rural constituency has religiously given a resounding vote to the ruling elite. The underlying question in this regard has been: What are the key background dynamics in the village that have made it so defiant to the winds of change and so decisive in Zimbabwe's electoral politics? To put it more practically, what are the underlying structural and/or institutional safety-nets that cushion ZANU PF from the corrosive role of economic decline and elite dis-cohesion on their electoral victory in the rural constituency? To answer this question, many studies (such as Chakaipa, 2010; Kurebwa, 2020; Mawere et al., 2022; Musekiwa, 2012; Rusinga, 2021) identify traditional leaders and their attendant partisan politics in servility to the ruling party as key actors impacting the nature and extent of the decisive capacity of the village vote. While the pro-ZANU PF role of traditional leaders in electoral politics has been given significant attention in existing literature (Chakaipa, 2010; Musekiwa, 2012; Kurebwa, 2020; Mawere et al., 2022; Rusinga, 2021), limited effort has been put to conceptualise this role, unpack the underlying historical and philosophical causal factors, how this has impacted their stance on elections and how this has determined the village vote. This study used comparative analysis to bridge this gap.

SECUROCRATIC STATE AND TRADITIONAL LEADERS RELATIONSHIPS

It is important to note that Section 281(1–3) of the Constitution of Zimbabwe and the Traditional Leaders Act form the legal framework which requires traditional leaders to be neutral, independent, apolitical in electoral politics and prohibits them from participating in partisan politics. The spirit of the constitution sought to address the corrosive outcomes of allowing traditional leaders to engage in partisan politics on electoral democracy. Since these clauses were introduced by Zimbabwe's 2013 Constitution, it is observed that prior to its adoption, traditional leaders were creating inter-party problems such as acting in unconstitutional ways, partisan politics that segregated the people opposed to their political choices and were sometimes being directed by one political party against the other (Chakaipa, 2010; Kurebwa, 2020; Musekiwa, 2012).

Using John Stewart Mill's method of difference in comparative analysis of the rural constituency and the urban constituency in Zimbabwe across the four electoral cycles, 2000–2005, 2005–2008, 2008–2013 and 2013–2018, this study found that the capture of traditional leaders by the securocratic state and their integration into a complex network of authoritarian consolidation infrastructures in the rural constituency has intensified the impregnability of the rural constituency. The securocratic state's capture of traditional leaders is an additional political infrastructure in the rural constituency that makes it different from the urban constituency. This conduct affects the minimum conditions that enable political transition through elections postulated in the agency theory that are: (i) free flow of contesting political narratives, (ii) free association and assembly by competing parties, (iii) presence of a fair legal and institutional environment involved in voting, vote counting and announcement of results and (iv) development of a tradition of elite compromise between moderate forces in the opposition and among ruling elites. This study posits that the political infrastructure for consolidating the securocratic state within which traditional leaders are captured and assimilated in the rural constituency has made compliance with apolitical conduct stipulated in section 281(1–3) of Zimbabwe's constitution either unthinkable or a very risky option for a traditional leader. How is the capture of traditional leaders and attendant impregnability of the rural constituency institutionally designed?

Three key political infrastructures consolidating the securocratic state are designed around the traditional leadership system in the rural constituency: (i) historical metamorphosis of rural politics; (ii) capture of traditional leadership and integration into a larger and securocratic/military pervasive infrastructure for coercion of rivals; and (iii) a pervasive infrastructure for perpetuating rural dependency on the ruling party. As shall be presented in detail later, these three infrastructures interact in many ways to produce high levels of electoral impregnability in the rural constituency.

Historical Metamorphosis of the Rural Constituency

A comparative analysis of Zimbabwe's electoral history and interview data collected in this study shows that the capture and assimilation of traditional leaders and conversion into forces promoting impregnability of the rural constituency to democratic forces is so deeply ingrained in history. Two main historical epochs contributed to the capture: (i) the colonial settler government's native settlement and governance policy and (ii) the spatial metamorphosis of nationalist liberation war and the military/authoritarian nature of attendant politics.

The colonial settler government's native settlement and governance policy created an authoritarian situation where traditional leaders and their people were forcefully driven out of their ancestral land, relocated to catchment areas that were underdeveloped, distanced from alternative information access. A system of strict traditional leadership and local government was created to force citizens to support the ruling elite and created over-reliance on state media (radio) as a source of legitimate political narratives (Mlambo, 2000; Moyana, 2002). A community with this kind of authoritarian politics becomes impervious to democratic transition agencies that rely on free flow of information, free association/participation and competition (Dahl, 1971; O'Donnell et al., 1986; Schumpeter, 1950). Three main legal instruments that bred this culture were the Matebeleland Order-in-Council of 1898, renewed from time to time, Land Apportionment Act (LAA) in 1930/1931 and the Native Land Husbandry Act (NLHA) of 1950/1951. The LAA compelled Africans who stayed outside communal areas (the then Tribal Trust Lands [TTLs]), to relocate, thereby dividing Zimbabwe into urban areas for the whites and rural areas for the black citizens (Kay, 1970; Government of Southern Rhodesia, 1961; National Archives of Zimbabwe,

S1194/190/1). This alienated black people from their ancestral land. Thus, there is nothing remembered with more hate than settler land policies among victims in the rural constituency. As a result, anti-settler political contestation led by founders of the ruling ZANU PF and military elites began from this point onward as these laws were viewed as symbols of white authoritarianism and exclusionary politics (Holleman, 1969).

Two key outcomes of these historical dynamics that ingrained the current impregnability of the rural constituency are noteworthy. First was the creation of animosity between the traditional leaders and their people in the village, on the one hand, and the colonial government in the capital, on the other. As Machiavelli warned the ruler, "above all he must refrain from seizing *the* property of others, because a *man* is quicker to forget *the death of his father* than *the* loss of *his* patrimony". This animosity transcended the decolonisation efforts and has been harvested by ZANU PF for use against opposition. ZANU PF has played a hero role by: (i) associating with the land redistribution programme in this situation; (ii) portraying the land reform programme as a violent eviction of former colonisers from ancestral land of the black majorities; and (iii) portraying the opposition, civil society and independent media as forces paid to reverse the land reform.

Thus, in the village, ZANU PF has strategically deployed propaganda and misinformation which have successfully branded the opposition, independent media and civic society organisations as conduits of imperialism who want to bring back colonialism and its ugly past (Interviews, November, 2022). The telos being to arouse and refresh the anti-colonial hatred among traditional leaders in the rural constituency so as to multiply defensive and/or punitive voting. With state radio being the main source of information, and without access to alternative media, the rural constituency so aroused, therefore, goes to vote to defend their liberty from the so-called return of colonialism and to punish opposition candidates for threatening to bring back the colonial hardships. This has worsened the impregnability of the rural constituency.

Propaganda and misinformation have for long been relied upon by ZANU PF to wrongly brand opponents, thanks to its monopoly of media narratives and limited access to alternative narratives in the rural constituency. The growing internet penetration, advent of alternative media and social media networks have increased the vulnerability of the village to alternative narratives. This is an opportunity to neutralise this pillar of impregnability. Nonetheless, this cannot be achieved if democratic forces do not engage in the business of intensifying these vulnerabilities and investing much time and resources in the manufacture and dispersal of alternative political narratives at a village level.

The second outcome has been a historical conflation between the ruling ZANU PF/military elite and traditional leadership in charge of the rural constituency. This is traceable to 1962 when the Rhodesian Front Party co-opted traditional leaders particularly the chiefs for two purposes (Ranger & Bhebhe, 2001). First being to use them as proof of support from the black population in its bid for independence from the British Government. Second was to use them to shield their subjects from supporting the liberation war fighters who are now in ZANU PF. As a result, some chiefs were labelled as sellouts and killed by liberation fighters whilst others were detained by the Rhodesian security for supporting the nationalists (Zamchiya, 2021). Studies, therefore, reveal that from the colonial period to independent Zimbabwe, the relationship has evolved into one where traditional leaders act as an "intermediary domination" between the state and the people (Kurebwa, 2020). Currently, the institution of traditional leadership comprising chiefs, headmen and village heads in order of hierarchy has been used to campaign for ZANU PF and facilitate the closure of their communities from opposition penetration (Musekiwa, 2012). For instance, in 2017 the President of the Zimbabwe Council of Chiefs, Fortune Charumbira (the highest ranking traditional leader) at an annual conference of chiefs stated that traditional leaders have been supporting and must continue to support ZANU PF and its presidential candidate (Mashininga, 2018). After being challenged in court in *Election Resource Centre v. Charumbira*, the court ruled the statements as unconstitutional but nothing substantive was done to dissuade others from implementing his political views. Actually, chiefs are given new cars by the ZANU PF government on the eve of most general elections as if to fuel them to continue with their partisan conduct (Tshuma, 2021; ZimEye Correspondent, 2018). In 2021, at a ZANU PF annual conference in Bindura, chief Charumbira defiant of the court ruling reiterated his original position that:

> On behalf of all chiefs in this country, I want to tell you that we are together. It's true we are together. We are behind you. I want to repeat this because there are people who ask us why we come here, [...] We're the owners of Zanu PF. The reason why Zanu PF exists is all about traditional leadership. So you cannot separate the struggles about land on this

continent from the traditional leadership. We will never leave Zanu PF. (Rushwaya, 2021, para. 2&4)

With these leaders captured in ZANU PF patronage networks, it is hard for the opposition, independent media and the civil society to gain permission to operate in their spheres of authority. One has to be authorized by the chief, headman and village head to access the villagers in the rural constituency. In many cases, traditional leaders have served as active and known local ZANU PF leadership. Although section 281 of the Constitution of Zimbabwe and sections 45–46 of the Traditional Leaders Act prohibit partisan conduct of traditional leaders, the culture continues. Instances of commandeered-voting, targeted intimidation of opposition supporters and economic sanctions through exclusion from food-handouts have ensued courtesy to this capture of traditional leaders (COTRAD, 2018). Access to land, residence and government social support is also run via the traditional leaders. This has been effectively used to punish rural voters for supporting the opposition and deter future opposition support.

The second historical factor that influenced the capture of traditional leaders and deployment to deepen the impregnability of the rural constituency to democratic forces is the spatial metamorphosis of nationalist anti-colonial war. A review of the history of the Zimbabwe People's Revolutionary Army (ZIPRA) a military wing of the ZAPU party and the Zimbabwe National Liberation Army (ZANLA) a military wing of ZANU party shows that they relied much on the traditional leaders and their rural constituency for mobilisation, recruitment, shelter, political support, intelligence gathering and food-handouts (Mlambo, 2014). For instance, soon after the failed 1966 and 1967 ZANLA and ZIPRA battles in Sinoia and Wankie Reserves, respectively, the nationalists war leaders resorted to massive mobilisation of the masses through night rallies raising political consciousness, creating and dispersing liberation political narratives and grievances as a new strategy of the liberation struggle. In this way, the grievances touched on everyone and thereby involving everyone in the war. For instance, James Chikerema summed ZAPU's liberation strategy as follows:

> We do not intend to finish in a matter of two, three, four or five years...this is a protracted struggle. The type of war we fight depends on changes of tactics and I can tell you that we have changed our tactics. We will combine

both, where they meet us and intercept us, we will stand and fight; where they don't see us, we will go to our own areas and infiltrate ourselves into the population and organise our masses. (Interview with Granada Television on 1 January 1970, as cited in Moorcraft & McLaughlin, 2008, p. 76)

Through this rural-based mobilisation, the nationalist movements ensured that their military won the support of the rural constituency, captured traditional leadership and become one of them. As Chung (2006) puts it, they merged into the people like "fish in water". Alexander (2006) states that:

> Some chiefs were active nationalists before occupying office, others turned against government, if not to nationalism, as a result of the disregard for their demands, notably for land, still others reluctantly obeyed nationalist dictums out of fear of retribution. Both nationalists and guerrillas preferred to use chiefs rather than to attack them: guerrillas were not opposed to chieftaincy per se but to its use in the services of the government (p. 106).

This marked the beginning of a long history of capture of the rural constituency and traditional leaders by military/ZANU PF. The village was thus militarised and pro-ZANU PF from this period till date. So, upon their retirement, these ex-ZANLA and ex-ZIPRA soldiers re-joined the rural community. They dominate the rural areas in form of war collaborators and war veterans with their descendants and dependents. Some of them have become traditional chiefs who are in charge of the administration of what enters and what leaves their jurisdictions. Some of them have become village heads, councillors and business persons which worsens the impregnability of the rural constituency to the democratic forces. The work of penetrating and winning the rural constituency requires democratic forces to go beyond rallies, hotel conferences and online activism.

Traditional Leaders in the Infrastructure for Coercion of Rivals

Traditional leaders form a key factor in the infrastructure for coercion of rivals deployed by the securocratic state. Traditional leaders have been assimilated into a network of bureaucratic/institutional coercion of rivals of the ruling elite. This is expressed through stringent regulations and screening processes done by a network of rigid partisan institutions from the Minister of Public Service, Labour and Social Welfare, Minister of State for Provincial Affairs in the Office of the President and Cabinet, Secretary for Provincial Affairs and Devolution (formerly called Provincial Development Coordinator (PDC)) (Herald Reporter, 2021), the District Administrator (DA)'s office, the councillor, the chief, headman and the village head aimed at fending off, dissuading and discouraging real and potential political rivals of ZANU PF from entering the rural constituency. Very close to a villager is a strict system of traditional leadership with the village head being the closest. Opponents of ZANU PF need land, access to government social support and farm inputs under the Presidential Input Scheme. Research participants highlighted that these have been very difficult to access outside ZANU PF. In addition, the village head has access to registration data of every citizen in the village. So, villagers fear that their information can easily be sent to the ZANU PF terror machinery in the event that the village head discovered that they support the opposition. In addition, traditional leaders need to be informed before CSOs and opposition parties can think of setting up their structures in the village. They need authorisation from the chief, headman and the village head. All these have to be authorised by the DA who also gets permission from the Minister of Local Government.

When research participants were interrogated about the role of traditional leaders in the accessibility of the rural constituency to the opposition, media and civic society ahead of the 2023 election, results were as displayed in Fig. 21.2.

Respondents were asked: How would you describe the role of traditional leaders in the accessibility of the rural constituency to the opposition, media and civic society ahead of the 2023 election?

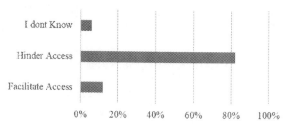

Fig. 21.2 How traditional leaders facilitate accessibility of the rural constituency

As shown above, 82% of research participants noted that traditional leaders hinder access to the rural constituency by the opposition, media and the civil society ahead of the 2023 election. Similar findings were presented in a survey report by Rukuni et al. (2015, p. 58) which revealed that 94% of traditional leaders in Bikita district were politically aligned to the ruling ZANU-PF and have used their positions to "punish those who belong to opposition political parties". During 2018 elections, the IRI/NDI Zimbabwe International Election Observation Mission Final Report (2018) also revealed that traditional leaders influenced the voting behaviour of villagers to vote in a certain way preferred by them. The IRI/NDI (2018) report noted that:

> In rural areas, traditional leaders and local chiefs were observed exerting influence over their respective communities by telling citizens whom to vote for, forcing people to attend ZANU-PF campaign events and threatening banishment from a village if a voter failed to vote for ZANUPF. Traditional leaders also played a role in the partisan distribution of food aid and contributed to fears about the lack of secrecy of the vote by recording voters' registration serial numbers and suggesting this information and data collected through the BVR process allowed their vote to be known (p. 34).

This entails that traditional leaders generally facilitate the impregnability of the rural constituency.

Infrastructure for Perpetuating Dependency

The ZANU PF government has created a culture of over-reliance on party assisted access to food handouts in the rural constituency such that most inhabitants view ZANU PF as an indispensable source of livelihood. Traditional leaders have been deployed as enforcers of this political climate in the village. 68% of interviewed rural citizens attested that they vote their political party for economic gain. One research participant noted that: "we cannot waste our time to fend for our families going to vote for empty promises. We need something on the table. My vote is something for something tangible". This "something-for-something" politics was reiterated across regional divides in the rural constituency. The ruling ZANU PF party has been doing this "something-for-a-vote" politics since 1980. It has become a deep-rooted political culture in the village.

Humanitarian relief Non-Governmental Organisations [NGOs] have also fallen prey to this patronage network of ZANU PF and traditional leaders in rural areas. NGOs usually rely on village datasets, registers and assemblies organised by village heads for recruitment of local representatives, beneficiaries and conducting vulnerability assessments before giving humanitarian aid. The Zimbabwe Human Rights NGO Forum (2021) notes that drought relief in the rural constituency flows through the following structure:

> There is a Ward Drought Relief Committee (WDRC) chaired by the Councillor and comprised of traditional leaders (mostly headmen and village heads, and sometimes chiefs) [...] followed by a Drought Relief Committee at village level which is chaired by the village head and comprised of members selected by villagers in the respective area as well as some members selected by the village head (p. 12).

This has made it very easy for NGOs to serve the ZANU PF patronage networks as beneficiaries are chosen from a list of names directly transferred from the ZANU PF cell register to the village head's register which is given to the representatives of NGOs (Zimbabwe Human Rights NGO Forum, 2021). With the harsh socioeconomic realities in the village, most citizens vote ZANU PF for economic gain. This has made it very hard for the opposition to win the rural constituency. This study also found that "being discovered by local traditional leaders that your child works for CSOs or independent media makes your life very difficult in the village as you are branded as a father of a traitor..." (Interviews, 2022). The net impact on an average villager has been an inculcation of a submissive and subject political culture which disdains opposition to the status quo. Table 21.2 presents selected interviews with traditional leaders in the rural constituency.

A comparative analysis of the above findings highlights four key observations that explain how dependency is mastered and prolonged in the rural constituency. First is that government programmes are paraded as ZANU PF programmes. The state/party conflation has made it very difficult for a villager since 1980 to tell the difference between the party and government. So, most citizens will continue to think government services that reach the rural constituency are ZANU PF services. Even NGO drought relief handouts have not managed to escape this. They have either been portrayed as NGO food brought by the ZANU PF party

Table 21.2 Political economy of dependency

Research constituency	A sample of key interview responses
Mt Darwin North	"Since year 2000 when I officially joined ZANU PF, my life has been far much better than before. My name comes first in all drought relief programmes, my children are given free education under the war veterans' scheme, I get farming inputs every year, our leaders make things happen for our children who need jobs in Harare. Its all about being connected to the right channel of a better life"
Insiza North	"Look around and see, those chickens were donated by the party to us as some livelihood incubation programme. Even this piece of land, I had to talk to our chairman to get it allocated to me. Those are my barns; they are filled with enough maize for me and my children and my chickens. What else could I want? Joining these people is better than fighting them because you will suffer and miss-out on opportunities. So do you think I can forgo all these things just for some dreaming opposition that has never given its supporters anything tangible?"
Hurungwe East	"When you are in the party and have harvested the benefits, you have to jealously guard against losing them. We are constantly reminded how we got all these benefits and to never change the circumstances that led us to get them. That is, remaining in the party to keep what has been given and to enjoy what will be given"

or NGO food benefiting citizens through registers compiled with ZANU PF influence. The net outcome is that ZANU PF's supporters benefit. This partly explains the sudden increase in impregnability of the rural constituency shown in the years that followed the GNU in Zimbabwe. When public services improved and NGO programmes increased, the rural constituency construed it as the improvement of ZANU PF and thus thanked them with a resounding 2013 election victory.

Secondly, the beneficiaries of government programmes believe they are being given a favour by ZANU PF. They do not see it as their right to have those services and the responsibility of a government to give drought relief to its citizens, subsidize farming, maintain roads and provide water to its citizens. Neglect of the rural constituency in development programmes has been so great to cause citizens not to demand services from government but to show gratitude to any politician who decides to do what he/she is expected to do by law and duty. Thirdly, it can be seen that rural citizens have naturalized commercialisation of politics and they see it as normal business. ZANU PF politics has become one of the business adventures that give the most cash-out in the village. To penetrate the rural constituency, democratic forces must begin to come to terms with commercialisation of politics and lack of civic education there.

Lastly, dependence on ZANU PF is prolonged through threats and/ or fear of loss of given or anticipated benefits. For instance, war veterans fear loss of their monthly pensions, school fees paid for their dependents, jobs given through ZANU PF connections and land given to them through ZANU PF patronage networks. The same applies to traditional leaders. Vehicles, land, salaries and connections can be lost if they turn against ZANU PF. If these two powerful social groups in the village are so captured and intimidated, what of the general villager who needs a place to lay his/her head and feed the family? It should be noted that the Communal Land Act gives occupants of communal land in the rural constituency no title deeds but stresses that their land is state owned. Section 4 of the Communal Land Act [Chapter 20:04] stipulates that the authority to allocate land and evict citizens vests with the president. Traditional leaders are given delegated "titular" powers to distribute land on behalf of the president. This president happens to be a ZANU PF president. Traditional leaders happen to be pro-ZANU PF people existing in a ZANU PF controlled land. This shows the risk taken by villagers to oppose ZANU PF in Zimbabwe. They might lose everything particularly those at the leadership helm of the opposition, they suffer the most so that their followers get some life lessons. Evidence of the suffering of Chief Nhlanhlayamandwe Ndiweni who opposed ZANU PF and found himself dismissed from chieftainship, imprisoned and government vehicle taken from him attests to this. For instance, Chief Nhlanhlayamandwe Ndiweni's dismissal by President Mnangagwa (Chidakwa, 2019) has been viewed as a punishment for his critical views against the government and a deterrence of such conduct among chiefs and traditional leaders under their control. Earlier before his dismissal, he was sentenced to 18 months jail after the ZANU PF secretary for administration witnessed against him in a court case between him and his subject (Mrewa, 2019). In this case, Judge Thompson Mabikwa gave him bail against state wish to jail him for 18 months. However, the judge was later relieved of his duties as well although the link between this case and Chief Ndiweni's dismissal is not clear. Chief Ndiweni was used as a life lesson to all other traditional leaders and their subjects on how to keep the ZANU PF benefits.

It is, however, important to observe that the relationship between the ruling ZANU PF and traditional leaders is based on the latter's cost–benefit analysis thereby making it situational, vulnerable and amenable to change. Traditional leaders bend to the whims of every ruler in power to secure their power. For instance, traditional authorities such as chiefs, headmen and village heads were a key conduit of the colonial authoritarian state as they were used to enforce settler politics in the native reserves (Keulder, 1998). In the colonial era, traditional leaders were salaried government officials accountable to the colonial government and some of them began to be appointed outside the relevant ruling clan or tribe (Ndlovu & Dube, 2012). Currently, section 283 of the Constitution of Zimbabwe, section 3, 8 and 11 of the Traditional Leaders Act give a framework on the appointment of Chiefs, headmen and village heads, respectively. These laws legally empower the President, Minister, Permanent Secretary to appoint and remove a chief, headman, village head, respectively, in accordance with prevailing culture, customs and traditional practices of the communities concerned. To those traditional leaders who oppose ZANU PF, the worse scenario has been public ridicule, threats and persecution (Mangwaya, 2022). The worst scenario has been loss of chieftainship as members with strong pro-ZANU PF views are prefaced. This, therefore, means they relate to ZANU PF based on a pragmatic cost–benefit-analysis. The manner with which they ditched the Smith government when it had become apparent that the nationalists were winning and the way they ditched Mugabe after the 2017 coup attests to this. The day they will see costs in ZANU PF and benefits in the opposition, they are likely to change camps overnight. In light of this background, the role of democratic forces is to find and use means to make traditional leaders and their subjects see the costs of voting ZANU PF and benefits of voting the opposition. Most importantly, the benefits of voting for the opposition must be perceived to outweigh both the costs of doing so and benefits of voting the ruling party.

Conclusion

The chapter presented the nature of capture of traditional leaders and how they are deployed by the securocratic state to intensify the impregnability problem in the rural constituency. The chapter reiterated that the problem is summed in terms of the colonial land and settlement setup, the spatial metamorphosis of the nationalist liberation struggle that naturalised the rural constituency as a ZANU PF zone, the political institutional setup that perpetuates coercion and dependency in the rural constituency. The chapter also highlighted key points of weakness in the impregnability problem which can be used by democratic forces as points of entry. The general argument is that the continuation of the capture of traditional leaders has been a key factor hindering a democratic breakthrough in Zimbabwe.

References

Alexander, J. (2006). *The unsettled land: State-making & the politics of land in Zimbabwe, 1893–2003*. Ohio University Press.

Bogaards, M., & Elischer, S. (2016). Competitive authoritarianism in Africa revisited. *Z Vgl Polit Wiss, 10*(2016), 5–18.

Carothers, C. (2018). The surprising instability of competitive authoritarianism. *Journal of Democracy, 29*(4), 129–135. https://doi.org/10.1353/jod.2018.0068

CCJP & LRF. (1999). *Breaking the silence, building true peace: A report on the disturbances in Matabeleland and the Midlands, 1980 to 1988 summary report*. Legal Resources Foundation. http://www.kubatana.net/html/archive/hr/990401ccjplrf.asp?sector=CACT

Chakaipa, S. (2010). Local government institutions and elections. In J. De Visser, N. Steytler, & N. Machingauta (Eds.), *Local government reform in Zimbabwe: A policy dialogue* (pp. 31–68). University of the Western Cape.

Chidakwa, B. (2019, December 14). Chief Ndiweni dethroned. *The Herald*. https://www.herald.co.zw/chief-ndiweni-dethroned/

Chung, F. (2006). *Re-living the Second Chimurenga. Memories from the liberation struggle in Zimbabwe*. Nordic Africa Institute.

Communal Lands Act [Chapter 20:04]. https://www.veritaszim.net/sites/veritas_d/files/Communal%20Land%20Act%2C%20Cap%202004%2C%20updated.rtf

COTRAD. (2018). *Traditional leaders intensify voter intimidation in Zaka*. https://ar-ar.facebook.com/Kubatana/posts/traditional-leaders-intensify-voter-intimidation-in-zaka-via-cotrad-trust-zimbab/1729665293711529/

Cox, G. W. (2007). *Authoritarian elections and leadership succession, 1975–2000*. https://www.haas.berkeley.edu/wp-content/uploads/cox_20071119.pdf

Dahl, R. (1971). *Polyarchy*. Yale University Press.

Diamond, L. (2002). Elections without democracy: Thinking about hybrid regimes. *Journal of Democracy, 13*(2), 21–35. http://web.pdx.edu/~mev/pdf/Diamond_470570.pdf

Duch, R. M., & Stevenson, R. T. (2008). *The economic vote*. Cambridge University Press.

Geddes, B. (2005). Why parties and elections in authoritarian regimes? *In annual meeting of the American Political Science Association* (pp. 456–471).

Government of Southern Rhodesia. (1961). *Second report of the select committee on resettlement of natives*. Government Printers.

Grugel, J. (2002). *Democratization: A critical introduction*. Palgrave. https://books.google.co.zw/books/about/Democratization.html?id=TyGIQgAACAAJ&redir_esc=y

Gumbo, B., & Ruhanya, P. (2022). The securocratic state: Conceptualising the transition problem in Zimbabwe. *Third World Thematics: A TWQ Journal*. https://doi.org/10.1080/23802014.2022.2099575

Hausken, K., & Ncube, M. (2014). Determinants of election outcomes: New evidence from Africa. *African Development Review*, 26(4), 610–630.

Hellwig, T. (2010). Context, information, and performance voting. In R. J. Dalton & C. J. Anderson (Eds.), *Citizens, context, and choice: How context shapes citizens' electoral choices* (pp. 149–175). Oxford University Press.

Herald Reporter. (2021, December 17). Provincial development coordinators elevated to new positions. *The Herald*. https://www.herald.co.zw/provincial-development-coordinators-elevated-to-new-positions/

Holleman, J. F. (1969). *Chief, council and commissioner: Some problems of government in Rhodesia*. Oxford University Press.

Howard, M. M., & Roessler, P. G. (2006b). Liberalizing electoral outcomes in competitive authoritarian regimes. *American Journal of Political Science*, 50(2), 365–381. https://doi.org/10.1111/j.1540-5907.2006.00189.x

Human Development Programme. (n.d). *Human Development Index (1990–2021)*. https://hdr.undp.org/sites/default/files/2021-22_HDR/HDR21-22_Composite_indices_complete_time_series.csv

IRI/NDI. (2018). *Zimbabwe international election observation mission final report*. https://www.ndi.org/sites/default/files/Zimbabwe%20ZIEOM%20FINAL%20REPORT%20Printer_updated.pdf

Kay, G. (1970). *Rhodesia: A human geography*. University of London Press.

Keulder, C. (1998). *Traditional leaders and local government in Africa: Lessons for South Africa*. Human Sciences Research Council.

Kubatana. (2005). *Parliamentary election results*. http://www.archive.kubatana.net/docs/elec/zesn_2005_elec_final_050422.pdf

Kubatana. (2008). *Parliamentary election results*. http://archive.kubatana.net/docs/elec/house_assem_results_080329.pdf

Kubatana. (2013). *Parliamentary election results*. http://archive.kubatana.net/docs/elec/harmonised_election_assembly_results_130806.xls

Kurebwa, J. (2020). *The capture of traditional leaders by political parties in Zimbabwe for political expediency*. Bindura University of Science Education.

Laakso, L. (2003). Opposition politics in independent Zimbabwe. *African Studies Quarterly*, 7(2&3), 119–137. http://web.africa.ufl.edu/asq/v7/v7i2a6.htm

Levystky, S., & Way, L. A. (2002). The rise of competitive authoritarianism. *Journal of Democracy, 13*(2), 51–65. https://scholar.harvard.edu/levitsky/files/SL_elections.pdf

Levystky, S., & Way, L. A. (2010). *Competitive authoritarianism: Hybrid regimes after the cold war*. https://doi.org/10.1017/CBO9780511781353

Lewis-Beck, M. S., & Stegmaier, M. (2000). Economic determinants of electoral outcomes. *Annual Review of Political Science, 3*(1), 183–219. https://doi.org/10.1146/annurev.polisci.3.1.183

Lewis-Beck, M. S., & Stegmaier, M. (2007). Economic models of voting. In R. J. Dalton & H. D. Klingeman (Eds.), *The Oxford handbook of political behavior* (pp. 518–537). Oxford University Press.

Mainwaring, S. (2012). From representative democracy to participatory competitive authoritarianism: Hugo Chávez and Venezuelan politics. *Perspectives on Politics, 10*(4), 955–967. https://doi.org/10.1017/S1537592712002629

Mandaza, I. (2016). *The political economy of the state in Zimbabwe: The rise and fall of the securocrat state*. https://www.theindependent.co.zw/2016/04/01/

Mandaza, I., & Sachikonye, L. M. (1991). *The one-party state and democracy: The Zimbabwe debate*. SAPES Books.

Mangwaya, M. (2022, September 11). Chiefs speak out against Zanu PF coercion. *The Standard*. https://www.newsday.co.zw/thestandard/local-news/article/200000359/chiefs-speak-out-against-zanu-pf-coercion

Maringira, G. (2017). Politicization and resistance in the Zimbabwean national army. *African Affairs, 116*(462), 18–38. https://doi.org/10.1093/afraf/adw055

Maringira, G. (2021). The military post-Mugabe. *Journal of Asian and African Studies, 56*(2), 176–188. https://doi.org/10.1177/0021909620986586

Mashininga, K. (2018, July 25). Traditional leaders in Zimbabwe must toe the ruling party line—Or else. *The Mail & Guardian*. https://mg.co.za/article/2018-07-25-00-traditional-leaders-in-zimbabwe-must-toe-the-ruling-party-line-or-else/

Masunungure, E. V. (2011). Zimbabwe's militarised electoral authoritarianism. *Journal of International Affairs, 65*(1), 47–64. http://www.jstor.org/stable/24388181

Masunungure, E. V., & Bratton, M. (2008). Zimbabwe's long agony. *Journal of Democracy, 19*(4), 41–55.

Matti, S. (2010). The Democratic Republic of the Congo? Corruption, patronage, and competitive authoritarianism in the DRC. *Africa Today, 56*(4), 43–61. https://doi.org/10.2979/aft.2010.56.4.42

Mawere, J., Matshidze, P. E., Kugara, S. L., & Madzivhandila, T., (2022) The role and significance of traditional leadership in South African local governance. In R. Tshifhumulo & T. Makhanikhe (Eds.), *Handbook of research on protecting and managing global indigenous knowledge systems* (pp. 249–273). IGI Global.

Merkel, W. (2004). Embedded and defective democracies. *Democratization*, *11*(5), 33–58. https://doi.org/10.1080/13510340412331304598

Mlambo, A. S. (2000). Manufacturing in Zimbabwe, 1980–90. In A. S. Mlambo, E. S. Pangeti, & I. Phimister (Eds.), *Zimbabwe: A History of Manufacturing, 1890–1995*. University of Zimbabwe Publications.

Mlambo, A. S. (2014). Nationalist movements to 1965. In *A history of Zimbabwe* (pp. 128–148). Cambridge University Press. https://doi.org/10.1017/CBO9781139128919.006

Moorcraft, P. L., & McLaughlin, P. (2008). *The Rhodesian war: A military history*. Collins.

Moyana, H. V. (2002). *The Political economy of land in Zimbabwe*. Mambo Press.

Moyo, G. (2014). Understanding the executive-military relations in Zimbabwe. *Journal of African Union Studies*, *3*(2/3), 69–86. https://www.jstor.org/stable/26893865

Mrewa, T. (2019, August 15). *Chief Ndiweni, 23 others found guilty of malicious damage to property*. Cite. https://cite.org.zw/chief-ndiweni-23-others-found-guilty-of-malicious-damage-to-property/

Musekiwa, N. (2012). The role of local authorities in democratic transition. In E. V. Masunungure, & J. Sumba (Eds.), *Democratic transition*. Weaver Press and IDAZIM.

Nadeau, R., Lewis-Beck, M. S., & Bélanger, E. (2013). Economics and elections revisited. *Comparative Political Studies*, *46*(5), 551–573.

National Archives of Zimbabwe [NAZ] S1194/190/1. *Land for native occupation*. Reports of the ad-hoc Committee, 1946/47.

Ndawana, E. (2020). The military and democratisation in post-Mugabe Zimbabwe. *South African Journal of International Affairs*, *27*(2), 193–217. https://doi.org/10.1080/10220461.2020.1791729

Ndlovu, M., & Dube, N. (2012). Analysis of the relevance of traditional leaders and the evolution of traditional leadership in Zimbabwe: A case study of amaNdebele. *International Journal of African Renaissance Studies*, *7*(1), 50–72. https://doi.org/10.1080/18186874.2012.699927

Ndlovu-Gatsheni, S. J. (2006). Nationalist-military alliance and the fate of democracy in Zimbabwe. *African Journal of Conflict Resolution*, *6*(1), 49–80.

O'Donnell, G. A., Schmitter, P. C. & Whitehead, L. (Eds.). (1986). *Transitions from authoritarian rule: Prospects for democracy*. Johns Hopkins University Press.

Ottaway, M. (2003). *Democracy challenged: The rise of semi authoritarianism*. Carnegie Endowment for International Peace. https://carnegieendowment.org/files/DemChallenged_Intro.pdf

Ranger, T., & Bhebhe, N. (2001). *The historical dimensions of democracy and human rights in Zimbabwe—Vol. 1: Pre-colonial and colonial legacies*. University of Zimbabwe.

Riley, M. F. (1982). *Zimbabwean nationalism and the rise of Mugabe*. Naval Postgraduate School.

Ruhanya, P. (2020). The Militarisation of State Institutions in Zimbabwe, 2002–2017. In: S.J. Ndlovu-Gatsheni, P. Ruhanya (Eds.), *The History and Political Transition of Zimbabwe: African Histories and Modernities*. Palgrave Macmillan. https://doi.org/10.1007/978-3-030-47733-2_8

Rukuni, T., Machingambi, Z., Musingafi, M. C., & Kaseke, K. E. (2015). The role of traditional leadership in conflict resolution and peace building in Zimbabwean rural communities: The case of Bikita District. *Public policy and administration research, 5*(3), 75-79.

Rupiya, M. (2005). Zimbabwe: Governance through military operations. *African Security Review, 14*(2), 116–118. https://doi.org/10.1080/10246029.2005.9627378

Rushwaya, S. (2021, October 30). 'Chiefs will never leave Zanu PF'—Chief Charumbira in shock new outburst. *Zimlive*. https://www.zimlive.com/chiefs-will-never-leave-zanu-pf-chief-charumbira-in-shock-new-outburst/

Rusinga, R. (2021). Zimbabwe's 2018 harmonised elections: An assessment of credibility. *Journal of African Elections, 20*(1), 90–114. https://doi.org/10.20940/JAE/2021/v20i1a5

Rustow, D. A. (1970). Transition to democracy: Toward a dynamic mode. *Comparative Politics, 2*(3), 337–363. http://www.jostor.org/stable/421307

Sachikonye, L. (1990). The 1990 Zimbabwe elections: A post-mortem. *Review of African Political Economy, 17*(48), 92–99. https://doi.org/10.1080/03056249008703864

Schedler, A. (2002). The nested game of democratization by elections. *International Political Science Review, 23*(1), 103–122. https://doi.org/10.1177/0192512102023001006

Schedler, A. (2006). The logic of electoral authoritarianism. In A. Schedler (Ed.), *Electoral authoritarianism: The dynamics of unfree competition* (pp. 1–23). Lynne Rienner.

Schedler, A. (2010). Democracy's past and future: Authoritarianism's last line of defense. *Journal of Democracy, 21*(1), 69–80.

Schumpeter, J. (1950). *Capitalism, socialism and democracy*. Harper & Row.

Stauffer, C. S. (2009). *Acting out the myths: The power of narrative discourse in shaping the Zimbabwe conflict of Matabeleland, 1980–1987*. [PhD Thesis, University of KwaZulu Natal]. http://hdl.handle.net/10413/8764

Tendi, B. M. (2013). Ideology, civilian authority and the Zimbabwean military. *Journal of Southern African Studies, 39*(4), 829–843. https://doi.org/10.1080/03057070.2013.858543

Tshuma, M. (2021, May 28). Zanu-PF accused of pampering chiefs with cars for political mileage. *Cite*. https://cite.org.zw/zanu-pf-accused-of-pampering-chiefs-with-cars-for-political-mileage/

World Bank. (n.d). *GDP per capita growth (annual %) (1960–2021)*. https://api.worldbank.org/v2/en/indicator/NY.GDP.PCAP.KD.ZG?downloadformat=excel

World Data. (n.d.). *Inflation—(1980–2021)* [Data set]. https://www.worlddata.info/africa/zimbabwe/inflation-rates.php

Yardımcı-Geyikçi, S. (2020). Democratic backsliding in a second-wave democracy: The strange case of Turkey. *APSA Democracy and Autocracy Newsletter, 18*(3), 21–27.

Zamchiya, P. (2021). *State politics & the customary power of chiefs in Zimbabwe. Institute for poverty, land and Agrarian studies*. Institute for Poverty, Land and Agrarian Studies [PLAAS].

Zimbabwe Democracy Institute. (2017). *Zimbabwe transition in a muddy terrain: Political economy military capture*. Kubatana. http://kubatana.net/2017/12/14/zimbabwetransition-muddy-terrain-political-economy-military-capture/

Zimbabwe Election Commission. (2018). *Parliamentary election results*. https://www.zec.org.zw/download/combined-verified-national-assembly-results-2018/

Zimbabwe Election Resource Centre v. Charumbira. https://electionjudgments.org/api/files/1560977137269u96zo5s54y.pdf

Zimbabwe Human Rights NGO Forum. (2021). *The politics of food: A contextual analysis of the distribution of food aid in Zimbabwe*. https://data.zimpeaceproject.com/api/files/1615803851127r38eqzh83co.pdf

ZimEye Correspondent. (2018, July 8). Zanu Pf lures chiefs: Promises cars if Mnangagwa wins elections. *ZimEye*. https://www.zimeye.net/2018/07/08/zanu-pf-lures-chiefs-promises-cars-if-mnangagwa-wins-elections/

List of Appendixes

Appendix 1.1 Evidence of Elections Without Democracy in Zimbabwe Fact-Sheet

Indicator	Mugabe Era	Mnangagwa Era
Capture of Legislature	Constitutional Amendment Number 7 (Act 23 of 1987) that conditioned the legislature to allow exercise of discretionary powers was that introduced an executive presidency in Zimbabwe. This amendment cushioned Mugabe's ZANU PF from the possibility of parliament control. He was now directly elected by electorates in the whole country as opposed to being elected by a single constituency as a member of parliament and then voted into office by members of parliament into the office of the prime minister. The legislature was captured by Mugabe's ruling ZANU PF party for purposes of enacting pieces of legislation aimed at creating an imperial presidency with unchecked powers. These pieces of legislation included POSA and AIPPA. These two pieces of legislation were enacted shortly before the 2002 presidential elections and were ostensibly aimed at solidifying and consolidating Robert Mugabe's hold on power through subrogating any opposition while claiming to uphold the rule of law. Three political machinations deployed pursuant of creating a legislature that serves as an enabler of exercise of discretionary power were identified by this study. First, the regime maximised on identity politics as a political culture in Zimbabwe that saw its resonance with the majority Shona-speaking ethnic groups thereby turning opposition politics into a direct opposition of the majority Shona ethnic group. This strategic ethnicalisation of electoral politics gave the Mugabe regime the blessing of support and affiliation to a major ethnic group that is beyond	Fielding of extremist supporters or retired members of the military elite to represent ZANU PF in parliamentary elections. The use of opposition political figures to ease and enable the process of enacting draconian legislation. For example, ZANU PF MPs connived with MDC Alliance aligned MPs to facilitate the promulgation of the PVO Amendment Bill. The use of ZEC to manipulate elections to ensure more ZANU PF MPs are elected. A shocking case has been the Chegutu West Constituency case where ZEC announced a ZANU PF MP Dexter Nduna as the winner despite having published that he got less votes than the opposing MDC Alliance (MDC-A) member

(continued)

(continued)

Indicator	Mugabe Era	Mnangagwa Era
	two-thirds of the national population and registered citizens on the voters' roll. The successive elections that occurred from 1980 till 1987 were more of an ethnic war and contestation between the two major ethnic groups, the Shona majority represented by the ruling Mugabe regime and the Ndebele minority voting the opposition PF ZAPU. Notably was the military operation code named Gukurahundi unleashed by the ZANU PF regime in Matabeleland and parts of Midlands provinces that are ethnically Ndebele speaking and were opposition strongholds that killed 20 000 citizens. Voting patterns from 1980 till 1987 illustrated this Shona/Ndebele divide. What this meant was that ZANU PF had an easy access to the two-thirds majority seats in the legislature which in turn was strictly pummelled by party whips to rubberstamp the decision of the ruling ZANU PF elite	

(continued)

(continued)

Indicator	Mugabe Era	Mnangagwa Era
Capture of Judiciary	President Mugabe and his ZANU PF party relied on three basic mechanisms: constitutional amendments, appointment of ZANU PF stalwarts into the judicial system and castigations on state media to emasculate the judiciary and control it. For instance, in 2001, the Supreme Court of Zimbabwe ruled that the ZANU PF invasion and redistribution of the land owned by commercial farmers to the blacks were unconstitutional. The government in 2005 amendment the constitution inserting Sect. 16A and 16B that legalised expropriation of land without compensation which was a rubberstamp of what ZANU PF had already started. The real political goal was to appease the disgruntled citizens yearning for land who were already falling for an emergent opposition MDC party. Another goal was to punish the white commercial farmers for sponsoring and siding with the MDC and civic society in the 2000 constitutional referendum that saw ZANU PF failing dismally. Many senior judges were forced to retire and were replaced with judges with strong links to ZANU PF and the liberation struggle. Examples are the current chief justice Luke Malaba who is a ZANU PF veteran of the liberation war and beneficiary of farm redistribution and the current Judge President George Chiweshe who is a retired Army General with strong ZANU PF links such as being used by Mugabe to take part in the 2008 election commission which ran disputed elections. These judges were very effective in buttressing ZANU PF staying power by handling disputes in a manner that advances the longevity of the regime. One example is the Tsvangirai petition challenging Mugabe's 2013 election victory that was tabled before the judges but was ignored until both Tsvangirai and Mugabe died in 2018 and 2019, respectively	The capture is evident in five different approaches targeting the composition, conduct and alignment of the judiciary: (i) the amendment of the constitution, through Constitutional Amendment (No.2) to give President Mnangagwa sweeping powers and influence in the appointment of judges and limiting the oversight role of the parliament and ending citizen participation in the process; (ii) the inertia and/or conniving attitude of the judiciary when a violation of the constitution is done by ZANU PF/military elite; (iii) ZANU PF government's public statements coercing judges to give judgements in their favour; and (iv) issuance of divisive judgements on internal fights within the opposition whose end give ZANU PF political advantage and (v) the chief justice's authoritarian capture tendencies towards other judges. The judiciary has executed its role of being an electoral court in a very contentious and politicised manner. The manner with which it handled the Konjana v Nduna and the Chamisa presidential election petition cases has left its credibility doubted. In the Konjana v Nduna case, the court ruled that the plaintiff failed to bring the case within a reasonable time (three months post-election) and therefore decided to ignore the fact acknowledged by ZEC that Nduna, a ZANU PF MP, lost the election. ZEC acknowledged that it made an error by proclaiming a candidate with fewer votes a winner but insisted that it cannot reverse or amend its proclamation. In the Chamisa 2018 election petition case, the constitutional court refused to open the ZEC saver to cross-check the authenticity of results proclaimed by ZEC agreeing with ZEC that there was no saver. This decision was shocking because the supply of the saver in question was done by an American Company IPSIDY Inc. after a tender competition process in 2018

(continued)

(continued)

Indicator	Mugabe Era	Mnangagwa Era
	The president's targeting and condemnation of impartial judges on state media has been a very instrumental apparatus in conditioning the judiciary to enable the Mugabe regime to exercise discretionary power to stay longer. Mugabe used intimidating tactics against the judges in a move that was seemingly aimed at influencing the judiciary decisions in court cases that involved the opposition. Prior to the 2002 elections, Robert Mugabe in his campaigning speeches churned out intimidating statements that were aimed at instilling fear into the country's judges. In one of his speeches pertaining to the land issue between white farmers and the government, Mugabe completely disregarded the role of the judiciary in administering justice in accordance with the law. He said: *Our party must continue to strike fear in the heart of the white man, our real enemy. They think because they are white, they have a divine right to our resources. The courts can do what they want, but no judicial decision will stand in our way. My own position is that we should not even be defending our position in the courts. The white man is not indigenous to Africa. Africa is for Africans. Zimbabwe is for Zimbabweans* – (The New York Times, 2000/12/22)	The amendment of the constitution through Constitution Amendment number 2 to enable the ZANU PF president to extend the Chief Justice Luke Malaba's term in office. The extension of Chief Justice Luke Malaba's term in office came as a remuneration for the job well done in running a judiciary that has been friendly to ZEC's electoral manipulation stated above and further manipulation of the judiciary for use as the last defence line for ZANU PF in the 2023 election Another manipulative evidence has been shown through ZANU PF government Ministry of Justice's public statements against the judiciary aimed at arm-twisting the judges to pass judgements in their favour. For instance, the Minister of Justice and Parliamentary affairs in opposition to a High Court ruling setting President Mnangagwa's extension of the Chief Justice's term in office beyond retirement age noted: "We have a serious situation of a judiciary that has been captured by foreign forces in this country. We are going to exercise our right in terms of the law and file an appeal against this baseless and meaningless decision of the High Court ... How does one judge, whose circumstances of appointment we are aware of, continue to make decisions that are against the government?" Such comments from a Justice Minister administering the judiciary result in intimidation, co-optation and erosion of the independence of the judiciary

(continued)

(continued)

Indicator	Mugabe Era	Mnangagwa Era
	When these statements were aired on state media, the chief justice and many senior judges were "white men" and resignations followed. In 2002, Zimbabwe's the most senior judge, Chief Justice Anton Gubbay, was forced to resign after Mugabe-led government said his personal safety could not be guaranteed. In October 2009, Judge David Barlett also resigned without giving reasons. His resignation brought the number of Judges who were forced to resign in the face of Robert Mugabe's threats to five. When Chief Justice Gubbay and two other Supreme Court Judges resigned, Mugabe increased the number of the Supreme Court bench from 5 to 8 Judges which was clearly a patronage-inclined decision to populate the superior court with his close associates in a bid to make sure that pro-government decisions were passed	
Capture of Media	The enactment of two restrictive statutes namely Access to Information and Protection of Privacy Act (AIPPA) compelling all journalists to register with the Zimbabwe Media Commission (ZMC) and the Public Order and Security Act (POSA) criminalising the reporting of falsehood went a long way in solidifying and consolidating Robert Mugabe's hold on power through "subrogating any opposition while claiming to uphold the rule of law"	The state media, ZBC and Zimpapers have been central in the manipulation of the electoral playfield by giving the incumbent president and ZANU PF above 70% coverage whereas giving the biggest opposition led by Nelson Chamisa limited coverage. The limited coverage given to the opposition is calculated to de-campaign and tarnish the image of opposition candidates. These institutions have been operating in a manner that ensures electoral certainty and procedural uncertainty

(continued)

(continued)

Indicator	Mugabe Era	Mnangagwa Era
Capture of the Electoral System	The militarisation of ZEC secretariat started with Mugabe. The symbiotic relationship between the security sector and ZANU PF makes such militarisation a derogation of ZEC's independence. The free and fair conduct of members of the security sector once appointed and/or employed by ZEC is unimaginable The unleashing of electoral violence and intimidation towards opposition parties and supporters prior, during and after elections has resulted in the prevalence of disputed elections in Zimbabwe under Mugabe regime. In the 1985 elections, Robert Mugabe's concerted efforts to change the political landscape were evident when ZAPU did not conduct pre-election rallies and meetings due to a war situation in which party supporters were intimidated, beaten, arrested and killed by ZANU PF and the police. The June 2000 elections were characterised by the highest number of political murders, beatings, rape cases, arson and wilful destruction of private property and have culminated into a disputed electoral process. The European election observers condemned Robert Mugabe for supporting a violent and intimidating campaign before the election and thwarting the work of thousands of local election observers and monitors. Fast forward to 2002 during the presidential elections, a repeat of political violence marred the whole electoral system	ZEC has been involved in the manipulation of the voters' roll, gerrymandering the process of voter registration process, and militarisation of the secretariat. The 2023 Delimitation Report showed capture of the electoral system by the ruling ZANU PF elite to influence the electoral outcome through gerrymandering, calculated to disorient the main opposition and benefit the ruling party. These include collapsing of constituencies with more registered voters to beef-up constituencies with less registered voters, multiplying constituencies with ZANU PF majorities in Harare to list a few The militarisation of ZEC secretariat has been admitted by the ZEC noting that such conduct is legally and morally permissible. However, the symbiotic relationship between the security sector and ZANU PF makes such militarisation a derogation of ZEC's independence. The free and fair conduct of members of the security sector once appointed and/or employed by ZEC is unimaginable Appointment of relatives of ZANU PF elites into ZECC. For example, the daughter of ZANU PF party Deputy President Kembo Mohadi, Millicent Mohadi, was on 7 June 2022 appointed by President Mnangagwa to become one of the commissioners of ZEC. The fact that Abigail Millicent Mohadi Ambrose's father Kembo Mohadi is an interested party in Zimbabwe's elections is enough to dismiss her appointment as part of a patron-client relationship which is detrimental to the conduct of credible elections in Zimbabwe

Appendix 1.2

Province	Constituency	% vote by party		Impregnability %
		ZANU PF	MDC	
Masvingo	Chivi South	70	25	46
	Mwenezi East	84	11	74
	Chiredzi South	63	27	74
Mash Central	Guruve North	87	9	79
	Guruve South	80	16	65
	Mt Darwin North	89	6	84
	Mt Darwin South	91	8	84
Mash West	Hurungwe East	74	22	53
	Hurungwe West	66	29	38
	Zvimba North	74	11	64
	Zvimba South	84	11	74
Midlands	Gokwe North	76	23	54
	Gokwe South	63	32	32
	Mberengwa	74	9	66

Appendix 1.3 FsQCA Scoring Sheet

fsQCA Scale	fsQCA Score interpretation	Criteria for scoring elite dis-cohesion
1 = (0.00)	Fully out of the set	No media reports/observable signs of elite disunity and disagreements in the eve of elections, no ruling elite joins the opposition
2 = (0.33)	More out than in the set	There are media reports of divisions, but there are no publicly observed internal division, no ruling elite forms the opposition party
3 = (0.66)	More in than out of the set	There are media reports of divisions, isolated publicly observable cases of internal divisions, and some ruling elites form their opposition parties but does not join alliance with the main opposition
4 = (1.0)	Fully in the set	In addition to media reports, there are many instances of publicly observed infighting among high-ranking elites, and some elites join the opposition party which makes alliances with the main opposition

Appendix 1.4 Sample Distributions Across Research Areas

Research area	Impregnability %	Number of interviews
Guruve North	76	125
Mt Darwin North	77	125
Mt Darwin South	72	125
Hurungwe East	79	125
Zvimba North	76	125
Zvimba South	37	125
Mwenezi East	71	125
Chiredzi South	61	125
Gokwe South	34	125
Mberengwa South	65	125
Umguza	34	125
Insiza North	65	125
Tsholotsho South	39	125
Mutoko East	76	125
Maramba Pfungwe	92	125
Mutoko South	75	125
Total		2000

Index

A
Agenda setting theory, 230, 231, 242

C
Clientelism, 12, 66, 118, 119, 289–292, 294, 298, 301, 313, 334, 343, 344
Commandment, 202, 219
Constitution of Zimbabwe, 7, 13, 61, 81, 110–113, 128, 144, 145, 150, 309, 311, 312, 317, 319, 325, 326, 339, 342, 346, 352–355, 360, 367, 383, 387, 402, 406, 413
Conviviality, 202, 218, 219
Critical Discourse Analysis (CDA), 7, 90, 96, 99, 100, 103, 193, 291
Critical thinking, 6, 74–79, 81, 85, 86, 156
Cultural Linguistics (CL), 202–204, 214

D
Democracy, 11–13, 20, 37, 41, 52, 143, 156, 174, 189, 229, 237, 239, 248, 249, 259, 263, 269, 290, 291, 293, 296, 297, 299, 303, 304, 313, 326, 340, 346, 371–373, 375, 381–384, 388, 395–397, 402
digital public sphere, 9, 164, 168, 171, 180
Disability, 2, 4, 21, 23–26, 30, 31, 34–36
Discrimination, 20–22, 29, 30, 33, 34, 37, 111, 112, 120, 128, 131, 135, 141, 156, 332, 346

E
Education, 6, 8, 21, 22, 27, 31–34, 36, 37, 64–66, 77, 78, 86, 109, 136, 143–146, 148–150, 153, 155, 156, 177, 178, 340, 367, 395, 411, 412
election violence, 89, 90, 96–99, 103, 104

electoral collusion, 14, 372, 374, 375, 379
electoral coverage, 11
Electoral illiteracy, 144, 145, 154, 155
electoral impregnability, 14, 393, 394, 399–401, 403
Electoral Participation, 2, 4, 5, 19–22, 24–31, 33–37, 153, 264
Electoral politics, 1–4, 6–10, 12, 14, 15, 41, 42, 45, 47, 49, 51, 73–75, 77, 81, 85, 86, 108, 110–123, 202, 204, 259, 284, 394–397, 400–402, 422
Electoral process/electoral processes, 2, 3, 5, 7, 13, 27, 30, 69, 109, 110, 112–114, 116, 117, 119, 120, 294, 304, 309, 310, 326, 331, 340, 351–353, 356, 357, 359–361, 363–365, 367, 377, 397
electoral violence, 5, 7, 32, 46, 47, 50, 52, 90, 94, 219, 396, 397, 427

F
feminism, 58, 59, 97, 109, 110
Framing, 230, 231, 233, 242, 243, 252, 265, 292

G
gender imbalances, 6, 30, 73, 74
gender relations, 8, 49, 95, 127, 136, 138, 141
Grassroots politics, 5, 55, 57, 59–61, 63, 66, 69

H
hegemony, 9, 43–45, 49, 164, 165, 167, 169, 172–175, 177, 179, 180, 188

I
ideology, 42, 188, 190, 194, 196, 213, 364, 387, 397

L
Legislative interventions, 7, 107, 109, 110, 122

M
mainstream media, 3, 11, 15, 169, 186, 264, 265, 267, 269, 270, 281, 283, 284
marginalization of women, 2, 7
melancholia, 3, 217
Militarism, 43, 45, 47, 52
Morbidity, 10, 229, 230, 233
music, 3, 9, 10, 186–189, 191–193, 197, 201–206, 210–215, 217, 219, 238, 282

N
name-calling, 9, 11, 130, 189–191, 193, 194, 196, 197, 248–250, 253, 259
national broadcaster, 179
Nationalist, vii, 42, 48, 205, 211, 218, 235, 236, 258, 334, 373, 374, 388, 403, 405–407, 413
new dispensation, 44, 52, 211, 228, 234, 235, 340

P
partisan politics, 12, 296, 316, 340, 341, 354, 401, 402
patriarchal mindset, 140, 141
Patriarchy, 8, 44, 46, 50–52, 58, 59, 63, 78, 89, 93, 110, 117, 118, 130, 135, 137, 141

polarisation/polarization, 6, 11, 74, 79, 95, 97, 99, 186, 191, 206, 241, 254, 257, 304, 365
Policy, 7, 12, 49, 68, 107–112, 115, 122, 174, 213, 291, 299, 315, 322–324, 379, 403
political discourse, 49, 252, 259, 264, 269
political transition, 393–399, 402
politics of naming, 253, 254
postcolony, 42, 202–204, 216, 219, 220
pragmatics, 250, 251
propaganda, 9, 10, 67, 74, 169, 177, 186–194, 196, 197, 228, 230, 232–236, 239, 243, 267, 272, 273, 364, 404

R
Responsibility, 8, 13, 83, 132, 135, 138, 153, 351, 360, 411
Rights, 8, 19–23, 25, 29, 30, 34–37, 56, 57, 67, 68, 75, 77, 81, 86, 94, 109, 111, 112, 122, 128, 129, 131, 133, 137, 145, 147, 148, 150, 152, 154, 155, 172, 173, 188, 192, 195, 255, 277, 293, 294, 296, 302, 313, 323, 340, 344, 354, 366, 373
rigid patriarchal theologies, 8
rural constituency, 14, 15, 393, 394, 397–413

S
securocratic state, 396–398, 402, 403, 407, 413
Shona women, 5, 55, 57, 60
social media, 3, 9, 11, 15, 93, 101, 119, 163, 164, 166, 171, 176–178, 180, 241, 264, 268–275, 277–284, 404
standpoint theory, 90, 95, 96, 99, 103
stereotypes, 64, 66, 74, 77, 81, 84, 110, 119, 120, 140, 205

T
traditional leadership, 4, 12, 154, 293–295, 300, 310–317, 320, 325, 333–335, 343, 352–355, 365, 403, 405–408
transformational politics, 228, 231, 232, 234

V
vote brokers, 12, 290, 293, 296, 297, 299, 302, 303, 313

W
women in politics, 8, 20, 57, 58, 61, 62, 66, 68, 69, 74–77, 81, 82, 86, 110, 112, 119, 120, 128, 130, 136, 139–141
Women political participation, 7, 107–111, 115, 116, 121, 122

Z
Zimbabwean experience, 13
Zimbabwean politics, 2, 7, 55, 60, 74, 75, 82, 83, 86, 91, 119, 121, 128, 133, 134, 145, 164–166, 227, 228, 230, 239, 251, 254, 256
Zimdancehall music, 10, 205